D0871729

C O L O N I A L
M A R Y L A N D

A HISTORY

A HISTORY OF THE AMERICAN COLONIES
IN THIRTEEN VOLUMES

GENERAL EDITORS:
MILTON M. KLEIN & JACOB E. COOKE

AUBREY C. LAND

COLONIAL MARYLAND

A HISTORY

kto press

A U.S. DIVISION OF KRAUS-THOMSON ORGANIZATION LIMITED
MILLWOOD, NEW YORK

First printing

Printed in the United States of America

Library of Congress Cataloging in Publication Data

Land, Aubrey C
  Colonial Maryland, a history.

  (A History of the American colonies)
  Bibliography: p.
  Includes index.
  1. Maryland—History—Colonial period, ca. 1600–1775.
2. Maryland—History—Revolution, 1775–1783.
I. Title. II. Series: History of the American colonies.
F184.L34   975.2'02   80-21732 ✓
ISBN 0-527-18713-5

FOR
ANNE,
ALISON,
AND
ALEXANDRA

CONTENTS

ILLUSTRATIONS

EDITORS' INTRODUCTION

The American colonies have not lacked their Boswells. Almost from the time of their founding, the English settlements in the New World became the subjects of historical narratives by promoters, politicians, and clergymen. Some, like John Smith's *General History of Virginia*, sought to stir interest in New World colonization. Others, such as Cotton Mather's *Magnalia Christi Americana*, used New England's past as an object lesson to guide its next generation. And others still, like William Smith's *History of the Province of New-York*, aimed at enhancing the colony's reputation in England by explaining its failures and emphasizing its accomplishments. All of these early chroniclers had their shortcomings but no more so than every generation of historians which essayed the same task thereafter. For it is both the strength and the challenge of the historical guild that in each age its practitioners should readdress themselves to the same subjects of inquiry as their predecessors. If the past is prologue, it must be constantly reenacted. The human drama is unchanging, but the audience is always new: its expectations of the past are different, its mood uniquely its own.

The tercentenary of John Smith's history is almost coterminous with the bicentenary of the end of the American colonial era. It is more than appropriate that the two occasions should be observed by a fresh retelling of the story of the colonization of English America not, as in the case of the earliest histories, in self-justification, national exaltation, or moral purgation but as a plain effort to reexamine the past through the lenses of the present.

Apart from the national observance of the two-hundredth anniversary of American independence, there is ample justification in this bicentennial era for a modern history of each of the original thirteen colonies. For many of them, there exists no single-volume narrative published in the present century and, for some, none written since those undertaken by contemporaries in the eighteenth century. The standard multivolume histories of the colonial period—those of Herbert L. Osgood, Charles M. Andrews, and Lawrence H. Gipson—are too comprehensive to provide adequate treatment of individual colonies, too political and institutional in emphasis to deal adequately with social, economic, and cultural developments, and too intercolonial and Anglo-American in focus to permit intensive examination of a single colony's distinctive evolution. The most recent of these comprehensive accounts, that of Gipson, was begun as far back as 1936; since then a considerable body of new scholarship has been produced.

The present series, *A History of the American Colonies*, of which *Colonial Maryland* is part, seeks to synthesize the new research, to treat social, economic, and cultural as well as political developments, and to delineate the broad outlines of each colony's history during the years before independence. No uniformity of organization has been imposed on the authors, although each volume attempts to give some attention to every aspect of the colony's historical development. Each author is a specialist in his own field and has shaped his material to the configuration of the colony about which he writes. While the Revolutionary Era is the terminal point of each volume, the authors have not read the history of the colony backward, as mere preludes to the inevitable movement toward independence and statehood.

Despite their local orientation, the individual volumes, taken together, will provide a collective account that should help us understand the broad foundation on which the future history of the colonies in the new nation was to rest and, at the same time, help clarify that still not completely explained melodrama of 1776 which saw, in John Adams's words, thirteen clocks somewhat amazingly strike as one. In larger perspective, *A History of the American Colonies* seeks to remind today's generation of Americans of its earliest heritage as a contribution to an understanding of its contemporary purpose. The link between past and present is as certain as it is at times indiscernible, for as Michael Kammen has so aptly observed: "The historian is the memory of civilization. A civilization without history ceases to be civilized. A civilization without history ceases to have identity. Without identity there is no purpose; without purpose civilization will wither."*

The history of colonial Maryland is closely connected with that of its larger Chesapeake neighbor, Virginia. The founder of Maryland, Lord Baltimore, was a stockholder in the Virginia Company, and he visited Virginia before deciding on the site of his own colony. Baltimore's earliest troubles were with Virginians: some sought to obstruct the grant of his charter, and one—the notorious William Claiborne—disputed Maryland's title to the upper Chesapeake. From Virginia came the Puritan refugees whose increasing numbers in Maryland prompted the passage of the famous Toleration Act of 1649, and from the Old Dominion, too, came the integral elements of Maryland's social and economic system: tobacco and slaves. So closely were the economies of the two colonies intertwined that exports from both were reported on the same customs return.

Much in Maryland's political culture mirrors that of its larger neighbor and in its lifestyle, as well. The politics of Baltimore's proprietary colony evidenced the same curious blend of aristocracy and democracy, deference and defiance, that Charles Sydnor thirty years ago identified as the distinctive quality of Virginia's system of government. And, as in colonial Virginia, our view of the social scene has been distorted by an overlarge focus on the great planters to the neglect of the more numerous yeomen, so in Maryland, historians seem to have passed by the small farmers who made up the vast bulk of its population in their preoccupation with the great planters—never more than five percent of the province's families.

The present account of Maryland's colonial history—the first new one in a century and the only one to treat more than politics—corrects many of the deficiencies arising from years of historiographical neglect. Aubrey Land, from his own detailed researches, brings to life vividly the habits and behavior of those whom contemporaries referred to as the "meaner sort" but who constituted the underpinnings of Maryland's society and economy. Their political power was always small; Maryland early saw the creation of a political elite—merchants, lawyers and planters—who dominated the government throughout its colonial his-

---

* Michael Kammen, *People of Paradox* (New York, 1972), 13.

tory. But the humbler citizens of Maryland were not without political influence, demonstrated most dramatically during the revolutionary era. The new constitution placed control of the state in the hands of the wealthy classes. The departure of the loyalists created only a temporary vacuum, quickly filled by new men whose views were remarkably like those of the persons they replaced. But while the new political structure remained conservative, Maryland enacted the most radical fiscal legislation of any of the revolutionary governments, permitting paper money to be used for meeting pre-revolutionary obligations. It was the "price of revolution" that Maryland's elite paid for its continued leadership of the humbler sort who had supported the movement for separation from the mother country.

In Maryland's colonial history may be seen many of the paradoxes of the new nation that emerged in 1776. Founded as the proprietary colony of a single individual who expected to make it a feudal seigneury, Maryland developed a vigorous Whig political system based on the principles of eighteenth-century English constitutionalism. Nevertheless, the colony's elite, though it bespoke the cause of whiggery, was careful to monopolize power, rejecting "simple Democracies" as of "all governments the worst" and insisting that a successful government must be one that was "steady, firm and respectable." A popular party led by conservatives moved Maryland cautiously into revolution, seeking independence but not at the risk of popular government. Maryland's elite succeeded brilliantly, as did their counterparts in other colonies, thereby making the American Revolution so different from the French that was to follow. The colonial history of Maryland—so ably delineated in these pages by Aubrey Land—viewed in conjunction with the history of the other twelve colonies, may thus help to clarify the meaning of a revolution whose inception, however fortuitous, produced consequences so momentous that they live with us still.

MILTON M. KLEIN
JACOB E. COOKE

PREFACE

When the American mainland colonies struck for independence in July 1776, only two were still proprietary. Maryland was unique, a successful proprietary colony. In contrast to neighboring Pennsylvania, Maryland represented an almost ideal type in the eyes of the proprietors, the Lords Baltimore: wealthy, orderly, and above all profitable to their Lordships. Such a splendid property was painful to lose. Even so, England lost far more: all of the seaboard colonies, each with its own history and resources.

The history of Maryland from first settlement to the final break with proprietor and crown is not told in the account that follows as a prelude to independence. Instead I have attempted to show the weaving of the pattern in the fabric of Maryland history as the weavers themselves performed the myriad tasks that slowly, and often without the foresight often attributed to them, completed the whole design. The Puritans who built the New England commonwealths had a sense of destiny, of fulfilling God's purpose; and they recorded the story, as events unfolded, with the consciousness of a chosen people preserving for posterity the early history of Zion. In contrast, Maryland grew out of a diversity of purposes, not always consonant, and no local historian compiled the chronicle.

Nevertheless Maryland history is not without pattern or themes, which seen in retrospect appear reasonably clear in a careful examination of these formative years. As I read the story, there are three.

First, and fundamental, the peopling of the Northern Chesapeake continued throughout the entire century and a half of colonial dependency. This very manner of speaking betrays an ethnocentric view, for Maryland had a native Indian population which for decades out-numbered the early white settlers. The whites, predominantly English, did not mingle with the Indians but merely displaced them. The next racial element to arrive in increasing numbers, the Blacks, spoke tongues as alien as those of the Algonquin and Iroquoian Indians. Although their African languages gradually perished, the Blacks multiplied and became an important segment of the provincial population, separate but not equal, yet integrated in a special way. Finally, well into the eighteenth century the last ethnic strains, the Germans and Scots-Irish pushed into the western parts of Maryland, first from Pennsylvania, then through Baltimore where some remained to give that city a Teutonic flavor. From the first landing in 1634 to the end of colonial dependency these immigrants—free and bond—augmented the broad labor base and, a few at least, brought talents to the professions and the economy.

A second theme, the evolution of a "provincial way," runs along in counterpoint to the peopling of Maryland. Visitors and newcomers found in the province much that was familiar: language, courts, houses, and even fashions. From the time of George Alsop (fl. 1659–1665), however, they also encountered something distinctive in economic arrangements, the social order, and politics. The business of making a living, arduous but uncomplicated in early years, altered continually. The introduction of slaves made possible a new planting order which functioned alongside the family farm that was almost universal in the first decades. Growing population and expanding tobacco production brought forth a mercantile element that "organized" the planting economy: moving crops to market in England, making credit available, and distributing imports returned after the sale of crops. Of course the merchants, or more accurately merchant-planters, fattened their purses from the services they provided until their personal wealth raised them into an elite, the leadership of provincial Maryland. In their political roles, they and their allies among the great planters formulated the legislation that supported the tobacco economy. To say that merchants and great planters formed the top layer of a stratified society could be taken to imply Marxian class conflict, which was never manifested in early Maryland. The adjective 'deferential' more aptly applies to social relations in the colony, where most people accepted the notions of "better sort" and "meaner sort." Yet British visitors in particular observed that the lesser folk acted in a far more familiar manner toward their betters than the English tolerated at home. Perhaps they were seeing the first sproutings of the determined egalitarianism that Tocqueville noted at the full flowering of Jacksonian democracy half a century after independence. But even in the Golden Age immediately preceding the Revolution, rank and station commanded respect as the outward and visible signs of inner worth.

A third figure in the pattern of Maryland colonial history may be described as a struggle for autonomy, or at least for a considerable degree of freedom in provincial self-realization. From the first years of settlement the people of Maryland had political institutions—courts, the apparatus of county government, and particularly the provincial Assembly—that voiced their "imperatives," a term I have used from time to time as a kind of shorthand for unarticulated social purposes. From the beginning, as provincial ways took a distinctive direction, political conflict was always potential and frequently overt, for Maryland was never a self-contained body politic. The head was always in England, especially during the twenty-five years of royal rule. When proprietor and province differed, Maryland leaders cast themselves in the role of defenders of the "provincial interest." Thus any threat from the proprietor or his agents created one of the constantly recurring constitutional crises, or what Marylanders very early learned to call "an invasion of our antient constitution." These frequent clashes have given Maryland political history extraordinary importance among the colonies. Consequently, I have given more space to politics than anticipated, not for the sake of detail but to lay bare the principles that provincials strove to maintain. The champion in matters political from first to last was the provincial Assembly. Individual leaders—the Cornwallises, Blakistons, Dulanys, Tilghmans, and Carrolls—came and went in the century and a half of Maryland colonial history. The Assembly remained on the field throughout. Here the great and wealthy joined in common cause with the less fortunate to ward off exactions of an absentee Lord Proprietor and to advance provincial well-being. If on first sight some of the clashes seem trivial, for example the supply bills, the English statutes controversy, or the Annapolis charter, be it remembered that these were tiny individual contests, which taken together made up the larger battle for freedom.

Near the end of colonial dependence, when an imperial Parliament took a hand in reordering affairs in the mainland colonies, including Maryland, the Assembly took on this additional antagonist with vigor. In the years immediately before independence antiproprietary politics merged with the anti-imperial movement. The end was independence and a kind of autonomy few had imagined.

———————

It is a pleasure to acknowledge the many helping hands extended along the route to completing this book. My foremost obligation is to Professor Milton M. Klein for his monumental patience and his infallible editorial eye. The late Dr. Morris L. Radoff gave both advice and assistance that proved invaluable. His staff at the Maryland Hall of Records have been unfailingly helpful. The Henry E. Huntington Memorial Library provided a season of welcome relief from other duties. The director, James Thorpe, and Senior Scholar, Ray Allen Billington, gave generously of encouragement and advice. To Mrs. Carol Lenox my thanks for preparing the typescript. Finally to my wife, Anne Wolfshohl Land, I owe a special debt for sound advice on many matters, literary and historical.

———————

All dates are in the form familiar to modern readers, who begin the New Year with 1 January instead of Lady Day (25 March). Thus a date that would at the time have been written 20 February 1688 or more commonly 20 February 1688/89 becomes in this text 20 February 1689 as we would write it today.

Aubrey C. Land

C O L O N I A L
M A R Y L A N D

A HISTORY

1

BEGINNINGS OF A PROVINCE

The history of provincial Maryland spans a century and a half. The chronicle proper begins on Annunciation Day 1634 and ends on 26 June 1776, when the last provincial governor sailed away from a colony that had committed itself to independence. Terminal dates, however, are little more than marks that chroniclers make before they cut the seamless web of history. Threads of the fabric run back into remoter times before English tongues spoke the name "Maryland." One strand in this endless warp touches explorers in the reign of Elizabeth, navigators who sailed Chesapeake waters and returned safely home to tell of soft air, lush forests, and broad rivers of the bay. But in 1634, Maryland, perched far away on the rim of Christendom, was little more than a new geographic name to Englishmen in the days of Charles I, whose reign saw the age of discovery give way to the age of overseas settlement and exploitation.

However dramatic and arresting this overseas expansion, sweeping changes at home distracted English eyes from distant zones and fixed them on great events close at hand. Vital concerns of politics, religion, philosophy, and economics were changing the very texture of their lives. If the seventeenth century was the century of genius, of Newton and the new philosophical outlook, it was equally the century of civil strife, when two English kings lost their thrones and one of them his head. While tensions racked the church, the economy of the island rocked to gusts of the new capitalism that was transforming medieval into modern Europe. Such great concerns of church and state, of the economy and society, preempted the attention of Britons and absorbed their vital energies.

Amid these distractions, a mere handful of Englishmen focused on the opportunities in overseas plantation. Prominent among them were the Calverts, a family indissolubly associated with a century and a half of Maryland history.

—1—

George Calvert (ca. 1580–1632), one of the threads reaching back into the Elizabethan past, played a key role in the founding of Maryland. Born into a Yorkshire country family, Calvert graduated from Oxford in 1597, had the grand tour of the Continent after the fashion of the day, and returned to England where he held several minor posts in government. After 1608 he was successively clerk of the Privy Council, member of Parliament, and special emissary abroad of King James I. To the king's favor Calvert owed his rapid preferment during the remaining years of his life. In 1617 he became a knight and in 1619 a principal Secretary of State. More substantially in 1620 he received a pension of £1000 annually from the customs, an income that fixed less adventuresome souls for life.

Calvert's interest in overseas enterprise developed quite naturally from investments that he had made in joint stock companies concerned with trade. He held shares in the East India Company and in 1609 he became a stockholder in the Virginia Company, which was then planting the first permanent English colony on the American seaboard. As a stockholder he quite naturally watched the fortunes, or more exactly the misfortunes, of the Jamestown settlement during the starving time and the hostile encounters with Indians. He also noted the constant costs to the Virginia Company, which put money—never quite enough—into the enterprise without realizing any profits for paying stockholders a dividend on their investments. Another man viewing this disheartening record might easily have lost interest, but Calvert seemed challenged, so much so that he even launched an independent venture of his own. In 1620 he purchased an interest in a patent granted some months previously to a syndicate "for the Colony and Plantation of Newfoundland." The next year at a cost of £25,000 he fitted out a small expedition to settle a place that he called Ferryland on the bleak east coast of Newfoundland. Two years later he obtained a patent from the crown to the whole southeast coast of the island, euphorically calling his grant "Avalon." At this point Calvert's career altered sharply. In 1625 he declared himself a Catholic and a few weeks later resigned his post as Secretary of State, selling the office in accordance with custom for £6,000. Immediately thereafter, the king raised him to the Irish peerage as Baron of Baltimore. Incapacitated for public office by his religion, George Calvert, now Lord Baltimore, henceforth devoted his attention to cultivating his private estate and his personal interests. He made two summer visits to his Newfoundland properties, decided that the climate—with "ayre so intolerable cold"— precluded a successful colony, and determined to transfer his activities southward. His letter to the king, dated Newfoundland, 19 August 1629, asked for "a precinct of land" in his majesty's dominion, Virginia, with the same privileges granted by the Avalon charter.

Calvert's activities during the next four years committed the family to planting a colony on the Chesapeake. Without awaiting the king's reply, Calvert sailed south to Jamestown where the governor and council received him courteously but without enthusiasm. As Lord Baltimore, a person of "eminence and degree," he commanded respect, but as a professor of the "Romish religion" he came under suspicion. According to the scanty evidence concerning his visit to Virginia, one pugnacious planter gave him the lie and threatened to knock him down. The more circumspect councillors rid themselves of their guest by tendering him the oath of allegiance and supremacy which, as a Catholic, Baltimore could not take. Nevertheless, before leaving he had seen enough to confirm his opinion that his future lay in the Chesapeake.

On his return to England, Lord Baltimore found further discouragement in the king's reply to the request for a "precinct" in Virginia. The king advised him "to desist from further prosectuing yo'r dessigns that way," observing with truth that new settlements "commonly have rugged and laborious beginnings." Undaunted, Baltimore began a campaign at court for his precinct in Virginia. He first inclined toward a grant southward from the James River but eventually fixed on the upper bay north of the Potomac. Tradition has it that Baltimore drew up the charter with his own hand and left blank only the name, which the king supplied—Terra Maria in the Latin of the charter; in English, Maryland—to honor the queen. The record supplies better evidence than the tradition, and it shows that Virginians used every artifice of the lobbyist to obstruct the charter. One interested party, William Claiborne, secretary of Virginia, played a leading part in the opposition to Baltimore. Over all protests Lord Baltimore carried his point and had his charter passed through a preliminary step, the privy seal, a few days before his death on 15 April 1632.

The charter of Maryland finally issued under the great seal of the realm on 20 June 1632. And it named as grantee Cecilius Calvert (ca. 1605–1675), second Baron of Baltimore, son and heir of George, the first lord. The twenty-three articles of the charter conferred on Lord Baltimore a princely domain and palatine powers. At the time no one could have told his lordship even the approximate size of the grant. The boundaries, apparently so clearly stated in Article III, traced the outline of Maryland from the ocean along the fortieth parallel "unto the true meridian of the first fountain of the river of Pattowmack," thence along the south bank of the river to a point "where it disembogues" into the Chesapeake, and then eastward along the parallel that runs through Watkin's Point to the Atlantic Ocean. Hidden in the future were the endless disputes and lawsuits that cost his lordship thousands of acres before provincial boundaries settled the final extent of Maryland at 6,769,290 acres, a princely domain even for lavish donors like the Stuarts. Lord Baltimore's powers within his palatinate were staggering: "as ample rights, jurisdictions, privileges, prerogatives, royalties, liberties, immunities and royal rights, and temporal franchises . . . as any Bishop of Durham . . . within the county palatine of Durham." In short, the Lord Baltimore was quite literally a monarch in his own New World realm. In return for this bounty the Lord Baltimore was bound to pay the king as rental "two Indian arrowheads of those parts" each year in Easter week. As the charter put it, King Charles I "of our special grace, certain knowledge, and mere motion" had created Baltimore and his heirs "the true and absolute Lords and Proprietaries" of Maryland. Henceforth, the title was shortened to Lord Proprietor.

It has seemed to some that in granting Maryland on these terms to Cecilius Calvert, King Charles abruptly set the clock back to an earlier feudal time. This view ignores both precedents and previous experiences with overseas plantations. The Stuarts had resorted long before to the practice of grants modeled on the county palatine of Durham, and the charter of Maryland followed in minutest detail the provisions of the

Cecilius Calvert, Second Lord Baltimore and First Lord Proprietor of Maryland, with the family arms, 1657. Courtesy of the Maryland Historical Society.

earlier patent that granted Avalon to the first Lord Baltimore. Quite possibly James I had adopted this ancient device at least in part because a more progressive arrangement—the joint stock company—had failed to cope with the problems of Virginia. At any rate the Baron of Baltimore was truly Lord Proprietor, actual owner of the soil and sovereign in government, subject only to his allegiance to the King.

—2—

Calvert set about exploiting his grant without delay, though twenty months passed before his first expedition touched Maryland soil. During the interval, he learned the meaning of the kingly precept imparted to his father, that colonies commonly have laborious beginnings. Preparations took time, both for raising money and for recruiting adventurers. Calvert estimated the cost of the Maryland venture at £40,000 sterling, a staggering sum for an initial voyage; but the company to be dispatched was large. According to Baltimore, he recruited some three hundred laboring men, nearly twenty gentlemen "of good fashion," and his two younger brothers for the party. He also advanced a large sum for ships, *Ark* and *Dove*.

Quite likely the figure of 300 exaggerates the actual number in the first expedition. A London official boarded the two vessels and found only 128 persons, all of whom took the oath of allegiance customarily administered to adventurers bound for overseas plantations. Once this formality was over the two ships, *Ark* of 350 tons and *Dove* of about 50 tons, sailed down the Thames to the narrow seas, westward along the southern coast, and put in at the Isle of Wight, where several Roman Catholic laymen and two Jesuit fathers came aboard to make up the company of slightly more than 150 souls.

The mystery surrounding the composition and embarkation of the expedition lends strength to the argument that Lord Baltimore founded his colony of Maryland as a refuge for his persecuted coreligionists. Certainly, the lot of Roman Catholics was unhappy in the England of Charles I. Successive editions of Foxe's *Book of Martyrs* (1563–1593) kept fresh in England the memories of the burning of Protestants under Queen Mary and gave incentive to zealous enforcement of the Elizabethan penal laws against Catholics. In public sentiment and in the eyes of the law, Roman Catholics were objects of suspicion and discrimination. Without doubt Cecilius, Lord Baltimore, wished to insure that Catholics in Maryland would be spared the discrimination they had suffered in England. But the whole pattern of his conduct, and his father's before him, resembled that of other colonial promoters of the day; he wrote constantly of profit and loss and of the prospects for future gain. He assuredly did not wish religious dissension to jeopardize the expedition, and he bade his brother Leonard, designated governor, to "cause all Acts of the Romane Catholique Religion to be done as privately as may be and . . . [to] instruct all the Roman Catholiques to be silent upon al occasions of discourse concerning matters of Religion." On the evidence a clear statement of Lord Baltimore's motives is not possible. Doubtless the religious haven figured in his thinking. Unquestionably too, he had in mind the enhancement of his family estate. The fairest statement of his motivation would include both.

Ark and *Dove* departed England on Friday, 22 November 1633, in good time for an early spring landing in the Chesapeake. The ships followed the usual route south, past Spain to the Canaries, then westward with the trade winds to the Indies. After a stop at Barbados the expedition turned north along the Atlantic coast to reach the capes at the mouth of the great bay of the Chesapeake on 27 February. A leisurely course up the bay brought the party to an island that they called St. Clements. There the company first came ashore on Lord Baltimore's own grant to perform a ceremony which posterity many generations later designated as Maryland Day. The very day itself seemed to call for solemn ceremonial: 25 March, Lady Day, the Feast of the Annunciation in the ancient cycle of quarterly church festivals; New Year's Day of 1634 according to the old style Julian calendar still used by the English. The company turned out to erect a huge cross hewn from a tree trunk and in its shadow to recite litanies "with great emotion."

Those adventurers who left records depict the accomplishment and the setting as moving experiences, and for good reason. Amid the hazards of winter seas, two small vessels had made the Atlantic crossing to a promised land, awesome in its majestic peace. Father Andrew White, one of the most literate of the voyagers, wrote with wonder of the Potomac: "The Thames seems a mere rivulet in comparison with it." He could not admire too much the grandeur of the forest. "You can drive a four-horse carriage, wherever you choose, through the midst of the trees." A quarter century earlier one of the first Europeans to describe this scene, Captain John Smith, had put it more succinctly: "All the Country is overgrown with trees." And so it must have seemed to men who carried with them the recollection of England's green and pleasant land, dotted with fields and pastures, laced with roads and pathways. Only here and there had the native Indians cleared patches for corn and vegetables and built their huts, or wigwams. These Indians proved friendly; when they shortly agreed to quit the area peaceably, leaving their fields and dwellings to the adventurers, Father White exclaimed, "The finger of God is in this."

From the outset Governor Leonard Calvert proved a practical sort. Once mass was concluded at St. Clements Island he set about the tasks of planting the colony. He put the men to work piecing together a barge, brought knocked-down from England, and the women to washing clothing, while he took a picked company of oarsmen to explore some sixty miles of the Potomac. Within two days he had visited various Indian tribes on the Maryland side and had concluded an agreement with a petty chieftain of the Yaocomico on the left bank of the St. Mary's River. Father White called the transaction a sale: "We bought from the King thirty miles of that land, delivering in exchange axes, hatchets, rakes, and several yards of cloth." Another eyewitness reported that Governor Calvert "presented" the chief and his advisers some cloth and implements to make the entry peaceable and safe. Whatever the technicalities, each side had given and received peaceably. The Yaocomico withdrew from their village with their goods, leaving the colonists houses of a sort and fields already partly planted with maize, all within gunshot of the governor's seat in the community that shortly came to be called St. Mary's City.

—3—

The beginnings had been doubly auspicious. At the outset settlers solved a food problem that earlier had almost wiped out Jamestown by raising enough corn during the summer for their own use and a small surplus for export. Besides foodstuffs they were able to begin planting tobacco, a cash crop for export, after the manner of the Virginians who had over the years brought cultivation through the experimental stage. At the same time friendly relations with the Indians of the neighborhood spared Maryland colonists the tensions that, below the Potomac, had culminated in the massacre of 1622. Occasional scares and almost continual disturbances grew out of thievery and murders perpetrated on each other by both Indians and whites. Though such blemishes spatter the record, Maryland never had an Indian "problem" in a century and a half of her provincial history.

The spectacular troublemakers were men of the same race as the colonists themselves. The deeds of William Claiborne, earliest and most notorious of them, fill many pages of Maryland records. A recital of all his doings would give him a disproportionate place in Maryland history at the expense of other and more enduring developments. Nevertheless Claiborne holds more than passing interest because he illustrates a type that surfaced in the outer reaches of Britain's overseas possessions, giving a turbulent cast to the early years of colonial history. Claiborne had fought unrelentingly against Lord Baltimore's charter. As secretary of Virginia, he had acted in his official capacity to prevent the king from granting land within the boundaries claimed by Virginia. But he also had personal motives. Several years earlier Claiborne had established something like a colony of his own halfway up the northern arm of the bay. He had selected his ground with an eye to both trade and plantation on Kent Island, the largest offshore body of land in the bay, flat, well drained, and cut off from the Eastern Shore by a "narrows" navigable only by an armed sloop or wherry designed for defence of the island. Here he had erected a fortified trading post staffed with retainers, who cleared the forest to lay out fields, orchards, and pastures. These properties clearly lay within the Maryland patent, but Claiborne stubbornly refused to acknowledge Baltimore's jurisdiction. On the other hand, Governor Leonard Calvert equally stubbornly determined to assert the Lord Proprietor's rights to the soil and government of the island. The impasse had complications touching Claiborne's financial backers in England, the mercantile firm of William Cloberry and Company, and his unscrupulous rival in the Chesapeake fur trade, Captain Henry Fleet, who sided with Baltimore.

Before an understanding could be negotiated, partisans of Claiborne and Calvert put the issue beyond amicable adjustment by an encounter sometimes described as the first naval battle in American history. On 23 April 1635, two proprietary vessels, *St. Helen* and *St. Margaret,* clashed with Claiborne's armed wherry, *Cockatrice,* at the mouth of the

Pocomoke River on the Eastern Shore. After Claiborne's commanding officer and two of his men fell, *Cockatrice* surrendered. A fortnight later another engagement between Governor Calvert's forces and Kent Islanders, fought near the same location, ended in Claiborne's favor.

Actual bloodshed ceased thereafter when English authority intervened in what appeared to be the beginning of civil war in the Chesapeake. First Cloberry and Company replaced Claiborne with another factor to supervise their investment, one George Evelin, who shortly came to terms with Governor Calvert. The Cloberrys acted in response to a precipitous decline in the fur trade, a result of the partisan warfare. The crown also took a hand in Chesapeake troubles to correct an even more dangerous threat that centered in Virginia, where the planters had "thrust out" their governor, Sir John Harvey, and elected Francis West to his place. Harvey had undoubtedly behaved in a highhanded manner toward Virginians and as an added offense had lent a helping hand to the infant colony of Maryland, already in disrepute with Virginians. The king could not countenance mutiny in his colony of Virginia and ordered Harvey's return as governor with increased authority. Accordingly at a critical moment Governor Calvert received a second assist in his struggle with Claiborne. For the time being Claiborne was stymied, but in neighboring Virginia he nursed his grudge, prepared to return to the fray at the first opportunity.

The contest between Calvert and Claiborne was far from an academic argument over a phrase, *hactanus inculta* (hitherto uncultivated), in Baltimore's charter. All such land within the boundaries described in his charter belonged to the Lord Proprietor by royal patent. Claiborne contended that his Kent Island establishment was in fact a cultivated and inhabited place, and that he had indeed at his own expense settled and cultivated the island before the charter issued under the great seal. Accordingly he claimed full ownership of the soil and exemption from Baltimore's jurisdiction or overlordship. In peopled countries such disputes are settled in courts of law. On the Atlantic frontier strong men often took matters into their own hands. In a country where a few hundred people had scattered themselves along the rim of millions of acres, some three thousand miles from the writs of long established courts, temptation to help themselves was almost irresistible. The first planting had ended on a note of triumph for the Lord Baltimore. Although he had encountered trials in the adventure, which had proved slow, costly, experimental, he had succeeded in the face of odds. Yet even greater contests—less dramatic perhaps, but more arduous—lay ahead for both proprietor and people as they tamed a wild land and brought into being a social order adapted to the task.

2

THE RIM OF CHRISTENDOM

The land within Lord Baltimore's huge grant was imperfectly known when the first settlers arrived. Whether George, the first lord, actually sailed up into the northern arm of the Chesapeake for a personal reconnaissance during his brief visit in 1629, the records do not clearly say. Certainly Cecilius, his eldest son and second lord, never laid eyes on Maryland soil. As heir apparent, Cecilius had remained in England to manage the family estates during his father's overseas ventures in Newfoundland and Virginia. In 1633 Cecilius was planning to accompany the first band of adventurers but at the last moment decided in favor of remaining at home to watch the moves of his enemies. The little he knew about his province he learned from maps and accounts of explorers to the area.

—1—

Neither explorers nor maps gave very much more than the vaguest information. Captain John Smith had reconnoitered the northern arm of the bay in the summer of 1608 and had left a verbal account along with the crude "Mappe of Virginia" as the entire Chesapeake area was called. Smith managed to convey an approximate idea of the shoreline but for hinterland he had only puffy trees interspersed with nude Indians and nondescript quadrupeds, the cartographer's conventions later satirized by Jonathan Swift in maps of another dark continent:

So geographers in Afric maps
With savage pictures fill their gaps;
And o'er unhabitable downs
Place elephants for want of towns.*

Imitators of Smith's map had done little to improve his cartography. A decade and a half after Leonard Calvert brought his company to Maryland, the Farrar Map (1651), drawn to support a hopeless hypothesis, might as easily have depicted the mountains of the moon. Farrar sought to prove that a ten day march of fifty foot and thirty horse from the headwaters of westward-reaching rivers would bring explorers to New Albion [California] "to the exceeding benefit of Great Britain, and joy of all true English." Not until 1670, in Cecilius Calvert's old age, did details of the bay area become familiar enough to enable Augustin Herman to produce a map that showed the waterways accurately. Even then the full dimensions of the shoreline were not perfectly known.

—2—

The shoreline of the Chesapeake from Cape Henry around the inlets and estuaries of the interior and back down to Cape Charles runs to the astonishing figure of 4,612 miles. The bay extends through two and one-half degrees of latitude, roughly from 36°55′ N. to 38°32′ N., or a linear distance of 184 miles from southern to northern extremities. The wide difference between rectilinear and coastal dimensions results from indentations in the shoreline, some quite small, others so immense as to be almost bays themselves at the estuaries of the Potomac and Patuxent. These larger estuaries thrusting far into the hinterland and a host of smaller ones divide the tidewater into the "necks" so common in Maryland geographical names. The bay, then, provided a potential access network to most areas of the tidewater. The northward extension of the bay proper was the main highway, dividing Maryland into Eastern and Western Shores. Estuaries and tidal rivers leading off the main stem on both shores were deep enough to serve

---

*"On Poetry: A Rapsody [sic]" (1733).

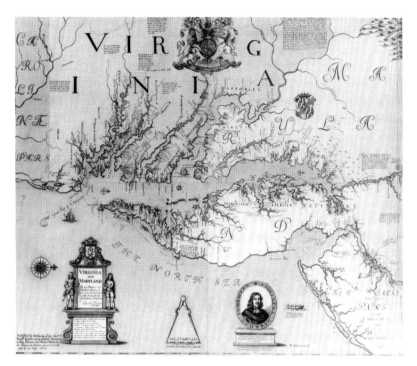

Augustin Herman's map of Maryland, 1670. Herman (pictured in the cartouche) included the three "necks" of northern Virginia in his finished work, though obviously he had little precise knowledge of the Potomac above the fall line, which he illustrates with graceful scrolls. Colonial Williamsburg Photographs.

as secondary or feeder routes. Ocean-going ships of the seventeenth and eighteenth centuries could penetrate far inland.

Urgently needing recruits to settle his palatinate, Cecilius, Lord Baltimore, immediately set out to publicize the geography and climate of Maryland. His first piece of promotional literature—*An Account of the Colony of the Lord Baron of Baltimore* (1633)—described the fauna, flora, and soil of Maryland enthusiastically, if somewhat inaccurately. Like any realtor, the Lord Proprietor sketched the rosiest picture, imaginative but not entirely mendacious, the stuff that dreams are made of. Much early promotional literature belongs to this lyrical period when Europeans played with visions of a new Eden, rich in opportunity, richer in romantic suggestion. Half a century later the magic had departed as the realities of the Maryland scene gave a more accurate view. The earliest settlers began to dispel promotional imagery. Like the explorers before them they found the country densely wooded. In his matter-of-fact way Captain John Smith had emphasized the difference between cultivated territories of Europe and the wild lands of the new world: "All the Country is overgrown with trees." A century later the Reverend Hugh Jones saw only slight change: "The whole country is a perfect Forest, except where the woods are cleared for Plantations." Beyond narrow sand and shingle beaches this immense forest of poplar, hickory, maple and black gum had for centuries enriched the soil beneath with an annual fall of leaves. The soils were light in texture, alluvial deposits of sandy loam rich with nature's mulch. Settlers easily made fields by the Indian method of girdling trees, thus sparing themselves the labor of felling the enormous trunks but leaving gaunt skeletons scattered about open spaces. These tidewater fields proved particularly suitable for tobacco, which Maryland settlers first saw growing about Jamestown on the route up the bay and quickly adopted as their staple crop. Between the dead hulks of girdled trees they had ample room for tobacco hills. But soil and staple, at first sight a happy combination, soon showed another and perverse aspect. The light soils washed easily in heavy rains, silting up streams and the upper reaches of the estuaries. Moreover, the greedy tobacco plant sucked out essential lime and potash within a tillage cycle of between four and six years. Planters then abandoned worn-out fields for fresh acres newly cleared. "Old fields" became as much a part of the landscape as the stark outlines of dead trees which newcomers found so depressing and commented upon in their letters home.

Along the tidewater the adventurers found a flat landscape, particularly on the Eastern Shore where the Dutch of Delft would have felt entirely at home. An elevation scarcely thirty feet above sea level became a landmark to be dignified by the name Windy Hill. The Western Shore tidewater lay a few feet higher, but there, too, level stretches ran from bayside and estuary in a wooded plain back to hilly terrain, a succession of rises that resembled a box of closely packed bonbons. These round-topped elevations often had steep sides, the result of water erosion that had cut ravines through what had ages before been nothing more than a slightly higher plain terraced upward toward the west. Light soils had given way before torrential rains that sometimes fall in summer. Once established, the stream beds cut downward until they reached a depth where the fall was so gentle that water flowed almost as placidly as in the tidal streams. Raw gashes that were once sides of the ravine had wooded over and all-weather springs at the bottom fed the streams with a steady flow of clear water.

For a low, level country Maryland's tidewater had excellent drainage. The early adventurers found some land on the Eastern Shore exactly at sea level, a marsh country of cattails and coarse grasses that made a paradise for nesting waterfowl and a breeding ground for the "muskeetoes" mentioned in so many travelers' accounts. But beyond, as the elevation rises a few feet, there is little swamp land of any extent. Even in the table-flat tidewater, without visible slope, the rain simply sinks through the light soil, as through a sieve, to drain just below ground surface into the bay or the nearest stream. A surprising number of springs bubble out along streamlines where surrounding land rises no more than a dozen feet.

Fresh water meets salt in the slow-moving tidal rivers. The largest of these—the Potomac and Patuxent on the Western Shore; the Nanticoke, Choptank, and Chester on the Eastern Shore—had channels deep enough many miles inland to accommodate any ship of the day. Thus the large rivers that drain the tidewater are in effect extensions of the bay with the characteristics of the Chesapeake itself: tidal activity, brackish water, and even the marine life of shell and fin fish. Eastern Shore rivers lose themselves in feeder streams miles inland. On the Western Shore, rapids at the border between tidewater and pied-mont—the fall line—abruptly change the character of streams.

Rainfall in the Chesapeake followed a pattern wholly unfamiliar to the English who settled the region. Accustomed to a gray overcast that brought almost continual light rains to Britain, newcomers found summer storms of North America novel and wonderful experiences. Lofty piles of clouds swept over the sky, the heavens crashed with lightning and thunder, and huge drops pelted down on the land below. Heaviest rainfall came in the warm months from April to September. From year to year planters could count on three-and-a-half to four inches of rain in each of these months, with the heaviest downfall in May, July, and August, when field crops most needed moisture. The somewhat drier winters still had sufficient rain to support natural vegetation: two-and-a-half to three inches each month were usual. The mean annual rainfall ran to about forty-one inches, a trifle more than precipitation in the county of Middlesex on the Thames.

Chesapeake temperatures complemented the favorable rainfall pattern to make a long and moist growing season suitable to a wide range of crops. Average temperatures stood near or slightly above freezing in the coldest months: December, January and February. Occasionally, however, blizzards sent the thermometer down to hover around zero. At this temperature estuaries froze, as eventually did the bay itself, sometimes with a sheet of ice so thick it could support ox teams drawing heavy wagons from shore to shore. Deep winter always brought shipping to a halt until the age of steel ships and icebreakers.

"The cold is extream sharp," observed Captain John Smith, "but here the proverbe is true that no extreame long continueth." February was the last winter month in which bitter cold was normally expected. After mid-March in the southern bay region and at the end of the month in the north those hard freezes, the black frosts, were exceptional. By mid-April planters could count on the possibility that the frost was past. Average temperatures rose from 52° in April to 75° in July, the hottest month, then fell to 55° in October. Daytime temperatures in summer went little above 90°, although unusual hot spells could send the thermometer as high as 105°. Relatively high humidity during these heat waves usually bore harder on people than on crops. Accustomed to a less violent English climate, new settlers paid in suffering until they became "seasoned."

By middle October early frost came to the tidewater, and once
settlements were made, windows were closed and woodsmoke scented
the autumn air. Long strands of migrating geese heralded colder days
ahead. By December winter had set in again.

Average seasonal levels of temperature tell the substantial story of
Maryland weather. But of course settlers remarked and recorded the
extraordinary. Winter blizzards with temperatures at zero or below
caused discomfort in the best built quarters and real suffering in more
primitive houses. Winds that blew at high velocity, as in occasional
"hyrrycanes," worked hardships on a population dependent on sails for
transportation. Even squalls could be dangerous. Ordinarily, however,
air currents moved along the bay at an average velocity of ten miles
per hour, safe for the smallest sailing craft.

Soil and climate, so far as he knew them, gave Cecilius Calvert the
expectation of a successful venture in the Chesapeake. But ultimately
success rested on the adventurers, the human agents that were to tame
this primeval land.

—3—

For the task of subduing the Maryland wilderness the hands were few.
Had Governor Calvert followed the example of Caesar Augustus and
numbered the people in the summer of 1634, he would have counted
fewer than 350 men, women, and children. Some 150 of these had
come on *Ark* and *Dove*. Upward of one hundred persons resided about
the fort on Kent Island, all of them retainers of William Claiborne
and at that moment an unpredictable element. For an unquantitative
age, hostile and even superstitious about numbering the people, no
more accurate estimate is possible. For that matter all population data
for the entire seventeenth century are unsatisfactory. Not until the
census of 1701 can demographers find a sound figure based on an actual
head count.

The size of the native Indian population is altogether a matter of
educated guesswork. Redskins never appeared in any contemporaneous
population statistics. Occasionally a provincial or a traveller described
a tribe or a confederacy vaguely as "a great nation and very populous,"
or similar words. These hazy contemporary references, added to the
informed conjectures of later anthropologists, give only a fair picture

of the Indian inhabitants in numbers and tribal organization. The bare outlines appear approximately as follows: Lower Western Shore tribes, the Doag, Mattawoman, Choptico, and Patuxent, belonged to a loose confederation dominated by the Piscattaway whose chief acted as "emperor" of the federation. These were the Indians Governor Calvert visited during his first days in Maryland. Sizes of the component tribes varied, but the largest appeared to number no more than a thousand and the smaller ones far less. On the Eastern Shore the Nanticoke, a more powerful "nation," numbered upward of 300 warriors, or 1500 souls altogether. According to contemporary estimates smaller tribes, the Choptank, Pocomoke, and Wicomoco, clustered about the dominant Nanticoke. Both groups—Eastern and Western Shore tribes—belonged to the great Algonquin stock that extended from Hudson's Bay south to the Carolinas. A third element, the dreaded Susquehanna around the northern end of the bay, spoke an Iroquoian language. The Susquehanna boasted some 700 warriors in a total population of possibly 4,000 persons as late as 1660. Altogether these three groups of Stone Age peoples totalled perhaps eight to ten thousand.* In 1634 they lived by hunting and fishing supplemented by primitive agriculture.

Throughout the first decades of Maryland history the native Indians were overwhelmingly the most numerous racial element. But the future belonged to the tiny band of whites who increased by geometrical ratio in the decades ahead while the tribes dwindled to mere remnants that eventually moved away leaving only place names—Patuxent, Nanticoke, Wicomico—as memorials to their existence. The process was gradual, never marked by cataclysms like the earlier massacre of 1622 in Virginia and the Pequot War in New England but continually blemished by scares and occasional murders committed by whites and Indians on each other. Far more lethal to Indian well-being than the infrequent murders, the white man's rum, diseases, and habits decimated once flourishing tribes. Smallpox struck down whole clans crowded into airless wigwams, totally defenseless against this unknown killer. Gradual encroachment on tribal hunting grounds by settlers who cleared the land struck at the delicate balance of Indian economy.

---

*Recent studies fault these estimates as being far too low.

Strong drink sapped native vitality and disrupted ageless tribal social controls. Within a half century Maryland Indians had ceased to be a factor in the tidewater.

—4—

Where the Indian coexisted with nature, the whites turned to subdue their environment in order to reproduce as nearly as they might the houses and husbandry they had known at home. Lord Baltimore had promised land grants to prospective adventurers in the Maryland enterprise as an inducement to "transport themselves thither." His promotional literature clearly indicates that he envisioned not only houses and fields after the European pattern but a similar social order as well which, even though already decaying at home, would be based specifically on the English manor with landlords and their tenants. In his "Conditions of Plantation" he promised to anyone who undertook to transport five laborers at a cost of £20 each a manor of 2,000 acres with all the rights and privileges "usually belonging to Mannours in England."

As it turned out few adventurers availed themselves of the opportunity to become manorial lords. Already the manor of medieval fame had seen its best days as a form of agricultural organization and had fallen into decline even in England. In Maryland it did not catch on permanently in its classic form with bailiffs, manorial courts, and the tight control of husbandry. By 1642 only sixteen private manors had been surveyed with a total of 31,000 acres, an average extent of less than 2,000 acres each. These few manors nevertheless accounted for 83 percent of the patented land, an imbalance that suggests that at least temporarily manors served a function. The manorial lords included Governor Leonard Calvert, Councillor Thomas Cornwallis, Thomas Weston, and Thomas Gerard, whose 6,000 acre manor made him the largest single landholder in these early years. The function of manorial organization in the first two decades of settlement seems clear enough in perspective: to provide a haven for the predominantly male population of these years. Single men preferred some form of communitarian life to the solitude of a hut at least until they could establish their own households. Moreover in the landlord's service—whether as indentured servants or leaseholders—they were in a position to accumulate funds for tools and seed against the day when they could find wives among incoming women servants. Finally, the manor served as a school for learning agricultural techniques totally foreign to English experience: the cultivation of tobacco and maize.

Once the manor had served its function in Maryland, it passed from the scene. The records of two manorial courts have survived the demise of this curious relic of medieval times. Themselves curiosities, these records read like the courts leet and baron of centuries before. At the court leet of St. Clement's Manor, the property of Thomas Gerard, held on Thursday, 17 October 1659, the constable, Richard Foster, presided. Residents, both freeholders and leaseholders, appeared in about equal number. The jury of "twelve good men and true" was sworn and made its presentments: "Wee present that about the third of October 1659 that Samuell Harris broke the peace and that there was bloudshed committed by Samuel Harris on the body of John Mansell for which he is fined 40 lbs of tobacco." Robert Cole has marked a hog belonging to the lord of the manor: fined 2000 pounds of tobacco, of which half is remitted. Luke Gardiner has caught "wilt hoggs" and has not given the lord of the manor his half "which he ought to have done and for his contempt therein is fined 1000 pounds of tobacco," which fine is reduced to 200 pounds. Finally the jury presents that "our Bounds are at This present unperfect and very obscure," wherefore with the lord's consent every man's land "shall bee bounded, marked and Layed out." These were understandable concerns of lord and retainers, settlers not yet adapted to an untamed land, but they looked to a past disappearing even in the mother country.

The greatest number of adventurers took less magnificent grants under a proprietary provision for the lesser person who was entitled to receive 100 acres of good land for himself, an additional 100 acres for his wife and each servant, and 50 acres for each child under the age of sixteen. This "headright system" enabled persons without retainers to obtain family-sized tracts, which from the first became the prevalent type of plantation. Men of modest means could acquire small but sufficient plantations, as did George Pye, founder of a notable line of descendants in St. Mary's. Pye came to Maryland with neither family nor capital, but as a freeman because he paid his own passage. Another immigrant, Thomas Passmore, who was also founder of a long line, moved to Maryland from Virginia in 1634 with his family and four indentured servants. An illiterate carpenter, Passmore nonetheless became a substantial landholder because he brought in several persons, each of whom entitled him to additional headrights. The type represented by Pye and Passmore was the most numerous element. Manors aside, most of the plantations fell below 125 acres.

Throughout the provincial period of Maryland history, land, both wild and cleared, was an important factor. During the first century at least, most of the free settlers crossed the Atlantic and peopled the province under the spell of almost free land in the gift of the Lord Proprietor. For his part, Baltimore stood to gain by every patent he granted. To be sure, he made grants in fee simple, but he reserved an annual quitrent of two shillings per hundred acres, payable to his local agent in the produce of the country, usually wheat, corn, or tobacco. Accordingly he could expect his gross income to be augmented by twenty shillings or £1 for every additional 1000 acres his officials patented to land-hungry settlers. For the settlers themselves their plantations provided immediately a livelihood and, in time to come, enfranchised them politically as freeholders in the literal sense. In future years property qualifications for voting were to be established. At the outset, however, all freemen or their representatives could attend the assemblies shortly to be called in successive years "to advise and consent of such things as shall be brought into deliberation," as the florid phrase for lawmaking went.

—5—

It is almost impossible to understand early Maryland history without a feeling for the fragility of the society that enacted the drama of these first decades. A tiny knot of settlers set down in the vastness of Chesapeake woodland was bound to have a sense of precariousness in the face of the overarching problem of mere survival. Wresting a livelihood from a raw wilderness, building a civil society to preserve harmony among men, insuring physical safety in the midst of unpredictable native tribes—all these concerns taxed to the limit the human resources of the adventurers who put their hands to these tasks.

Perhaps the most striking feature of Maryland society is the size of the population base in early decades. A mere 150 had disembarked at

St. Mary's from *Ark* and *Dove*. Add to these roughly the 100 more already on Kent Island, retainers of rebellious William Claiborne, and the total population in 1634 comes to about 250 persons, from gentlemen down to unfree servants bound in articles of indenture to work a few years for their masters before gaining their freedom. These and others who followed them to the province during the next half decade had the good fortune to make their start in prosperous years when high tobacco prices offered an inducement to immigrate and then to produce crops once they had arrived. Consequently, within six years population increased more than 250 percent but still remained numerically small. Most of these huddled about the original settlement at St. Mary's in civil subdivisions called "hundreds" after an ancient English jurisdiction. By 1642 five such hundreds had come into existence, each rated according to "taxables," a somewhat vague designation until defined precisely by statute a few years later. In any case a poll tax was due on every taxable and the size of the tax base gives a clue to the sparseness of population. St. Michael's Hundred headed the list with fifty-nine taxables, followed by St. Mary's with forty-four, St. George's with thirty-three, St. Clement's with twenty-nine, and Mattapany with seventeen. Only two of the hundreds lay any distance from St. Mary's City—Mattapany on the Patuxent to the north and St. Clement's westward on the Wicomico River. Population had as yet made little impression on the environment.

Of the nearly seven million acres in the Maryland palatinate, surveyors had by 1642 laid off a mere 37,000 in patents. Sixteen surveys, 31,000 acres altogether, were manors. The remaining 6,000 acres were marked off in small plantations. Curiously, over four-fifths of the freemen had failed to take up land in the first years. In 1642 some 136 out of the total of 173 freemen living in the area of St. Mary's owned no land at all. They either leased plots from holders of manors or entered into wage agreements with landowners.

The striking number of landless freemen resulted from a powerful combination of two factors. First, the Lord Proprietor favored large grants to investors who adventured their money in bringing indentured labor to Maryland, and in consequence he made surveys of manors prompt and easy for them. Thomas Cornwallis, John Metcalfe, and Thomas Greene not only had funds to ease the financial burden of peopling the vacant country but, as men of some learning especially in the law, they promised a kind of natural leadership for overseeing the immense task of clearing, building, and planting. Certainly they had nearly complete sway over their own indentured laborers. Secondly, the bulk of the settlers themselves, whether free or servant, lacked capital for tools, seed, or livestock and, just as important, the discipline to operate a viable plantation on the Atlantic frontier. Both freemen and servants came from middling English backgrounds, younger sons of farmers, artisans, or craftsmen. They differed chiefly in the ability of freemen to pay their passage to the colony. About half made their marks instead of signing their names. All had grown to mature years in the English work habits—short hours of labor, frequent holidays, and a leisurely working pace. Some years earlier at Jamestown, this ethic of "idlelesse," so ill-adapted to frontier demands, had kept Virginia perpetually on the brink of starvation. In Maryland during the first decade the laboring element adjusted to the exacting requirements of a virgin land during an enforced apprenticeship. Freemen typically entered into wage agreements with landlords while they earned their nest eggs, or they leased acreage on terms similar to sharecropping. Either arrangement subjected them to some discipline and prepared them for independent careers later.

The initial settlers in Maryland had genuine advantages over their earlier counterparts in Virginia. First, they had a record to instruct them: Captain John Smith had written two vivid accounts of the early troubles in Virginia, including the starving time when famine almost destroyed the Jamestown settlement. As a hedge against food shortages, the first expedition had brought slips of fruit trees for orchards and maize for the initial crop, which they planted immediately. More important they had the benefit of John Rolfe's experiments that had given Virginia a cash crop. Rolfe had judged the harsh native tobacco of the Chesapeake unsuited to European tastes and had imported seeds of the milder *nicotiana tabacum* from the Spanish West Indies for trial in Virginia soil. His experiment succeeded only too well. A tobacco craze among Virginians had led to overproduction and a glutted market that sent initial high prices tumbling in the late 1620s for a few years at least. In the early 1630s the market corrected itself and appeared more favorable for Maryland settlers. In the year Lord Baltimore dispatched the first expedition, tobacco prices had gone up sharply from one penny to around four to six pennies a pound, depending on quality, and they remained high until a market glut in the early 1640s sent them plunging down again. These bonanza years put early Maryland settlers on a firm footing for the difficult years ahead that were to be the time of troubles. By 1639 Maryland was exporting 100,000 pounds of tobacco, an average of 600 pounds per taxable. At prevailing prices this level of production meant an average income from the cash crop of between £10 and £15 sterling per taxable. Already Maryland was engaged in commercial agriculture. In 1637 tobacco had become the money of account in Lord Baltimore's province. Inhabitants reckoned their taxes, fees, and private debts in pounds of tobacco.

—6—

Within less than ten years the Maryland economy had taken the direction it followed for decades into the future. Not surprisingly some human types later so familiar in Maryland also appeared in the first years: planters, squires, and merchants.

In the seventeenth century the term "planter" had more than one meaning in the mother tongue of immigrants to Maryland. Back home in England men on occasion referred to all the adventurers in Lord Baltimore's province as planters, meaning that these hardy souls had gone out to plant a colony overseas. "Planter" continued to have this reference for years to come. But from the first years another and more technical meaning attached to planting: a functional reference to cultivation of the staple crop, tobacco. Since the overwhelming majority of freemen in Maryland planted tobacco—a little or a lot depending on their labor force—most thought of themselves as planters. In the earliest official records, the proceedings of a general Assembly of freemen held at St. Mary's in January 1638, nearly two-thirds of those attending were listed as planters. The remainder carried over their English designations: esquire, gentleman, or craftsman of some kind: cooper, carpenter, or brick mason.

Almost to a man planters lived in circumstances that a later age would call deprived. The majority wrung their entire living from field and forest with their own hands. For crops they cleared primitive fields, usually by the Indian method of girdling trees, where they planted tobacco and corn. One "hand" could produce a maximum of 1500 to 2000 pounds of tobacco a year working full time in season at that task alone. Practically, production averaged far less, more nearly 600 pounds, because distractions were many. A wise law required each taxable to plant two acres of corn as insurance against famine. Kitchen gardens for common vegetables such as beans, peas, and squash also cut into planting time. Meanwhile, planters had to find time to construct dwelling places. An observer in early years reported that all colonists lived in "cottages," a term for cramped wattle and daub affairs that housed the rural poor back home in England.

Altogether, the first generation of planters faced formidable tasks of erecting a new society with a minimum of help, not even wives and children for the most part. Population was dominated by young adult males who outnumbered women by about four to one. Where families were the exception, population increase depended on immigration. Lacking opportunities to set up households, ordinary freemen without capital did not exercise their headrights to take up land of their own but either entered into long-term wage agreements with large landholders or leased acreage for a plantation. High wages—fifteen to twenty pounds of tobacco a day—enabled the poor freemen and recently freed servant to obtain tools, seed, and livestock of his own over a short period of years. However beneficial to the poor, the practice of leasing favored large landholders even more by giving them annual returns on their surplus acres and ultimately the added value of improvements—cleared fields, orchards, tobacco sheds, and dwellings—made by tenants on the property.

Enriched by these short term and long term returns, a class of landlords emerged in the early decades. Above the ordinary planters in social rank and well beyond them in wealth, these select few are identified in the public records as esquires or gentlemen to distinguish them from the common run. Governor Leonard Calvert and Thomas Cornwallis, his chief lieutenant, both received manors for their investment in the expedition of 1634 and provided political and economic leadership from the beginning. A year or so later John Lewger, who became provincial secretary, and Thomas Gerard, swelled the ranks of manor holders. As men of some means they extended credit to lessees for essential tools and livestock. Between them, Cornwallis and Lewger counted almost half the planters of early Maryland among their debtors. In 1642 Cornwallis had debts due him in the amount of 40,056 pounds of tobacco, at prices then prevailing the equivalent of £664 sterling.

Whatever their descriptive titles such as esquire or gentleman selected from English tradition, colonists of this stripe in fact performed the function of entrepreneurs, an expression not current at the time. Enterprise won them position and fortune in a society as yet fluid. Thomas Gerard started in Maryland with capital of £200 sterling borrowed from a relative. From this modest beginning he went on during his active life to amass a considerable fortune.

The gulf between small planter and manorial lord was wide but not unbridgeable. Just as the holders of manors in early years owned 83 percent of the patented land, so these same privileged few—some 10 percent of the freemen—owned 63 percent of the personal wealth in Maryland. But small planters, often newly freed servants, could rise from the very bottom to the top rank of wealth and position. Robert Vaughan came to the province as an indentured servant, but beginning in 1638 he attended the Assembly as a freeman. Thereafter he held official posts such as sergeant of militia and constable of St. George's Hundred, and represented St. Clement's Hundred as burgess in the elective Assembly of 1640. In 1642 he moved to Kent Island where he sat as a justice of the peace for twenty-six years and held the position of militia officer for an equal term. In 1648 he became a member of the council and served for a time in this prominent position. Another indentured servant, Zachary Wade, outdid Vaughan in substance at least if not in honors. During his long career Wade amassed 4000 acres of land, one of the largest holdings in Maryland, and personal property of more than £400. At his death in 1678 he ranked among the top five percent of his contemporaries in wealth.

Other indentured servants had less striking careers. But in the first quarter century in Maryland upward mobility remained high for men of talent. Once freed, servants acquired land without much delay, usually in plots of 50 to 400 acres. As freeholders they became jurors, minor office holders, justices of the peace, and sheriffs. Such planters were forming the skeleton of Maryland society and creating a tradition of the Chesapeake as a land of opportunity.

—7—

If "fragile" best describes the society of this numerically tiny band of English set down on the vastness of the Atlantic frontier, the vigor of its individual members must not be overlooked. Mere seeds of a population, they faced, sometimes awkwardly and falteringly, the tasks of organizing politically for the purpose of exploiting the resources of their new home. As they were learning the extent and potentialities of a virgin land they were beginning to weave the strands of a social and economic fabric that could withstand the rigors that lay ahead. For Baltimore's adventure had hardly begun when a time of troubles descended on the infant colony.

3

A TIME OF TROUBLES

In old age Cecilius, Lord Baltimore, looked back justifiably on the years between 1642 and 1660 as a time of troubles. The epoch coincides almost exactly with the ferment in England that brought his benefactor, King Charles I, into disagreement with Parliament, then into civil war, and finally to the executioner's block in 1649, when England began an eleven year experiment with the Commonwealth. In Maryland as in England, the time of troubles was compounded of politics and religion, an explosive combination even in a stable society. But for the province still small in population and fragile in social texture, the turmoil that racked the colony threatened to destroy Baltimore's adventure entirely. Beset with rebellion and plundering on his Maryland premises, Baltimore eventually faced the sobering prospect of losing his province altogether. As a leading Roman Catholic he could hardly expect forbearance from a government of English Puritans accustomed to calling his church "the whore of Babylon." When the Commons won the initiative and Puritans assumed the seats of power, his security against losing his province and all his investment in it rested on the ancient tradition of property rights safeguarded by the common law of tenures which protected landholders of the realm against spoliation. During the trying years of civil war and interregnum Baltimore could never fly to sanctuary in his palatinate for fear of exposing himself to proscription and his property to confiscation. Of necessity he watched provincial doings from his somewhat precarious seat in England and consigned direct management of Maryland affairs to lieutenants who sometimes failed him disastrously.

—1—

The forum to which the tiny population of Maryland brought troublesome problems of every description in the first decades of settlement was the provincial Assembly. First called within twelve months of the landing as a gathering of all freemen, the Assembly within a decade became an elective body representing a populace dispersed over the southern tip of the Western Shore and up to Kent Island in the bay. The early career of the provincial Assembly provides an instructive commentary on contemporary political thought and on the actual conditions of life on the Atlantic frontier.

The first Assembly convened at St. Mary's City on 26 February 1635, when the settlement was exactly eleven months old. No records of the meeting have survived, but later references clearly indicate that the freemen enacted several "wholesome lawes and ordinances then made and provided for the welfare of this Province." Assemblymen had justifiably taken the initiative: they knew local problems at firsthand and they acted on the plain words in Article VIII of the charter providing for an Assembly of freemen or their delegates who "shall be called together for the framing of lawes, when, and as often as need shall require."

Lord Baltimore seized upon other phrases of the same Article VIII and came out with a different conception of the lawmaking process, one more congruent with his authoritarian political theories. The Lord Proprietor fixed on words that, by his interpretation, plainly indicated an intent of the king to "grant unto the said now baron of Baltimore . . . free, full, and absolute power, by the tenor of these presents, to ordain, make, and enact laws . . . with the advice, assent, and approbation of the freemen of the same province" or their delegates. By his reading Baltimore had authority to propose laws while provincials had nothing more than the right to approve or suggest changes generally. Accordingly Cecilius refused to ratify the wholesome laws enacted by the Assembly and instead transmitted his own "draught of Lawes" for assent and approval by a new Assembly called to meet at St. Mary's on 25 January 1638.

During the intervening three years several occurrences had altered the complexion of Maryland affairs. William Claiborne had resisted proprietary jurisdiction and had done battle with the proprietor's officers. Local leaders had emerged, men capable of speaking their minds on policy questions: Thomas Cornwallis, a pillar of the Council, Captain Robert Evelin, commander of Kent Island, and Sergeant Robert Vaughan, high constable of St. George's Hundred. Already the amorphous body of freemen was coming under political discipline in recognizable units, those subdivisions anciently known to Englishmen as "hundreds." Consequently the Assembly of 1638, the second in Maryland history, followed anything but a docile course.

At first glance the session of 1638 resembles a primary Assembly of all freemen. On 25 January the Lieutenant General, as Governor Calvert was styled, took his place, followed by two senior councillors, designated as "esquires," nine other leading persons denominated "gentlemen," and a large body of planters varied by an occasional carpenter or bricklayer. Altogether thirty freemen appeared personally, but several among them brought proxies for some others who did not or could not attend. Obviously not every free male from the scattered hundreds and from Kent Island could leave livestock and houses untended for six weeks to sit in solemn conclave making laws. Fewer than half the eligible freemen appeared at all, and many of these gave their proxies within a day or so to return home. Clearly this second Assembly was no primary body, a gathering of all free men. About a dozen regulars sat through all the sessions until adjournment on Saturday, 24 March. Without formalities or declarations the Assembly had in fact become representative. It was also unicameral; councillors and delegates sat together in a single chamber.

These regulars, the essential leadership of the province, did the real work and their chief task revolved about the impasse created by the Lord Proprietor's veto of the acts passed by the first Assembly and his dispatch of a code drawn with his own hand. Who, then, was to legislate, Lord Proprietor or Assembly? To this question the freemen gave an unambiguous answer. On the second day "was read out the draught of the Lawes transmitted by the Lord Proprietor . . . and were severally debated by the house." Next day on the question, "whether they should be received as Lawes or no," the Assembly voted two to one against the proprietor. Then after their flat veto of the Lord Proprietor's proposed laws, the Assembly appointed a committee to draw up its own slate of acts to be debated and forwarded to Lord Baltimore.

This action apparently set the stage for perpetual stalemate: the Assembly refusing to accept the Lord Proprietor's laws, the proprietor disallowing Assembly legislation and denying the right of local initiative in law-making. Actually the apparent impasse resulted in a kind of tacit compromise. The committee appointed to develop the Assembly's draft did in fact produce twenty-six acts—for punishing criminal offenses, for securing titles to land, for the liberties of the people, and the like—all matters of urgent local concern. But then the committeemen recommended inclusion of several acts submitted by the proprietor as also useful for the welfare of provincials. In the end the Assembly accepted seventeen proprietary "bills": for bounding manors, for assigning freeholds, for military discipline. Altogether the Assembly of 1638 passed forty-three acts, a fair start toward a much needed code of laws. The Lord Proprietor could see that a sizable portion of the measures he had submitted had met approval; provincials had maintained the principle of local initiative and had themselves developed a number of laws much needed for punishing "enormous offenders." The compromise thus offered must have seemed even more palatable to Lord Baltimore when he found among the acts initiated by the Assembly two particular measures: "An Act for the attainder of William Clayborne" and "An Act confirming the sentence against Thomas Smith [Claiborne's Agent]." The Assembly had punished these proprietary enemies by declaring the goods and chattels of both forfeit to his Lordship. The representatives could hardly have offered more tempting bait.

—2—

The saga of the Assembly did not end with winning of the initiative in legislation. Other questions remained to be settled, for instance the form and organization of the lawmaking body. The Assembly of 1638 met as a unicameral legislature, with Governor Calvert sitting as president surrounded by councillors and the freemen of the province all in a single room. It was this apparent formlessness that gives an illusion that most eligible provincials gathered in a primary Assembly. Actually by the wholesale giving of proxies the freemen had created a kind of informal representative system. As yet, however, the internal structure of the Assembly and the formalities of legislative procedure remained to be determined by a process of trial and error. Already during the day-to-day meetings in the session of 1638 occasional differences appeared. On one occasion, Thomas Cornwallis had a sharp disagreement with Governor Calvert and the governor gave way to his senior councillor, who was fast becoming the political leader he was destined to be for many years in the future.

Transactions of the third Assembly held in February and March 1639 carried the legislative branch a long step forward. Previously the governor had merely called all freemen to make their "personal repair" to St. Mary's City. Now for the first time his writ directed freeholders to meet and choose "discreet honest men" as their "burgesses" to represent them. Calvert designated as electoral districts five clusters of settlement, the Hundreds: St. Mary's, St. Michaels, St. George's, Mattapany, and Kent Fort. The election returns are among the most revealing documents in early Maryland history for the commentary they make on the numbers and status of the population exactly five years after the first settlers arrived. In Mattapany Hundred, a few miles north of St. Mary's City, seven voters chose their single burgess; five signed the writ by making their marks. St. Michaels's Hundred to the west elected two representatives from their fourteen eligible voters, seven making their marks. Altogether the four Western Shore hundreds sent six burgesses to represent an electorate of forty-eight freemen. Kent Fort Hundred up the bay chose two of their fifty-three franchise holders.

Besides the elected representatives, Governor Calvert summoned five others by writs directed to them personally: Thomas Cornwallis, Giles Brent, Fulk Brent, Thomas Greene, and John Boteler [Butler]. As a special group whose counsel the governor considered essential, these five were the seed of the later Council of State. In this Assembly, however, they still sat with the eight elected burgesses in a unicameral body with the governor as presiding officer. And in a law passed during the session this elective process was formalized as a permanent part of the provincial constitution, with the exception of the confused years of the middle 1642s when the province was convulsed by internal strife and outside meddling.

The unicameral arrangement soon came under criticism. In 1642 a representative from Kent Island, Robert Vaughan, "in the name of the rest" asked that the burgesses "be by themselves" as a separate house, "but it was not Granted by the Lieut General [Governor Calvert]." During the troubled years following, the question, if it came up at all, took second place to annual emergencies. But finally in the session of April 1650 the elected representatives had their wish: their own chamber and their own speaker. Within less than two decades the basic structure and procedure of the Assembly took permanent form.

—3—

The executive branch proved easier to adapt to the needs of a community destined to increase in numbers and complexity. Here the Lord Proprietor had a free hand. His initial arrangements had been simple and functional to a colonizing expedition. He had sent Leonard Calvert as governor, assisted by two "commissioners," Captain Thomas Cornwallis and Jerome Hawley. Then in 1637 Baltimore dispatched an official commission that erected the framework of a proper executive department. The commission made Calvert both governor and chancellor, John Lewger the provincial secretary, or custodian of all records, and the trio—Lewger, Hawley, and Cornwallis—councillors. When Governor Calvert began appointing sheriffs shortly thereafter the executive branch was substantially complete.

Lord Baltimore left no doubt about his conception of government or the source of political authority. To brother Leonard he wrote, "Certainly I have the power to revoke any authority I have given you, either in whole or in part . . . for you are but meerly instrumental in those things to do what I direct." With the Assembly the Lord Proprietor had to compromise his authoritarian conceptions. To his younger brother he could take the stern line. As long as Leonard remained obedient to his Lordship's commands, the governor enjoyed the extensive powers of a viceroy: head of the military establishment as lieutenant general and admiral, keeper of the great seal and judge in equity as chancellor, and finally the source of grants and writs.

Though subordinate to the governor, the secretary had even more duties: all the functions not assigned to the governor and chancellor. And these were considerable. The secretary's position became the mother of offices which were differentiated into separate posts as the province grew in numbers and as the pressures of work augmented over the years. Seven official posts eventually derived from the secretary's office in this process of subdivision: surveyor general in 1642, agent and receiver general in 1651, attorney general in 1657, commissary general in 1673, naval officer in 1676, rent roll keeper in 1689, and judge of the land office in 1738. But initially all these duties were the responsibility of the secretary, who exercised them by clerks until the labors outgrew these subordinates and clearly necessitated independent offices each with its own appointed chief.

Of all the secretary's cares none took precedence over the land system, a principal concern of both proprietor and people. For the proprietor his land obviously meant potential income and ultimately the success of his colonizing enterprise. In his "Conditions of Plantation" Baltimore had promised 2,000 acres of land to every adventurer who transported five adult males as settlers and proportionately smaller acreage to those who brought fewer people. As a quitrent—to "quit" tenants of all feudal dues and services—he asked ten pounds of good, merchantable wheat each year for every fifty acres granted. During the next fifty years his Lordship altered specific details such as the size of grants and quitrents, without changing the "headright system" of parcelling out land according to the numbers of immigrants coming in. Then in 1683 he abandoned headrights and made cash payment of "caution money" the basis for acquiring title to land. At first he fixed the rate at two hundred pounds of tobacco (equivalent to sixteen shillings sterling) for every 100 acres. His successors increased this caution money from time to time until 1738 when the price reached a peak of £5 sterling per 100 acres.

In order to distribute as much land as possible and hence realize maximum revenues from the annual rent collections, proprietary officials established a simple mechanism for operating the land office. Land hungry settlers could perfect a grant in three steps. First on establishing a headright, or in later years on paying caution money, a warrant issued entitling the holder to have the surveyor lay out a stated number of acres on vacant land anywhere in the province. Next the certificate, returned by the surveyor with metes and bounds of the survey drawn on plat, authorized the holder to proceed to the third and final step: obtaining a patent under the seal of the province conveying title in fee simple subject to an annual quitrent.

Ironically the success of the land system undermined one of Lord

Baltimore's initial designs for his province. He had clearly hoped to establish in Maryland the kind of landholding aristocracy familiar in the English countryside, a gentry that would support his own palatine overlordship. The idea of lords and retainers had appeared in his first conditions of plantation and later had explicit expression in his offer to erect manors for his chief tenants with all the trappings of a medieval fief. But the few manors that were actually laid out with courts leet and baron, quaint relics of a feudalism, soon withered in new world soil. Instead of manorial lords and faithful tenants the single family freehold prevailed. Only during the first two decades did freemen show a marked preference for work contracts and tenancy on these larger estates subject to manorial rules. When tenancy did develop years later on a large scale the system differed fundamentally from the copyhold tenancy of the manor. Once the settlers had broken the solid expanse of raw wilderness and had acquired capital for tools, the freemen of Maryland turned to the small family plantation, which soon outnumbered manors many fold.

—4—

During these promising beginnings of institutional growth officers of the tiny proprietary establishment found themselves grappling with a pair of troublesome problems: the Jesuits and the Indians.

Two Jesuit priests had accompanied the expedition of 1634, Fathers Andrew White and John Altman. Between them they brought a host of servants, with headrights entitling them to a grant of 6,000 acres. According to the conditions of plantation they held this property in their own names, exactly as other gentleman adventurers like Cornwallis who came in the first expedition. Father White had little interest in such secular matters as improving his lands, which he left to his colleague and to overseers. Like his French counterparts in Canada he turned to missionary work among the Indians. Leaving what rude comforts the primitive huts of early settlers afforded, he went directly to the even cruder dwellings of the natives.

Running through Andrew White's saintly character was a decidedly practical streak. He not only learned the native language, he learned it thoroughly enough to compile a dictionary and a grammar, the first philological work in British North America, and finally a catechism for instructing his converts. Father White lived at various times among the Patuxent north of St. Mary's, the Portobago to the west, and, even further along the Potomac, the Piscattaway. His greatest triumph, the conversion of the Piscattaway Chieftain Kittamaquund and his wife, was recognized by attendance of the governor and secretary at the elaborate baptismal ceremony. Father White had exerted himself mightily to achieve his goal: he had persuaded the chieftain to forego native dress forever in favor of English clothing, to put away all his concubines, to learn English, and to change his name to Charles. The final act of the day, marrying the newly baptized couple according to Christian rites, consumed his vital energies. He contracted fever and lay ill for weeks before recovering.

Other Jesuit activities met with less approval from the authorities. By 1637 the mission had grown beyond the two fathers who had come with Governor Calvert's expedition. Additional priests and their retainers had acquired headrights entitling the Jesuits to thousands of acres, at least in the opinion of a newcomer who superseded Father White as head of the Maryland mission in 1637. Known in his order as the Reverend Philip Fisher, the new head took over the management of secular affairs and held the bulk of the land under the secular name Thomas Copley, Esquire. From his seat at St. Inego's Manor near St. Mary's, Copley made his presence felt immediately. Without delay he dispatched a letter to the Lord Proprietor demanding special privileges for the Jesuits: freedom from quitrents and from taxes for public service, exemption from the civil courts, permission to trade with the Indians without a proprietary license, and the right to determine which of their ecclesiastical privileges they would surrender to the government. Directly on the margin of Copley's letter Lord Baltimore set down his reaction, "Herein are demands of very extravagant privileges."

If Copley's letter disquieted proprietary authorities, his actions gave them genuine cause for alarm. Without further notice Copley entered into direct negotiations with the Indians for a grant of land within the Maryland patent. This open threat to his authority as absolute Lord and Proprietor stirred Baltimore to action. He stiffened the Conditions of Plantation by adding a prohibition on landholding by any "corporation, society, fraternity, municipality, political body (whether it be ecclesiastical or temporal)." Even then the battle with the Jesuits had not ended. Determined to guard the monopoly of his order, Copley attempted to frustrate proprietary efforts to send secular clergy for the ministry to whites who were peopling the province. Ironically his coreligionists had created unforeseen dangers for Lord Baltimore, who finally had to present his case to the English Provincial of the Society, Henry More, before abrogating Jesuit land cessions from the Indians. On the Maryland side Governor Calvert had been unable to resist the highhanded actions of Copley. Against their private land cessions from the natives he had no recourse short of hailing them into court, an action that he feared might expose him to excommunication, because the Jesuits claimed exemption from civil jurisdiction under the papal bull, *In coena Domini.* But he saw, too, the risks of an *imperium in imperio,* a Jesuit domain within Baltimore's province, and he welcomed the helping hand of his brother, meekly accepting a stern rebuke for permitting the purchase in the first place.

Without the Jesuits Governor Calvert had already found distractions enough as white and native cultures met and, all too often, clashed. Calvert had taken considerable care to acquaint himself with the tribes on the lower Western Shore when the colonists first landed and had established especially friendly relations with the Yaocomico, who sold their huts and cornlands at St. Mary's to the whites. But within a decade these amicable beginnings had deteriorated as misunderstandings, thefts, and shootings followed with monotonous regularity.

Skilled interpreters might have prevented some of the more serious ruptures. But persons with even rudimentary knowledge of native tongues were rare, and almost none were fluent. One exception, a Virginian, Captain Henry Fleet, had learned the Piscattaway dialect during five years as a captive of that tribe. After his ransom he had entered the fur trade and had doubtless found means of communicating with other tribes around the southern bay area in spite of dialectal differences among them. Fleet had encountered the first expedition and had pointed out the desirability of the St. Mary's site, where he remained for sometime at the request of Governor Leonard Calvert, carrying on his trade with "trucking axes . . . howes . . . Dutch cloth . . . Irish stockings" and a miscellany in "one chest containing some beads, knives, combes, fish hooks, jewsharps, and looking glasses." As a trader, Fleet had his own interests to safeguard and more than once created suspicions of playing a double game. His own contradictory accounts raise doubt about his reliability as a faithful interpreter.

Settlers, with only a few words and whatever signs they could muster, easily fell into misunderstandings with their Indian neighbors, occasionally with fatal results.

Causes of trouble were on every hand. Settlers ordinarily let their swine and cattle roam freely in woods and grassy places. To the Indian these edibles appeared no different from deer or bear, except in unwariness toward the stalker. White owners first complained, then retaliated directly on the predators by destroying their crops or firing on Indians, especially strangers, in the vicinity of plantations. Private ownership of roving animals had no place in the conceptions of tribesmen, who continued to kill cows and pigs that strayed any distance from the planter's clearing. All attempts to place physical distance between red man and white failed as plantations multiplied. Territorily the Indian was the injured party. Several tribes complained that continued encroachment left them with hardly "Land Enough to make their corn fields on." But the final touch, an order that Indians fence their fields to keep out ranging cattle, must have seemed both unreasonable and unfair.

Property rights posed conceptual difficulties for the Indian, but the white man's hard liquor presented a different kind of problem. Fur traders first learned of native susceptibility to hot and fiery waters, and other settlers quickly followed their lead as soon as they found that in drink an Indian would part with his lands as well as his furs. The Nanticoke on the Eastern Shore complained that "the English bring strong Drink to the Towns and sell it among their Indians to their great Prejudice." Though forbidden by law, the practice became so notorious that Maryland authorities eventually authorized "the Great men at the Indian Towns . . . to break and Stove the Bottles, Casqs and Barrels, or oversett and Spill such other Vessells wherein such Liquors shall be." Nevertheless thirsty natives came to planters' houses in search of rum or brandy and sometimes ran amok after overindulging. Sternly warned against selling liquor to natives, individual planters still continued to serve strong drink, often to their own detriment.

In these encounters the Indian almost uniformly came off second best. The records contain occasional gory descriptions of planters, their wives, and their children being brutally murdered or sometimes scalped alive. Frequently, strange Indians, visiting parties of Delawares or Iroquois, were blamed for these outrages, and within a few years after first settlement planters acquired a wholesome fear of these outsiders, who could not always be distinguished from local tribesmen. Consequently whites distrusted any native who approached without giving a locally recognized sign of peaceable intent. Inevitably a double standard came to prevail in punishment of offenses. Acting on instructions from the Lord Proprietor, Governor Calvert attempted to punish crimes committed by whites with the same even-handed justice he meted out to Indians, only to be frustrated by local sentiment. In 1642 one John Elkin, indicted for murdering the "King" of the Yaocomico, was prosecuted by the attorney general, who produced in evidence Elkin's signed confession that he had killed the Indian. In spite of this incriminating evidence the jury brought in a verdict of not guilty with the explanation that they did not consider killing a pagan a breach of "his Lordship's peace or the King's." As presiding judge Governor Calvert informed the jurors that the Indians of Maryland "were in the peace of the King and his Lordship's peace" and sent them back to reconsider. Their revised verdict—"guilty of murther in his owne defence"—infuriated the governor who told the jurymen it "implied a contradiction" and again sent them out to deliberate. In the third verdict the jury announced "that they found that Elkin had killed the Indian in his owne defence." Calvert thereupon ruled against entering the verdict on the record and ordered another jury empannelled to "enquire and try the same evidence." Meanwhile he levied fines on the dismissed jurymen for returning unreasonable verdicts. The governor imposed a particularly stiff fine on one of the dismissed jurors, George Pye, who openly reproached the whole court for making too much over the death of an Indian. If Calvert had intended to impress the new jury with his determination to maintain a single standard of justice, he failed. The second jury brought in a verdict, "guilty of manslaughter." Quite clearly no jury was ready to convict a white man of murdering an Indian, no matter how obvious the guilt of the accused.

Against this background of disharmony most of the tribes came under suspicion of hostile intentions toward whites, still numerically small. Governor Calvert concerned himself chiefly with the Susquehanna at the northern end of the bay. Legends of their prodigious physiques, their hollow voices, and their ferocity as warriors, current among smaller and weaker tribes of southern Maryland, kept governor and colonists in awe of their northern neighbors. Calvert planned expeditions against the Susquehanna in 1639 and again in 1640, though neither of these forays actually took place. Not until 1643 did a punitive force, commanded by Thomas Cornwallis, sail north to settle accounts with "the Susquihannas or any their aiders." Unfortunately the records contain only a few delphic scraps of information about this expedition, which certainly ended without glory and left in enemy hands goods and arms, including "two field pieces." The net result, an uneasy truce between Susquehanna and colonists, lasted on through the upheaval of 1644 in Virginia, when Opechancanough led the Powhatan confederacy in a massive retaliation that resembled the massacre of 1622. The Maryland tribes did not join Opechancanough and, though tense, Maryland planters did not experience the horrors that racked Virginia.

After 1644 Maryland had little trouble with the Susquehanna. During the next few years an epidemic of smallpox ravaged their villages and reduced the fighting force of this feared tribe to a sorry remnant. Furthermore attacks from neighbors to the north neutralized Susquehanna striking power. Like other Maryland tribes the once mighty Susquehanna experienced the slow process of decay and demoralization that left their former hunting grounds undefended against white settlement. Meanwhile danger to Lord Baltimore's palatinate, still tiny in numbers, came not from the red man but from whites, within and without the colony.

—5—

The long shadow of troubles in England presaged the beginnings of new and more critical misfortunes for the Maryland palatinate. Tension between king and Parliament had come to an open break in 1642 when, on 22 August, Charles I raised the royal standard at Nottingham and proclaimed the commons and their soldiers in rebellion. In dismally wet weather loyal cavaliers rallied to the king's arms, but never in numbers sufficient to offset a parliamentary lead in money, men, and arms. On land the fortunes of war, after many vacillations, turned inexorably against the royalists until the king's final defeat. But from the very first, Parliament had secured the fleet and with it control of the seas.

It was by sea that Maryland received the shock waves of civil war back home. A principal agent was one Richard Ingle, shipmaster and early adherent of Parliament, who first appeared in Maryland in 1641. During his first known visit Ingle ran afoul of the talented Brent family—Giles, Fulke, and their two sisters, Margaret and Mary—in his business transactions. Accordingly when Ingle returned on a second voyage in late 1643 breathing maledictions against royalists—"The King is no King" and similar words—he found himself facing serious trouble. Governor Leonard Calvert had recently returned briefly to England for a personal report to his brother, the Lord Proprietor, leaving Giles Brent acting head of state. As acting governor, Brent ordered Ingle's arrest on the charge of "high treason to his Majesty," a dangerous move because Ingle had come to the Chesapeake with parliamentary letters of marque authorizing him to seize any ships in the king's service. Ingle did suffer arrest but found a friend in Thomas Cornwallis, who contrived to set him free from the sheriff's custody and return him to the quarter deck of his ship. Ingle promptly sailed for England, taking along as a passenger Cornwallis, who now felt impelled to "flie" with him.

Maryland next saw Ingle in February 1645 when he appeared in the bay aboard a vessel appropriately named *Reformation*, heavily armed and manned by a hardy crew. Ingle gave the broadest interpretation to his letters of marque. His proceedings—highhanded to say the least—in time acquired the name "Ingle's Rebellion." Certainly the ensuing turmoil deserves a descriptive name, though not rebellion in the technical sense. Ingle landed a crew from *Reformation,* took possession of St. Mary's City by force, and tendered "an oath of submission" to provincials. Several, Catholic and Protestant alike, refused the oath and became victims of the pillage that followed. Ingle adopted the contemporaneous practice of rewarding his men with plunder in lieu of money payments, and they took full advantage of the opportunity. Among others they set upon the properties of Ingle's sometime benefactor, Thomas Cornwallis, joined his rebellious servants, and despoiled his affluent estate—burning fences, driving off cattle, even wrenching locks off the doors—in the amount of £3000, according to Cornwallis's statement. Thereafter the looters went off to prey on other provincials. In Ingle's self-serving statement, "It pleased God to enable him to take divers places from them." For a season Ingle had his way. Governor Calvert fled to Virginia, and William Claiborne returned to Maryland to reassert his claim to Kent Island. Between them Ingle and Claiborne had unopposed control of Lord Baltimore's palatinate.

The plundering time, as many colonists called the reign of Ingle, lasted until Governor Calvert raised an armed force in Virginia and returned to Maryland with soldiery at his heels. Ingle had sailed for England by that time, leaving part of his leaderless band to continue their depredations. Confronted with Calvert's organized force, the despoilers melted away, and the governor arrived at St. Inego's Fort in time to meet an Assembly called for late December 1646. Claiborne attempted unsuccessfully to persuade Kent Island residents to move across the bay and take the governor prisoner. Thereafter he retired a second time to Virginia and Governor Calvert "reduced" Kent Island to obedience with no more lethal weapon than the offer of a general pardon. Calvert had recovered Maryland for the house of Baltimore in adverse circumstances, and his magnanimous conduct in victory worked in favor of the proprietor. By contrast the days of Ingle bit deep in the memory of provincials. The Assembly distilled popular sentiment to a vivid, if overdrawn, statement in an address to Lord Baltimore: "Great and many have been the miseries calamities and other suffering . . . undergone here since the beginning of the heinous rebellion first put in practice by that pirate Ingle and afterwards almost for two years continued by his accomplices and confederates . . . Most of your lordship's loyal friends here were spoiled of their whole estate . . . plundered and deprived in a manner of all livelyhood . . . under that intolerable yoke which they were forced to bear." In the popular mind Ingle had become both a pirate and rebel.

—6—

Ingle had stepped off the Maryland stage, but his disappearance took away only a single disturbing element from the troubled scene. The dates 1640 and 1660 embrace one of the most complicated and crucial periods of Maryland history. Beneath the surface turbulence strong currents were sweeping out channels that contained the flow of provincial history through the remaining years of the century. Proprietor and country still had much to learn about the functioning of the executive branch and general Assembly, and about the role of religion in this frontier province.

When Governor Leonard Calvert returned from Virginia he could not have known that his mortal span had less than a year to run. Wisely he forebore a policy of proscription on the tiny population and instead issued general pardons, insisting only on an oath of fidelity to the Lord Proprietor. Before leaving Virginia he had promised his soldiery money payment for their service to prevent wholesale pillage, the common compensation for troops. Now that he had accomplished peaceful investiture, he found himself without funds and, fearful of mutiny, prepared to satisfy pay claims from his personal assets or, if necessary, even proprietary monies. In the midst of these arrangements Calvert sickened and on 9 June appeared in the last extremity. He had already commissioned Robert Vaughan as captain general and commander, under himself, of Kent Island. On his deathbed he named Thomas Greene, a leading Roman Catholic, his successor as governor, and to administer his estate and personal affairs he nominated his kinswoman, Margaret Brent. The same evening he died after a ten year term as governor of his brother's province.

To this triumvirate—Greene, Vaughan, and Margaret Brent—fell the task of restoring tranquility to an unsettled province. Vaughan, once an indentured servant, had the job of securing Kent Island, now a separate county and something of a frontier march but still claimed by Claiborne. Governor Greene inherited the complexities of administering a province still small in population but dangerously unbalanced in religion, with Protestants outnumbering Catholics by three to one. But Margaret Brent had the most pressing and ticklish task of the three: satisfying the soldiers' demands for pay with something less than adequate funds in her hands.

This remarkable woman proved herself intrepid as well as resourceful. When Governor Greene summoned his first Assembly Margaret Brent marched in to the gathering and "requested to have vote in the house for her selfe and voyce allso for that att the last Court 3d Jan: it was ordered that the said Mrs. Brent was to be looked uppon and received as his Lordship's Attorney." When the governor as presiding officer "denyed" her request she protested all proceedings "unless shee may be present and have vote as aforesaid." Frustrated in her political demarche, Margaret Brent moved ahead in her most critical job of quieting the pay claims of the soldiery, whose murmurs threatened to grow into mutiny. She took the necessary assets from the estate of the late Governor Calvert and, when these proved insufficient, turned to the properties of the Lord Proprietor himself to stave off possible mutiny. When Lord Baltimore later objected to sequestration of his funds the whole Assembly rallied to her and vouched for her justification in view of contemporary tensions.

In vividness and accomplishment Margaret Brent outmatched Governor Greene, whose administration lasted only fourteen months. In August of 1648 the Lord Proprietor superseded him with a Protestant governor, William Stone, a resident of Southampton County, Virginia, who guided the province through nearly a decade of perils that appeared almost as soon as he assumed his post.

—7—

Governor Stone could hardly have been ignorant of recent troubles in Maryland. Ingle had actually compelled Baltimore's duly commissioned chief magistrate to flee from the colony, a bit of news that spread throughout the Chesapeake even in a day of imperfect communication. Neither could Stone have easily previsioned the troubles in store for his administration, though they grew out of one of his earliest decisions.

> In the yeer 1649, many, both of the congregated Church, and others well-affected people in Virginia, being debarred from the free exercise of Religion under the Government of Sir William Berkeley, removed themselves, Families and Estates into the Province of Maryland, being thereunto invited by Captain Stone . . . with promise of Liberty in Religion and Priviledges of English Subjects.

Stone's invitation was consonant with Baltimore's desire to attract immigrants and with his policy of religious toleration in that intolerant age. The people of the congregated church—Puritans to use their common name—had incurred the wrath of Governor William Berkeley, a staunch Anglican, and some three hundred of them removed from Virginia to settle an area they named "Providence," in good Puritan tradition, at the mouth of the Severn River. Their leader, Richard Bennett, had preceded them by a few months when banished by Governor Berkeley and had selected the spot.

Stone had promised the Puritans land, toleration, and full civil rights. On each commitment he made good. His first Assembly passed the famous "Act Concerning Religion," which provided stiff fines for such expressions of religious opprobrium as "heretick, Scismatick, Idolater, puritan, Independant, Prespitarian, popish priest, Jesuite, Jesuited papist, Lutheran, Calvenist, Anabaptist, Brownist, Antinomian, Barrowist, Roundhead, Sepratist" or any other. The operative clause of the act read, "no person or persons whatsoever within this Province . . . professing to believe in Jesus Christ, shall from henceforth bee any waies troubled, molested or discountenanced for or in respect of his or her religion nor in the free exercise thereof . . . nor any way compelled to the beleife or exercise of any other Religion against his or her consent." The language and intent are strikingly similar to the instructions Cecilius, Lord Baltimore, had given his brother for guidance at the time of first settlement. Equally protective of Catholic and Protestant confessions, the Act Concerning Religion enjoys the status of the earliest legislation in the English-speaking world explicitly granting toleration to all Christians. The Puritans themselves at the moment professed satisfaction with the "freedom and liberty in the exercise of our religion, under his Lordship's government and interest."

Before long their tune changed. Like their Puritan brethren elsewhere the men of Providence showed remarkable talent for discovering faults. They found in the oath of fidelity to Lord Baltimore certain pretensions to royalty, at a time when the king himself was standing trial for his life in England. Worse still they saw in the oath a commitment to support "that government and those officers who were sworn to countenance and uphold anti-Christ . . . the Roman Catholic Religion." Many among them "exceedingly scrupled" to take the oath.

Against this background of growing uneasiness a single untoward accident set off an avalanche of misfortunes for the proprietary establishment. In England the protracted struggle between the king and a Puritan-dominated Parliament ended when Charles I went to the executioner's block in 1649. Parliament immediately issued a decree making it treason to acknowledge "Charles Stuart, son of the late Charles, commonly called the Prince of Wales . . . to be king or chief magistrate of England or Ireland, or of any dominion belonging thereunto." Nevertheless Thomas Greene, acting as deputy governor during a visit of Governor Stone to Virginia, proclaimed Charles II as lawful sovereign. Stone hurried back to reverse his error but he could never expunge the memory of the blunder. Maryland stood condemned of defiance along with Virginia where Governor Berkeley had declared for King Charles II.

Parliamentary retaliation came in the form of a commission "to reduce all plantations within the Bay of Chesapeake" to obedience. The commission included two members well acquainted with Maryland affairs, Richard Bennett and William Claiborne, who lost no time proceeding to St. Mary's to accept the submission of Governor Stone and his acknowledgment of parliamentary authority. Actually Claiborne acted with considerable restraint. Instead of plundering and otherwise punishing men who had deprived him of Kent Island properties and had passed an act of attainder against him, he joined Bennett in placing the province temporarily in the hands of a "council" and a short time later restoring Governor Stone to office "until the pleasure of the State of England be further known." Bennett and Claiborne then returned to duties in Virginia. But the general effect proved to be a confusion of authority for many months in the future. Rumor and uncertainty left administration of the province in a state of near chaos, with Stone nominally the governor but the Puritans maintaining their autonomy on the Severn.

Not until 1654 did the stalemate disappear and then only to dissolve into civil war. In July the Puritans of Providence urged Bennett and Claiborne to return to Maryland on the pretext that Governor Stone had fallen into "rebellion" against the Commonwealth established by Oliver Cromwell at home. Late in the month Bennett and Claiborne in effect set Stone aside and appointed "for the conservation of the peace and public administration of justice" ten Puritans "to be Commissioners for the well ordering, directing, and governing the affairs of Maryland."

The new Puritan Commissioners convened an Assembly at Patuxent, miles away from St. Mary's City but more convenient to settlers at Providence. Without delay the Assembly overturned the proprietary and his policies, substituting for them a genuinely Puritan regime. Among six laws that members voted to repeal were the toleration act and the act outlawing William Claiborne. The forty-five acts put on the books at the end of the session included the usual Puritan blue laws against sabbath breaking, adultery and fornication, swearing, drunkenness, slander and tale-bearing. But more pointedly an "Act of Recognition" officially sanctioned the Puritan commissioners as the government, a new "Act Concerning Religion" restrained Catholics from the exercise of their religion, and legislation under the title "Concerning Rights of Land" excused provincials from taking the oath of fidelity to Lord Baltimore. In one brief session during October of 1654 the Puritans had effectively wrested control from proprietary authorities and placed it in the hands of a commission headed by William Fuller, a leading Puritan of Providence.

Thus the stage was set for civil war in provincial Maryland, for Lord Baltimore had successfully appealed to the highest authority back home. Oliver Cromwell had dismissed Parliament and under the title Lord Protector had taken the government of Britain and the dominions into his hands. Lord Baltimore put his case before Cromwell and moved the Lord Protector to reprove the Puritans and to command them to desist from "disturbing the Lord Baltimore, or his officers, or people in Maryland." Once Cromwell had decided in his favor, the proprietor bestirred his governor, William Stone, to reassert his authority in Maryland.

The first step toward restoring proprietary authority proved easy. Governor Stone dispatched one John Hammond to Patuxent where the Puritans had deposited the provincial records at the house of Richard Preston, speaker of the Assembly that had seized control the previous October. Hammond recovered the records without serious difficulty and brought them back to St. Mary's. But the next steps toward restoring authority were less clear. Evidently Governor Stone thought his personal appearance with the symbols of authority most likely to impress the Puritan element in Providence. In March of 1655 he assembled upward of a hundred men, embarked them in a dozen small craft, and moved toward the Severn River.

In the prevailing state of tension and distrust a clash became almost inevitable. The detailed accounts of what happened and how contain much conflicting evidence, but the outline of events emerges quite unmistakably. Both sides sent messengers to the other; both sides received the messages with distrust. On Saturday, 24 March 1655, Stone moved his force close to the Severn River. The Puritans opposed him with even larger numbers of troops, assisted from the water by Roger Heamans, master of the armed ship *Golden Lion,* lying near the shore. As soon as Governor Stone led his men in formation toward the Puritan settlement, Heamans fired a volley with the ship's guns, and William Fuller, commander of the Puritan ground force, gave the word—so an eyewitness recounts—"In the name of God fall on; God is our strength." Outnumbered and outmanned, Governor Stone yielded upon promise of quarter after losing nearly half his men as casualties.

The aftermath of the Battle of the Severn, described by the most objective of the witnesses as a "skirmish," did nothing to ease bad feelings between proprietary partisans and Puritans. Within three days the victors condemned ten prisoners to death and actually executed four of the number. Governor Stone, slightly wounded in the fighting, was held prisoner along with his council for over a month. Even the interposition of Cromwell himself, who ordered the Puritans to desist pending a hearing of both sides, did not end the uncertain outlook for the proprietary regime.

For more than two years final disposition hung in abeyance until late November of 1657 when a "treaty" between Lord Baltimore and Richard Bennett for the Puritans effected a settlement of the "very sad and distracted condition" of Maryland. Baltimore received confirmation of his patent and agreed to a general amnesty. One of the articles of agreement restored the toleration previously provided in the first "Act Concerning Religion" of 1649. To all appearances Maryland returned to the status quo ante bellum. And yet tribulations had not ended.

—8—

It may have seemed to Lord Baltimore in 1658 that he had finally succeeded in his protracted effort to maintain his patent to Maryland and to keep the lid on the boiling cauldron there. Certainly he had seen the end of imprints in the fierce war of polemics published during the time of troubles. The controversy had produced five major pamphlets, beginning in 1653 with *The Lord Baltimore's Case,* a short piece cast in the form of objections and answers, the answers wholly favorable to the Lord Proprietor. After the fashion of polemical warfare of the time the rejoinder came two years later under the verbose title, *Virginia and Maryland, or the Lord Baltimore's Printed Case Uncased and Answered.* The tone and thrust are clearly indicated in the 218 word subtitle, which includes such phrases as "the illegality of his Patent . . . The Injustice and Tyranny practiced in the Government . . . the Papists late Rebellion against the Government of his Highness the Lord Protector . . . assault on the Protestants . . . the oppression of the poor," and so on. Pamphleteers of the day pulled all the stops. Another imprint,

Babylon's Fall (1655), by one Leonard Strong, "Agent for the People of Providence in Maryland," gave a dramatic, anti-proprietary account of the Battle of the Severn and had its counterpart in John Langford's *Refutation of Babylon's Fall,* containing a contradictory but more temperate story of the battle. Exchanges came to a close in 1656 with the longest of these writings, *Leah and Rachel, or, The Two Fruitful Sisters Virginia and Maryland,* by John Hammond, who had been a resident in both colonies. Hammond's piece contained vivid descriptions of both provinces, frequently quoted by later historians, and, as a kind of coda, a brief homily enjoining the provinces to live in peace and fruitfulness as the two sisters Leah and Rachel did in biblical days.

And indeed peace did come to Maryland and Virginia. After signing the agreement with Bennett, Lord Baltimore was finally rid of that "pestilent enemie to the welfare of the Province" as he called William Claiborne. It was among his own people and specifically his own subordinate, Governor Josias Fendall, that the Lord Proprietor had his next vexing problem.

A sturdy supporter of his lordship, Fendall became governor, in name at least, during the months between Stone's imprisonment and the "treaty" with Bennett in late 1657. But not until February of 1658 did Fendall shed his purely nominal role and perform the actual duties as appointed first magistrate. In the following two years he took the province a considerable distance away from the worst disorders of the decade. He managed to persuade the Puritans in the Severn area, now erected into a new county named Anne Arundel, to send representatives to an Assembly that he tactfully held in recently established Calvert County, halfway between their seat and St. Mary's City. Now that the turmoil appeared past, the legislature, formerly unicameral, sat as two separate bodies, an upper house consisting of the governor and council and a lower house of elected delegates from each of the four counties: St. Mary's, Kent, Calvert, and Anne Arundel. At last Maryland had a miniature parliament. Fendall showed legislative skill in shepherding several much needed laws through the Assembly, and he pressed forward in administrative organization of the province when he erected two additional counties, Charles to the west and Baltimore in the frontier area at the head of the bay.

Just as Maryland regained a degree of tranquility a novel occurrence brought fresh trouble. The overt act that gave the name Fendall's

Rebellion to the new disturbance came during a meeting of the Assembly in February and March of 1660, a momentous year for both Maryland and the mother country. As the Assembly convened, General Monck, Cromwell's successor in power, was marching toward London, and a revived Parliament at Westminster was restoring its excluded members preliminary to the recall of Charles Stuart as rightful monarch. These decisive events back home could not have been known on the Chesapeake when Fendall and his council met the elected burgesses for a session unique in Maryland history.

From beginning to end the transactions of this Assembly were unprecedented and obscure. The meetings took place not at St. Mary's City in formal chambers but at "Mr. Thomas Gerrard's howse" for two initial days and thereafter at the house of Robert Slye, elected delegate from St. Mary's County. On the tenth day the elected delegates sent a message to the governor and council, namely, the upper house:

> The Assembly of Burgesses judging themselves to be a lawfull Assembly without dependence on any other power in the Province now in being is the highest court of Judicature And if any Objection can be made to the Contrary, Wee desire to heare it.

To this startling manifesto the upper house returned a message posing two main questions. Did the burgesses mean that the lower house was a complete Assembly without governor and council? All present could easily remember the day when the Commons of England had abolished the House of Lords and made themselves alone the Parliament of the realm. Secondly, did the burgesses mean that they were wholly independent of "the Lord Proprietary yea or nay?" Again Parliament had dethroned the Stuarts, as all could remember.

Two days of conferences did little either to bring the two houses into rapport or to clarify the aims of the burgesses. On Wednesday, 14 March, the only formal record, the upper house journal, abruptly ends with the governor and council sitting in a single body with the burgesses, as demanded during the conferences. Maryland had slipped back to the primitive unicameral legislature of earlier times. Governor Fendall accepted these conditions and the further stipulation that the speaker of the house, not the governor, have power to adjourn the

Assembly. One important member of the council refused: Secretary Philip Calvert, brother of the Lord Baltimore and a recent arrival in the province, protested these proceedings as "a manifest breach of his lordship's Right Royall Jurisdiction and Seiniory." Calvert demanded that the reasons offered be entered upon the record, "but was denied it by the Governor." Whereupon Secretary Calvert asked permission to leave. "You may if you please, we shall not force you to stay," replied the governor.

With these words the record ends; but speculation continued and there were further consequences. Two sober witnesses later charged, in sworn depositions, that Fendall aimed "to change the Government into the forme of a Commonwealth." They went on to accuse Fendall of two overt acts of rebellion, namely of surrendering his commission from Lord Baltimore in exchange for a new one from the Assembly, and subsequently of attempts to "rayse a faction against his Lordship's Jurisdiction." Whether he physically handed over the proprietary commission or not, he certainly did so by implication when he assented to lower house hegemony. He did not, however, have time to consolidate a supporting party. If, as an early chronicler tells us, Fendall conspired to "play the part in Maryland which Cromwell had just performed in England," he failed miserably. On 24 June Lord Baltimore commissioned his younger brother, Philip Calvert, as governor. This commission and an order from King Charles II, recently restored to his throne, cut short Fendall's "pygmie rebellion," as Baltimore liked to call it.

The time of troubles had, at long last, ended.

4

THE FORMATIVE YEARS

From his vantage point in England, Cecilius, Lord Baltimore, could look with some satisfaction on the prospects at home and abroad during the closing months of 1660. His liege Lord, Charles II, now firmly seated on the throne of his ancestors, had begun a reign that was to last a quarter century and was to imprint on his country that combination of astuteness, dissimulation, depravity, and creativeness associated with Restoration England. From the restored monarch Lord Baltimore expected no direct threat, and as long as Charles II ruled there was none. In his overseas province of Maryland the prospects appeared tolerable, at least by comparison with the times of troubles. Baltimore's younger brother, Philip, had treated the author of the "pygmie rebellion" leniently, allowing Fendall to retire to his estate in Charles County on promise of good behavior. Thereafter Philip had addressed himself to restoring proprietary authority in the province, now organized in six counties, all of them along the Western Shore except Kent which served as the administrative division for the entire Eastern Shore. These six counties and their subdivisions, the hundreds each presided over by a constable to keep the peace, appeared top-heavy in administrative structure for a still tiny population. This arrangement could be justified only by the thin distribution of the inhabitants along the bayside from St. Mary's to the Susquehanna, over a hundred miles as the crow flies. Peopling his province and at the same time maintaining his palatine authority were among the chief concerns of Cecilius, Lord Baltimore, in the remaining fifteen years of his proprietorship. The two objectives were not always harmonious.

—1—

The population of Maryland was actually declining by the time of Ingle's rebellion and, during the years following, increased only slowly. One careful student counted only 168 taxables out of about 350 people in the year 1648, not a significantly larger number than this vast area contained immediately after the landing of *Ark* and *Dove* in 1634. Civil War back home had reduced emigration to a trickle, and live births hardly equalled deaths in the local population. By far, the larger portion of people who had migrated were males, and among them the mortality rate ran high. The New World had a way of shaking the strongest constitutions before the immigrant had passed through the "seasoning" period. Some of those who did survive fevers and ague, the most frequently mentioned causes of death, in time married and established families. But women were few and those who migrated did not take husbands until they were well advanced in their childbearing years. Consequently the earliest immigrant population failed even to reproduce itself fully.

Nevertheless the children born to these marriages played an important role in transforming the demography of Maryland. Native born children lived longer and suffered less sickness than their immigrant parents. Among the native born, males and females were about equal in numbers. Most important, the native born women began their reproductive careers at a younger age than their immigrant mothers and usually in better health. If travelers' reports are to be credited, these native born women were prodigies of fertility. Even though they could not escape entirely the perils of death in childbed or their progeny avoid the high rate of infant mortality, these "country born," as they soon began to style themselves, helped to work a change in population direction toward a more balanced ratio between the sexes.

Still population growth depended heavily upon immigration through the remaining decades of the seventeenth century. Just before the restoration of 1660 a count of the inhabitants put the total number at about 2,500. In the quarter century since the landing of *Ark* and *Dove* the population had increased tenfold from the original 250. Even so, for the millions of acres and hundreds of miles of shoreline the absolute number was insignificant, a few seeds in a vast wilderness.

Within the next fifteen years the number increased to approximately 13,000, chiefly by the arrival of new immigrants, again predominantly male. A few migrated in family units, ordinarily with sufficient resources to become immediately small independent land owners able to play a role in county politics. Larger numbers came as indentured servants, who earned their freedom within a few years to swell the ranks of freemen in the province. The Lord Proprietor took considerable interest in the movement of indentured servants to Maryland and in all probability gave financial encouragement to a remarkable bit of promotional literature, George Alsop's pamphlet, *A Character of the Province of Maryland,* published in London during 1666.

Alsop had excellent qualifications, he told his readers, for describing the province and for evaluating the quality of society there. He had himself served a four-year term as an indentured servant on a plantation in Baltimore County and spoke from direct experience. Then in grandiloquent style, a bit coarse at times and spiced with touches of innuendo, he proceeded to a wholly favorable account "of the situation and plenty of the Province of Mary-Land," of the mild government and absence of crime. The heart of Alsop's pamphlet is found in his chapter on "the common usage of Servants in Mary-Land, together with their Priviledges," a description of the bondsman's lot from initial indenture to ultimate freedom. While technically correct in most statements, Alsop is misleading. His account suffuses a rosy glow on an institution that other commentators show in a grim, sometimes even cruel, light. In Alsop's version any person without passage money needed only to sign an indenture, or agreement, to serve three or four years with a merchant bound for Maryland. The merchant provided everything "necessary and convenient" for the voyage and on arrival allowed the servant some time to find a purchaser of the indenture, or as Alsop glibly put it, "after their curiosity has picht on one whom they think fit for their turn, and that they may live well withall." He found it necessary to condemn a rumor "That those which are transported over thither, are sold in open Market for Slaves, and draw in Carts like Horses; which is so damnable an untruth, that if they should search to the very Center of Hell, and enquire for a Lye of the most antient and damned stamp, I confidently believe they could not find one to parallel this."

Once situated, Alsop continued, male servants had relatively easy duties in summer: five and a half days of labor a week and on hottest days three hours at midday to "repose themselves." In winter they worked still less, only cutting wood used for the fires and hunting the plentiful game. Servants with special skills, either "Handicraft or Mechanick," received preferential treatment as well as their masters' esteem "above measure." At the expiration of their time, servants became freemen and received "by the Custom of the Country," fifty acres of land, corn enough for a year, three suits of clothing, and tools of his trade." Thereafter, he concluded, "they live passingly well." Women had the best time of all: "For they are no sooner on shoar, but they are courted into a copulative Matrimony."

The records do not bear out all of Alsop's claims. Talented servants had always fared well after their terms. In earlier decades Zachary Wade and Robert Vaughan had acquired estates in land and chattels and had held posts of honor and profit. Men of their calibre continued to appear and to rise to prominence, examples of the American success story. For the majority, opportunities to advance were fuller in the early years; most could attain a competence and participate to some small degree in public life, even if no more than doing jury duty. But each passing decade after the Restoration witnessed a decline in opportunity for the freedmen, in part because the economy fell on hard times, in part because society became increasingly structured. Dominant planters, particularly the county justices and sheriffs, established harsher relations with their former servants and demanded greater deference from them. Complaints of inadequate food, clothing, and shelter and of brutality from overseers were most frequently levelled against this group. Often the planter-justices retained their ex-servants as laborers, as tenants on their own extensive lands, or as overseers of newly indentured servants. Facing barriers to social integration, many freedmen left the county to seek their fortunes in another part of the province, and a few removed to Virginia or North Carolina in the hope of improving their lot. Those who remained locally rooted often took their wives from former maidservants of their own masters or neighboring planters and established families that further increased the population. Altogether for the vast majority, life in the province fell short of Alsop's rosy description.

—2—

Philip Calvert presided as chief magistrate over Maryland for a year and a half. In late 1661 he was superseded by Cecilius's own son and heir, Charles, then only twenty-four years of age. Except for two brief absences for business in England, Charles Calvert administered the proprietorship until 1684 when he returned permanently to the homeland. For nearly a quarter century, then, Calvert stood at the head of provincial affairs during a period of unprecedented growth and multiplying complexities. In his first years as governor young Charles Calvert could turn for immediate advice to his uncle Philip, who became provincial secretary and chancellor and sat as senior member of the council. Ultimately, of course, as governor he looked for guidance to his father, whose authoritarian philosophy he shared and applied in his conduct of provincial affairs.

In administration Governor Calvert showed considerable technical skill. He organized the Eastern Shore, hitherto the single county of Kent, into four new counties as population advanced: Somerset and Dorchester in the south, Talbot in the center, and Cecil in the north. Aside from obvious convenience to settlers in conducting their local affairs, the new counties, each empowered to elect four delegates to the Assembly, brought Eastern Shore representation into reasonable balance with the older counties on the main. Calvert also continued executive reorganization by further dividing the provincial secretary's office. In 1673 he established a separate office for testamentary and probate business headed by a "Judge or Commissary General." The papers of the commissary general's office, an immense series of folio volumes housed today at the Maryland Hall of Records, contain in the last wills and testaments, the inventories of estates, and the final accounts of executors a store of treasure almost beyond belief for the social history of colonial Maryland. The Calverts had in mind more practical purposes: assuring proper descent of property to heirs and securing creditors of deceased planters from loss. With equally practical intent the Calverts took another function from the secretary in 1676 and put it in the hands of three "Naval Officers" charged with entering and clearing all vessels to insure collection of revenues. Altogether the

Restoration proprietary showed real ingenuity in ordering administration for more efficient and more profitable operation.

During his administration young Charles Calvert discovered that good government involved much more than clear apportionment of duties and operation of offices. As population grew and the province took on the appearance of permanence the Assembly showed signs of developing a will of its own, not always consonant with proprietary policy. After the Restoration the provincial Assembly met as two houses, the governor's council as the upper house and the elected "burgesses," four from each county and two from St. Mary's City, as the lower house. From the upper house the governor expected no difficulties. He chose his councillors carefully from a select group of wealthier provincials, most of them blood kin or allied by ties of marriage and consequently sympathetic to proprietary policies and ready to do the proprietor's will. Understandably the Calverts had adopted this rule of exclusiveness in appointments to higher office as a proper personnel policy to maintain tight control of provincial administration. But the elected members, soon to acquire the title "delegates," came to sessions unencumbered by any obligation save to their constituents. As the decade wore on this representative element showed a disturbing independence of thought, occasionally grumbling at the authoritarian proprietary administration. In 1669 the delegates neared a confrontation with what they called "his Lordship's prerogative."

The April session of 1669 opened with a rousing sermon by Charles Nicholett, chaplain of the lower house, who told receptive delegates that they were "chosen or elected both by God and man and have a power put into their hands." He reminded them that the Commons of England had done "brave things" and exhorted them to assume "a Liberty equal to the people of England." Evidently Nicholett's words had a tonic effect on his hearers, for a committee of delegates waited on the upper house to demand a copy of Lord Baltimore's charter "that they may the better proceed," adding diplomatically "and not intrench upon his Lordship's prerogative."

The governor and upper house were not to be put off by this show of tact. They hailed Nicholett before them, listened to his explanation that some delegates had asked him "to stir up the Lower House to do their Duty," then in their most formal manner fined him forty shillings and ordered him "to Crave the pardon of the Lord Proprietor, the

Lieutenant General, and the Assembly" for his meddling with matters pertaining to government. Nicholett complied, but the fat was in the fire. The session proceeded along a stormy course, climaxed by a manifesto from the lower house entitled "The Publick Grievances," a catalog of several specific charges so serious that the frustrated upper house labelled them "mutinous & seditious" and demanded them "razed out of the Journalls." What appeared complete deadlock resolved into compromise: the lower house erased from its journal three of the most offensive "grievances" and the upper house agreed to strike from its "Journal Book the words (Mutinous & seditious)," which the delegates found intolerable. Thereafter the session moved along with less thunder and lightning to produce a respectable body of legislation. But the Assembly of 1669 marked the beginning of a new era in provincial affairs, at once a reflection of growing vitality in the body politic and of emerging polarity between proprietor and country.

On the proprietary side reaction followed inexorably. Some months after the session Governor Charles Calvert issued an order to the sheriffs of the several counties disfranchising all freemen of the colony who had less than fifty acres of land or a personal estate within the county of less than £40 sterling. By a stroke of the pen the proprietary government had established a property qualification for voting, a questionable interpretation of charter rights not unnoticed by the lower house of the Assembly. A few years later in 1676 a similar edict reduced the number of delegates elected from each county to a mere two, half of the former representation, again in the teeth of lower house protest. This second exercise of the prerogative gave an earnest of things to come, for in 1675 Cecilius, Lord Baltimore, had died and Charles had succeeded as Lord Proprietor. For nearly a decade thereafter, proprietor and governor were united in a single person, a resident of the province. In these ten years, the Lord Baron, wielder of the prerogative, lived and labored in direct contact with the people that he was pleased to call his "faithful tenants" in the travail of bringing forth a society.

—3—

Over the religious complexion of Maryland society the proprietor exercised no control whatever. From first settlement Protestants had outnumbered Catholics, but during the time of troubles and especially in the decades after the Restoration immigrants tipped the balance so much further that Catholics became increasingly a minority element. Moreover, the newcomers, who represented many confessions, gave Maryland a polyglot character religiously. One commentator mentioned "Presbyterians, Independents, Anabaptists, Quakers," and Catholics, without covering all the ground.

Members of the Society of Friends—"people called Quakers"—found asylum in Maryland in small numbers before 1661, when one of their missionaries reported several settled meetings in the province. At first the government took a dubious view of two Quaker traits: "diswading the people from complying with the Military discipline in this tyme of Danger, as also from giving testimony or being Jurors in Causes between party and party." But neither Quaker pacifism nor aversion to oaths visited upon the Friends the savage punishment they suffered in other colonies, notably Massachusetts Bay. The number of meetings multiplied, particularly in Anne Arundel County on the Western Shore and in Talbot County directly across the bay. In 1672 George Fox, founder of the Society of Friends, visited Maryland to convene the first general meetings at West River near Annapolis and at Tred Avon in Talbot County. Fox's *Journal* notes that the Eastern Shore meeting attracted not only Friends but "many of the World, both Protestants of divers sorts, and some Papists," on some days as many as a thousand persons altogether, including "several magistrates, and their Wives, and other Persons of chief Account in the Country." Looking back on his experience as he left the province, Fox thought the meetings "wonderful glorious."

Fox dwelt on the devotional character of the meetings, the conversions or "convincements," but other Quakers observed that the meetings had another side. "Many people resort to it and transact a great deal of trade one with another," said one Friend, "so that it is a kind of market or change where the captains of ships and planters meet and settle their affairs; and this draws abundance of people of the best rank to it." The Quaker community produced a number of country merchants, reputed for their sobriety and honest dealing. Over the next hundred years the Quaker merchants of Maryland, on both Eastern and Western Shores, formed a kind of network that had affiliations with Pennsylvania and Virginia, but most importantly with the great Quaker merchants of London. In Anne Arundel County an official report dated 1697 listed as a "preacher" at one of the weekly meetings the wife of Samuel Galloway, whose descendants of the next three generations stood at the head of the provincial mercantile aristocracy. Meeting house and counting house established almost from the first the symbiosis that gave Quaker merchants an edge in business.

Another Protestant element, the Presbyterians, came in small numbers even before the Quakers, perhaps as early as 1649. Sometime in August of 1657 Francis Doughty left Accomac County, Virginia, after an altercation with local authorities to preach on the lower Eastern Shore of Maryland. Somerset County in time became a Presbyterian stronghold, particularly after the arrival of the Reverend Francis Makemie (ca. 1658–1708), regarded by historians of the church as the father of American Presbyterianism. Whether Makemie was in fact the first regularly ordained minister of the confession in America has been disputed, but he did establish the first presbytery within his own lifetime, a generation before the great wave of Scots-Irish Presbyterians that swept through Philadelphia and Charleston to flood the back country in the eighteenth century.

At the other end of the Eastern Shore a colorful though numerically unimportant group, the Labadists, added to the religious mosaic. Originally followers of Jean de Labadie, this sect dispatched as pioneers to America Peter Sluyter and Jasper Dankers to seek a haven for their communal society. According to their journal, Sluyter and Dankers met and converted the son of Augustin Herman when they landed in New York. Soon thereafter they received a portion of Herman's estate, Bohemia Manor, in Cecil County where at long last they found their refuge. Eventually the Labadist experiment in communal living failed and the property went to individual members. However others fared, Sluyter at least died a rich man by Maryland standards.

Quite possibly Anglicans, like Catholics, were a minority element in restoration Maryland. Charles, Lord Baltimore, assured the King's Privy Council in rather unclear language: "The greatest part of the inhabitants of that Province (three or foure at least) do consist of Presbiterians, Independents, Anabaptists, and Quakers, those of the Church of England as well as those of the Romish being the fewest." At the time Baltimore was arguing that in his province "a Tolleration is given to all persons beleeving in Jesus Christ freely to exercise theire Religion." Accordingly, he said, people have settled there at once expecting this liberty and expecting to provide for their ministers "by a voluntary contribution of those of their own perswasion." Consequently "it will be a most difficult task to draw such persons to consent unto a Law which shall compel them to maintain Ministers of a contrary perswasion to themselves." In short the Lords Baltimore opposed establishing the Anglican church by statute.

Baltimore's argument to the Privy Council had resulted from a letter of 1676 of the Reverend John Yeo, Anglican minister in Calvert County, to the Archbishop of Canterbury. Yeo presented the primate with a grim picture: "The province of Maryland is in a deplorable condition for want of an established ministry. Here are ten or twelve counties, and in them at least 20,000 souls, and but three Protestant ministers of the Church of England . . . The Lord's day is profaned. Religion is despised, and all notorious vices are committed; so that it is become a Sodom of uncleanness and a pest-house of iniquity."

The Yeo letter, patently designed to arouse attention, ultimately led the Privy Council to enjoin Lord Baltimore to propose some means of supporting a competent number of clergy. The Privy Council meant, of course, clergy of the established church to read the prescribed prayers for the king's grace and to baptize, marry, and bury the dead according to the rites of the Anglican church. The councillors in their wisdom surely had in mind the benefits of correct formalities to Englishmen transplanted overseas. Whether they comprehended even vaguely the conditions of pioneer life—the primitive communications and the isolation—is doubtful. Maryland was an aural society, almost wholly dependent for news, practical information, and ideas on word of mouth. Immigrants, many of whom could read and write after a fashion, had neither necessity nor opportunity to exercise or improve these skills where books were rarities and where no printing press existed even to turn out legal forms and notices. The minister's sermon alone brought the planter in touch with the world of ideas and, if the clergyman had correspondents locally or abroad, news of the world beyond parish horizons. Church services, at once social and intellectual occasions, lifted ordinary provincials above the tedium of physical labor and neighborhood gossip. Whenever held, services were well attended and the minister became a personage of importance to the community.

The mandate of the Privy Council designed to bolster the state of religion came to nothing. Other concerns such as boundary disputes and Indian scares seemed more pressing at the time. Moreover both his Lordship and the people of the province were in the throes of an economic crisis that threatened local prosperity and proprietary revenues alike.

—4—

The first crisis of the Maryland economy resembled creeping paralysis. No dramatic indicators heralded the onset of the malaise. The effects proved drastic nonetheless, and for a time the political doctors treated the symptoms without either understanding the disease or appreciably affecting it.

One obvious symptom was the shortage of money. "The general way of traffick and commerce there is chiefly by Barter, or exchange of one commodity for another," said an informed commentator. To meet the shortage of money for circulation the Lord Proprietor proposed his own coinage: silver shillings, sixpences, and groats.* A cooperative Assembly passed the necessary legislation for putting the coins in circulation, and Baltimore had dies cut with his bust on the obverse and on the reverse his arms circumscribed by the hopeful motto *Crescite et Multiplicamini.*** After the initial shipment of the new coins to Maryland, British officialdom brought the whole scheme to a halt as a violation of English law. If the province profited little from the good intentions of the proprietary, collectors of a later age have rejoiced in the search for specimens of these rare and handsome pieces. Tobacco remained almost exclusively the money of account in provincial transactions until well into the eighteenth century. As the contemporary historian, John Oldmixon, put it in 1708: "Tobacco is their Meat, Drink, Cloathing, and Money."

Devotion to tobacco as a cash crop lay at the root of Maryland's economic plight. High prices during the first years of settlement had enabled planters to make ends meet even with the small crops they were constrained to produce while so many toilsome days went to clearing the interminable forest and to erecting houses. But almost as

---

*An English silver coin worth four pennies
**"Increase and multiply"

soon as these precarious times passed prices began to decline, almost simultaneously with the restoration of the proprietor, when the auspices seemed most favorable for renewed economic growth. The end of civil war in England brought a fresh influx of immigrants, some freemen and a larger number of indentured servants. More hands and larger fields meant larger crops. An age of affluence appeared in prospect. But then over a period of three or four years supply outgrew demand and ushered in Maryland's first great depression. Around 1660 Maryland tobacco averaged some fourteen shillings sterling per hundred pounds. At that price a small planter who produced a crop of 600 to 1,000 pounds could count on a cash return of between £5 and £7 sterling for his tobacco alone. But by 1666 tobacco had fallen to roughly seven shillings six pence a hundred, a trifle over half the price five years previously. Poorer planters faced disaster and even those better off felt the pinch.

The whole Chesapeake was caught up in depression, for markets were controlled three thousand miles away in the mother country. After the Stuart restoration in England, Parliament had seen fit to regularize the commerce of the colonies in accordance with the prevalent economic theory of the day, mercantilism. Among other tenets, mercantilist thought held that the strength of an empire depended on mutual support and self-sufficiency among its several parts. Following this idea, mercantilists believed that colonies ought to concentrate on commodities the mother country could not produce: tobacco, rice, indigo, and other suitable cash crops. Quite naturally it followed that such exotic products should be sent "home," certainly not to foreign countries to enjoy at their pleasure. In brief, mercantilism envisaged both exclusionism and regulation in commerce and industry. To this end Parliament enacted in the early 1660s a series of laws collectively known as the Acts of Trade and Navigation.

The Navigation Acts, as they are commonly called, embodied three chief principles: the "bottoms principle," the "staple principle," and the "principle of enumeration." Together they neatly brought enforceable legislation into a single design. Certain specifically named or "enumerated" commodities such as tobacco, sugar, cotton, and dyestuffs which were produced in the colonies overseas were to be shipped only to Britain or another British colony. Shipment of these commodities was restricted to English "bottoms," that is to say British owned and built ships, commanded by a British captain and manned by a crew at least two-thirds of whom were British. Finally, England was made the staple for all foreign products—wine from Spain or France, cloth from the Low Countries—coming into the empire. Such products could be transported only in British bottoms and, before proceeding to ultimate consumers in the colonies, had to pass through England: "laid on the shores of England," in the wording of the act. Seemingly arbitrary, the Navigation Acts had a kind of logic and benevolent intent. The bottoms provision aimed at stimulating ship-building in the empire, including New England, and the employment of British sailors. The Staple Act focused commerce on England, principally London, to the advantage of the rising merchant class. Even the distasteful channelling of the enumerated colonial products to England, admittedly designed to secure adequate supplies to the mother country, had a compensatory side. The colonial "staples," so called because they, too, had to be laid on the shores of England, were to enjoy a monopoly there. England placed prohibitive duties on Spanish tobacco and French sugar.

Nevertheless the Navigation Acts irked colonials, who felt, with some justification, that the laws placed them at the mercy of the British market. And when low prices came, the Chesapeake colonies threatened retaliation with the only weapon ready at hand: the first crop limitation program in American history. Virginia, older and more populous, took the lead with a drastic proposal, the "stint," a total cessation of tobacco planting for a year. Governor William Berkeley strongly favored the stint and carried the message to Maryland, without whose cooperation the plan was bound to fail. Accompanied by several of his councillors, Berkeley journeyed to Maryland "in the depth of winter to the very great hazard of his health" as he later put it. From preliminary talks between 1664 and 1666, by letter and by negotiating committees, the stint gradually developed.

Not everyone shared Berkeley's enthusiasm. Cecilius, Lord Baltimore, urged the difficulty of enforcement in terms familiar to the twentieth century: "There will be no means of convicting Transgressors without either encouraging servants to inform against their masters; or next neighbors, one against another, both which will be odious and dangerous for perjury and setting families in combustion both within themselves, and one against another." Moreover, he pointed out, inspection would require a huge bureaucracy with all the risks of "negligence, corruption, or partiality." Elected delegates to the Maryland Assembly came down on Baltimore's side with arguments to justify their foot dragging. Certainly they would have agreed with his Lordship's clinching argument: "It would wholly ruin the poor, who are the generality of the Provinces."

Nevertheless proponents of the stint won the day. Governor Charles Calvert and his councillors committed themselves to Berkeley's plan and applied pressure enough on delegates in the lower house to get through the Assembly in May of 1666 "An Act for Encouragement of Trade." This curiously named law provided that "noe tobacco shall be sowen, sett, planted, or in any way Tended within this province of Maryland" in the twelve months following the first of February 1667, on condition that the other tobacco planting provinces to the south enacted similar legislation.

Before the stint could take effect its abettors had a rude jolt. In the showdown, Cecilius had sided with opponents of the stint and overridden his son, the governor, in an exercise of the proprietary veto. In a fit of anger, Berkeley described this setback as "an Instrument under the signature and Seal at Arms of the Lord Baltimore in absolute and Princely terms prohibiting the execution of the Act." At the time no one could have predicted the sequel. In the summer of 1667 the most catastrophic hurricane of the century swept across the Chesapeake. Two days of violent gales accompanied by rain and hail left the tobacco provinces a shambles. Fifteen thousand homes and outbuildings went down before lashing winds in Virginia alone and three-fourths of the tobacco crop was destroyed by the combined fury of wind, rain, and hail "as big as turkey eggs." The disaster lingered in folk memory for half a century as "the hurricane of 1667."

Freakish weather reversed the decline in tobacco prices for two years, but the secular downward trend continued for decades. Lord Baltimore gave the matter considerable thought, but his analysis failed to read correctly the Maryland scene. "If there be any that live in a poor manner, it is not from the low price of tobacco, but from their own sloth, ill husbandry, and profusely spending the crops in Brandewine, and other liquors, it being evident . . . that such as are industrious and frugal, live in great plenty in comparison with husbandmen in England." He added that "a painful and able man will in a summer make his four hogs heads of tobacco which, at the rate as it now is, will produce in England fourteen or fifteen pound, which will buy him clothes and another servant clear, besides which he will plant corn enough to find himself [food], and to sell four or five pound more, and rear a stock of cattle." Such armchair philosophy, a blend of fact and fancy, looked backward to a day when prices had permitted the "painful and able man" to acquire at least a competence and possibly even moderate affluence by provincial standards. Without doubt some planters deserved Baltimore's accusation of sloth; almost all practiced poor husbandry or at least showed little imagination in improving farming techniques. But Baltimore's reading ignored the deeper truth: population growth during restoration decades was creating a new economic order and a new society, fixing in both of them problems that endured for more than a century.

The manor had failed as a device for organizing agricultural production or, more accurately, had never caught on. Individual holdings—the family plantation—won the day. Very large holdings and very small holdings both declined relatively. Moreover the concentration of wealth, notable in earlier days, levelled off: in 1640 the top 10 percent of freeholders owned around 63 percent of the wealth, in 1670 they owned 50 percent. Clearly increasing numbers of small planters were altering the statistics. And yet these small producers, many of them freed indentured servants, failed to do as well as those who had come to the colony before Ingle's rebellion. Somehow genuine prosperity eluded them.

Baltimore's strictures on their slovenly husbandry contain an element of truth. Maryland planters took their methods of raising tobacco from Virginians and made no improvements. The entire operation proceeded in a spirit of routine, static and unchanging. First the planter "made" a field by clearing the trees or frequently simply killing them by girdling. Then in early spring he sowed his seed in a rich bed sheltered from north winds and covered with cloth against nipping frost. When warm weather arrived he transplanted slips from his seedbed in hills made with a broad or "hilling" hoe. Thereafter cultivation consisted of keeping down weeds around the hills by hoeing, picking off green horned tobacco worms, and removing superfluous shoots called "suckers" that grew from the base of the stalk. In late summer, planters cut the fully grown stalks, dried them in curing barns, and finally prepared the crop for shipment by packing the leaf in hogsheads that held five hundred pounds and upward. From seedbed to hogshead the planting cycle covered almost the calendar year, from late February until November.

The planting cycle at once limited the size of crops and exacted unremitting care. Planters used a single implement in tilling, the hoe, which served for hilling tobacco and, astonishingly, for breaking fields to be sown with wheat. Plows, virtually unnecessary in light tidewater soils, almost never appear in inventories of estates. But a hoeing husbandry limited the number of tobacco plants a single householder could tend. Wives and children assisted in worming, suckering and other light tasks, but the toil of preparing fields, both initial clearing and making hills for tobacco plants, required adult male strength and endurance. For really large crops planters needed additional "hands" capable of heavy work.

Hands meant indentured servants, the type Alsop hoped to entice. Slavery made little headway in Maryland for decades after the Restoration. In 1663 Governor Charles Calvert told his father that he had tried in vain to find one or two hundred "responsable men" who would guarantee to purchase one slave each if the Royal African Company would send a shipload to the province. "I find wee are nott men of estates good enough to undertake such a businesse, but could wish wee were for wee are naturally inclin'd to love neigros if our purses would endure it." Inventories of estates reinforce Calvert's statement: only fifteen of 151 estates probated between 1658 and 1670 listed slaves. A certain John Nuthert owned thirteen, more than twice as many as any of the other fourteen. But these same 151 households had 260 white indentured servants. The demand for hands, then, helped to people the province even in these years when opportunity had lessened and when progress up the economic ladder had become slower and more difficult for freed servants.

Everyone, high and low, felt the hard times that had descended on Maryland. But neither provincial planter nor Lord Proprietor clearly conceived the dimensions of the depression or accurately predicted its long duration. Living in a difficult present, each wrestled with immediate and pressing problems. Yet some signs of changing circumstances were too plain to miss, even when their bearings were not so obvious. The Navigation Acts had brought the province permanently into the British commercial system. As visible symbols, revenue agents of the crown appeared in the Chesapeake to enforce the acts. Royal officers, present and active, put provincials in mind of their dual allegiance, immediately to his Lordship but ultimately to the king. But to Lord Baltimore, crown agents represented an intrusion into the bailiwick where his charter made him the true and absolute lord and proprietary. These arrangements had insensibly introduced a new factor into Maryland affairs and touched matters of high concern to the society slowly coming into early maturity along the bay.

—5—

The actors in the pageant of early Maryland hardly formed a society in the usual sense at all. An assemblage of immigrants uprooted from their native heath and transplanted to a boundless wilderness, they had cleared land for the first plantations and had maintained their beachhead against interlopers like Ingle. But only continuing immigration had kept the predominantly male colony alive. Without opportunities for family life the population had for many years not even reproduced itself. After the Restoration a true society evolved to assure the permanence of Baltimore's enterprise. Its growth in an era of depression left indelible marks that later overlays obscured but never erased.

This first genuine social order might have remained hidden from view altogether but for the fortunate preservation of an extraordinarily complete set of records unique in the planting colonies, the court records. The pages of county court proceedings, the probate records, and the all-important land records tell in mountainous detail of the mighty and the humble in a social fabric as it was actually being woven. With a little coaxing the entries reenact the dramas of their lives: transgressions and punishments, purchases of real estate, suits to recover debts, down to last wills and testaments bequeathing goods and chattels to heirs with an exact accounting of both. Year after year, the hitherto invisible people of Maryland march out of the yellowed pages, each to add his bit toward sharper definition of types and classes.

At first view the people of Maryland appear almost to a man a single type: the planter. Every household produced a tobacco crop for the excellent reason that tobacco was not merely the cash crop but the actual money of the province, essential for paying taxes, court fees, settling debts, and making purchases. Functionally almost every adult male was a planter, though not the planter of legend: the man of leisure, owner of a mansion house, elegant furnishings, and hordes of servile laborers who did the work. The reality of his lifestyle differs so radically that minds accustomed to the romantic connotations of the term, "planter," can hardly accept the true picture.

Yet the testimony of the records etch a scene as sharp as a photograph in details. Frequently the planter's house had a single room, in one recorded instance twelve feet square. Some dwellings ran to more ample dimensions, as large as sixteen by thirty-two feet. Windows are described as "unglazed," that is mere apertures in the wall covered by shutters to keep out wind and rain. The very poorest had dirt floors, but the abundance of timber afforded most families the comfort of wooden planking. Detailed inventories of furnishings almost never mention a carpet or a rug, but they do catalogue utensils: a cook pot or two, occasionally a skillet, sometimes a metal spoon, perhaps a pail for milk. Otherwise poorer planters improvised household necessities: bowls and cups from dried gourds, tables from hewn boards laid on supports, chairs from short sections of a log, spoons from bits of wood whittled into shape by men and boys in long winter evenings about the fire. Often bedding, listed in almost every inventory, consisted of nothing more than a flock mattress and coverlets, though one or more feather beds appear in plusher households.

With living quarters cramped and privacy inside the house out of the question, planting families lived out of doors, at least in mild weather. Members spent their leisure under the shade tree and even did many chores outside, like shelling peas from the kitchen garden that provided a good part of the food for the table. Hunting, sometimes for sport but mainly for pot, occupied many hours. Chiefly the unremitting demands of husbandry took household males to tobacco and corn fields or to the forest. At first the forest was an obstruction, an impediment to be cleared to make way for a plantation. But once a household was established, the woodlands supplied firewood and timber, not only for building but for making useful home furnishings and utensils from crude tables to wooden spoons.

Both field and forest rewarded the planter and put bounds on his lifestyle. The essential tobacco crop provided his income, but hardly enough to make ends meet. With only the labor of his own family planters marketed crops of between 750 and 2000 pounds, worth in money £3 to £10 sterling. This return covered every purchase made by ordinary planters: tools, clothing, and such foodstuffs as sugar and condiments. A bad crop year or extravagant buying could plunge the family into debt, for most purchases were made from local merchants who noted the amounts on their ledgers as "book debts" to be settled when crops came to market. Two or three poor years in succession could put the planter in permanent debt from which total escape seemed almost impossible. Almost every estate had more or less indebtedness to be paid off when settled at the planter's death by his administrator. With incomes of these dimensions few planters accumulated more than a bare competence during a lifetime. According to the inventories, over four-fifths left personal estates of £100 or less, many encumbered with debt.

These are the planters as the records show them. A later age would call them deprived or disadvantaged. Though their lifestyles seem dreary and their sumptuary surroundings bleak, many enjoyed a kind of rude plenty from kitchen garden and orchard, from their farm animals and their pot hunting. Moreover there is another side of their life and labor not clearly reflected in the records. They cleared the fields, built the houses, planted the orchards, erected the barns, made fences and crude roads: all those improvements that technical economists lump together under the heading, capital formation. These works, almost heroic in magnitude, laid solid foundations upon which the well-being of the province rested in future years.

Not every planter, of course, conformed to the common model. A few, perhaps one in twenty, rose well above the average in personal estate, even in the depressed years. These favored ones also clash with the moonlight and magnolias imagery of the planting society. A telling example, William Worgan from Dorchester, one of the newer counties on the lower Eastern Shore, fairly represents the wealthy planter. When Worgan died in late 1676 the probate court sent two officials to inventory and value his estate. The appraisers found Worgan's total assets worth 202,616 pounds of tobacco, the equivalent of £844-4-8 sterling, obviously a wealthy estate. Among these assets were debts due the estate, seventy-three in all, good debts that the administrators could collect, because appraisers did not list among assets those "doubtful" or "desperate" debts due from men who had "run away" or "left

Maxwell Hall, Charles County, situated on a bluff overlooking the Patuxent River, is an eighteenth century exemplification of vernacular houses built in the second half of the seventeenth century by affluent planters as their country seats. Excepting the porch, a later addition, this house retains its original appearance with gambrel roof and massive chimneys. Courtesy of the Maryland Historical Trust.

the province" and thus could not be called to account. Altogether the sums due Worgan came to 143,246 pounds of tobacco, well over half of the value of his personal estate. This is the record of a merchant who had sold on credit goods from his store such as cloth, hoes, axes, sugar, and perhaps rum, setting down on his ledger the sums due. These "book debts," as the statutes described them, enabled planters like Worgan to gain a special foothold in the expanding economy of Maryland: to distribute imports among consumers, to consolidate the dozens of small tobacco crops into a return cargo for shipment to London consignment houses that had sent him merchandise in the first place.

As for planting, Worgan did little more than his poorer neighbors. He owned no slaves; his total work force consisted of five indentured servants, one woman and four men, all duly listed as assets by the appraiser. But compared to his customers, the poorer planters, he was wealthy. His stature as an economic man was greater than his neighbors' by the height of his mercantile business.

In every county, types like Worgan moved to the top, planters like Edward Lloyd, Robert Slye, Benjamin Rozer, Thomas Notley, William Stevens. Hard driving and enterprising, they organized the commercial agriculture of the province and made possible the outward movement of crops and inward flow of goods. All began as petty merchants, then, as opportunities arose, diversified their activities with money lending, land speculation, and sometimes law practice. Some came to the province with sufficient capital to set up in business immediately. William Stevens described himself as "formerly of London, Ironmonger now of Somerset County in the Province of Maryland Esquire." Stevens operated three plantations, kept a store, and speculated in land. In 1679 he became a member of the governor's council and died in 1687, after adding the title esquire to his other dignities and hundreds of pounds to his pocketbook. Others like William Burgess and John Hammond rose by their own efforts from the ranks of small planters to the top bracket of wealth. Both founded dynasties. A few—Philip Lynes and Nicholas Gassoway among them—came to the province as indentured servants and followed the road of enterprise to wealth and honor. Both Lynes and Gassoway founded families that continued the tradition of affluence for generations.

Clearly an elite was developing to answer the needs of a society growing in numbers but still fluid. As the decades slipped by, the merchant-planters moved toward positions of leadership in provincial affairs. Their function as organizers of the provincial economy understandably led them toward politics, either as elected representatives to the lower house of the Assembly or as appointed officials: from justices of the county courts up to the high dignity of the council. Whom God had prospered in worldly goods, mortal man, noting this sign of divine favor, preferred to stewardship in the affairs of the world. As self-made men, the elite leadership never lost touch with their humble origins. Even in affluence they retained the planter outlook of less fortunate neighbors and by instinct and reason represented his views, even his prejudices, in high places. Moreover their ranks remained accessible to talent, never entirely closed off by barriers or artificial lines. Social mobility marked Maryland as an open society.

—6—

After the death of Cecilius in 1675 the new Baron of Baltimore, Lord Charles, with the benefit of long experience as resident governor in Maryland, might have looked more carefully at the burgeoning society of his province. But though sensitive on some matters, especially questions of his prerogatives, Baltimore occasionally handled certain practical problems with unaccountable obtuseness. In 1676, shortly after he inherited Maryland, he went to England on business that he thought would detain him a mere six months but which dragged along for two years. He placed the province in the hands of his son, Cecil, then nine years old, with a trusted advisor as deputy governor in charge, first Jesse Wharton, then after his death, Thomas Notley. Both timing and action spelled trouble.

Within the province critics accused the proprietor of pretentions to "an absolute prince in Maryland, with as absolute prerogative Royall Right and Power." Even worse, they said, he "assums and attracts more Royall power to himself over his tennants than our gratious Kinge over his subjects in England." The accusations referred not only to their nine year old resident ruler—after all, boy kings with regents were well known in England—but to a host of other actions: Baltimore's tampering with the franchise, impressing soldiers, mishandling provincial revenues, and the like. The case against Baltimore was recited at length in one of the most remarkable documents in provincial history, "Complaint from Heaven with a Huy and Crye and a petition out of Virginia and Maryland." Half literate and charged with emotion, the "Complaint," asked King Charles to "take the Government of Maryland unto his gratious selfe" and give the province Protestant rule.

However ominous this note to the proprietary away in England, other events pressed harder on his governor, now Thomas Notley. On a Sunday in early September 1676, some sixty persons, most bearing arms, met at the plantation of Thomas Barnbury on the Patuxent River in Calvert County to discuss their grievances against the proprietary regime. Their catalogue of complaints, considered seditious by the council, listed the highhanded doings of Lord Baltimore, particularly his interference with voting and high taxation during these hard years. Since William Davyes, a militia ensign as well as a prosperous planter, had emerged as a leader of this irregular assemblage, the council at first merely demanded they lay down their arms and disperse. Then, when the insurgents refused to obey and marched away with drums beating and colors flying, the council pronounced them mutinous, pursued Davyes and his co-partner John Pate all the way to Delaware, and brought them back to be hanged at the "Cliffs" near Annapolis as a public spectacle.

Even as the councillors congratulated themselves on nipping sedition in the bud, more serious trouble arose in Charles County, a frontier land to the west adjacent to Stafford County, Virginia. Indian raids in Stafford had touched off Bacon's Rebellion in the early summer of 1676. Planters in Charles, related by blood and sympathy with neighbors in Stafford, had also tasted Indian wrath. Moreover, they had in their midst at least two restless spirits, John Coode, clergyman turned planter, and Josias Fendall, former governor now disbarred from office. Though not at first in collusion, Fendall and Coode kept Charles County planters in a state of agitation for several years. When Lord Baltimore returned to the province he feared they had "been tampering to stirr up the inhabitants of Maryland and those of the north part of Virginia to mutiny." He found no more appropriate description of Coode and Fendall than "two rank Baconists."

But unrest in Charles County proved endemic, not merely the handiwork of two intriguers. Genuinely frightened by occasional Indian atrocities, planters in Charles continued to gather at the dwellings of Fendall and Coode to discuss their forebodings and to generate new rumors about a Roman Catholic conspiracy to keep the Protestants subservient to the proprietor and his cronies.

In sober fact Governor Notley had virtually eliminated the Indian threat, one of the few accomplishments of his administration in the name of his young ward. Proprietary negotiators signed treaties with the once powerful Nanticoke on the Eastern Shore and with several tribes up the Potomac, formerly a threat but now decimated. Finally, with Colonel Henry Coursey as ambassador, Notley's government reached agreement with the Iroquois at a conference in New York. Actually all the Maryland tribes, even the fearsome Susquehanna, had withered to shadows of their former strength. Only the Iroquois, well removed from direct contact with Maryland, retained any real striking power, and they had promised "an absolute covenant of peace," giving as a token a wampum belt of thirteen strands. Accordingly when Lord Charles returned from England in the closing weeks of 1678 Notley could report this bulwark of treaties against further Indian hostilities. Planters, however, did not fully comprehend how low Maryland Indians had fallen in numbers and spirit. The days when isolated settlers fell to the tomahawk lived in their recollections as a reality more potent than paper with all the marks of signers and accompanying wampum tokens. Still a bogey to inflame imaginations, Indians had actually ceased to figure in Maryland affairs, an inactive state they were to retain until the last French war nearly a century ahead. Nevertheless the Indian threat, however unreal, remained a factor in the complex of suspicions directed toward Baltimore and his administration.

—7—

Lord Charles learned in his eighteen year administration that Maryland did not live unto herself alone. First as his father's governor and then as Lord Proprietor in his own right he had seen the Navigation Acts draw the province under the umbrella of the British mercantile system. He had also witnessed provincial involvement in an Indian problem that touched relations with neighboring Virginia and remoter New York. But the question of his boundaries—the actual extent of his

Maryland palatinate—increasingly occupied his energies during his proprietorship and eventually took him permanently back to England.

The Virginia boundary, with fewest thorns, had come into contention in 1663 as settlers moved into the lower Eastern Shore. After five years of some uncertainty, commissioners of the two colonies agreed on a line, "due east from Watkins Point," to divide Somerset County in Maryland from Accomac County, Virginia. The actual task of laying off the line fell to the surveyor general of Virginia, Edward Scarborough, who ran it not due east but five degrees and fifteen minutes north of east, at a cost to Baltimore of nearly 15,000 acres, as he discovered later.

But the most worrisome threat came from the Dutch along the northern reaches of Maryland. Before 1664, while the Dutch still maintained a foothold at New Amsterdam, complications enough had appeared, for Holland had taken over a tiny Swedish colony on the Delaware River along the fortieth parallel, which by charter provision formed the northern boundary of Maryland. But the snarl became hopeless when King Charles granted the Dutch possessions on the mainland to his brother, James, Duke of York, in 1664. As high admiral of the navy, James sent his fleet to New Amsterdam and without firing a shot seized his property, which he promptly renamed New York. The Duke of York claimed the widest extent for his domain, including an Eastern Shore area—the lower Counties, or Delaware— where a few Dutch had settled. This area, clearly below the fortieth parallel, lay within the charter boundaries of Maryland. To Baltimore's potential dispute with a powerful duke, heir apparent to the throne of England, Charles II added another in 1681 when he granted Pennsylvania to William Penn.

Following the Pennsylvania grant, events pressed hard on Lord Baltimore. Penn lost no time sending colonists to settle his domain but neglected to ascertain his boundaries. Accordingly the first settlers actually laid out Philadelphia at the confluence of the Schuylkill and Delaware Rivers a few miles below the fortieth parallel claimed by Baltimore as his northern limit. The king meanwhile wrote to Baltimore, telling him of the Pennsylvania grant and commanding him to meet with William Penn "to make a true division & separation" of their provinces.

By steps Lord Charles was drawing toward confrontation with powerful antagonists. His initial meeting with Penn at a private house in Anne Arundel County during December 1682 proved fruitless. The transcript of their exchanges explains why Baltimore mistrusted Penn: "oily" was his characterization. A second meeting at New Castle the following May turned out even worse, because Baltimore had in the meantime discovered that Penn had acquired the Lower Counties from the Duke of York. Now at least the House of Baltimore had a single antagonist, William Penn, claimant to hundreds of thousands of acres that once seemed so secure under the Maryland charter. With such stakes in jeopardy Baltimore could no longer tarry in his province. On 7 May 1684 he commissioned his second son, Benedict Leonard, now four years old, as resident governor with George Talbot, Henry Darnall and William Digges, senior councillors, as the actual administrators and sailed for England the following week.

Both externally and internally the posture of his province was far from satisfactory. In deciding to go to England Baltimore had by implication concluded that the territorial threat outweighed domestic disaffection to his proprietorship. He left an infant son nominal head of state as an earnest of his intention to return. All his calculations went awry. Internal vexations soon turned into crises beyond the control of his resident managers. Baltimore, himself, never again set foot on Maryland soil in the thirty years of life remaining to him.

5

THE ROYAL ADMINISTRATION

"Maryland is now in torment and not only troubled with our disease, poverty, but in very great danger of falling in pieces; whether it be that old Lord Baltimore's politic maxims are not pursued or that they are unsuited to this age." Lately returned to England from a tour as a resident governor in Virginia, Lord Culpeper wrote with keen discernment of the twin maladies besetting Maryland: economic depression and political tension.

Twice in half a decade the pot had boiled up, first in 1676 during the Baconian troubles and later in 1681 when an ancient foeman, Josias Fendall, again became active in Charles County. According to charges brought against him, Fendall had hatched a plot to seize and imprison the Lord Proprietor and several of the council. Baltimore had been present in Maryland during both these outbursts and had managed to keep the lid on firmly. His departure for England in 1684 to defend his boundaries against Penn left the province leaderless at a time when it was smouldering with discontent.

—1—

The abortive "rising" of 1681 vividly illustrated the high state of tension that mounted rather than abated over the next few years. For the first time the names of Josias Fendall and John Coode were clearly linked. Fendall had long been a spectre, but Coode had yet to show the traits that made him a chief villain to the Lord Proprietary. Fendall's trial for sedition at the November session of the provincial court has the full detail of a stenographic report, made by John Llewellin, "who writes shorthand," as Baltimore carefully pointed out. The proceedings remind anyone likely to forget that the seventeenth century was "an age of oaths, perjurers, and informers," when "plotting was one of the spare-time occupations." From the evidence laid before the jury two main impressions came across: the uncertainty about the facts of Fendall's alleged misdeeds and, even more strongly, the dread and prejudice of Protestants toward Roman Catholics. Nevertheless the court found Fendall guilty of a design to imprison Baltimore and others and sentenced him to a fine of 40,000 pounds of tobacco and banishment. One of the judges, Secretary William Calvert, bluntly told Fendall that the court could have given him a harder sentence, "boaring of the Tongue, cropping one or both ears, and other corporall punishments, but wee have forbourne and taken this moderate and less shamefull way."

Fendall disposed of, the court turned to others for alleged complicity in the plot. John Coode, recently elected to the Assembly, first came to trial for suspected conspiracy with Fendall, but the jury speedily acquitted him. The chief judge, Chancellor Philip Calvert, gave Coode some gratuitous advice—"keepe a Guard upon your Tongue" and the like—then ordered him to give security "for his good abearance" and for his appearance at the next court meeting. Coode immediately produced as cosigner of his peace bond, Nehemiah Blakiston, a rising lawyer related to the oldest families in Maryland. Another Fendall partisan, George Godfrey, a county court justice and militia officer in Charles, did not come off as well. Godfrey had attempted to organize a troop "to rescue and sett at large" the person of Fendall while he was languishing in jail awaiting trial. The jury found Godfrey guilty and the court sentenced him to "be hanged by the neck untill he be dead." A week later Charles, Lord Baltimore, commuted the sentence to life imprisonment.

Patently, discontent had been strong in 1681, and men of some influence had already given forewarning of their concern for the direction Lord Baltimore seemed to be moving the province. The administrative arrangements Baltimore made, particularly his appointment of George Talbot as president of the council when he sailed for England in May of 1684, offered no hope for change. Discontent in Maryland centered around three matters: the patronage, the church, and the customs service, the latter now complicated by royal officials actually at work in the colony. On each subject the discontented made their views known at the seats of power in London: Whitehall and Lambeth Palace. Baltimore spent anxious months answering the questions raised by privy councillors and the Lords of Trade and Plantations.

On patronage, provincials claimed that the Lord Proprietor packed the administration with his relatives and with Catholics. Baltimore countered with lists of Protestants whom he had appointed to the council and to county offices. Nonetheless close scrutiny of the provincial establishment shows tight control of the council, land office, secretary's office, and the apparatus for collecting the proprietary revenues. These posts were in the hands of blood relatives or persons related by marriage to the proprietary family and, of course, all Catholics. Collectively the officials holding them constituted a power group to the exclusion of outsiders, however influential or wealthy. To ambitious provincials outside this charmed circle, opportunity seemed limited by religious and family qualifications nowhere officially stated but obviously everywhere observed.

The church, or more precisely the estate of religion in Maryland, had become a cause for concern. The Reverend John Yeo had already memorialized the Bishop of London on the deplorable provision for Anglicans in the province. Baltimore could, and did, restate the official policy of toleration and blamed the absence of priests and chapels on the Bishop of London, whose see included the American colonies. But the age was not tolerant. The Spanish Inquisition still rankled in British memories. Louis XIV was preparing to revoke the toleration granted Protestants by the Edict of Nantes and to subject them to the pitiless dragonades. Politics and religion could hardly be divorced. And Englishmen shortly were to rouse from uneasy endurance of the Catholic Stuarts to active revolution once hope of a Protestant succession was cut off by the birth of a male heir to the throne. It was easy to impute hostility toward protestantism to Lord Baltimore and, with a little casuistry, to make his patronage policy a plot against the well-being of honest Protestants, who were now the overwhelming majority in Maryland. Religion offered fertile subject for the innuendo that always figured in the discourse of discontent.

The most definite charge against Lord Baltimore, interference with royal customs officials, was also the most damaging and first to explode. In late October of 1684 Baltimore's hot-headed nephew, George Talbot, murdered Christopher Rousby, collector of the King's customs, on board the royal ketch, *Quaker,* anchored in the Patuxent River. The gory details of the fatal stabbing "with a dagger newly prepared and sharpened" created an unprecedented stir in Maryland, where Talbot was president of the council governing in the name of Baltimore's infant son. Understandably British officialdom became interested in the murder of the king's officer by a leading magistrate of a proprietary government already accused of obstructing revenue collections. For the next two years Lord Baltimore had to endure the consequences of his nephew's rash and ill-timed act.

However sorely pressed at home in England, the Lord Proprietor had no intention of loosening his hold on Maryland affairs. To restore stability and unity of command he chose one William Joseph, a Roman Catholic in religion and an advocate of divine right in politics. On 14 November 1688, soon after his arrival in Maryland, Joseph met his first Assembly. From his opening address to his adjournment of the lawmakers Joseph made one blunder after another. In his opening speech he set an authoritarian tone. "There is no power but of God and the Power by which we are Assembled here is undoubtedly Derived from God, to the King, and from the King to his Excellency the Lord Proprietor, and from his said Lordship to Us." On this text he preached a sermon, the like of which had never been heard by the astonished Assemblymen. He excoriated provincials for sins of drunkeness, adultery ("the Land is full of Adulturers," he said), and sabbath breaking. He referred to certain royal orders that were to be obeyed on pain of royal wrath for disobedience. He commanded the Assembly to pass an act of thanksgiving for the recent birth of a prince to King James and his Catholic queen and to keep holy the day of birth during the prince's lifetime. He ordered the Assemblymen to pay without complaint money due the proprietary, to suppress sin and scandal, and to sink their animosities in concern for the welfare of the Proprietor and— whatever that meant—the people in general. Finally he demanded that every delegate take an oath of fidelity to the Lord Proprietor. He closed his remarkable harangue with an insulting precept: "before you Begin to make Laws you do not begin to breake Laws."

Joseph's first Assembly was also his last. Resentful delegates, who had already taken the oath of fidelity, refused to take it again during session time. Throughout the proceedings they declined to be intimidated during the interminable wrangling between upper and lower houses. Even so the Assembly passed eleven acts, none of them major legislation but nevertheless a remarkable record when considered against the background of tension and suspicion in the province. On 8 December Joseph prorogued the Assembly just as rumors of impending revolt in England filtered into the province. Through the early months of 1689 he declined to call the delegates into session even when firm news of revolution in England arrived. In an atmosphere heavy with suspicion the provincial rumor mill ground away vigorously. The talk was of insurrection.

—2—

The proprietary establishment in Maryland fell with astonishingly little resistance. Whatever vitality had carried it through two earlier uprisings evaporated after the December adjournment of the Assembly. Two developments, one in England and one in Maryland, hastened the end.

In early November of 1688 a "protestant wind" had brought William of Orange to England's west country, where he began his advance on London. As the husband of Mary, elder daughter of James II and a Protestant, William had brought Dutch troops to join English Protestant regiments in displacing the Catholic monarch and his infant son. By Christmas James II had fled to France and William had arrived without bloodshed at the seat of government. One further act completed this bloodless revolution and forever gave it the name Glorious Revolution: during the first three weeks of February 1689, Parliament effected a settlement that bestowed the crown upon William and Mary and assured a Protestant succession to the crown.

News of these high affairs, arriving piecemeal in Maryland, started anew the rumors of Catholic plotting with Indians to destroy the Protestant population. Suspicion increased during the spring and summer when no official word came from Lord Baltimore. Other colonies were proclaiming the new monarchs: Virginia on 26 April and Jacob Leisler's revolutionary government in New York on 22 June. In this supercharged atmosphere the Protestant Association was born.

The Protestant Association coalesced dramatically in the last two weeks of July 1689 around a half dozen Maryland leaders. On 16 July John Coode began "raising men up Potowmack" to preserve the country from Indians and papists and to proclaim the new king and queen. Coode's allies, distributed through the southern counties of the Western Shore, included a trio whose names could command respect: Kenylm Cheseldyne and Nehemiah Blakiston from St. Mary's County and Henry Jowles of Calvert. While these three, along with Coode, comprised the most determined leaders, several others added their prestige and talent: John Addison and John Courts, both of Charles County, and from Calvert County, Ninian Beale, at 64 the oldest of the group.

Certain similarities among the top leaders afford an insight into the rebellion they headed. All but one were immigrants, young men with some capital when they arrived. Only John Courts of Charles County was "country born." All of them were outside the charmed circle of proprietary favorites, though all had prospered as they had acquired plantations and stocked them with goods and chattels. By provincial standards, they belonged among the men of substance. All of them, too, had been county justices, as had many of their chief adherents, their lieutenants who led the rank and file of the Association. But only a few had held posts as Assemblymen, and still fewer had risen to places in the civil or military establishment, and those only recently. In short the prime movers of the Association were the natural leaders in their counties: the most affluent, talented, and ambitious, but hitherto cut off from larger opportunity in higher provincial affairs.

Fullest testimony to the abilities of Association leaders comes from subsequent years when they compiled an impressive record of accomplishment. In the summer of 1689 they were largely untried, though energetically organizing opposition to a do-nothing policy of Governor Joseph and developing their platform. On 25 July the rebels issued a "Declaration of the reason and motive for the present appearing in arms of His Majesties Protestant Subjects in the Province of Maryland," a summary of their complaints against the Catholic Lord Proprietor and a pledge "to pressure, vindicate and assert the Sovereign Dominion and right of King William and Queen Mary to this Province; to defend the Protestant Religion among us and to protect and shelter the Inhabitants from all manner of violence, oppression and destruction that is plotted and deseigned against them." The "Declaration" proved excellent propaganda. Coode's force grew appreciably in the march to St. Mary's City, where William Digges, the Proprietor's kinsman by marriage, surrendered on 27 July without firing a shot. One other pocket of proprietary resistance remained, at Mattapany where Baltimore's councillor-kinsmen, Sewall and Darnall, had organized a defensive unit of some 160 men. When confronted with Association forces outnumbering them fivefold, they, also, capitulated on 1 August, on promise of safe conduct to their homes and full enjoyment of their rights and privileges "equall with the rest of their Majesties Subjects." The articles of surrender contained one portentous statement: henceforth no papist was to occupy any office, civil or military.

In a bloodless coup the Associators had toppled the palatine authority of Charles, Lord Baltimore, in Maryland and, although they could not know it, had inaugurated a quarter century of royal government. Immediately before them loomed two tasks: to obtain recognition for their revolution from the crown and to establish their authority locally. With an eye to crown favor, the victorious "loyall Protestant Subjects Inhabitants of the Province of Maryland" dispatched an address on 5 August to King William and Queen Mary with congratulations on their accession. The same document explained that the associated Protestants had taken up arms in their royal names and had "rescued the Government from the hands of your Enemies" in order to effect "the publick and general acknowledgment of your Majesty's undoubted right thereunto." Then followed a prayer for settlement of a Protestant government on the colony.

The Associators did not rest on prayer alone for the success of their cause. They moved without delay to oust subordinate proprietary officials in the counties and to install persons sympathetic to their own cause, particularly in the county militia. To give their power some legal foundation they summoned an Assembly, later to be called the Associators' Convention, to meet at St. Mary's on 22 August. Elections met some local resistance in the counties outside the lower Western Shore, but only one, Anne Arundel, failed to send delegates. Once assembled as a "convention of the people" the delegates formally petitioned the crown for "a deliverance to your suffering people" and "a Protestant Government by your Majestyes gracious direction especially to be appointed." Then on the last day of the session they passed the ordinance that was to give Maryland its government for the next two and a half years. The ordinance officially named the civil and military officers for each of the counties: the sheriffs, coroners, and justices of the peace, the majors and captains of horse and foot. There was no attempt to seize the powerful and lucrative offices of the central provincial government left vacant by the deposition of Lord Baltimore's appointees. The convention even turned down John Coode's suggestion for an executive committee to act for the convention after adjournment. One witness thought this refusal grew out of the delegates' desire "to be all alike in power."

Certainly the elected delegates to the convention did have much in common. They closely resembled the leaders who had precipitated the rebellion. Almost to a man the delegates had entered the colony as adults, had prospered materially, and had held lesser offices. Ordinarily, however, political careers for them ended with minor office. Until the crown could speak they appeared content with a monopoly of county posts. An outspoken opponent called them and their works "rebellion in the highest degree." But for well over two years this substantial group, supported by sympathetic lawyers and merchants, remained the government of Maryland.

—3—

Although the Associators had prevailed, their two year hold on the reins of authority lacked something in security. They spoke a simple truth when they complained of "the unsettled state of our present constitution not having any orders from England or knowing your Majestys pleasure." Yet they had no alternative but to await their turn for royal attention while the new monarchs dealt with high problems of the realm including a war with France, which supported James II and unrelentingly opposed William. "King William's War," as the colonists spoke of it, was the beginning of a series of conflicts that, with brief intervals of peace, were to last nearly a century and to acquire the name the Second Hundred Years' War. Immediately and practically, the new war merely added a high priority concern to others that delayed a decision on the Associators' prayer for a governor appointed by the king rather than the Lord Proprietor. With whatever time they could spare from pressing demands of the war, the king's advisors dealt with Lord Baltimore, who energetically opposed a royal governor for his palatinate. Whatever their frustrations, the Associators had to preserve their tenuous hold until the ponderous machinery back home ground out a decision.

As it turned out, Lord Baltimore's furious burst of energy merely prolonged the Associators' anguish. He offered to replace all "Deputys, Councill & Justices" with "profest Protestants" and promised "all the satisfaction the Inhabitants in general there can desire." But already, without his knowledge, the scales had tipped against him. On 1 February 1690 King William signed a letter prepared by the Lords of Trade commanding the Associators to continue their administration of the government "in our name" until the crown could make "full examination of all matters." The king's letter removed any taint of rebellion from the Associators' coup and, by tacit recognition of their actions, encouraged them to consolidate their revolution in Maryland.

Thereafter events in England moved inexorably toward the royal government desired by the Associators. By May of 1690 the crown had settled on a governor, Lionel Copley, and on 27 June 1691 made his appointment official when the Lord Keeper affixed the great seal to his commission. Two days later the Lords of Trade decided that the lucrative and powerful post of provincial secretary should go to Sir Thomas Lawrence, a baronet in his middle forties without any previous contact with Maryland. Then followed the tedious process of choosing a Council to accommodate the interests of governor, secretary, the merchant community, and Lord Baltimore, who retained extensive property rights in Maryland both in the soil and in revenues given him by law. But no one could doubt that Copley's commission effectively suspended Lord Baltimore's charter "by reasons of great neglects and miscarriages," as the commission put it. Moreover the Queen had explicitly told the Associators that "having since heard what your deputies and Agents have offered to us, Wee have thought fitt to take our Province of Maryland under our immediate care and Protection."

—4—

Lionel Copley, agent of the crown's care and protection and Maryland's first royal governor, made port in early April 1692 to receive a heart-warming welcome from the people of the province. The winter crossing had been a "very ill passage" but even before that he had experienced some hazards of another sort. A loyal Protestant, lieutenant-governor of Hull, he had played an important role in securing his bailiwick for William of Orange. The government of Maryland was to be his reward, an opportunity to repair his personal finances, which had fallen into disarray. Copley's debts had almost cost him his liberty before he could leave England. Lord Baltimore made a determined effort to purchase these debts from Copley's creditors in the hope of confining him to debtor's prison. Even with an advance of £500 from the Privy Council, Copley narrowly escaped the Proprietor's "arbitrary, unchrystian and ungentlemanly practices," as he put it.

Warm welcome from Maryland partisans notwithstanding, Copley had problems pressing upon him within a week of his landing. For some months a power struggle had been going on within Associator ranks. In this covert internecine fighting Nehemiah Blakiston had emerged as the strong man, provisional chief executive, and commander-in-chief of the military. Correspondingly, John Coode and Henry Jowles had lost stature. In no time at all Copley and Blakiston reached an understanding, an accommodation that lasted through the new royal governor's brief administration. Their alliance contributed to the polarization that marred the first years of royal rule in the colony. Blakiston's success left several of his former coadjutors disappointed and hungry for a share of the spoils of power.

Fortunately the polarization did not inhibit the transition from the extralegal Associator government to fully constituted royal administration. Governor Copley promptly dissolved the Association Assembly and issued writs for election of a new house. The writs called on each county to elect four delegates, a return to the arrangement that Lord Baltimore had curtailed in 1676 when he had arbitrarily reduced the number to two over the protest of provincials. A clear majority of the new delegates had supported the Association and now put their hands willingly to the task of setting the royal house in order.

During its first session, the Assembly produced the astounding number of eighty-six acts. To be sure some of these were nothing more than short bills continuing certain acts that were about to expire by time limitation. But others made fundamental changes, for example, an act establishing the Anglican Church. Neither the sheer bulk of legislation nor the importance of particular acts properly gauge the stature of this first royal Assembly. Yet the matters that raise this Assembly so far out of the ordinary seem prosaic to the point of dullness. In the technical terminology of political science, the Assembly of 1692 created a permanent committee infrastructure. In earlier days, before the revolution, the elected lower house had appointed ad hoc committees for almost all tasks. In 1692 the delegates established four permanent committees that transformed their body into the first modern legislature in Maryland history. The committee on elections and privileges in time gave the lower house control of its membership. The committee of laws brought together expert legal talent in its membership for the chore of drafting legislation. To hold hearings and examine petitions the house established a committee of "aggrievances," soon to be one of the busiest committees of the lower house. Finally a committee of accounts brought under the perpetual scrutiny of knowledgeable members the financial affairs of the province. The power of the purse eventually became the essential force in self-government, giving the initiative to the elective branch of the legislature. In brief, the lower house had without the slightest fanfare or memorable utterance crossed its Rubicon: it had in fact made the Assembly a miniature parliament. As an initial gesture the lower house quietly ignored the clerk selected by the governor in accord with traditional practice and referred to the delegates for acceptance. Then without response or explanation they chose their own clerk, the keeper of their records. Quietly, without antagonizing Governor Copley, the lower house of Assembly carried off its part of what later commentators labelled a "revolution of government."

On the whole, the Assembly worked well with Copley. The real problem for the first royal administrator was the new provincial secretary, Sir Thomas Lawrence, whose constant self-seeking and greed for financial perquisites kept delegates and officials from the governor down to the petty clerks in a perpetual boil for years to come. Lawrence's incessant bickerings with any and all who opposed his ruthless pursuit of fees fill many pages of the public records. Doubtless, too, these sordid battles consumed both time and moral energy that might have gone to more important matters in these years of change. The death of Governor Copley on 9 September 1693 and the arrival the following year of Francis Nicholson as his successor, however, brought to Maryland a dominant figure who could rise above the petty personal squabbling to a view of larger concerns facing the province.

—5—

When Francis Nicholson landed at St. Mary's on 26 July 1694 he was a debonair bachelor aged thirty-nine. His experience in administration included a tour as lieutenant governor of the Dominion of New England immediately before the Glorious Revolution and shortly thereafter two years as lieutenant governor of Virginia. Nicholson's administration of Virginia had been remarkably peaceful, in contrast to the hubub he had witnessed in Maryland first hand on an inspection tour of the province in 1691 while compiling a report for official eyes back home. His record of supporting the church in Virginia and his hand in the establishment of the College of William and Mary suggested a creative talent in administration sorely needed in the turbulent province of Maryland. Moreover he had shown himself efficient and methodical, qualities essential to charting a steady course.

From his Virginia observation post Nicholson had already seen enough of Maryland politics to arouse his suspicions about the motives of certain Maryland leaders, among them John Coode. Furthermore, he had an acute sense of the economic depression that had steadily deepened during the years of King William's War. But before dealing with any problem, Nicholson needed accurate information on the state of affairs in the province. On the day he took office he shook the establishment by demanding reports from incumbent officers and sound record keeping for the future. Maryland records, hitherto poorly kept, sometimes not even kept at all, improve noticeably from that date. With reports in hand he turned his attention to the church and military, both in sad estate, and to abuses in all branches of administration. He found tasks aplenty.

One of Nicholson's innovations, his "progress" into the upper counties, brought him into direct contact with local officials and, more important, the citizenry who never ventured as far as the provincial capital. These tours kept militia officers mindful of their responsibilities to render exact accounts of equipment and training and made vestrymen aware of their duty to maintain their parishes. On occasion, Nicholson did not hesitate to turn out an entire panel of county justices for irregularities in holding court or for violations of their commissions. In his words, these visits to outlying officials aimed "to keep up their drooping Spirits," and doutless they did, but they also gave the governor a lively sense of provincial needs: the relocation of the capital, the establishment of public schools, and the appointment of more competent staff to provincial offices.

—6—

St. Mary's City had served as the seat of provincial government since Leonard Calvert brought ashore the first band of settlers in 1634. At the bottom point of the Western Shore, the community had excellent anchorage in the Potomac for Atlantic ships but poor access to the hinterland where tobacco fields produced the wealth that gave Maryland its economic base. As planters made the clearings for their plantations further up the bayside and into the virgin lands behind the water's edge, ships increasingly bypassed the capital to trade at locations more convenient to producers who were their customers. Though enthusiastically named, St. Mary's City failed to develop as a metropolitan center. Instead it remained a pleasant, somewhat sleepy hamlet distinguished from other settled places by the presence of the governor and by annual meetings of the Assemblymen, who made their visits from ever increasing distances as new counties further up the bay came into existence. Governor Nicholson's proposal to move the capital to a more central location nevertheless met stiff opposition from householders in St. Mary's City and from officials already seated in the surrounding countryside. But even before Nicholson's arrival the disadvantages of the old capital had become so evident that the council had been scheduling its meetings at more accessible locations. Early in his administration the new governor signed into law an act to designate the ancient Puritan stronghold of "Arundell Towne" at the mouth of the Severn River as "the Chief place and Seat of Justice within the Province for holding of Assemblyes and Provinciall courts."

Governor Nicholson left an indelible mark on the new capital, which acquired the name Annapolis in 1695. As a student of landscape architecture, he turned his hand to designing the circles, squares, and street system of Annapolis after the baroque school in vogue back home. He had brought with him a copy of the imposing French manual, *The Compleat Gard'ner,* recently translated by John Evelyn, and from it drew a striking city plan: a large circle, "State Circle," on the brow of the highest elevation; behind it a smaller "Church Circle" slightly less elevated, and the radial streets extending outward at the cardinal points of the compass. Then, north of Church Circle he added an open square with twelve lots forming its perimeter, apparently hoping from the designation, Bloomsbury Square, for a development similar to the fashionable place of residence in London with the same name.

The act establishing the new capital specified in some detail the architecture of the building to house the Assembly and courts in State Circle: "Forty six foot in length, from Inside to Inside, and Twenty two foot wide from Inside to Inside, Brickworke two story high, the lower story to be Eleven foot in Pitch, and the upper story to be Eight foot in Pitch and plastered on the Inside." Some nemesis plagued this first statehouse. Colonel Casparus Herman, the builder, proved dilatory, and recurrent shortages of funds delayed occupancy until 1698. About a year later a bolt of lightning severely damaged roof and wall, a portent of its complete destruction by fire in October of 1704. But for a time the statehouse stood as crown of the provincial capital which Governor Nicholson pushed ahead as a residential as well as a commercial community.

As insurance against industrial blight the town act provided that "any Baker Brewer Tanner Dyer or any such Tradesmen That . . . may any ways anoy or disquiett the neighbors or Inhabitants . . . Exercise . . . such Trade a sufficient Distance from the said Town" to avoid becoming public nuisances. The same act created a board of commissioners and conferred on them important powers, including oversight of wharf construction essential to making the town a proper port. Together the governor and Assembly made some progress toward creating a metropolitan center, however small. One observer in 1699 commented:

> Governor Nicholson hath done his endeavour to make a towne. . . . There are in itt about fourty dwelling houses . . . seven or eight whereof cann afford good lodging and accommodations for strangers. There is alsoe a State house and a free schoole built with bricke which make a great shew among a parcell of wooden houses, and the foundations of a church laid, the only bricke church in Maryland. They have two market daies in the week.

Survey of Annapolis by James Stoddert, 1718, from a copy made in 1743.
This plat shows the characteristic circles with radial streets and Bloomsbury
Square dear to the heart of Governor Nicholson. Courtesy of the Maryland
Hall of Records.

—7—

The "free schoole" was another Nicholson effort to improve the quality of life in the province. The governor had complained of "the great scarcity of good Clarks," a consequence of meagre attention to education. Only once previously, in 1671, had the Assembly gone the length of proposing legislation to provide for a school, and that act had failed to pass. Nicholson had better luck with his first Assembly. He offered from his own purse £50 toward a building and £25 a year toward maintaining a master. The Assembly speedily produced the legislation which, with amendments over subsequent months, established at Annapolis in 1696 King William's School with the Archbishop of Canterbury as chancellor. Both governor and Assembly had hopes for one free school in every county, and the act gave the trustees authority to proceed on the county schools as soon as they could find adequate financing. But this proposed expansion had to wait more than two decades and for a more prosperous period.

Education and religion went hand in hand. The Act of 1696 establishing King William's School spoke of "the popagation of the gospel and the education of the youth of the province in good letters and manners." As yet the propagation of the gospel, at last Anglican, was far from flourishing and in pathetic condition, to the distress of the governor who was himself a strong churchman. Nicholson found only three fully ordained and properly inducted Anglican ministers in all of Maryland, though a few other parishes had lay readers. Meanwhile Catholics and the dissenting sects showed greater zeal. Quakers boasted seventeen active weekly meetings. More threatening in the governor's eyes, eight Catholics officiating in some ministerial capacity actively proselytized among county families. During an epidemic that raged for a season in the lower counties, priests "made it their business to go . . . to persons' houses when dying and frantic, and endeavor to seduce and make proselytes of them, and in such condition boldly presume to administer the sacrament to them." Whatever the allegations, the Catholic clergy could not be charged with shirking their duty in times of peril. But the Assembly urged action on Nicholson, and he in turn threatened severe penalties for converting Protestants. Later he launched an investigation to determine "how many people have within this twelve months been brought over to the Romish persuation and by what means."

Negative measures alone could not retain the allegiance of professing Anglicans and attract a larger membership. Nicholson's positive answer, a revitalized and expanded church program, began at the grass roots. He personally offered to contribute £5 to every parish that would build a house for its minister and to pay the full cost of surveying a glebe. At the top level he worked closely and successfully with the Bishop of London to find priests to supply empty pulpits. Together they provided eighteen parishes with ministers. Nicholson also obtained from Bishop Henry Compton the appointment of a commissary, young Thomas Bray (1656–1730), as supervisor of the Maryland church and its ministers. Although Bray did not immediately come to the colony, he aided the governor's program by recruiting clergy and by organizing valuable parish libraries to be shipped to Maryland. These were the beginnings of Bray's interest in the colonial church that a few years later led him to found the Society for the Propagation of the Gospel and its twin, the Society for the Promotion of Christian Knowledge.

Just as Nicholson appeared in sight of his goals he received a setback that threatened his entire program and the very existence of an established church in Maryland. The attorney general back home had discovered in the Act of 1692 establishing the Anglican Church words that, in his opinion, seemed "to establish the Great Charter of England to be the law in Maryland." The offending clause read "where the Laws of the Province are silent Justice shall be administered according to the Laws of England." British policy did not deny colonials the rights of Englishmen, but officials had set their minds against wholesale adoption by any province of the statute law of England, including Magna Charta. All attempts by colonial legislatures to claim British statute law consistently met rebuff. The attorney general's doubts passed to the king, who disallowed the Act of 1692 and all subsequent acts of establishment that contained this provision, so threatening to his Majesty's royal prerogative.

Nicholson learned of the catastrophe in the late spring by private letter from Thomas Lawrence, the provincial secretary, then visiting in England. The moment was particularly inauspicious for the governor. His had been a reform administration and his policies as well as his tactics had touched provincials on sensitive spots. At once he saw months of patient work toward putting the church on a sound footing totally ruined. In his distress he made a wrong decision. He dared not be candid with the Assembly, he wrote the Bishop of London, for fear the delegates would decline to pass a new church act and the related school laws without the offending clauses. Accordingly he called them back into special session only forty-five days after adjournment of the regular meeting and tried to gain his objective by stealth. He opened the session by disclosing news of a conspiracy against the king, proceeded to a discussion of war news and trade developments, then almost casually referred a dozen proposals to the Committee of Laws, among them a recommendation that the delegates "draw up the Acts of Religion anew and abbreviate the same."

The ruse failed. The abbreviated legislation still contained the objectionable clause, and when Nicholson stiffened, suspicious delegates began to balk. Nicholson pulled the last stop in an emotional appeal: "As God Almighty moved the hearts of the Children of Israel so he hoped their hearts will be opened to consider the Drawing up of this Bill in that nature as it may obtain His Majesties Royal Assent." But their hearts were not opened and the frustrated governor had to settle for an act that recited the litany, "where the Laws of the Province are silent Justice shall be administered according to the Laws of England." Even more galling, he had to explain to his English superiors that the delegates traditionally associated the "libertys and priviledges of the church and subject together." The bitterest dose of all, Nicholson had to lobby among his English friends for royal approval of the act, which in the end met the doom of its predecessor, the royal veto. The church was still not legally established.

The royal vetoes, which Nicholson still had not dared disclose, inevitably came to light. The Assembly reacted with "ill-humor" at subsequent sessions and before long had developed so much resistance to any recommendations from the governor that his optimism evaporated. His program had ground to a halt. "So please God there don't come better times," he wrote, "I may shutt up Shopp."

But worse days lay ahead. Within a year and a half an administration that had promised much and had actually accomplished more than a little was in a shambles. Outward manifestations first catch the eye: Governor Nicholson indignantly caning John Coode for unseemly conduct when the old rebel appeared at divine service. But beneath the surface ran a strong current of determination among the elected delegates to maintain an initiative they had won as responsible spokesmen for the provincial imperative. At times they engaged the governor in petty bickering, but at others they stood on broad principle, when they insisted on control over their own membership. A case in point, the election of John Coode to the lower house brought on a confrontation. Coode openly boasted that he had taken holy orders in the Anglican Church, a disqualification for holding civil office. Nevertheless the lower house by majority vote seated Coode and backed down only when Nicholson summoned them to his presence, displayed his evidence, and challenged them to deny it. The chastened delegates rescinded their former vote, dismissed Coode, apologized to the governor. Nicholson had won a pyrrhic victory; the real trial of strength had yet to come.

The stage was set for the last act, a coalition to unseat Nicholson. Philip Clarke, a firebrand from St. Mary's county, joined forces with Coode to smear the governor's reputation. They soon recruited Gerrard Slye, merchant from the lower counties, who prepared a slate of seventeen charges, complete with the innuendo and absurdities of contemporary polemics. Inevitably the governor, drawn into exposing the follies of Slye's attack, faced a network of opponents, some of them prominent leaders, bound by ties of kinship and interest. Consequently Nicholson accomplished little during his last year, though his reputation remained unscathed with the Board of Trade, which promoted him to the governorship of Virginia, a richer and more populous province. And when he turned over the seals of office to his successor, Nathanial Blakiston, on 2 January 1699 even the lower house, no doubt happy to see him go, voted a congratulatory message acknowledging that his administration had been "one of our greatest Temporall Blessings."

—8—

Flowery hypocrisy became in years ahead a tradition in farewell addresses to departing governors. Nicholson had come to Maryland with a program and a sense of mission. He had made enemies, some bitter, because his reforms frustrated their personal ambitions. The colony was to have other able governors during the quarter century of royal administration. But none brought anything like Nicholson's talents nor his combination of cosmopolitan outlook and a program for advancement of the province.

Nicholson's administration had begun during one of the dreariest war years. The War of the League of Augsburg, or as colonials called it, King William's War, had dragged along into its fifth year when he took office. French privateers had disrupted the usual movement of merchant ships to Chesapeake waters, and vast quantities of tobacco spoiled on Maryland docks. In the depth of the consequent depression Nicholson took positive steps to revitalize the tobacco trade and thus restore prosperity in the province, which depended almost solely on this cash crop for its economic well-being. He lobbied, effectively as it turned out, for regular fleets escorted by British warships to protect helpless merchantmen against marauding privateers. At the same time he obtained a British patrol boat to combat an invasion of illegal traders—Scottish merchants and Quakers from the north—while he put the tobacco trade in order. He maneuvered through the Assembly new export taxes designed to pay public debts and at the same time to retaliate against the Pennsylvania Quaker merchants, whose sharp practices had created a constant drain of hard money from the province. Even before the war's end Nicholson could point to clear improvement in the economy and refute his critics with proof that public debts were paid for the first time in more than a decade. When peace came in 1697 a veritable boom started, lasting five years, well beyond Nicholson's term.

The postwar boom ended when England and France took up the cudgels again in 1702 over the succession to the vacant throne of Spain. The new phase of strife between two ancient enemies, the War of the Spanish Succession, again received in the colonies the name of the ruling monarch, Queen Anne's War. The five year peace between 1697 and 1702 appeared in perspective a truce while the opponents recuperated sufficiently to commence hostilities again. But the interim of peace, though a mere half decade, witnessed not only boom times but along with the new affluence the beginnings of a shift to slave labor in tobacco culture.

The first recorded mention of Negroes in Maryland occurs in 1642 with the delivery of thirteen Blacks to St. Mary's. But for the next fifty years importation of the unwilling immigrants was never brisk. In 1697, Blacks numbered about 3,000 in the total population of above 30,000 persons. The seventeenth century had been the century of the indentured servant, those immigrants without capital who sold their labor for a term of years and who, when freed, established themselves as small planters, often tenants at first. They continued to come in appreciable numbers during succeeding decades—more than 600 in 1698 alone—but in that same year the tide turned when during the summer some 470 Blacks "from Guny" came ashore in Maryland.

Once started, the importation of bondsmen from West Africa into Maryland continued through the boom time between the wars and on into the less prosperous years of Queen Anne's War (1702–1713). The majority went to the southern counties of both shores. But even in Baltimore county, less suited to slave labor than the richer lands to the south, the number of Blacks jumped from 52 in 1695 to 204 in 1704 and to 438 in 1710. By 1710 the total slave population of Maryland had increased to almost 8,000, over two and a half times the number in 1697.

With the influx of Blacks came a change in the Maryland economy. New and larger units of production, different in kind from the "plantations" of earlier decades, appeared here and there in all of the counties. Alongside the familiar family plantation, tended by a single householder with the assistance of his children and a few indentured servants, emerged the great planter. Owner of a dozen to a score of servile laborers, he set a new lifestyle based on landholdings larger than anything previously known and a pattern of husbandry unfamiliar in earlier years. Slaves and land were the conspicuous signs of the new elite. Already a few county families had begun, during Nicholson's administration, to amass landed estates that later formed a solid base for their descendants. John Addison patented over 4,000 acres of choice wild land up the Potomac. Councillor Thomas Brooke received patents for 11,000 acres. Others took smaller acreage: William Coursey patented 1,900 acres, Thomas Ennals 1,600, Robert Smith over 2,000. The same men were purchasing the new slaves. Bartholomew Ennals owned a single slave when he died around 1700; his son Thomas had thirty-eight at his death in 1718.

The new breed of planter stemmed from these modest beginnings in Nicholson's time. They continued to accumulate land and slaves even during the harder years of Queen Anne's War. But not until peacetime did they exercise extensive power in Maryland; from then on, though few in numbers, they had disproportionate weight in the economic and political scales.

—9—

Ironically Francis Nicholson, the ardent churchman, left Maryland without realizing his hopes for a sound Anglican establishment. He had personally contributed to the building of churches and had made a start toward attracting ministers to Maryland. All this work seemed vain when the crown struck down the laws underpinning the establishment. Not until 1702 was legislation satisfactory to the crown finally passed and then only through the good offices of Thomas Bray, a stranger to the province.

Bray had earlier assisted Nicholson in finding ministers to fill the many vacant pulpits and had shipped valuable libraries to several parishes in Maryland. At last in January 1700 he actually sailed for the province in company with a Quaker agent who secretly carried the order in council that voided the latest Maryland legislation establishing the Anglican Church. The unsuspecting Bray stopped for a brief visit in Virginia, where his coadjutor Nicholson was governor, then proceeded to Maryland. There a group of prominent Quakers sprang the council order on him. At the same time they demanded an immediate halt in collection of church taxes, which had started as soon as the Assembly had passed the act of establishment but which had no legal justification after the law was disallowed. With energy and astuteness not usually associated with men of the cloth, Bray at once put his hand to obtaining new legislation, purged of objectionable provisions, and raced the agents of opponents of the act back to England to lobby for its acceptance. This time crown officers found new difficulties in the law and again recommended disallowance. The process seemed never ending. At this point Bray came forward with the suggestion that crown lawyers themselves revise the act in order to put it in acceptable form. He then joined forces with his far-away Maryland friends in a successful effort to persuade the Assembly to enact the crown draft into law. Thus in 1702, after more than a decade, the Church of England became the established church of the colony, supported by an annual tithe of forty pounds of tobacco on each taxable in the province.

Quakers had been the most determined and far the most effective opponents of establishment. But already by 1700 Quaker influence had begun to decline, and thereafter Roman Catholics became the disturbing challenge to Anglicans. The renewed war with France, a leading Catholic power, evoked in colonial minds the associated evils of "popery" and arbitrary power. While the best numerical estimates of professed Catholics at the time—eight fathers and three brothers officiating for 600 to 700 communicants—indicates no real menace, Protestants viewed with misgivings a swelling stream of migration by "Irish Papists" coming in as indentured servants. Accordingly, the Protestant majority rallied to the heavy-handed crackdown on Catholics by a new royal governor.

John Seymour (?–1709), descended from an old Gloucestershire family, came to his post in 1704 from a military career that included service in the campaigns of the great Duke of Marlborough. Almost immediately he found cause for offense when he discovered that two Catholic priests had publicly celebrated mass and gave them a tongue lashing that gauges at once the arrogance of Seymour and the intolerance of the age:

> It is the unhappy Temper of you and all your Tribe to grow insolent upon Civility. . . . You might methinks be Content to live quietly as you may and let the Exercise of your Superstitious Vanities be confined to yourselves without proclaiming them at publick Times and in publick places unless you expect by your gawdy shows and Serpentine Policy to amuse the multitude and beguile the unthinking weakest part of them, an Act of Deceit well known to be amongst you. . . . In plain and few words Gentlemen if you intend to live here let me hear no more of these things for if I do and they are made good against you be assured I'll chastise you. . . . I'll make but this one Tryal. . . . You are the first that have given any disturbance to my Government and if it were not for the hopes of your better demeanour you should now be the first that should feel the Effects of so doing.

Pray take notice that I am an English Protestant Gentleman and can never equivocate.

A month later Seymour induced the Assembly to pass "An Act to Prevent the Growth of Popery," which prohibited all Catholic services—baptism, marriage, and mass—either public or private. At the same time Irish servants brought into the province were subjected to an import tax of 20 shillings per person to discourage Catholic immigration. A few months later cooler heads prevailed to lift the ban on private family services, but the prohibition on public functions remained.

Governor Seymour went with a popular current when he penalized the Catholics. He quickly found himself in trouble when he moved counter to a trend apparent enough in retrospect but not clear to him at the time. For a decade and a half the Assembly had become a power in provincial affairs beyond anything known in proprietary days. Seymour's brusque authoritarian manner, natural to a military man accustomed to command, struck a sensitive nerve. Possibly provincials sensed an attitude toward them that he disclosed explicitly in periodic reports to the Board of Trade: "The Natives who are ignorant and raw in business and naturally proude and obstinate, are not only the Representatives in Assembly but Justices of the County Courts; and by the name of Country borne, distinguish themselves from the rest of her Majestys Subjects, and run into great heats and divisions which may be of ill Consequence; for as they know little of the laws and good Manners they practice less." The phrase, "country born," frequently on the tongues of provincials, seemed specially irritating to Seymour, who dragged it into his letters home time after time.

On its side the Assembly had won an initiative that members refused to relinquish. Even Nicholson had accorded the assembled delegates decent respect during frequent disagreements. Nicholson's successor, Nathaniel Blakiston, had gone further and practiced a policy of deference in his brief term as governor. Then during three years prior to Seymour, while the governor's office stood vacant, the Assembly had no royal factor as a counterpoise. Understandably Seymour clashed with the elected representatives whom he regarded not only as "proude and obstinate" but altogether too much inclined to regard themselves "independent of the Queen's Governour." Tension between governor and

legislature thwarted many well-intentioned proposals from both con-
testants as the struggle between royal prerogative and popular aspi-
ration ran its course.

The royal prerogative became the issue in one rather minor battle,
which however touched an important principle. St. Mary's City, now
sinking into the semblance of a country hamlet, had by Seymour's
time ceased to send the two delegates allotted to it while still the
capital city. As viceroy, Seymour conferred on Annapolis a special
charter of incorporation, which set up a municipal government of
mayor, aldermen, and common councilmen, collectively entitled to
elect two delegates to the lower house of Assembly. When the Annapolis delegates appeared, the lower house promptly expelled them
on the ground that the governor lacked authority to grant Annapolis
a charter that included provision for sending representatives to sit in
their midst. Seymour responded in a furious message to this "infringement upon Her Majesty's Royal Prerogative." The lower house stubbornly maintained that the governor alone had no power to grant the
charter but offered to concur in awarding two seats to Annapolis provided all the freeholders and not merely the tight body of municipal
officials "have their equal Priviledges in choosing their Representatives." In the end the lower house had its way by simply refusing to
seat the Annapolis delegates until the governor consented to sign a bill
qualifying all freeholders of the city to vote for the two representatives.

The battle over the Annapolis delegates had been short and sharply
focused. Another struggle, over the Maryland courts, dragged on for
years, a campaign rather than a single battle. Almost from the first,
Seymour had criticized shortcomings in the administration of justice
in the colony. Lawyers fell far below his standards for learning and
professional decorum. Justices of the several courts ranked even lower
on his scale. Obviously reforms were in order, but Seymour began
rather cautiously for a man of his authoritarian outlook and direct
methods. He offered his improvements step by step.

Seymour's first target, the lawyers, had indeed frequently acted
unprofessionally and, worse, had violated both the letter and spirit of
the law. The records were spotted with examples. In Prince George's
County, two prominent attorneys had abandoned all restraint in arguing a case and descended to the depths of personal vituperation too
violent for even the tolerant justices. The court fined each attorney

two hundred pounds of tobacco "for giveing one another Abusive Languig before the Court." Seymour mentioned the "ill behavior of Several Attorneys practiceing in the provinciall County Courts" and catalogued their abuses: "corruption Ignorance and Extortion," "Stirring up of Vexatious and Litigious Suites," and "Multiplying them to the private Lucre and Gaine." In short, he said, "by senseless and insignificant brawles, Repetitions, impertinent Cavills the time of the Courts is Consumed and taken up for the most part in trifles."

For all these sweeping accusations the records bear Seymour out in detail. One instance particularly offended the governor. Thomas Macnemara, an impetuous and successful attorney on the Western Shore, had been assigned by the court to plead in behalf of a petitioner *in forma pauperis* and thus entitled to free counsel. Nevertheless, Macnemara had exacted from the pauper twenty shillings and one hundred pounds of bacon before taking the case. When he learned of this infamy Governor Seymour decided to move. By proclamation he established two methods of ascertaining an attorney's qualifications to practice. The attorney could present evidence that he was a member of one of the Inns of Court or of Chancery in London. Such trained lawyers were few in Maryland. Any others, and they formed the great majority, could submit to an examination for fitness before the governor and council.

On the afternoon following Seymour's proclamation four prominent attorneys present in the capital, William Bladen, Robert Goldsborough, Wornell Hunt, and Richard Dallam, applied for examination and immediately received certification. They constituted the first official bar in Maryland.

Macnemara also applied. His petition stated that without the income from his many cases pending in the courts he would be unable to support himself and his family and concluded: "Your petitioner hereby promising a reformation of his former past behaviour." The governor and council declined Macnemara's plea, "reflecting on the many misdemeanors of the petitioner . . . and how often he had promised Reformation but had yet given so little proof thereof . . . having often Contemned and Affronted the Justices as well as abused his Clyants." Macnemara had trapped himself. Disbarred from appearing for his pauper client, he bluntly refused to return the money and bacon he had extorted. While the pauper was complaining to the council, Mac-

nemara stood at the door awaiting the outcome. The sheriff, sent out
to ask whether he had taken the fee, brought back Macnemara's reply:
"He reserved the Answer untill he knew whether it was a Crime, And
what he had got none should take it from him." Seymour disposed of
Macnemara with military directness: "Upon [this] Sawcy Answer and
other Audatious behaviour His Excellency ordered the Sheriff to put
him in the stocks one full hour bare breeched of which his Excellency
was pleased to remit half an hour a great Gust arrising."

The age knew indelicacy in conduct and punishment alike. Fortune
favored the bold and aggressive types like Macnemara. But Seymour
had scored points in curbing the least creditable element of the legal
profession. His proposals for court reform met less public approval and
in the end came to naught.

Seymour had in his letters home described the provincial court as
"a mere Jest." He had a low opinion of the twelve justices of this
central court, men "not knowing any Rules to guide their Judgment."
Of the county justices he held a meaner view. Many of them also sat
as delegates in the lower house of Assembly and "on all occasions have
sought to corroborate and establish their jurisdiction and Administration tho they are never so meanly qualified for the Trust."

Seymour proposed to accomplish the seemingly impossible task of
reform by a simple plan, which he disclosed piecemeal. First he sought
to reduce the provincial court to fewer but more dependable judges.
This central court would hear the important cases: capital offenses and
suits involving large sums of money. Then when not holding court
in Annapolis, the justices would go on circuit through the counties
to hold assizes and thus bring to these outlying districts the kind of
knowledge and decorum sadly lacking outside the capital. Finally he
proposed to restrict the jurisdiction of county courts drastically, leaving them little more than breaches of the peace and suits for small
sums. Altogether his reforms aimed at more centralization and greater
executive control of the judicial system. Seymour claimed several merits
for his plan, among them more competent judges, more efficient dispatch of justice, and above all more responsible discharge of duties.

But instead of support he met resistance. His plan undercut provincial traditions matured considerably since the Revolution of 1689.
Inhabitants of the several counties had not only grown accustomed to
the ample jurisdiction of the county courts but had adapted them into

their very lifestyles. During court sessions, three or four consecutive days every quarter, the male population converged on the county seat, often not even a hamlet but merely a courthouse and an adjacent tavern. Here planters great and small went about a routine of serious judicial business in a pattern familiar to both participants and spectators.

First the public prosecutor opened with crown cases, frequently female indentured servants accused of bastardy, a serious offense that not only resulted in loss of valuable service to planters while their servants' physical condition kept them from work but also flagrantly violated accepted morality. Ordinarily female servants convicted of bastardy were punished by twenty-five lashes on the bare back "well laid on" and additional service tacked on to their indentures as compensation to the owner. Occasionally the offender gained a certain local notoriety. Jane Addison of Charles County established something of a record within a very few years. Earlier the grand jury presented her for "incontinent Liveing" with a Negro, Sawcy Jack. A short time later she was convicted of bastardy and received the customary lashing. Finally she came to the dock to face a charge of murdering her latest bastard child, though this time the prosecutor failed to uncover evidence to convict.

After the criminal docket the court turned to the more numerous civil suits. Maryland planters were already making the reputation that led a later observer to call them a "most litigious people." Everyone seemed to be suing everyone else, mainly for debts but also for the recovery of stray animals and all manner of petty concerns that made up the warp and weft of rural life. Students today look at the court proceedings and wonder how the justices could adjudicate the astonishing number of cases on the docket each quarter.

The judges not only tried the suits before them but also performed other kinds of work that today would be considered administrative or supervisory. Every year the justices appointed an overseer of public roads for each precinct and received complaints about the condition of thoroughfares. From public funds they paid bounties for killing crows, squirrels, and wolves, the pests of an agricultural community. They committed orphans to custody during their minority; established rates to be charged by inns for lodging guests, stabling their horses, and serving food and liquor in the public rooms; determined expenses arising from county disbursements and apportioned them among the taxable inhabitants of the county. And finally the court had jurisdiction

over local records, including the all-important county land records.

These activities alone gave the courthouse the intensity of a beehive.
Out of doors another round of activities went on as planters bought
and sold crops, traded horses, purchased land, and talked politics. At
the end of the day's formal session, justices, litigants, and the merely
curious spectators gathered in whatever inns or lodgings the place
afforded to slake their thirst and to continue talking crops, politics
and law, often to the accompaniment of horseplay and occasional fis-
ticuffs over matters that could not be decided more decorously.

Against these settled folkways Seymour's plan for reforming the
court system simply could not prevail. When the governor issued
commissions to the county justices he lowered their jurisdiction to
suits involving a maximum of 2000 pounds of tobacco or £10 sterling.
Lawyers and clients raised an unmistakable outcry at this drastic cut-
back, which meant taking all but the smallest cases to distant provincial
justices with the attendant hardship of travel and consequent higher
costs. But Seymour had another card to play: the justices of the assizes
making the circuit through the counties were to hear the larger suits.
Here too he met resistance from a formidable opponent, the Assembly.
Delegates to the lower house—some of them justices of the county
courts—refused to pass legislation paying the salaries of the itinerant
assize judges. Seymour found himself compelled to establish his circuit
system by executive action and to ask the Queen to pay each justice
£120 annually out of royal revenues. In the end, Governor Seymour's
judicial reforms failed. He gave way to popular pressure by raising the
maximum jurisdiction of county courts first to 8,000 pounds of tobacco
or £40, then later to 10,000 pounds of tobacco or £50 where it had
originally stood. When he died unexpectedly in 1709 the assize justices
continued to make their circuits through the counties but the lower
house clamored for a return to the "old common ordinary way" of
justice. Delegates characterized the assizes as "very ill Convenient to
the country and imposed . . . without their Consent."

—10—

After the death of Seymour the province had no royal governor for half
a decade. The senior councillor, always styled Major General Edward
Lloyd (1670–1719) in the records, presided as chief magistrate through

the six years while the province awaited a royal appointee. Head of an old and wealthy Talbot County family, Lloyd dutifully attempted to comply with the Queen's instructions to Seymour. The majority of the councillors stood with him. Accordingly, they had to oppose a vociferous lower house of Assembly whose members prepared to eradicate the unpopular policies and acts of the Seymour administration. A crown official who periodically toured the American colonies during these years found unexpected tension in the province when he passed through in December 1709: "Maryland, which I allways took to be the most quiet and easyest Government of the Maine, the freest from all factions and partys, is now by the ill conduct of the last Governor run into as great extravagancy as any of the rest." Patently Major General Lloyd and the council were trying to hold the line in a nearly impossible position: attached by inclination to the local interest while bound by oath to royal policy.

Understandably the "native" interest prevailed. Unrelenting pressure from the lower house wore down the most sincere resolution of the councillors. As months passed, then years, without the expected governor, delegates pushed the council into violating its instructions on important matters: the courts, for example, and the patronage. The lower house put the case bluntly to their colleagues in the upper house: "Since you must own we more immediately represent the people than your Honorable Board, you must allow us to know more of their Oppression and we offer the Properest Remedies we can to relieve them." Essentially the elected delegates openly invited council acquiescence and even cooperation in ordering provincial affairs toward a native interest. Clearly the lower house had discerned its role and was learning how to proceed toward realizing its aims. It had established its identity and had begun to reach for power.

The times favored this clear direction in Maryland politics. England was similarly going through a period of transformation that later scholars labelled the Age of Queen Anne. The queen had inherited a war, on the surface a dynastic struggle over the succession to the Spanish throne. On the European front her great captain, John Churchill, Duke of Marlborough, had raised English arms to glory at Blenheim, Ramillies, and Oudenarde. Wits spoke of "Marlborough's war" against Louis XIV. But the war dragged on after his great victories into an international conflict, a world war in which the colonies of three empires—English, French and Spanish—played an increasingly important role. Beyond the coasts of Europe private warships, the celebrated privateers, flying the colors of each nation, preyed on the merchant vessels of the other. War trade became indistinguishable from trade war. French privateers lurked about American coasts to seize British and American merchantmen that ventured on blue water. And vessels of the tobacco fleet trading to the Chesapeake figured among the richest prizes.

For Maryland, Queen Anne's War brought depression. The loss of European markets forced down tobacco prices, while risks of wartime shipping boosted freight and insurance rates to exorbitant levels. After 1705, freight rates averaged £15 a ton, double the pre-war figure. High shipping costs not only ate up much of the profit on cargoes of tobacco sent to England; the same costs raised the prices of imports: the textiles, tools, and other manufactures vital to the commercial agriculture of the planting colonies. With no end to war in sight the options appeared grim. Many feared wholesale emigration from Maryland to some unspecified place where living would be easier. Others talked of diversifying the agriculture of the province or even attempting some kind of industrialization in order to decrease dependence upon trade with England.

Nothing of the kind happened, neither general exodus of population nor radical alteration of the economy. Merchants and planters endured the prolonged hardships, but they fought back through their elected representatives in the Assembly. The desperate plight of Maryland economically steeled delegates to resist directives and blandishments of governors and even commands of the queen's own majesty. Disagreements between Whitehall and Annapolis at times threatened stalemate. For seven years after 1704 crown and province contended over the size of tobacco hogsheads, at first sight a trivial matter but of genuine concern in hard times. Maryland planters had long felt at a competitive disadvantage beside Virginians in the tobacco trade. Virginia leaf was heavier and standard gauge hogsheads held an appreciably greater weight of Virginia tobacco. Yet shippers assessed freight rates by the hogshead without regard to weight. Maryland producers preferred a larger gauge hogshead to equalize weights and in 1704 pushed an act through the Assembly requiring the larger size. English merchants promptly protested on the ground that their ships were constructed to carry the size hogsheads employed by Virginia and complained that the Maryland law adversely affected their carrying capacity. The queen obligingly vetoed the act and at the same time another Maryland act to prevent "cropping and defacing" tobacco, an abuse of shipmasters that sharply decreased the sale value of Maryland leaf on the English market. With the queen's veto came instructions that the Assembly pass an act requiring planters to ship in the same size hogsheads used in Virginia. To this flat command delegates in the lower house responded with a lesson in reciprocity. In a series of rebuttals and memorials they temporized until 1711 before striking what amounted to a bargain: the crown agreed to approve a bill to prevent cropping and defacing tobacco in return for an act of Assembly requiring standard gauge hogsheads. Even this arrangement did not come easily. Edward Lloyd told crown officials that the act for regulating the size of hogsheads "was Gained with great Difficulty."

The journals of the Maryland Assembly, the official proceedings, do not make exciting reading. The endless morning meetings and afternoon adjournments, messages between the upper and lower houses, the readings of bills and amendments all seem lifeless and somehow stereotyped. But beneath the turgid prose something alive stirs, surfacing occasionally in a disagreement between the elected delegates of the lower house and the appointed members of the upper chamber. The resulting exchanges, at first tart and then by degrees more and more bitter, bring into focus a principle, an imperative too dear to provincial hearts for their spokesmen—the elected delegates—to relinquish. If their messages lack something in literary grace, they burgeon with determination to promote the native interest. The note was strong and clear.

In the twenty-five years of royal government Maryland experienced many changes. Some were obvious and abrupt. Royal officers replaced proprietary officials, and writs ran in the monarch's name, not the Lord Proprietor's. The capital moved from the Potomac north to Annapolis. After several false starts the Anglican church came to stay as the established religion. Other changes were less visible and more gradual. These years of almost continual international warfare, though beyond question hard on planters, did nevertheless witness some economic growth. An increasing population prevented total stagnation. Even in the worst years a few planters managed to find cash or credit for the costliest of investments: Negro slaves. But subtlest and least visible of all, a political transformation had occurred, so gradual that at no one moment in time can a line be drawn to mark the date of maturity. Yet when the royal administration ended in 1715, the provincial Assembly no longer resembled the body of the earlier proprietary period, uncertain of its constitutional position and flabby in its internal organization. The lower house could not turn back the calendar.

6

THE SECOND RESTORATION
(1714–1734)

The royal government of Maryland ended abruptly in early 1715 on the heels of great changes in the western world. Just two years previously at Utrecht the European powers, aligned in two hostile coalitions, had signed the treaties that ended the eleven year War of the Spanish Succession. The coming of peace brought hope to a world weary of a war that had extended to the utmost reaches of the empires of England, France, and Spain at the cost of much life and treasure. The British colonies on the Atlantic seaboard had always attached the name of their reigning sovereign to the fighting, and in their mouths the struggle had been Queen Anne's War. Begun as a dynastic war, the battleground had become international, extending to trade and colonial possessions. Shortly after the peace of Utrecht the titular chiefs of state at the head of each coalition had come to their ends. In August 1714 Queen Anne died, last of the Protestant House of Stuart; a year later Louis XIV, the grand monarch, reached the end of the longest recorded reign in European history, and one of the most warlike. Within two years Europeans and their relatives overseas in the colonies witnessed the kind of changes that mark the close of an era and the beginning of a new epoch.

—1—

Of immediate interest to colonials, the death of Queen Anne brought a new reigning family to England, the House of Hanover. The new dynasty traced its claim to the English throne to a daughter of James I, who had married her to the Elector of Hanover a century before.

Thus in September 1714, a great grandson of this union, Georg Ludwig, a minor German princeling who spoke no English, ascended the throne of the Conqueror and Elizabeth, subscribing himself George I.

In Maryland these high ceremonies were duly announced by the first resident governor in half a decade, John Hart (governor 1714–1720). Queen Anne had appointed him on the first day of January 1714, and he had arrived in Annapolis in late May to take up the office left vacant since the death of Seymour. It fell to Hart to proclaim the new monarch and to preside over other changes touching the affairs of the new king's subject, Lord Baltimore.

Charles, Lord Baltimore, had lost his palatine government in the uprising of 1689, but he had retained his palatine property: his rights to millions of vacant acres and quitrents to all patented lands. Almost eighty-five years of age and recently married to his fourth wife, Baltimore was currently experiencing serious problems with his son and heir, Benedict Leonard (1679–1715). The son had renounced his Catholic faith, received communion in the Church of England, and had taken his young children out of Catholic schools to have them brought up as Protestants. By these acts Benedict Leonard had removed the only obstacle to recovery of the family claim to civil government in Maryland. Through his lawyers he began a campaign to have the province fully restored to his family. On the death of his father in February 1715, Benedict Leonard, now Lord Baltimore, succeeded in his project. The crown restored to him the desired rights of government, subject to royal approval of the govenor he appointed for his province. The new Lord Proprietor immediately notified John Hart that he would continue in office, wearing the hat of proprietary governor.

But the succession of changes that marked the early administration of Governor Hart had not ended. Eight weeks almost to a day after Benedict Leonard succeeded to the title, Lord Baron of Baltimore, he died at the early age of thirty-five. His son Charles (1699–1751), still a minor, became the fifth Lord Baltimore with Lord Guilford as his guardian. Under the aegis of Lord Guilford acting for the new Lord Charles, Governor Hart was to serve out his term during the years of external peace that prevailed in the reign of George I.

—2—

Though again proprietary in name, Maryland in important ways remained a royal province. Certainly there was no complete return to the old days. The Assembly held fast those legislative powers captured during twenty-five years of royal administration. When proprietary officials later attempted to tamper with the machinery, lower house leaders mounted a preventive action that lasted half a century, the anti-proprietary movement. But in 1714, when John Hart began his six year term, these constitutional battles were in the future. Both governor and provincials were living in a period that was free for the first time in a quarter century of war or rumors of war. Internally as well, the province seemed tranquil. Governor Hart said as much in an official letter to the Board of Trade.

But Hart erred. Just as Assemblymen had progressed along the road of no return, so had their constituents, the people of Maryland. Not only had the outlook of provincials changed, the physical circumstances of their lives had similarly altered during the twenty-five years of royal rule. The change had occurred almost insensibly in the tidewater, the oldest settled area of the province, where the marks of an earlier and more primitive existence had given way to a scene more civilized in both outward and inward aspects. In good part change had been a consequence of sheer growth in population and wealth, but alongside these easily visible signs went the more intangible alterations: in society the beginning of the formation of an elite and in the economy some signs of growth despite the blight of almost constant warfare.

Somewhere around 1700 population growth experienced a takeoff after a slow and uncertain course in earlier years. Just before the restoration of 1660, the population of the province of Maryland had not exceeded 2,500, and in 1675 there were no more than 13,000. These early statistics, the best available from an age inhospitable to head counts, are little more than informed guesses. Governor Blakiston provided the first reliable census when he numbered the people in 1701 in a remarkable document that listed by name every man, woman, and child, both free and bonded, in Maryland. Unfortunately the Board of Trade, which commissioned the census in response to increasing interest in "political arithmetic," destroyed the bulky compilation of names and kept only the totals by counties. These abstracted figures give the first accurate idea of population distribution within the province and the first reliable grand total, 32,258. From this date at the beginning of the 18th century onward, population increase can be calculated with reasonable certainty decade by decade. In round numbers the figures are impressive. By 1710 population had grown to 43,000, by 1720 to 62,000, and in 1730 to 82,000. These increases appear even more striking expressed as growth rates or, in the terminology of demographers, as percentage decennial increases: for the first decade 39 percent, for the second 44, and for the third decade 32. Though the growth rate continued at a high level for years to come, these three decades set a record never again equalled. Population had at last substantially filled the tidewater, obliterating wide vacant spaces between plantations. The vast hinterland, however, remained largely in a state of nature.

New realities resulted from the enlarged population base. For the first time Maryland experienced something that can be called urban development, not as yet significant but a beginning. Back in the 1660s and 1770s the Lord Proprietor had encouraged the establishment of urban places by proclamation, and somewhat later the Assembly had passed acts laying out waterside town sites to serve as ports of call for tobacco ships. This town movement accorded with English thinking, which held that civil society could not permanently survive without towns and cities where merchants and tradesmen could follow their callings. Nevertheless the attempts of Proprietor and Assembly proved abortive. Population did not follow edicts and laws: the sites remained ghost towns and even their exact location became to later generations a matter of conjecture.

On the larger population base of the eighteenth century a successful era of town building began. The town and port of Oxford on the Eastern Shore at the mouth of the Tred Avon dates from an act passed in 1706. Next year the Assembly established a new site for a town already on paper but uninhabited, Chestertown in Kent County on the broad, placid Chester River. Somewhat later legislation called into existence other towns: in 1724 Joppa on the Gunpowder River in Baltimore County, in 1729 Port Tobacco on the Potomac in Charles County, and finally in the same year a small community named Baltimore Town on the Patapsco, more nearly a harbor than a river.

In the Golden Age that lay ahead all of these communities attracted some residents. Chestertown, which lay in a particularly lovely countryside threaded by a river that could easily accommodate ocean-going ships, became the residence of merchants who built splendid townhouses along the waterfront. Showplaces in the twentieth century, these mansions were in their day the homes of active traders who fattened their purses on the commerce that made this center one of the most active ports in eighteenth century Maryland. Oxford, too, located on the bay, attracted several merchants. Among them, Henry Callister, a factor of the Liverpool house, Foster Cunliffe and Company, left in his letters an inimitable picture of life in a small port town on the lower Eastern Shore. But neither Joppa at the head of the bay nor Port Tobacco in extreme southern Maryland grew to greater size than villages. And several other places called towns, but which must have struck visitors as too optimistically named, qualified as nothing more than hamlets. A real future was reserved only for Baltimore, which quickly eclipsed neighboring Joppa and became an essential strand in the web of Maryland history.

Nevertheless, nascent urbanization brought a new flavor to an overwhelmingly rural province. The towns, villages, and hamlets were signs of inner economic strength in an expanding population. They also were to alter cultural and social ways in the province.

—3—

The second restoration followed on the heels of a difficult epoch in Maryland history. During almost the whole twenty-five years of the royal period the empire had been at war with France. Added to the ordinary perils of the seas, the threat of seizure by enemy privateers had inhibited the passage of tobacco ships from colony to mother country. Exports grew hardly at all during the years 1700 to 1715 while the population increased appreciably. Accordingly, provincial planters, lacking commodity exports, could not import the capital and consumer goods they desperately needed. Reliable officials reported these hard times, using such adjectives as "necessitous" and "naked" to describe the condition of the people.

Peace brought better times for Maryland and quite as important a new feeling of opportunity. Tobacco production and export began a secular rise that lasted until the end of the colonial period. At the war's end in 1714 the entire Chesapeake exportation stood at about 30,000,000 pounds of tobacco a year, roughly the amount exported in 1700, fifteen years previously. Within the next twenty years Maryland and Virginia were exporting nearer 40,000,000 pounds per annum and at better prices. The portion of the Chesapeake crop produced in Maryland cannot be exactly determined because British customs officials combined Virginia and Maryland in a single series of entries. But well-informed contemporaries estimated that Lord Baltimore's province provided about one-third of the total, an estimate borne out in the analyses made by historians of a later age using quantitative methods.

This rising curve of production had a tonic effect on the economy. The thirty percent increase in tobacco exports, enhanced by higher prices, meant a rise in planter income unparalleled for decades. Seasonal variation made for bad years, and characteristic short term fluctuations caused real hardship, especially to small planters caught in the downswing of a cycle. Since their numbers made them a force at the polls, the small planters helped create the political unrest that ran through these two eventful decades of the second restoration.

—4—

Poor planters furnished the solid electoral base in all seasons and in years of depression their discontent put pressure on their representatives in the Assembly. But articulation of their woes came from a new elite paradoxically growing prosperous in the same economy that bred disaster among the less fortunate. The poor had predominated in the population since the first years of settlement. Their lifestyles had improved somewhat as decades passed, though in degree rather than in kind. The oldest inhabitants, whose memories stretched back over fifty years, could recognize all around themselves the type that had peopled the colony in the days when old Lord Charles had first become Proprietor in 1675: planters who tilled a few acres of tobacco for their cash income, often not more than £10 to £20 a year, who raised corn, vegetables, and fruit to supply their food, and who lived in the crudest houses furnished in spartan style. At the end of their days most such

Cedar Park, Anne Arundel county, like many vernacular houses of the eighteenth century, was enlarged by additions as their owners prospered after tobacco prices rose and their possessions outgrew the modest dimensions of the original plan. Courtesy of the Maryland Historical Trust.

persons left total estates of no more than £25, and the rest not more than £100. Some owned small plantations, others leased their land from landlords.

But out of the mass of small producers a few improved their economic status sufficiently to leave their heirs assets larger than the vast majority of their less fortunate neighbors. This breed was not wholly new. There had always been an enterprising and energetic planter here and there pulling away from the common run. Time has destroyed whatever personal records they kept that might enlighten later generations about the exact steps in their rise to fortune, but inventories of their estates show signs of income beyond that derived from planting pure and simple. For almost all those who came to the top—the £1000 men and larger—merchandising or trading provided the economic momentum toward wealth. The first four decades of the eighteenth century, with good times and bad, with times of war and times of peace, saw the multiplication of these substantial men, the Maryland squirearchy.

As a rule, a small portion of their income came from the public offices they held. Captain Thomas Tasker (died 1700), first of a distinguished Maryland line, had been a justice of the county court in Calvert County in 1685, then under the revolutionary regime a justice of the provincial court, and the following year treasurer of the province. His son, Benjamin (1690–1768), followed in his footsteps as justice of the peace in Anne Arundel County at the age of thirty-two. The Lloyds of the Eastern Shore had a parallel record. Colonel Edward Lloyd (died 1697) had moved to Maryland in the Puritan exodus from Virginia in 1649. The next year he became Commander of Anne Arundel County and a member of the council in 1658, a post he held for eight years. His son, Philemon (died 1685), commanded the horse of Talbot, Kent, and Cecil Counties before his premature death at thirty-nine. Philemon's son, Edward (1670–1719), represented Talbot County in the Assembly and in 1707 commanded the whole Eastern Shore militia with the extraordinary title of major general which followed him through his career as senior councillor and *de facto* governor of the province after the death of Governor John Seymour. Richard Smith (died 1689) of Calvert County also founded a dynasty of public servants after arriving in the province in 1649. He held the post of attorney general from 1657 to 1660. His son, Colonel Walter Smith of Hall's

Craft (died 1711) and in turn his son, Walter Smith of the Freshes (1692–1734) continued the tradition of officeholding and planting. A score of such families, including the Addisons of Prince George's County, the Platers of Charles County, the Dashiels of Somerset, and the Frisbys of Cecil, had come to form an upper crust of wealth and position by the end of the royal period.

Social stratification did not, however, inhibit the rise of the lowly to greater estate. Even the penniless could aspire to wealth and position provided they had talent and perseverance. One immigrant, Daniel Dulany (1685–1753), who came from Ireland as an indentured servant in the tobacco fleet of 1703, completed his term of service and became an established lawyer in the southern Maryland county courts within ten years. His education at the University of Dublin had equipped him for better things than toiling in tobacco fields, and his manners gave him entree into the better families. He married into the family of John Courts, a well-to-do planter in Charles County. On the death of his first wife, Dulany won the hand of Rebecca, daughter of Walter Smith of Calvert County, whose family line went back to the earliest years of the province. Dulany's income as a lawyer permitted him to buy several modest plantations and to take out patents on vacant tracts. By the time he moved to Annapolis around 1720 he had become a large landholder, held several petty offices, and earned a reputation as a successful lawyer. Even then he had become an example of the rags to riches theme, but greater things were still to come.

Thomas Macnemara, a business associate of Dulany, had by coincidence arrived in the same fleet of 1703. Macnemara's success outstripped Dulany's in part because of this relationship to Charles Carroll, the Settler. Carroll purchased Macnemara's indenture and brought him into his family as a servant but freed him shortly to marry one of the Carroll nieces, whom the irresistible Macnemara had deflowered. Macnemara earned a reputation for ruthless pursuit of fees in the law practice, which he immediately entered, and for personal conduct that almost passes belief. His indictments for murder, sodomy, rape, and various lesser offenses never ended in a conviction and seemingly enhanced his reputation with the country folk whose cases he almost invariably won, to the gratification of his clients. In time Macnemara's conduct became an embarrassment to his business associates and to his

Daniel Dulany the Elder, attributed to Justus Engelhardt Kuhn, who painted the portraits of the wealthy as adornments for the mansions they built in the decades just before the Golden Age. Courtesy of the Peabody Conservatory on deposit at the Maryland Historical Society.

relatives by marriage, the Carrolls, but he accumulated a fortune before his premature death in 1720. His career was an example of success following the bold stroke, even the ruthless stroke.

Less theatrical than Macnemara, Thomas Bordley had greater success in law and in accumulating a fortune. Son of a Yorkshire clergyman, Bordley came as a youth to the province with an older brother who followed the calling of their father. Thomas served a term of years as apprentice to a country lawyer and eventually entered practice himself. Widely known for his resourcefulness, Bordley could make his own terms with clients and did so to his financial advantage. His only peer at the Maryland bar was Daniel Dulany, who opposed him in some of the most important cases of his career.

Though this trio left their marks on their times as lawyers and officeholders, all three were planters: owners of extensive lands and numerous slaves, and producers of tobacco. Each had his earliest associations in the countryside. But their legal practice eventually brought them all to Annapolis where the central courts of the province convened and where the Assembly met to legislate once or more each year. And inevitably each became involved in politics. Dulany and Bordley played notable roles as leaders in the lower house during the decade following 1720.

—5—

In the lively turn of politics during Hart's administration the future leaders had almost no part. Economic discontent stood in abeyance for a time, now that ships could move to British markets without danger of marauding privateers and deliver tobacco at prices improving year by year. But other causes of unrest attended the transition from royal back to proprietary rule, among them the uprising in Scotland in support of the exiled Stuarts, the jacquerie of '15, which revived fears of "Catholic menace" in Britain and Maryland alike.

Marylanders, suspicious of a proprietary family only recently converted to the Anglican Church, took alarm when Lord Baltimore's guardian appointed Charles Carroll, a leading Roman Catholic, to three lucrative posts. Plural officeholding, common enough at the time, concerned provincials hardly at all. Nor could anyone deny that Carroll deserved a reward for devoted service to the proprietary family during its twenty-five year eclipse. But one of the posts, receiver general of the revenue, had a public character in the eyes of provincials, always sensitive to fees and taxes. When Governor Hart tendered Carroll the usual oaths of abjuration and supremacy the new receiver general refused, as a Catholic, to take them. Fiscal administration seemed stalled.

A pair of pranksters brought matters to a head. On the evening of 10 June 1716 they loaded the cannon installed for defense of the capital and fired a resounding salvo in the silent darkness. In "extreme surprise, dread, and disquiet" townspeople recalled that the day was the Pretender's birthday and that a shipload of Jacobite rebels, convicted for attempting to restore the exiled Stuarts, had recently arrived in Maryland. By morning it was clear that the cannon fire had been merely a prank, but the humor was lost on the community. The perpetrators received whippings and the pillory, while two other persons charged with drinking the Pretender's health drew fines of £100 sterling.

Here real trouble began. Receiver general Carroll, though technically disqualified, proceeded anyway to collect the fines, one of them against his own nephew. Moreover, Carroll announced, he intended to collect *all* the revenues for remittance to Lord Baltimore. Governor Hart flew into a rage at Carroll's "insnaring and insolent" conduct and invited the Assembly to deal with Carroll's collecting of fines before qualifying himself by taking the required oaths, a plain inroad upon the Maryland constitution. The delegates agreed that Carroll's behavior indeed violated the constitution, but they declined a show down. As yet they were not ready to trench on the great issues between crown and proprietor. But they did share Hart's animus against Catholics and in the following months kept their grievances alive. Then suddenly two years later, in response to a rousing harangue by Hart on the machinations of priests and lay Catholics, both houses rushed through legislation depriving all Catholics of the franchise until they qualified themselves by oath. Thus disappeared in 1718 the last vestige of the toleration that Cecilius Calvert had established in 1634 by instruction and that the Assembly had embodied in the "Act Concerning Religion" of 1649.

The rest of Hart's administration appears as a jumble of personalities, clashes, and alliances which the governor eyed as conspiracies directed against himself. Intrigue was by no means absent, but the shifting alliances and occasional demarches were in fact little more than a restless search for personal advantage in the post-war prosperity. For

Hart himself, untutored in Maryland ways, the scene was a puzzle for which the solution continually eluded him. His most succinct analysis, that in his final report to the Board of Trade, misread the six years of his administration: "[Maryland] is administered in the same manner, as when I formerly had the honour to be Governor by commission immediately from the Crown, save that in enacting of laws, holding of Courts, issuing of process, and granting of Commissions, the Lord Proprietor's name is solely made use of: as was done by his Lords's noble ancestors." Like some of his successors, Hart saw no further than the forms. He missed the substance: ambitions and discontents feeding on new prosperity and greater population. He made his report in 1720, met his last Assembly in the spring, and sailed for England.

As succeeding governor the proprietary family dispatched "our Cosen" Charles Calvert, actually a remote relative of Lord Charles, with the mission of soothing tempers and making peace. The beginning was far from propitious. Calvert arrived at the end of summer 1720 and, shaken by the new world climate, lay ill when his first Assembly met on 12 October. Unable to appear in person, Calvert communicated his instructions and his first message through the senior member of the Council, Colonel William Holland. Calvert assured the lawmakers of the Lord Proprietor's "Benign sweet disposition" and of his Lordship's aim to treat "the good People of Maryland as a Bountifull Indulgent Father towards a dutiful Deserving son." This ceremonial language came, of course, not from the Proprietor, who was still a minor, but from Lord Guilford, his guardian and the real policy maker. But then the governor went on to define the delphic father-son reference. Baltimore had commanded him as governor to bring "our Prerogative" and "your Privileges . . . into Ballance." Exactly what his Lordship meant by "our Prerogative" became clear when he informed the Assembly of the Proprietor's dissent to an act passed at the preceding session and of his displeasure with another. Clearly the new administration was to rest on the ancient palatine authority claimed by the Lords Baltimore before the Glorious Revolution, benevolently exercised, to be sure, but nevertheless paternal.

Equally clearly the Assembly had to ponder the possible inroads on what they had habitually called "our happy constitution." That constitution they had developed during the quarter century of royal rule, when the dissent, or veto, was sparingly exercised. The lawmakers well knew that since the triumph of the Whigs in England the crown had ceased to use the veto over acts of Parliament altogether. Queen Anne exercised the royal veto for the last time in 1707 when she refused assent to the Scottish Militia Bill. The new doctrine announced by Governor Calvert had an ominous sound: he spoke of "prerogative." The Assembly spoke not of "privilege," but of "our happy constitution."

Calvert's first two years were, nevertheless, peaceful though not prosperous. After five years tobacco prices began slipping during the autumn of his arrival and went steadily down in the two following years. After a half decade of heavy production, supply had overtaken demand. Post-war prosperity ended in depression. In 1722, as the pinch became painful and planters restless, the governor dissolved the standing Assembly and issued writs for new elections.

Results of the poll showed nothing like a wholesale turnover, but in several counties new representatives unseated veterans and in the City of Annapolis, which elected two delegates, new men made a clean sweep. More important than the fresh faces, a different mood permeated the lower house. Responding to the complaints of their constituents, delegates made tobacco legislation the first order of business.

The law currently in force, usually called the "trash act," prohibited shipment of any tobacco unless "in good condition and of a clear and clean leaf free from any ground Leaves, trashy Leaves, suckers or otherwise damnifying leaves." Praiseworthy in aim, this act worked a real hardship on all but large planters who could discard low grade tobacco and still have a rewarding market crop. The poorer majority complained that they had hardly enough good leaf after paying fees and taxes to provide the barest necessities of life. With the shipping season almost at hand the first step the lower house wished to take was to repeal the burdensome trash act. Without delay the Committee of Laws reported a repealing act to the floor, where members pushed it through in record time. They had faithfully discharged their obligation to their constituents.

The repealing act met instant opposition in the upper house. Its members received their appointments from Lord Baltimore as his governor's "Council of State," which in Assembly sessions sat as the upper house, not accountable to the electorate. Since they held posts at his pleasure, they listened respectfully to the governor, who often used them to emasculate bills by removing essential provisions or in the last resort to reject the legislation outright. Resentful delegates downstairs once openly accused them of being "Assistants to Prerogative and Dependent on it, Rather than a State in which the people place a Confidence." At any rate the upper house did not respond to pressures felt in the lower house and flatly refused consent to the repealing act.

Neither house could have previsioned the full consequences of the upper house decision. It opened an era of bad feeling between the two houses that was to last ten years and then, after a brief hiatus, break out again for another decade. For twenty-five years the "tobacco question" remained in contention, never without touching some sensitive spot: the constitution, the ecclesiastical establishment, proprietary officers, the economy, and, quite naturally, personal egos. But immediately, the response to upper house intransigence was an act of retaliation by the frustrated delegates, a declaration formulated by new leaders of the lower house that made the session of 1722 memorable until the Revolution half a century ahead swept away proprietary assemblies altogether.

The declaration was the handiwork of the Committee of Laws. Always a central committee of the house, the Committee of Laws counted among its members two newly elected delegates, Daniel Dulany and Thomas Bordley. Within the week following upper house refusal to repeal the trash act this pair took the lead in hatching a scheme that was to reverberate in local politics for years to come and more than once send echoes into the proprietary closet in England and beyond to Whitehall itself. On 25 October the committee perfected its work and presented it to their brethren in the form of a resolution.

On its face the resolution appeared innocent enough. However, there were three main sections which when taken together added up to something close to provincial autonomy, under lower house domination of course. The first section moved the house to appoint a standing Committee on Courts of Justice to act as watchdog on the judicial system of the province. Section two provided that the committee formulate a special clause for insertion into the judges' oath binding the judges "To Do equall Law and right to all the Kings Subjects rich and poor" without exception even when commanded by "Letters of the King, Lord Proprietary, or of any other." The final section charged the new committee to insure that the oath bound the judges to "Try and Determine [cases] According to the Laws Statutes Ordinances and reasonable Customs of England and of this province." The resolution concluded with the assertion that "this province hath allwaies hitherto had the Common Law and such Generall Statutes of England As are not restrained by words of Locall Limitation in them."

The intention was plain: to settle in favor of provincials vital constitutional questions that had been in doubt since the Lords Baltimore had retrieved their ancient rights from the crown. The clause binding judges to render decisions according to the laws, statutes, and ordinances of England and Maryland aimed at opening the vast reservoir of English statute law and common law, which the Proprietor could not veto as he could ordinary acts of the Assembly. The clause binding the courts to disregard commands of the king or Proprietor freed the justices from domination or interference by authority outside the province. The new Committee on Courts of Justice provided local supervision and insurance against royal or proprietary meddling. In a nutshell the resolution gave the judiciary of Maryland unmatched autonomy and whittled the proprietary prerogative down to size. Altogether the resolution gave a novel twist, a New World solution, to the age-old conflict between authority and self-determinatiion.

The lower house proceeded with deliberation. After sitting on the resolution for a week the delegates sent it upstairs with a non-committal message. The councillors acted with equal deliberation. They declined to betray their consternation at the innocent-looking bomb placed on the council table. On the last day of the session they acknowledged the "resolves" and, noting their considerable consequence to the Lord Proprietor and province, referred them to more mature consideration at the next session.

—6—

The session of 1722 ended with ominous quiet. But the ingredients of an explosion lay on the council table during the period of adjournment. The council remained in no doubt of the Lord Proprietor's posture. In a clear message he gave the councillors, acting as the upper house in legislative sessions, permission to adopt any particular English law—subject to his veto, of course—but he categorically refused to permit introduction "in a Lump." In the same message Baltimore let the council know that their colleagues downstairs had hoodwinked them during the memorable session of 1722. Without the slightest fanfare Bordley and Dulany, both legal craftsmen, had inserted in an otherwise innocent act a clause that introduced the English statutes "by implication." Both upper house and governor, who had signed the act, had overlooked the clause, but keen-eyed proprietary lawyers spotted it. On their recommendation Lord Baltimore gave the act a resounding veto. In effect he threw down the gauntlet.

The lower house picked it up in the session of September 1723. On learning of the veto the delegates appointed a select committee to search "the Ancient Records of this Province" for precedents supporting the extension of the English statutes to Maryland. Then, while the committee dug into the old folios, the house proceeded to bait their colleagues upstairs. As an opening gambit the delegates moved to strike the per diem allowances for meetings of the council in the interim between legislative sessions from the journal of accounts. Over the protests of the upper house, expressed in stinging language, the delegates won the day by simply omitting the per diem expenses from the accounts. They transformed the committee report, which was wholly favorable to the lower house position, into an argumentative address to Lord Baltimore, resorting to the old fiction that he had been misled by false counsel.

At the session of 1724 the delegates learned that their efforts had proved fruitless. Baltimore simply ignored the address. Without effective alternatives the lower house returned to tormenting their colleagues upstairs, who attempted to pose as protectors of "the good people of this Province." Downstairs strategists found no difficulty exposing the sophistry of this pose as protector of the "good people" while in fact thwarting the elected representatives of these same "good people." First the house proposed the "free election of sheriffs according to the common law of England." The ruse worked perfectly. Appointing sheriffs, responded the upper house, "has been hitherto thought a branch of our Proprietary's prerogative." Next the delegates suggested a drastic reduction in officers' fees, a real challenge to the councillors who practically monopolized offices with the fattest fees. When the upper house tried a tone of offended righteousness, someone downstairs maliciously pointed out that the proposed reduction had been submitted for their Honors' "consideration as part of the legislature," and not as officers. Obviously stung, the harassed councillors complained in the last exchanges of the session that the delegates "turn everything into banter and ridicule."

The clear value of these proceedings as propaganda was not lost on the lower house. Dulany and Bordley had stood in the forefront of the battle since 1722. When the governor dissolved the Assembly in 1725 and ordered new elections, they made copies of the record, including the blistering messages between the two houses, for publication by Andrew Bradford, a Philadelphia printer. As an introduction Bordley wrote a lengthy "Epistolar Preface to the Maryland Readers," explaining the lower house position. The entire production made a superb campaign document for the new elections that were to be held shortly.

The newly elected Assembly of 1725 met in the autumn for two months. It was destined to be the last real legislative session during Governor Charles Calvert's administration, but anti-proprietary forces in the lower house made it a memorable one. For the first time they involved the governor in the game of exchanging messages. "I am afraid some Evil Spirits walk among us," Governor Calvert told the delegates, "and it would be a matter of Great pleasure to such, to have your house and me att Variance, but for my own part, I defy the Devill and his Works to do it." Brave words but vain, for once Calvert had taken a hand all his defiance could not extricate him from the quarrel provoked by the evil spirits. Again the lower house scored.

Although they did not yet use the term in common speech, Marylanders witnessed in these sessions between 1722 and 1725 the beginnings of a political alignment one day to be called the "country party." In America as well as in England "party" still had the connotation of faction, and factions, as everyone knew, aimed at protecting and furthering special interests. But in Maryland the "interest" transcended narrow lines and the country's interest could hardly be stigmatized as either narrow or selfish. And once that interest was defined as emerging leaders like Dulany and Bordley intended it to be, namely, as the welfare of the whole province, the few in opposition clearly grew to appear as the self-serving, the greedy, and the obstructionist element. Since opponents of the country interest centered in a tiny coterie of councillors, higher officials, and placeholders around the governor, they gradually became known as the "court party." With these alignments sharpening, the day of partisan politics approached.

For two years after the session of 1725, politics abated. Governor

Charles Calvert prevented tumultuous meetings by simply not calling the legislature into a working session where leading troublemakers could create problems. But no footdragging could either make outstanding problems disappear or stop the cultural growth of the province.

—7—

Annapolis on the Severn, capital of Maryland, provides a kind of barometer for the cultural progress of the colony. Laid out during the administration of Governor Francis Nicholson, the community had two assets—a charming location and an unusual city plan—but little else. It grew in defiance of history and geography.

In earliest years a pair of sharp speculators had trumped up a claim to all the city lots around State Circle and Church Circle, heart of the incorporated area. On the dubious authority of some old and vaguely worded grants, they managed for a time to unsettle titles to city lots surveyed for sale. Their machinations failed just as another threat to security occurred. Brigands afoot in the province threatened to seize the provincial arms magazine and destroy the town. No one could tell for certain whether the threat was serious, but everyone knew that while the outlaws still roamed at large the statehouse had mysteriously caught fire one night and burned to ashes with the loss of valuable provincial and county records. Daytime fires were ordinary occurrences among wooden dwelling houses that still outnumbered brick structures.

In 1708 Ebenezer Cook put his impressions in doggerel verse:

> Up to Annapolis I went,
> A City situate on a Plain,
> Where scarce a house will keep out Rain:
> The Buildings fram'd with Cyprus rare
> Resemble much our Southwark Fair.

Hardly flattering even to a city in the wilderness, Cook's description came uncomfortably close to the mark. Some forty houses, mostly wooden and probably similar in appearance to the temporary fabric of English fair stalls, dotted the 140 acre extent of the town. Up the

gentle slope from the Severn an irregular line of buildings sketched
a rough circle around the new brick statehouse, erected after the fire
of 1704. Beyond, in Church Circle, masons were laying the foundations
of St. Anne's.

However unpromising in 1708, Annapolis had flourished over the
two following decades. Cook described a totally different community
in his mock heroic poem, *Sotweed Redivivus* in 1730:

> Bound up to Port Annapolis,
> The famous Beau Metropolis
> Of Maryland, of small Renown
> When Anna first wore England's Crown
> Is now Grown Rich and Opulent
> The awful Seat of Government.

Obviously location and man-made handicaps had not prevented
growth. Though beautifully sited, Annapolis lacked first-rate harbor
facilities. The largest sea-going vessels had to anchor in South River
several miles away and even there found only a tolerable port. Moreover
the shallow Severn tapped no extensive hinterland, as did the Patuxent
River further south or the meandering rivers of the Eastern Shore.
Annapolis was never to become a city of docks and quays but paradoxically was leaning toward a commercial center nonetheless or, more
exactly, a financial center, as the wealthy either moved there or maintained mansions for special seasons of the year. Cook's phrase, "beau
metropolis," fixes on the dominant impression created in the minds
of visitors: a community of official-class residents and affluent merchant-planters who could afford the luxury of town life.

Already in 1730 Annapolis showed signs of the oasis culture that
was to prevail in the Golden Age in years ahead. Town life had become
safer than in earlier days and at the same time afforded diversions
denied country gatherings. The Assembly came around to doing something about household fires when it voted public money for a fire
engine "to Work with four Hands to play with a Brass Spout only
(without Leather Trunks) and three dozen good Strong Leather
Buckets." The city itself established an annual fair to be held in September with the usual frolics: wrestling, gander pulling, and cudgelling
(complete with eye gouging) to amuse both country folk and the

citizenry. In 1720 merchants subscribed a silver prize for the feature event of the fair, a horse race "Run according to the Antient Rules." The city fathers held a special meeting to decide whether to offer both a first and second place award or a single prize in a winner-take-all contest. The single award won favor, and on fair day newly elected Mayor Benjamin Tasker made a ceremonial progress to the racetrack just outside the city limits to witness his favorite sport and to present the winner "a fine New fashiond two handled Cup with a Cover."

City elections were scheduled to coincide with the fair, when voters, many of whom were large planters, would be in town rather than at their country seats. The only incorporated community in the province with a municipal constitution, Annapolis had for several years enjoyed a relatively stable and smoothly working administration. A Philadelphian, Benjamin Mifflin, took home a particularly favorable impression of the "Excellent Constitution" which his own city had "great reason to envy." He noted with approval that the ten councilmen and six aldermen held their posts for life. Certain local citizens had a different view of this cozy monopoly but for the moment held their peace.

Culturally, too, Annapolis was the focus of the province. On one fundamental matter, education or the transmission of culture from one generation to the next, both city and province lagged. Virginia had long before founded the College of William and Mary (1693) to bring the education of youth above the level of the three "Rs," but Maryland procrastinated. More than once the subject had come up for discussion, as in 1671 when the Assembly considered "An Act for the Founding & Erecting of a School or College . . . for the Education of Youth in Learning and Virtue," only to have it fail because of disagreement between the two houses. Then in 1732 similar legislation became entangled in squabbles. Only private tutors for the well-to-do and home instruction among literate families kept the rudiments alive. Surprisingly basic literacy was reasonably high; few people made their marks on official documents.

But another facet of culture and the dissemination of knowledge had come to the province, the newspaper. Printers had not been entirely unknown in Maryland. As far back as 1686 William Nuthead had set up at St. Mary's City as the first printer in Maryland and had earned a slender livelihood by practicing his trade there. During the troubles of 1688–1689 Nuthead had printed the "Declaration" of the Protestant

Association, thus insuring wide circulation for that manifesto and at the same time winning favor with leaders who dominated Maryland politics for years to come. Quite naturally he received government orders for printing legal forms, as well as occasional sermons preached at the beginning of legislative sessions or on fast days. Nuthead died the year Governor Nicholson moved the provincial capital to Annapolis. His widow, Dinah, the first known woman printer in America, moved the press to Anne Arundel county where she continued to enjoy government patronage, at least for some months. Thereafter Thomas Reading, an enterprising protégé of the rising young lawyer William Bladen, assumed the responsibilities of public printer.

Thomas Reading made printing a profitable undertaking. With Bladen's help in obtaining approval of the Assembly, Reading brought out in 1700 *A Complete Body of the Laws of Maryland*, a vast improvement over the handwritten copies currently used by county justices. Then in 1704 under government contract he began printing the laws passed at each session of the provincial Assembly. These "session laws," printed at public expense for distribution to all government offices and to county courts, became a mainstay in the budget of Maryland printers and two centuries later among the most eagerly sought items for collections of early American imprints. But even with official patronage Reading and his successors found the printing press something less than the high road to fortune, and at times the province was without a printer altogether for a year or so at a time. Lacking local facilities, the Assembly periodically contracted with northern firms to have the session laws printed. For two years an immigrant from the Rhineland, John Peter Zenger, plied his trade at his house on the Eastern Shore, though not a single imprint from his years in Maryland has come to light. Zenger printed three sets of session laws in 1720–1722 before moving to New York and fame in the celebrated "Zenger Case," a milestone in the freedom of the press.

Printing came to its own in 1726 with the arrival of William Parks (c. 1698–1750) in Annapolis. English born and trained, Parks answered the urgent invitation of Thomas Bordley to settle in Annapolis on the promise of government patronage, principally printing the session acts. On this basic income, together with fees from the post office commonly attached to local printers, Parks set up shop and immediately began publishing the session acts. The next year he brought out a large folio

The Maryland Gazette

From Tuesday June 17, to Tuesday June 24, 1729. (Numb. XCIII.)

Mr. *Parks*,

THE *College* at *Williamsburgh* is obliged to pay Two Copies of Latin Verses, to the Governour, every Fifth of *November*, as Quit-Rent for Land. The *November* after Col. *Spotswood*, and his Train, return'd from their Progress amongst the Mountains (when the *Tramontane Order* was instituted) Mr. *Blair*, the President, chose for his Subject, The Suppression of the *late Rebellion*; and Mr. *Blackmore*, the Humanity Professor, composed an excellent Poem on this *Mountain Expedition*; which the late Rev. Mr. *George Seagood* turn'd into *English*.

I have sent you the Translation, which (having gain'd the Applause of several good Judges) may probably contribute to the Satisfaction of your Correspondents, that are poetically inclined.

" When his bless'd Influence shall the Globe controul,
" And the Messias reign from Pole to Pole,
Unwearied are his Pains, unshaken is his Mind,
To spread this Good to all of *Adam's* Kind :
In this, ambitious of eternal Fame,
T' advance his Sov'reigns and his Saviour's Name,
That *GEORGE's* Fame may thro' the World be read,
And *CHRIST's* and *Britain's* Cross in faithless Nations
(spread.

Now then, the Hero for his March prepares,
And t'wards the *Indian* Parts his Course he steers :
And thus begins to move by GOD's Command ;
As once did *Joshua* to the Promis'd Land,
All Things and Places full of GOD appear,
And both his Goodness and his Power declare :
And all his Creatures his Commands fulfil
And aft ' ' ' ' ' ' or his permissive Will.

Masthead of the first *Maryland Gazette*, 24 June 1729. The verse printed in this issue is typical of the local product that William Parks published for his readers. Courtesy of the Maryland Historical Society.

of 312 pages, *A Compleat Collection of the Laws of Maryland*, sumptuously bound at his own shop. None of these, useful as they were, matched his most significant enterprise, the first newspaper in the southern colonies.

Parks printed the initial issue of the *Maryland Gazette* on 12 September 1727. The sixty-four earliest issues are lost, but No. 65, the first extant, gives a fair impression of his journal. Paid advertising occupied a considerable amount of space: notices of ship's cargoes for sale, runaway slaves, and the like. But the space reserved for what the publisher called "Speculative Letters, Poems, Essays, Translations, etc. which may tend to the Improvement of Mankind" takes pride of place. Parks copied freely both prose and poetry from British papers as well as from journals published in other colonies, but his most informative pieces were locally produced letters and essays that came in numbers to his office, usually signed with a pseudonym. The "P.P." series arguing the case of the Maryland planters against the English merchants stirred readers with ringing rhetoric and plain reasoning designed to touch planter sentiment. In brief, Parks provided a forum for *belles lettres* and for social commentary, often with political implications. His printing office became a part of the political battle which was about to enter a new phase.

—8—

In June of 1727 Governor Charles Calvert disclosed the reason he had delayed calling the Assembly into session for two years, as he began preparing a lavish reception for his successor, Benedict Leonard Calvert, the Lord Proprietor's younger brother. During the two year lapse, the political scene had been quiet while the economy went deeper into the doldrums. Pressure was building, however, against the inevitable day the new governor would convene his first legislature.

An unknown quantity in Maryland, Benedict Leonard (1700–1732) had already acquired by age twenty-seven a family reputation for letters and "antiquities," absorbed in part from Thomas Hearne, the noted antiquarian, while he was attending Christ Church College at Oxford. Yet on the grand tour, a common capstone to the gentleman's college career, Calvert had not only indulged his love for the old and curious but had displayed considerable talent for business. In Paris he had negotiated a tobacco contract with the French Farmers General much to his brother's satisfaction. Throughout the tour Lord Baltimore's private secretary had kept him informed of current events in Maryland and had briefed him on the proprietary views of political doings in the province. Accordingly when Calvert arrived fresh from the glories of Paris and Venice he brought an up-to-date knowledge of Maryland affairs, colored of course with the prejudices of the proprietary closet. Not surprisingly he dubbed Maryland "this unpolished part of the Universe." More specifically, he wrote, "Our Conversation runs on planting Tobacco and such other improvements of trade, as neither the Muses inspire, nor Classic Authors treat of." The fault, he thought, lay in the character of the people who had neither antiquities nor the learning to appreciate them.

Calvert's views on the province he was to administer boded ill for the trials ahead. He could not long avoid calling an assembly, which immediately resurrected the judge's oath and addressed itself to tobacco legislation. Planters called on their representatives to play the doctor to the sick tobacco trade. Angry knots of men gathered to damn individual legislators thought to be lukewarm for laws to raise tobacco prices, and in Prince George's County one band threatened direct action by mysterious summonses posted to trees and chapel doors calling all "honest men [to] meet at Queen Ann Town . . . to assert our Rights armed in a Suitable manner." Spurred on by these pressures, the Assembly passed an act limiting the number of plants each grower could tend, an austerity measure designed to raise prices by decreasing the supply of tobacco. Other clauses in the act, however, broke new ground and gave the legislation much wider bearings. On the assumption that tobacco prices would rise with increasing scarcity, the Assembly undertook to scale down officers' fees and ecclesiastical tithes, both paid in tobacco.

Proprietary officers had always received payments in the form of fees, a cumbersome system and for some provincials very costly, because at every step in a legal process the officer concerned exacted a fee. In court actions, land office business, customs collections, and probate proceedings, these fees were assessed and often amounted to a considerable sum. Officers' fees had always fallen within the prerogative of the Lord Proprietor, who had designated the amount due for each service rendered when he established the office. Individually fees were not large, but they were numerous and therefore costly to persons involved in litigation, taking up land, or registering deeds. The Assembly simply inserted in the planting limitation law a new table scaling down the fees by about twenty-five percent. Every proprietary officer from constables of the hundreds up to the governor felt the pinch of the cut, and not one of them was happy.

Another group, the clergy, neither as numerous nor as powerful but certainly articulate, also came in for reduction of income. Since the act of 1702 establishing the Anglican Church, each clergyman had received as his salary forty pounds of tobacco from each taxable in his parish. Quite naturally these "livings," as they were called, varied considerably among parishes. In the more populous parishes, such as St. Anne's at Annapolis, income from the sale of the "church tobacco" came to a tidy sum, in some years as much as £200. Parishes in less thickly settled areas provided a bare living and often entailed on the incumbent considerable travel to visit his scattered communicants, especially in the frontier regions where the boundaries took in an enormous extent of land. Nevertheless ministers had answered the call to Maryland, and the number of parishes with rectors in residence had grown on both shores. Population growth, and consequently the multiplication of taxables, had brought decent, if not lordly, livings to most incumbents. Now the clergy also were to experience a cut, from 40 pounds per poll to 30 pounds, in expectation of rising tobacco prices resulting from crop limitation.

These were the complications of tobacco legislation. Planters, clergy, and officers alike were involved. Most important, the Lord Proprietor felt himself touched, both in his prerogative, which seemed threatened, and practically, because his officers would suffer. Accordingly he returned the act, passed by the representatives of the people and signed by his brother, the governor, with a peremptory veto. In the same message he disallowed another act that again proposed a judges' oath binding the justices to adjudicate cases according to British law where provincial legislation was silent.

Baltimore's double rebuff touched off understandable talk about breaches of "our happy constitution." The lower house threatened an investigation "in the proper place" of the Lord Proprietor's disputed authority to veto acts of Assembly signed by the governor. This thinly veiled threat to drag Lord Baltimore into hearings before the Board of Trade and possibly the attorney general touched a sensitive proprietary nerve. But more directly, desperate planters finally carried out their threat to form armed bands that took enforcement of planting limitations into their own hands, roaming the countryside to cut excess tobacco. Certain to attract attention in the province and in England, the tobacco cutting riots were nevertheless an inappropriate response, not because they were extralegal but because they could not get at the root of the problem in a systematic way.

One response of a quite unexpected kind to country and proprietor alike did serve to put one of the constitutional questions in perspective. In mid-December of 1728 William Parks advertised for sale a pamphlet by Daniel Dulany, *The Right of the Inhabitants of Maryland to the Benefit of the English Laws*, at a price of two shillings. Through thirty-one pages of remorseless logic Dulany drove toward his conclusion: that the people of Maryland, being English, are entitled to "the Enjoyment of English Liberties; and to the Benefit of the English Laws: Which I take to be are . . . convertible Terms." These liberties, he argued, are secured by the common law, "the best and most Common Birth-Right," to quote Lord Coke. But to admit the common law and deny the statute laws that declare, alter, and amplify it is surely contrary to reason. "If we may be deprived of any Part of that Right, without our Consent . . . We may by the same Reason, and Authority, be deprived of some other Part; and our Lives, Liberties, and Properties [rendered] Precarious."

Dulany's legal argument, one of the earliest in colonial America to be adorned with references to natural rights, never had a rebuttal. Lord Baltimore carefully preserved his copy, the only one that has survived, which today remains in the Calvert papers. Neither in a message or letter did he ever so much as mention it.

The premature death of Thomas Bordley left Daniel Dulany the undisputed leader of the opposition to Lord Baltimore's pretensions to the palatine authority exercised of old by the earlier lords. But even his leadership and ingenuity availed little against the continual vetoes from England. When provincials began to consider issuing paper money, badly needed as a means of exchange in a colony chronically short of specie, the proprietary court returned a stony negative. Other colonies, notably Pennsylvania, had tried paper currency with considerable success for commercial and business enterprise. Maryland had to make shift with the unwieldy tobacco currency which was difficult to manage almost to the point of impossibility for ordinary transactions.

Without hope of constructive legislation, Maryland was once again at impasse. No one suffered greater frustration than Governor Benedict Leonard Calvert, whose pacifying mission had failed along with his health. Calvert had cherished the ambition of writing a history of the province, an enterprise that took him deep into a study of the ancient records. The projected history fell victim to the relentless obligations of office, but the research gave Calvert a clear insight into the constitutional problem and the background of the current economic plight of the colony. In late October of 1729, after a summer of misery from his "cholick," Calvert sharpened his pen and sat down to write his brother the Lord Proprietor a twenty-nine page letter that set forth in minute detail the plight of the colony and the outlook for the future. He described the background of each problem as carefully as if his brother had never heard of the province of Maryland at all. His letter probably made a greater impact on the proprietor than the unwritten history would have had he actually completed it.

First Calvert took up the question of the all-important money returns, certain to catch the proprietary eye. These monies grew out of the quitrents due on all patented land. In fact, however, since 1717 no patentee had actually paid quitrents as such, for in that year the Assembly had granted the Lord Proprietor a two-shilling duty on each hogshead of tobacco exported as an equivalent for his rents. The "equivalent act" had initially run three years and had been periodically renewed since. Calvert pointed out the advantages of this arrangement: it saved the expense of collectors, of compiling and maintaining up-to-date rent rolls on land that frequently changed hands, and of supervisors to keep the collectors honest. All these costs—the overhead expenses—would cut into the quitrents, which he estimated to be worth approximately £6,000 annually. On the other side, each renewal gave demagogues an opportunity to harp on the great bargain the two-shilling duty gave the Lord Proprietor.

But a further complication, Calvert warned, could not be overlooked. Tied to the equivalent act was an additional duty of one shilling per hogshead on exported tobacco originally granted to the royal governor in 1704. In 1717 this export duty had been incorporated into the "equivalent act" as salary for the proprietary governor. Now should the

Lord Proprietor allow the equivalent act to expire and return to collecting his quitrents directly from owners of land, the governor would lose his salary and become dependent for his support on annual grants from the Assembly, which might put pressure on him. Calvert proposed a solution to this distasteful prospect. He recommended that his brother take counsel with his legal advisers to determine whether the act of 1704 settling the salary on the Queen's governor could be construed as having devolved on the Lord Proprietor "or be invested in you and for the same purpose." If the duty could be collected under the act of 1704, the governor would maintain his independence of legislators' whims.

Officers' fees came in next for analysis in Calvert's letter. Since proprietary officers received their incomes solely from these service charges or fees, the ability of the Lord Proprietor to attract talented and responsible administrators depended on the size of the fees and the ease of collection. An act regulating fees and providing legal methods of collecting them, originally passed in 1719, had expired in the twenties. Thereafter the Assembly had passed acts every year scaling down payments during these bleak years. Lord Baltimore had prevented the reduction by disallowing the acts, but by the same token he deprived his officers of any statutory ground for collecting them. "Every insolent fellow thinks himself free to refuse payment, and browbeat, as it were, the officers," Calvert reported, "And it is besides a continual bone of contention, and a specious handle to amuse the ignorant." Again he proposed a solution, prerogative action. If Lord Baltimore could create the offices, he could assign fees for supporting the incumbents and thus remove the whole matter from Assembly interference.

All this sounded high-handed enough and indeed was congruent with Calvert's conception of government: "This Superiority, as I may term it, of the people over the Government, seems unaturall, and is I am sure repugnant to the very End for which Government was Instituted, Viz, an Authoritative Influence for the good order of Society." In his view the proprietary establishment could never function as long as the "proud, petulant and Ignorant planters kept the Common necessary Support of Government so much under their Thumb."

Undemocratic in his outlook, Calvert was not blind to the realities. He wrote of the limitations of the staple crop system. "Tobacco, as our Staple, is our all, and indeed leaves no room for anything Else:

It requires the Attendance of all our hands, and exacts their utmost labour, the whole year round." But tobacco, once shipped to England, brought back only merchandise, never money.

> Money, or somewhat to answer its Current Effects in trade, is certainly much wanted here; we may Barter one Another our Staple Tobacco; but to Carry on and Inlarge our trade Abroad & to Invite Artificers, Ship wrights, etc. to Settle amongst us, another Species of Currency in payments, seems very desirable.

Calvert made it plain that in principle he favored the paper currency demanded by provincial legislators.

Exactly what effect Benedict Leonard's letter had on his brother, Lord Baltimore, can only be surmised. The arrival of a twenty-nine page letter was something of a novelty. Actually it more nearly resembled a full and quite penetrating report on a province, which, if not exactly in torment, was at least sorely troubled. Frequently Charles, Lord Baltimore, now of age, made marginal notes on similar reports from higher proprietary officers from whom he demanded intelligence of Maryland affairs. But the pages of brother Benedict Leonard's are without marginalia to indicate the proprietor's reaction. Plainly government had almost come to a halt, the economy was sickly, and his governor desperately—as it proved, fatally—ill. Without delay his Lordship dispatched a new governor to replace his ailing brother.

Samuel Ogle (1702–1752) put in at the port of Annapolis on 2 December 1731 after what he described as "a very ruff passage" to find the resident governor bedfast and unable to attend the welcoming ceremonies. Within a month Ogle had assessed the local situation. The sad state of proprietary affairs, he hinted to Lord Baltimore, could be attributed to Benedict Leonard's neurosis and lack of energy: "The extream bad state of health he enjoys is much worse than I imagined, and which I believe has not been mended very much by the help of Physick, which he takes more of than anyone I ever knew in my life."

Ogle himself had boundless energy and unlimited confidence in his ability to set the proprietary house in order. To provincials accustomed to Calvert's ways, Ogle represented a new species. Moreover the new governor apparently enjoyed the confidence of the Proprietor. He certainly spoke freely to him.

I find plainly that nothing in the world has hurt your interest more than your Governors declaring open enmity to such men as Bodeley [Bordley] and Delany [Dulany] who were capable of doing you a great deal of good or harm, and trusting your affairs to such as could not do much one way or another. . . . I think the places you have ought to be managed as much as possible to keep up your interest with the Country Gentry but likewise be given to such people as are capable of serving within their particular posts, which is as good a way as I know to retreive your Lordships affairs in several points where they have been but too much neglected.

Quite naturally this new doctrine, the philosophy of a political realist, was confidential and not disclosed to provincials. But they soon saw the results in a general reorientation. The old days of inertia and the politics of impasse were gone, sailing away with Benedict Leonard who died at sea on the way home. Indeed it shortly became apparent that Ogle was merely the herald of momentous things to come: a visit of the Lord Proprietor himself.

Since old Lord Charles had left for England in 1684 no Lord Proprietor had set foot on Maryland soil. The visit of his grandson, Charles, Baron of Baltimore and Absolute Lord and Proprietor, was therefore of considerable interest to his "faithful tenants," as he always referred to the people of Maryland. On his arrival in late November of 1732 the ancient cannon boomed a royal salute, and after nightfall the populace danced about bonfires that burned cheerfully on the beach while they drank deeply from barrels of rum punch always provided for such occasions. William Parks struck off a four page effusion, *Carmen Seculare for the Year MDCCXXXII*, composed by Richard Lewis, the local schoolmaster, to honor Lord and Lady Baltimore. Surely their Lordships must have been flattered with Lewis's salute:

If in wish'd Progress, thro' these wide Domains,
Our Lord shall pass, to cheer his Tenant Swains;
With Pleasure will be seen th'extensive Land.
Adorn'd by Nature with a lib'ral hand.

And certainly the flourish that ended this remarkable performance could not have failed to please:

An hundred Suns thro' Summer Signs have roll'd.
An hundred winters have diffus'd their cold'
Since Maryland has Calvert's Race obeyed
And to its noble Lords her Homage paid;
This, for the Year of Sacred Jubilee:
This Year, distinguish'd far above the rest,
That Time hath sent, shall be forever blest!
From your kind Visit, shall the People date
An happier Aera, marked by smiling Fate,
To raise the Province from its languid State.

Lord Baltimore had, indeed, in the forefront of his mind the idea of raising the province from its torpor and for very practical reasons. Perhaps a couplet tucked away in the middle of the Lewis panegyric impressed him more than all the fulsome flattery:

And ev'ry future Year that runs his Race,
Shall to your Revenue add large Increase.

Certainly throughout the most brilliant social season in the history of the province Baltimore kept steadily at the task of setting the proprietary household in order with his own hands. His purpose was plain from his first meeting with his Council of State: he called for accounts of his revenues and went over them minutely.

When the Assembly convened on 13 March 1733 Baltimore had matured his plans. Already he had effected an accommodation with Daniel Dulany, whom he had singled out as the person most likely to serve his interest. He had offered, and Dulany had accepted, three important "places" in the proprietor's gift: agent and receiver general, judge of the court of vice-admiralty, and attorney general. Ogle alone had objected on the grounds that this bountiful reward to a single person cut into the patronage which, in his opinion, ought to be more widely spread. But as a leader in the lower house Dulany had his uses when the political weather clouded. At first the climate seemed favorable: the Assembly passed the long-desired paper money bill, an act emitting £90,000 in paper notes ranging from one shilling to twenty shillings, to which Baltimore readily assented.

With the currency act the honeymoon ended. When the lower house offered to renew the "equivalent act" compounding for the quitrents, Baltimore flatly refused. He directed his agent and receiver general, Dulany, to compile new rent rolls and organize the collection service. Then to the dismay of the delegates, his Lordship ordered payment of the governor's salary from the duty of 1704, exactly as Benedict Leonard suggested, claiming this revenue as successor to the crown in the government. Finally in April he settled the matter of officers' fees by naked exercise of his prerogative: by proclamation he established a table of fees for all his appointed officials.

When he sailed for home in the early summer of 1733 Baltimore had in his own fashion settled the outstanding political issues. Dazed provincials hardly realized when he left exactly what his Lordship had done to their constitution. Baltimore had acted the role of Absolute Lord and Proprietor as no Calvert had done since 1689. Much of the ground the Assembly had gained in nearly a half century of constant aggression was lost in a six-weeks session presided over by his Lordship in person. The settlement of 1733 completed the second restoration.

7

THE POLITICS OF TENSION

During the summer following Lord Baltimore's departure provincials had the opportunity to assess the immediate effects of his visit. How the policies he had established would finally work out few could guess, but no one could doubt that he had left behind an able cadre of lieutenants for their detailed implementation. Samuel Ogle again became governor on the departure of his Lordship. For subordinate administrators Ogle had Edmund Jenings as provincial secretary, Benjamin Tasker, his near relative by marriage, as senior councillor, and Daniel Dulany as agent and receiver general. On this corps of talent rested the success of the new dispensation.

—1—

The one obvious benefit of Baltimore's visit to Marylanders had been the paper currency act. A few had objected to paper money during the half decade of preliminary agitation only to be lampooned by Ebenezer Cook, self-styled poet laureate, in *Sotweed Redivivus*, a 1730 sequel to his earlier poem. Cook joshed the witless lower house delegates for

> Alleging *Planters*, when in drink
> Wou'd light their Pipes with Paper Chink;
> And knowing not to read, might be
> Impose'd on, by such Currency.

He made jocular reference to the clergy and office holders who

> Held Predial Tythes, secure in Bags
> Better than Paper made of Rags.
> The Scribes likewise, and Pharises,
> Infected with the same Disease,
> On Paper Money look a squint,
> Care not to be made Fools in Print.

Cook puts in the mouth of his hero, the hard-headed planter, a reply to such folly and hypocrisy:

> It's Money, be it what it will,
> In Tan-Pit coin'd, or Paper-Mill.

Certainly the Assembly had taken every precaution to prevent the kind of depreciation that plagued paper money in some other colonies. Legislators levied a tax on exported tobacco for a sinking fund to be invested by three trustees, all British merchants, in Bank of England Stock. Perhaps this arrangement for gradual redemption of the paper bills in sterling had made the act palatable to Lord Baltimore, for he accepted designation as supervisor of the trustees and thus came into legal and functional connection with other Englishmen who had financial stakes in the province. At any rate paper money proved a boon to planters and merchants in need of a stable circulating medium. When the last paper money of the 1733 issue was redeemed thirty years later the bank stock had appreciated sufficiently to leave a surplus of £25,000 in the hands of the trustees.* This sum was available as the nucleus of a new sinking fund when the Assembly decided to float new paper currency issues in 1766 and 1769. In Maryland paper money was a success: debtor and creditor admitted as much. After 1733 the province was never without sound paper in circulation.

Other legacies of the proprietary visitation were less happy. Baltimore's decision against renewing the equivalent act brought his faithful tenants back to direct payment of quitrents. Daniel Dulany energet-

---

*The trustees held this surplus through the War for Independence and decades beyond until the sovereign state of Maryland finally recovered it in the famous Bank Stock Case (1804–1806).

ically pushed compilation of the rent rolls by his two principal sub-ordinates, the rent-roll keepers, one for the Eastern and one for the Western Shore. Below them the receivers, one for each county, per-formed the laborious task of compiling the actual tabulation of land-holders, the acreage each owned, and the amounts due the proprietor. After that came the task of calling directly on each landholder to collect rents due. For these services the receivers took 25 percent of the proceeds, commissions they doubtless earned during the first years while they perfected the rolls. In 1736 commissions of the receivers were reduced to 20 percent and in 1753 to 15 percent. Two years later the proprietor dismissed all the receivers and put collection in the hands of county sheriffs at 10 percent. Within two decades his Lordship raised his personal revenue system to near perfection, at least from his point of view.

Provincials soon took a different view. Too late planters and their elected delegates quite clearly saw the advantages they had enjoyed under the old equivalent act, and, before the new system had run two years, made the first offer to compound for quitrents again. Over the next ten years the lower house made various proposals. First, the delegates suggested flat sums in lieu of direct payment of rents. When the first offer of £4000 brought a flat no, they raised the amount to £5000 with the same result. Then they moved to the more enticing proposal of an export duty of two and a half shillings per hogshead, to run for seven years. This arrangement had the merit of keeping payments in some kind of relationship to increasing tobacco produc-tion. The Proprietor refused each proposal on this or that pretext. He had in his files a letter from Dulany dated 1736 clinching his case for continuing direct collection: "I am perswaded that when all the Lands under grant in the Province are brought to the rent-roll that your quitrents will amount to ab[out] eight thousand pounds per annum . . . which sum must increase and never decrease." At least this part of the settlement of 1733 remained intact as long as the proprietary regime lasted.

The same cannot be said about the fee proclamation. The new table of fees had given proprietary officers clearly defined payments and a legal basis for collecting them. But Baltimore's naked exercise of the prerogative galled provincial leaders nurtured on the philosophy of legislative control over such matters. Hardly a planter, however modest his estate, could escape the impact of the pervasive fee system for compensating public officials. Later ages, accustomed to salaried officers, find it difficult to realize either the number of separate fees payable for official transactions of every kind or the nuisance of meeting them in tobacco money. The chancellor, keeper of the great seal, collected fees for thirty-two services, ranging from five pounds of tobacco for sealing an original writ up to ninety pounds of tobacco for sealing a land patent. The provincial secretary's fees, one hundred twenty-seven in all, ranged from five to two hundred eleven pounds of tobacco. Sheriffs were entitled to sixty-six fees for their various duties of summoning and swearing; they received nine pounds of tobacco for swearing in each witness in the many cases before county courts. Virtually every official in the establishment had his table of fees; the commissary general forty-three, judges of the land office thirteen, clerks of the county courts sixty-one, and on through the judge of the court of vice admiralty, the register and the marshall of the same court, the examiner general of the land office, and the cryer of the provincial court. The list seems nearly endless. Provincials could transact no official business without satisfying the incessant demands for fees over which they had no control whatever. In time legislators were bound to question the Proprietor's right to establish fees unilaterally.

—2—

One striking result of the settlement of 1733 was the demoralization of the nascent country party. Bordley's death and Dulany's defection left delegates in the lower house without leaders to direct their strategy or to pen the trenchant messages that at once tormented the councillors and brought them into opprobrium as "servants of the prerogative." Moreover the chief negotiable issues—quitrents, officers' fees, and paper money—had vanished, temporarily at least, under the heavy hand of the Lord Proprietor. Without either leaders or issues, the lower house could not mount the attacks that had kept the governments of the two Calverts, Charles and Benedict Leonard, in turmoil.

For half a dozen years, then, initiative lay with the proprietary forces. Governor Samuel Ogle proved an adept administrator, energetic and realistic, and his principal subordinates carried out under his eye the policies laid down in 1733. Yet, however able and dogged the proprietary staff in the province, its drive might easily have diminished but for a constant force, new in the system, from the English side. Above Ogle and the chief officers of the Maryland establishment stood a higher authority, the Lord Proprietor's "court," invisible to Maryland eyes but ever present to the minds of provincial officials within the charmed circle of favorites. Never a clearly organized group, the membership of the proprietary court in England varied somewhat but usually included Lord Baltimore's personal secretary, his official secretary (usually called the Principal Secretary), and one or more legal advisers. This tiny staff, with the Proprietor himself as the axis, formed the "court" and actually presided over the destinies of Maryland, establishing policies, issuing instructions, distributing patronage, examining laws, and above all enjoying the revenues from the province.

In the years before his Lordship's visit the "court" had compiled a poor record, particularly during Baltimore's minority. Principal Secretary Thomas Beake, a London lawyer, held his office for life as a reward for his role in effecting the restoration of Maryland to the Calvert family in 1715. As his associate in office, Beake had a proprietary relative, Charles Lowe, who actually did much of the work. The spirit informing this office appears in a letter from Lowe to Governor Benedict Leonard Calvert on patronage appointments. Lowe said he cared nothing about the character of Maryland appointees "so you are pleased, and I paid [a gratuity]."

These lax ways disappeared with the death of Beake, shortly before the proprietary visit to Maryland. His Lordship appointed as sole secretary his brother-in-law, Sir Theodore Janssen (1658–1748), a political economist who had won fame as the author of *General Maxims of Trade* (1713) and had acquired some notoriety for his connection with the South Sea Bubble, the speculative mania that ruined many English investors in 1720. Janssen accompanied his superior to Maryland in 1732 and there personally sized up provincial problems and leaders. The advice he offered revitalized the proprietary court.

Charles, Lord Baltimore, himself appeared changed after he brought Janssen's fresh mind into the proprietary closet. Though lacking in the noble qualities of the first two lords, Charles had a clear head and personal presence that later was to impress as keen a critic as Frederick the Great, who had only praise for this English Milord after the two had spent a few days together. Moreover Baltimore had the patience to study personally his Maryland officials' reports, annotating them with pithy comments for future reference. In the margin of one boastful letter from a provincial officer he wrote, "I judge every man by his actions."

With the support and prodding of the Proprietor's court, Ogle and his lieutenants kept the game in their hands for several years. Doubtless improved economic conditions contributed to diminish provincial unrest and its expression in the House of Delegates.

—3—

The upswing in the economic cycle during the mid 1730s came gradually, far too slowly for provincials who had suffered the depression of the previous decade and a half. Fortunately the roots of the new prosperity were sound and their growth steady, though agonizingly slow after the years of dearth.

The first beneficiaries of this growth, the tobacco planters, could hardly have known the mechanisms at work in their favor. Small producers still sold their crops to native merchants in their neighborhood or to factors of English houses trading in their counties. Larger planters more often consigned to London merchants, or occasionally to those of Bristol: John Hyde and Company, leader in the Maryland trade, Jonathan Forward and Company, John Hanbury, John Falconar, or William Hunt. These had been the traditional consignees for Maryland tobacco and these, or successor firms, were to continue in that role for decades to come.

The new element that touched off the gradual improvement in price was the entry of the Scottish factors into the Chesapeake trade. Glasgow merchant houses had imported some tobacco from the colonies since the union with England in 1707, but in the middle thirties their purchases commenced a steady rise. Except from the borderlands along the Potomac, the Scots took little Maryland tobacco because it did not suit the taste of their chief customers, the French. But their purchases in Virginia, particularly in the James and Rappahannock basins, effectively stabilized prices throughout the entire bay area. Economically, Maryland and Virginia had always been a single unit, a fact recognized as far back as the days of Governor Berkeley and the abortive stint.

Now Maryland planters became indirectly the beneficiaries of Scottish buyers in neighboring Virginia and in the riverine lands of the Potomac on the Maryland side.

Entry of the Scots by no means revolutionized the tobacco economy. Their business methods offered an alternative to the traditional consignment system. Glasgow merchant houses sent their own buyers to the Chesapeake where, as factors of the parent house, they opened stores to sell British goods to planters and take their tobacco in return. Operating on ample credit, factors offered their customers terms that London could not always match. Over the years the Scottish houses pushed their chain of stores up the rivers, on the Maryland side of the Potomac as far as Bladensburg, to claim the riverine tobacco for the Glaswegian houses of Cunninghame and Company and Glassford and Company. The heroic age of the Scots, however, did not arrive for many years to come, until the decades after 1750. In the thirties and forties their purchases merely stimulated a trade that observers had hitherto called sickly. In 1730 the Chesapeake exported 40,606,000 pounds of tobacco to Great Britain: 35,080,000 to England and 5,526,000 to Scotland. By 1742 total exports rose to 53,206,000 pounds of tobacco: 43,467,000 to England, 9,739,000 to Scotland. This 30 percent increase in exports did wonders for Chesapeake planters. But the best was yet to come. Volume escalated to about 100,000,000 pounds in the middle of 1770s, the share going to Glasgow each decade becoming proportionately larger until the Scots claimed almost half the total.

Maryland planters and merchants alike shared the blessings of better times. For planters steadier prices and the opportunity to expand production were the obvious benefits. Merchants also stood to gain by the greater volume of business and the lessened fear of sending their consignments to glutted markets. Except along the Potomac, where they were displaced, native Maryland merchants suffered little from the Scottish intrusion. In the Patuxent basin and further on up the bay they held their own, continuing to consign to London or Bristol throughout the provincial period.

Merchants who had struggled through lean years of the twenties found larger opportunities for personal enrichment in the post-1735 prosperity. Some of them ended their days in relative affluence. Marsham Waring of Prince George's County died about 1750 leaving a personal estate of £1175-9-0 currency in addition to his real estate. In Somerset County, Colonel George Dashiel left even ampler personal assets, £2301-10-0 currency in store goods, debts due, and other chattels. The Dashiel family had a tradition of trading that ran back to the beginnings of the century. Another Eastern Shore merchant, John Conner of Kent County, had an estate of £2625-17-4 currency at his death in the early 1750s. By standards of earlier years these qualified as fortunes. But greater opportunities and larger accomplishments lay ahead.

—4—

The merchant community of the Golden Age was already outstripping the levels of wealth attained by these prototypes. Few records survive to document the exact route each individual took toward riches; for most the cold figures in the final accounting of their estates in the probate records measure the levels of their fortunes. But one remarkable man, Dr. Charles Carroll (1691–1755), left behind a complete set of letter and account books that disclose the details of his progress. Carroll immigrated to Maryland from Ireland sometime about 1715 and set up in Annapolis as physician and surgeon. Apparently he prospered in his medical practice and soon began investing his capital in land and in mercantile ventures. Within a decade Carroll's interests as a merchant completely overshadowed his medical practice, which he did not give up entirely until the last decade of his life. As a tobacco producer on his own plantations, he consigned his crops and those of smaller planters to his correspondents in London and Bristol. Eventually his business contacts included all the great London houses in the tobacco trade such as John Hyde and John Hanbury, and many of the lesser merchants like Thomas Colmore, Philip Smith, William Hunt, John Philpot, William Black, and Robert Myre. But soon he spread his commercial net wider to include contacts in the West Indies, the Iberian countries, and the Wine Islands. His correspondent in Barbados was the merchant prince Coddrington Carrington, to whom he sent cargoes of lumber, barrel staves, grain, and other foodstuffs for cash in the form of bills of exchange or for return cargoes of sugar and molasses. Even more profitable, his trade to southern Europe and the Wine Islands included outbound shipments of grain and barrel staves, always in demand in wine producing countries, and return ladings of wine that could be sent to England, the West Indies, or back to Maryland.

Carroll's letter books do not make engaging reading. The pages are filled with detailed directions to his local agents around the bay about the quantity and quality of barrel staves or headings, about the grain, flour, or beans for a particular vessel, or about the pickled pork or beef, to complete the assorted cargoes he dispatched. All these goods had to be assembled by a particular time at a specified location for loading. The reader patient enough to plow through the outpouring of commands, queries, and cajolery comes away with the impression of Dr. Carroll as a man in a frenzy to get all the bits and pieces together for a single profitable venture. Yet Carroll needed several such voyages a year, some of them concurrent, to satisfy his quest for profits. Then, as soon as he had those profits in hand, he could not rest until he had reinvested them, for idle money that earned nothing was anathema to him. Altogether he led a strenuous life.

The picture of Dr. Carroll would be incomplete without reference to other enterprises allied to his counting house. He commissioned shallops to ply the bay collecting cargoes for overseas shipment, and he purchased shares in larger vessels that made the voyages to England and the West Indies. All the smaller craft and some of the larger ships came from shipyards in the bay, where builders produced modest tonnage for local sale and occasionally for British buyers. And, like every man of means in Maryland, Carroll acquired land. He purchased several producing plantations outright, thirteen in all with a total acreage of 3,049, but by far his largest acreage he patented in vacant stretches of wild land still available in Baltimore County and toward the west. In all he took out patents for 28,480 acres. Carroll's wild lands brought him into the company of land speculators, who made immense sums after 1750 trafficking in family farms to new immigrants and younger sons without plantations of their own. Finally Carroll invested heavily in a new industry for Maryland, iron production, which in the end proved highly profitable. At his death in 1755 Dr. Carroll left to his son and namesake, Charles Carroll, Barrister, a "handsome fortune," as the current phrase went.

—5—

Nearly every county on the Eastern and Western Shores shows a counterpart to Dr. Carroll, several even more affluent. Thomas Ringgold of Chestertown in Kent County was extensively involved in the West Indian and Portuguese trades. In Anne Arundel County, Samuel Galloway, a leading Quaker, towered over the Western Shore mercantile community. Galloway consigned his tobacco to the London house of Sylvanus Grove, also a Quaker, but had business connections with Joseph Galloway of Philadelphia, with Ringgold, and occasionally with Dr. Carroll. Besides his mainstay, tobacco, Galloway successfully operated in the trade to Jamaica and Barbados, to Madeira, Lisbon, and Ireland, usually in "mixed cargoes" of grain and staves. To the south in Calvert County the smaller establishment of Kensey Johns made a moderate fortune in tobacco. The Johns family belonged to a Maryland network of Quaker merchants with close ties to Sylvanus Grove and Thomas Philpot. The elder Philpot sent his son to learn the tobacco business in the Johns household.

The gridwork of merchants like the Ringgolds, Galloways, and Johns held their own in Maryland while the Scots penetrated southern regions of the bay. These merchants formed a kind of county elite, leaders in local affairs as vestrymen, justices of the peace, delegates to the Assembly, and, of course, bankers—or more accurately creditors—of smaller fry who made up the bulk of the population in the new age of prosperity as they had in earlier and harder times.

—6—

The small producer remained a remarkably constant element in Maryland throughout colonial times. The highly visible merchant-planter elite, few in numbers, dominated the economy. His kind organized the marketing of tobacco and the distribution of imports. And, as foremost citizens, they dominated political and social life as well. But in a sense the elite rested on the far more numerous small planters, whose estates in personalty amounted to less than £100 sterling. Many planters in this lowest bracket of wealth were tenants or, if they owned real estate, at best holders of modest acreage. Reliable data taken from

Gray's Inn Creek Shipyard, one of the few industrial scenes of eighteenth century Maryland, shows the variety of small vessels that sailed Chesapeake waters. The unfinished hulk on the ways is obviously an ocean-going craft. The painting is the mantelpiece of Spencer Hall, Kent County. Courtesy of the Maryland Historical Society.

inventories filed in the testamentary court show the numerical pre-
ponderance of small planters over the years from the late seventeenth
century well into the Golden Age.*

Percentage Distribution of
Gross Estates in Maryland
(Pounds Sterling)

Size of Estate	1690–1699	1710–1719	1730–1739	1750–1759
0–£100	72.5	69.4	59.9	50.8
£101–£1000	25.7	28.2	36.7	41.9
£1001 and above	1.7	2.1	3.4	7.2

(Source: Inventories and Accounts, Maryland Hall of Records)

Clearly the small producers, men with visible personal estates of
£100 or less, still made up half the heads of households near the end
of the colonial period. Like their forebears a century before, they lived
in tiny houses, usually one room and never more than two. Whether
they owned their land or leased modest plantations from a landlord,
most of their property was in livestock, tools, bedding, and a few
household utensils. Later ages described this type as "deprived." In the
records of their day they qualified as planters, though certainly not
the planters of romance.

The small planters are the invisible people of the Chesapeake. Travelers rarely noted them, perhaps because most lived away from the
choicest waterfront locations or the main roads. Doubtless Henry Callister, factor of Foster Cunliffe and Company at Oxford on the Choptank
River, had them in mind when he wrote his jingle,

> Our fires are wood,
> Our houses good,
> Our diet, sawny and hominy
> Drink, juice of the apple,
> Tobacco's our staple.
> *Gloria tibi Domine.*

---

*The testamentary court or probate court was, in Maryland, the province of the
commissary general.

A younger member of the elite on an itinerary to the northward left a rare snapshot that catches the lifestyle of a couple he met on his journey. His personal comment is as revealing as his description. The couple had just sat down to their dinner, "a homely dish of fish without any kind of sauce," when he passed by:

> They desired me to eat, but I told them I had no stomach. They had no cloth upon the table, and their mess was in a dirty, deep, wooden dish which they evacuated with their hands, cramming down skins, scales, and all. They used neither knife, fork, spoon, plate, or napkin because, I suppose, they had none to use. I looked upon this as a picture of that primitive simplicity practiced by our forefathers long before the mechanic arts had supplied them with instruments for the luxury and elegance of life.

Both observers give parts of the picture; further details can be teased out of the probate court records, where the inventories and accounts contain enough data to furnish sketchy biographies of every person of property however lowly. The "primitive simplicity" of seventeenth century forebears had persisted into the luminous mid-eighteenth century, at least for half the people. Planters at the bottom of the scale had a "country living": a saddle horse, half a dozen or fewer cows, swine to furnish fresh or salt meat for the table according to the season, and bare essentials of housekeeping, sometimes no more than a cookpot or skillet. Curiously, the most valuable household furnishing was often the bed and bedding, occasionally appraised at a figure of £1–0–0 up to £3–0–0, as much as all other household goods together. Frequently all the rest was little enough. Many essentials are missing in half the inventories, for instance plates and cups. Such omissions suggest makeshifts: wooden bowls and gourds in their place. Appraisers of estates overlooked no articles, even a cracked cup without a handle or a single glass bottle. Certainly cutlery rarely appeared and napkins never.

Planters at this level, then, still lived not much more sumptuously than their counterparts a hundred years before. Some houses still had dirt floors, packed hard and worn smooth by constant tramping, though most had wood or more rarely brick. Tables still were boards placed across trestles, and chairs nothing more than sections of log cut to comfortable sitting height. Windows are described as unglazed or, put another way, mere apertures in the walls with only shutters to keep out winter winds. In summer they admitted light and inevitably insects. For light in cold weather the family depended on the blaze from the hearth or a wick floating in fat. Understandably, during clement days of spring and summer planting families lived largely out of doors, where a shade tree afforded more comfort than the cheerless interior of a stuffy house.

Indoors or out menfolk contrived utensils—wooden bowls, gourd cups or shallow dishes—with no more sophisticated tool than a sharp knife. Or they made traps and snares for small game, some of them from patterns handed down from medieval times. Supplementary hunting for sport and pot kept the household in fresh meat around the calendar.

Of course the chief concern from early spring onward was tobacco, the entire cycle from seed beds, through hilling and transplanting, worming, weeding, to the final cutting and curing. But planters also had to devote some time to the kitchen garden for fresh vegetables in season, drying any surplus for winter consumption. Equally important, and even more time consuming, they "put in" field crops: corn, wheat, and rye. Until after mid-century the hoe served as the sole cultivating tool, including initial ground breaking. Not only did field crops furnish the cereal component of the family diet—bread, hominy, and mush— but any surplus could be sold to merchants assembling cargoes. Even a few bushels brought in some cash to supplement the returns from the main tobacco crop.

Beside their tobacco and grain, more enterprising small producers had another source of income. In winter males of the household cut the supply of wood for fuel and for the staves required to pack cured tobacco in hogsheads. The simplest tools, a frow and mallet, served to manufacture barrel staves, which split off easily along the straight grain of white oak logs. A pair of energetic workmen could turn out hundreds in a single day, enough to meet the family need for tobacco casks and a surplus to sell. A few planters used their spare staves to make barrels for pickled pork and beef that went into the West India trade. Altogether, small producers had several opportunities to make spare money beyond the returns from their staple crop, mostly by selling tiny plantation surpluses to merchants.

Their chief shortage was "hands" to do the work in field and forest.

The planter who could find the cash or credit bought an indentured servant or better still a slave to augment his labor supply. The very act of acquiring an asset as valuable as a bondsman moved him upward to another bracket of wealth intermediate between the small producer and the affluent merchant-planter. But this step upward in the scale, though not impossible, was too difficult for most. Consequently the small planter bred his own increase by the strength of his loins and perpetuated his kind and class. The statistics are clear: he remained the most numerous element in the population even through the age of affluence, when the more prosperous types almost hide him from view and consign his kind to the status of invisible people.

—7—

Bond labor—indentured servitude and slavery—marked the line between small producer and larger planters. In the records almost no inventory of an estate below £100 includes bond labor. A high percentage of the estates above £100 list bond labor, either indentured servants or slaves.

Before 1690 indentured servants far outnumbered slaves, but increasingly after 1700 slaves displaced indentured servants as field labor. Servants tended to be costly, anywhere from £10 to £20, depending on their qualifications, and served for a four year term before becoming free persons. Each also cost the owner something in freedom dues— an extra suit of clothing, a hoe, two barrels of corn—the "custom of the country" in local speech. Slaves cost more, depending on age, sex, and health, somewhere between £5 and £35, and in rare instances even higher for the specially qualified. But their terms were for life and their offspring became the property of the planter.

Through the early years of the century, slaves arrived in some numbers, even during the wartime depression. By 1720 approximately one quarter of Maryland planters held slaves, but in small numbers, usually four or less. In fact only 6 percent of the planting families had more than ten slaves, and a mere 2 percent held the twenty Blacks that Professor U. B. Phillips set as the number marking the lower limit of slave power for the classic plantation. Not surprisingly the two estates probated in the year 1720 with the largest number of slaves were those of merchant-planters: Richard Bond with twenty-nine and

Philemon Hemsley with thirty-seven. Of course the small planters, those with estates below £100, held no slaves at all though they made up well over two-thirds of the population around 1720.

In the four decades after 1720 both slaveholders and slave population grew by leaps and bounds. By 1760, 46 percent of the planting families had slaves. More than half these planters had five or fewer, enough, however, to quadruple tobacco crops on their plantations. But large slaveholders catch the eye far more insistently. A few planters held twenty to fifty Blacks, and a much smaller number owned a hundred or more distributed among several "quarters." The day of the great plantation had arrived.

The definitive scholarly work on Maryland slavery remains to be done. Doubtless when the bits and pieces are put together the mosaic will resemble the pattern of neighboring Virginia. The twentieth century, without illusions about the nature of chattel slavery or the feelings of Blacks themselves toward their condition, rejects the basic assumptions on which the peculiar institution rested. Men of the mid-eighteenth century accepted the governing assumption of Black inferiority and kept their slaves in bondage by naked force as a final resort. Here and there a voice expressed grief when Black families were broken up during settlement of estates, but no crusaders appeared to attack the system, not even among the Maryland Quakers, who did not own slaves as a matter of conscience and church discipline. A learned Anglican divine, the Reverend Thomas Bacon, preached a series of sermons to Blacks, explaining to them that God had placed their race under the domination of whites as He had put children under a loving father. But frequent runaways, advertised in the *Gazette* with a tiny figure going at top speed, and the occasional plots or rumors of insurrections left no illusions among the master class that the Negro enjoyed his lot. A conspiracy of slaves centering in Prince George's County during the winter of 1739–1740 convulsed the Western Shore and stirred the citizens of Annapolis to raise an Independent Troop of forty horse and sixty foot to turn out at fifteen minutes notice to protect the arms magazine from rebel seizure.

The Independent Troop of Annapolis lasted until local fears subsided a few weeks afterward. Maryland ordinarily had no need for the systematic patrols used in South Carolina. To be sure, planters kept an eye on strange Blacks moving along the roads and stopped them to inspect the passes that their owners were required to give them for absences from the home plantation. Surveillance and the threat of whipping or branding served to keep slaves in subjection in all but a few extreme cases. When necessary, however, the machinery of the law could visit terrible punishment on offenders and make them horrible examples to the rest of the slave community. In 1723 the attorney general brought to trial a slave, Hannah, under indictment for a brutal ax murder. On conviction the court decreed that she be sent to a gallows erected on a ridge in plain view of slaves passing along the public highway, there to be hanged until dead "and that after She is Dead she be hanged up in Chains on the said Gallows there to remain Until She be Rotten."

Indentured servants experienced the rigors of the law as well, though not quite so cruelly. At the same term of court in 1723 one Mary Reed, an indentured servant, convicted of stealing a nightgown worth forty shillings, six bottles of French brandy worth eight shillings, and other goods to the value of thirty shillings, went to the gallows for her crime. Justice was harsh for the servile class, but for the Black slave was reserved the ultimate. Not only were slaves valuable property, they often were intransigent property that, in the eyes of society, needed rigid curbs.

—8—

Beside their role in agriculture slaves figured importantly in the beginnings of industry in Maryland. About 1715 the English Quaker economist and entrepreneur, Joshua Gee, and his backers had sent a cadre of iron workers with indentured servants for laborers to the upper bay where they erected an iron works on Principio Creek. The Principio Works prospered from the start, beneficiary of the high grade ores lying almost on the surface of the ground, limitless forests for charcoal, and water transportation at the furnace site. In 1719 the provincial Assembly passed *An Act for the Encouragement of an Iron Manufacture, within this Province*, establishing a procedure for condemning land to be used for iron works and exempting laborers from tax levies during the first four years of their employment. Five years later Parliament drastically reduced the duty on colonial iron to stimulate importation of American pig into England, where fast disappearing forests threatened future production. The stage was set for the most ambitious local industrial experiment in provincial America.

The Baltimore Iron Works began in 1731 with the covenant of five wealthy provincials to enter "into a Copartnership or Company" for carrying on the business "at their Equal Charges and by Equal Dividends." The partners, Benjamin Tasker, Daniel Dulany, Dr. Charles Carroll, Charles Carroll of Annapolis, and his brother, Daniel Carroll of Duddington Manor each subscribed £700 sterling to the initial capital of £3,500. In actuality each partner contributed to this common stock not cash but ore lands or slaves to the value of his subscription. With these assets they began building a furnace, forge house, coal houses, and quarters for the laborers.

Their technical consultant, the Pennsylvania iron manufacturer Clement Plumsted, had warned them in advance that the business had many hazards, chief among them incompetent management. Doubtless the partners had expected difficulties but surely not as many as they encountered in the first year and a half. Their building contractors, rare enough in the Chesapeake, did shoddy work and never once met a construction deadline. One contractor quickly mastered the art of padding accounts at company expense. Laborers rioted and supply contractors delayed delivery of charcoal and "oar." Finally the partners themselves fell into petty quarrels by attempting to keep a tight rein on Stephen Onion, their resident manager. Instead of delegating authority to Onion they maintained control of the most minute decisions, though they rarely agreed on instructions to be sent.

Possibly the partners denied Onion reasonable latitude, even for emergencies, because he came to them with a doubtful recommendation from his former employer, Joshua Gee. "As thee well observed, Stephen Onion was a pleasant man and talked well to ye purpose," Gee wrote, "but when thee has said that thou has said all." Nevertheless the partners had no ground for complaining that their superintendent was talkative rather than active. Within two years Onion brought normal production to fourteen tons of pig iron a week and assured the owners that he could raise output to twenty tons provided his ore arrived on schedule. His frequent, concise reports written in a fine copperplate hand not only kept the partners informed of output, labor troubles, and delivery delays by contractors, and of failures to stockpile raw materials, but also warned them of the results of their own folly. "Too much Strong Liquer daily disorders more or less of the workmen and is the occation of Bad languige and Quarrels . . . prudence in dilivering of rum is necessary."

From the beginning of production the Baltimore Iron Works returned a profit to the investors. Each partner shipped iron to his correspondents in England and about the bay. At a meeting on 30 December 1733 the gross profits reported came to £2,642–4–7 sterling (sales to Britain) and £3,531–17–7 ½ currency (local sales). The partners took modest dividends in these first years, plowing back part of the profits into the business. Other iron works in the province also did well: the Principio Works, the Lancashire Company, Snowden's Iron Works, and smaller concerns like the Ringsberry Works. The Baltimore company outdid them all. Within thirty years the value of a share rose from the initial £700 to £10,000 in the 1760s. Long before this peak each of the shareholders counted on an average annual dividend of £400 sterling.

—9—

The promise of wealth in iron was only one of the reasons for the interest in the northern reaches of the Chesapeake shown by Lord Baltimore and his official family. Last of bayside areas to attract settlers, the lands in Baltimore and Cecil Counties offered less to planters devoted to tobacco than the light friable soils of the lower tidewater. But the heavier clays in the north proved ideal for cereal crops and, as the West India trade expanded, demand for wheat and corn encouraged settlement and cultivation of grain in the north. By midcentury other markets for cereals developed in southern Europe where growing population created a demand for American grain and flour.

Charles, Lord Baltimore, learned in detail about the infant iron industry around Jones Falls and the hamlet of Baltimore on his visit to Maryland in 1733. He also became aware of his precarious tenure of the upper bay. By his charter the northern boundary ran from "Delaware Bay" west along the "Fortieth Degree of North Latitude from the Aequinoctial, where *New England* is terminated," a fair enough description for the year of grace, 1632. Meanwhile the crown had made other gifts that touched Baltimore's domain and had taken old Lord Charles back to England in 1684 to clear up his boundary with William

Antietam Iron Furnace, Antietam Creek. This pig iron smelter, built after the Baltimore Company's plant, produced cannon for General George Washington's army and operated as late as the 1840s. Like many furnaces it stood against a hillside to permit loading of ore and charcoal from ground level. Courtesy of the Maryland Historical Trust.

Penn. By the 1730s both Penn and Charles, Lord Baltimore, had died, but the Penn heirs still claimed a strip some fifteen miles south of the fortieth parallel containing two million acres, which now stood in jeopardy.

The Penn-Baltimore boundary dispute shows both parties in an unlovely light, arrogant and deceitful throughout the seemingly endless litigation in British courts and meetings between the proprietors themselves or their representatives. In the disputed zone itself the human drama proved more dramatic than the tedious court cases and arid conferences.

Understandably Lord Baltimore encouraged settlers to take up lands in the upper counties as a way of establishing his right by actual occupation. With proprietary approval, assorted Germans, Irish, and Welsh took Maryland patents to land along the Susquehanna several miles north of nearby Pennsylvania settlements and, according to Lancaster County officials, actually above the parallel running through Philadelphia itself. In this polyglot community one Thomas Cresap quickly became the dominant personality, commanding total loyalty from his unlettered neighbors, who never raised overnice questions about the military and magisterial authority he exercised. Born in Yorkshire around the turn of the century, Cresap had migrated to Maryland at fifteen and settled on the Susquehanna, where hard work and ever-present danger had moulded him in the cast that turned out the great pioneers, tough of fibre and dauntless in courage. Cresap's first test came in January of 1733 when he and a couple of retainers administered a bloody repulse to a posse from Lancaster sent to bring him to trial. Thereafter he bade defiance to the whole province of Pennsylvania and undertook counter raids on his own initiative.

Cresap's doings earned him a title, the "Maryland Monster," among Pennsylvanians. The raids and reprisals through the following three years were dubbed the "Conojacular War," a guerilla conflict that became semi-official as the governors of each province gave additional incentives to their partisans by offering rewards for the capture of their more aggressive opponents. Late in 1736 the Pennsylvanians decided on an all out effort to take the Monster and bring him to trial. At midnight on 23 November the sheriff of Lancaster County with a posse of twenty-four armed men at his heels crossed the Susquehanna to

Cresap's barricaded house and, at a safe distance, called on him to surrender.

> Cresap with several horrid Oaths and the most abusive Language against the Proprietor and People of Pennsylvania, answered that they should never have him till he was a Corpse, and filling a Glass of Rum he drank Damnation to himself and all that were with him if ever he or they surrendered.

Professing great offense at Cresap's swearing, the posse set fire to his house and captured him as he fled to his boat. Once in Philadelphia, manacled with a heavy chain, he gave the crowd that turned out to see the Maryland Monster in the flesh a show worth its trouble. Turning to one of his guards Cresap croaked out, "Damn it, Aston, this is one of the Prettyest Towns in Maryland."

Secretary Edmund Jenings and attorney general Dulany went immediately to Philadelphia to obtain Cresap's release. There they experienced some of the wiles that have made lawyers of the Quaker capital proverbial. In the end they succeeded only in having Cresap's chains removed. His release had to wait until the crown took cognizance of the bloodshed along the border and issued a cease and desist order that released prisoners on both sides.

Here the fate of the boundary and the career of Thomas Cresap divide. Cresap returned to Maryland on a new frontier pushing westward in the province. The boundary dragged along a course as prosaic as the preliminaries had been boisterous. In 1750 Lord Chancellor Hardwicke decreed the formula for establishing a definitive line: a joint commission of Maryland and Pennsylvania representatives to review the evidence and work out the final details. Eighteen more years elapsed before the commission completed its report. Its decisions wrote a chapter in provincial as well as American history. An early historian compacted hundreds of pages of tedious prose into a single descriptive sentence.

> The boundary adjustment provided for a line drawn due west from Cape Henlopen across the Peninsula, from the center of which another line should be drawn tangent to a circle twelve miles from New Castle, while a meridian from the tangent

point should be continued to within fifteen miles south of Philadelphia, whence should be traced the parallel that was to divide the provinces.

The results show on any modern map: the curious circular bulge at the top of Delaware, the boundary extending westward along the line 39°43'26".

In time the line became famous under the names of the mathematicians employed in 1763 by Lord Baltimore and the Penns for surveying it: Charles Mason and Jeremiah Dixon. Along their surveyed line Mason and Dixon placed stones at the end of each mile showing an M on the south front and a P on the north. Every fifth marker bore the arms of Lord Baltimore on the south face and the Penn arms on the north.

—10—

During the middle years of the 1730s Samuel Ogle had presided over a province not only increasing and prospering but also well-behaved, at least from his point of view. The election of 1738 augured a change from a dispirited state to a truculent mood in the Assembly. Prominent among new faces, Dr. Charles Carroll appeared as delegate from Anne Arundel County. Carroll had converted from the Roman church to the Anglican and, now a prominent Protestant landholder, merchant, ironmaster, and intellectual, prepared to take a leading role in the lower house where the dispirited country party outnumbered the court party by an overwhelming margin. The election of Carroll and half a dozen likeminded delegates was an omen of trouble for Ogle.

True to the signs, the lower house rose to something like its old form. The Committee on Courts of Justice, quiescent since 1733, brought in a report attacking the fee proclamation. Investigating further, the committee turned up damaging evidence that Eastern Shore courts were straying from the path of justice. In Talbot County, for instance, the judges had refused to subpoena witnesses for the grand jury before consulting the attorney general. Forthwith the house summoned the Talbot justices and sharply reprimanded them for having "misdemeaned yourself in your Office as magistrates." Immediately afterwards a witness reported that one of the censured judges had slandered the lower house in general and Nicholas Goldsborough, Talbot County representative, in particular, using the term "son-of-a-bitch" and less printable language. The offending judge was instantly ordered into custody until he agreed "to make his submission to this House."

This show of aggression brought the session to an abrupt end. Governor Ogle refused to let the house get the bit in its teeth. He peremptorily prorogued the session before a single act could be passed and shortly after dissolved the Assembly with an order for new elections in the winter.

The winter elections returned an even more determined panel of delegates, among them Philip Hammond who, along with Dr. Carroll, qualified as a "chief incendiary" in Ogle's eyes. The contretemps could not have come at a worse time for the governor. After twenty-five years of peace, war clouds had appeared on the horizon. Spanish *guarda costas* and English traders were colliding more frequently in the Caribbean. Crown officials had already instructed colonial governors to put their provinces in a posture of defense for any emergency. Specifically Ogle had to ask the Assembly to renew an act levying a duty for the purchase of arms, an act due to expire at the termination of the current session.

In this predicament Ogle chose to open the session with a patronizing address. He had already affronted the lower house by his recent prorogation; now he irritated them further by speaking of the "ill effects of heats and animosities" and referring unguardedly to "the most malicious enemies of government." In reply the delegates mounted a broad attack, the first of its kind, on the privileges and powers inherent in the proprietary system. They spread on their journal the Resolutions of 1722, questioning the legal right of the proprietary element to most of its claims: the tonnage duty, fees set by proclamation, and the like. Furthermore the resolutions criticized the practice of selling clerkships and even the operation of the land system.

This unexpected onslaught infuriated Ogle, unaccustomed to either radical ideas or truculence in manifestoes from the lower house. Five weeks of acid exchanges between the two houses finally disabused him of any notion that his administration was to continue indefinitely the placid course of the preceding five years. While displaying this new aggressiveness the lower house also taught Ogle a pointed lesson in tactical maneuver.

Many years previously, elected representatives had learned to put limitations on the life of legislative acts, particularly tax laws. Any piece of legislation without time limitation could be kept in force indefinitely as long as the governor or Lord Proprietor had veto power over acts to repeal. Accordingly draftsmen on the Committee of Laws included in every bill a verbal formula that limited its operation to a three year period or to the end of the next session of Assembly following that date. If the law was accomplishing its intended purpose, the Assembly could, and usually did, renew it for another three years by a short bill with the simple wording, "An Act renewing an Act entitled . . ." These renewals could go on indefinitely and had the effect of making certain desirable laws semipermanent. Though somewhat cumbersome the practice had merit. In the first place the Assembly continually reviewed these temporary acts to determine their effectiveness, renewing those still needed and allowing those that no longer served the public good to expire. Moreover renewal time of such acts as those levying duties or taxes gave the lower house the opportunity to exact concessions from governors as the price of continuing the act for another period of time.

This practice of periodic renewals had actually given a kind of structure to legislative sessions. Immediately after the opening formalities, the Committee of Laws in the lower house customarily drew up a list of acts due to expire and prepared the short renewal bills for introduction to the floor. Early in the May session of 1739 the committee set to work at its task. But before debating renewal of the arms levy, so important to Ogle, the house gave the governor a jolt that brought the session to an abrupt end. The delegates demanded the appointment of a colonial agent to represent the province in presenting to the crown its case against the Lord Proprietor's fee proclamation and his tonnage duty. No governor could sanction such a deadly threat to the Proprietor. Neither could he prevent the delegates from turning the message demanding an agent into propaganda by spreading it on the record to be printed with the *Votes and Proceedings* for distribution throughout the province.

In fury Ogle put an end to the meeting. He prorogued the Assembly, saving the precious arms levy by a none-too-velvety stratagem. The levy was due to expire immediately after the next session of Assembly following the election of 1739. But, Ogle argued, the meeting just ended had been a "convention, since no laws had been enacted, and not a regular legislative session at all. Hence the arms duty remained in force.* By this sophistry he kept the duty for another year but at the cost of permanent estrangement from the elected representatives.

—11—

Ogle's expedient had been a thinly disguised exercise of the prerogative, now under full attack by the lower house. Over the two years that followed, the last shred of prestige he had with the delegates vanished. His next Assembly marked a definite stage in his declining effectiveness.

Before the Assembly convened in April of 1740 fighting had actually begun in what came to be called the War of Jenkins' Ear. England had "warmly engaged" Spain, Ogle told the delegates, and was acquiring "much Glory" in other parts of the world. As a plea for granting arms money the patriotic note failed dismally. The meeting came close to an exact repeat of the "convention" of the preceding year. Six weeks of wrangling produced a solitary law, "An Act for Issuing . . . the Sum of Two thousand five hundred and Sixty two Pounds ten Shillings Current money . . . for the Encouragement of Persons Voluntarily Inlisting themselves in his Majesty's Service." This single act, with the pittance offered, did prevent the meeting from ending as another convention and so erased nine temporary laws from the books, including the arms levy and an act regulating the militia. Half a dozen new bills passed by the house and sent upstairs for consideration also died when Ogle prorogued the Assembly. One of these, an act for the limitation of officers's fees, anathema to the Proprietor, had determined Ogle to end the session. Unable to provide for provincial defense, he had come to the end of his rope. His effectiveness had gone even before the Lord Proprietor announced his replacement by a relative, Thomas Bladen.

Shortly after Bladen's arrival in 1742 Ogle had a final brush with the delegates, still mindful of his stinging rebukes and summary dis-

---

*Ogle made good his claim, both practically and formally. The duty was collected for another year. The Votes and Proceedings, when printed, were superscribed "At a Session held at Annapolis May 1–June 12, 1739. Being a Convention of the Assembly Elected in 1739."

missals, and by no means in a forgiving mood because he was about to depart for England. Learning that Ogle had committed an unparalleled breach of parliamentary privilege—challenging a delegate to a duel—the house commanded its sergeant-at-arms to take him into his custody "in Order that he answer to this honorable house." Fortunately Ogle was temporarily residing at the home of his father-in-law, Benjamin Tasker, who delayed the sergeant-at-arms in the parlor long enough to warn Governor Bladen what was afoot, before returning to announce, "Mr. Ogle was not to be spoken with." Bladen saved his predecessor the ordeal of craving pardon by requesting the delegates to drop the matter as a personal favor to him. The delegates complied, with a reservation saving their rights and privileges, and the incident closed with Bladen in debt to the lower house.

—12—

Initially popular, Bladen accomplished little during five years in office. His qualifications gave him every advantage: his American birth, his ties with the local squirearchy (he was the brother of Mrs. Benjamin Tasker), and his family relations with the Lord Proprietor whose sister he married. Nevertheless no move that he made could shift the balance of power. The lower house had laid the foundation of an anti-proprietary movement that lasted as long as the province. Some accommodation occurred within the polarization of country party and court party, but the fundamental antagonism remained. For instance, Bladen's instructions called for construction of a proper mansion for the resident governor and he took the project to the Assembly, which obliged with an appropriation of £4,000 currency. The ambitious house plan outran the appropriated funds before the second story was completed and Bladen was back asking for an additional £2,000 to complete the building. Rather than bow to what appeared extortion, the lower house preferred to leave the building unfinished. Townspeople quickly made the governor the butt and dubbed the empty hulk "Bladen's Folly," open to wind and weather and symbol of a futile administration.

In sum, before the decade had run its course a revived country party had developed a permanent repertoire of tactics resulting in the politics of tension. To proprietary eyes the confrontations, delays, and bargaining appeared nothing more than parochial intransigence, the mind-

less resistance of stubborn provincials pursuing their own selfish designs. On their side, the delegates who led the antiproprietary
movement felt and expressed the imperatives of a constituency growing
in maturity and sophistication, ready to question ways their fathers
had accepted. Already tensions inherent in the proprietary system were
approaching irreconcilables.

8

BEGINNINGS OF THE GOLDEN AGE

The term, Golden Age of Colonial Culture, is usually associated with the history of an elite, the upper stratum of society whose members possessed the fortunes, built the great houses, and enjoyed the good life. These were a fraction of the population. Probably most of the people in Maryland, men and women, free and bond, did not realize they were living in a golden age at all. Immediately about them they saw half the population with little more than the bare necessities of life. From outside the province, but certainly touching their daily existence, they heard tidings of war exactly half the time if the golden age is dated from 1740 to the end of colonial dependency in 1776. In 1739 the empire clashed with Spain in the War of Jenkins' Ear; by 1744 conflict had extended to France in the War of the Austrian Succession, or on American tongues, King George's War. The peace of 1748 was in fact a truce, a breathing spell before the last intercolonial conflict, the French and Indian War, which began in the backwoods of Maryland and Pennsylvania in 1755 and eventually spread northward and southward along the whole frontier before the peace in 1763.

Yet in these years certain outward signs of inward vitality did appear: the great town and country houses of the wealthy minority, the clubs, and a revitalized press. These were the crown of a society entering a mature phase within the old colonial system. And like any crown it depended for its security on a solid economic base.

—1—

As long as tobacco held sway as the staple crop the prosperity of Maryland stood in special jeopardy. Planters in both Chesapeake provinces had long understood the connection between the quality of their staple and its price in England. During the 1720s the legislatures in Virginia and Maryland had debated practical measures to improve the quality of exported tobacco and thus enhance its price. In 1730 Virginia had passed a tobacco inspection act and had benefited from the elimination of trash from shipments to British markets. In Maryland tobacco inspection, though much needed, was entangled with officers' fees and clergy tithes. Maryland planters refused to accept any inspection act that did not scale down payments to officers and clergy by about the amount of the expected rise in the value of tobacco resulting from removing trash. The Lord Proprietor on his side declined to allow any legislation that presumed to tamper with fees. Maryland did not share equally with Virginia in the improved tobacco trade of the thirties. To some thoughtful provincials Maryland actually appeared to be losing to Virginia.

During the barren years of Bladen's administration one observer, Daniel Dulany, occupied a position that enabled him to make proposals for ending the loggerheads. In letter after letter to the proprietary court in England, Dulany argued that officers and clergy would have to give way and accept a reduction in their fees in the interest of getting a tobacco inspection act which would put Maryland on an even footing in the trade again. Himself an officer, Dulany could hardly be accused of self-interest at the expense of the common welfare. At last Lord Baltimore saw it Dulany's way and instructed the governor he sent as Bladen's replacement to proceed in that direction.

In March 1747, Samuel Ogle returned to Maryland after five years rustication in England. Though he had left the province under a cloud, his return was happier. At Annapolis he was "received at his Landing by a Number of Gentlemen, and saluted by the Town Guns, and from on board sundry Ships in the River." Incoming governors always raised hopes: they brought new instructions and, equally important, fresh minds to old problems. The first problem was tobacco legislation and Ogle's initial Assembly addressed it.

Even with proprietary blessing a proper inspection law proved anything but easy to formulate. More than twenty record votes were taken before all questions of officers' fees, clergy's salaries, and tobacco inspection were settled. As finally perfected "An Act for Amending the Staple of Tobacco, for Preventing Frauds in his Majesty's Customs, and for the Limitation of Officers' Fees" marked a combined economic and political achievement: it had something for everyone and from each it exacted a sacrifice. The inspection provision established eighty public warehouses with officials in charge to view all tobacco. On approved tobacco they issued negotiable tobacco notes, acceptable for all payments due in tobacco. Trashy tobacco they burned the same day as rejected, to prevent its export. Inspecting officers were nominated by vestrymen and church wardens and supervised by the county justices of the peace. The machinery represented a step in self-government with new and important authority in local hands. If planters could not ship anything they pleased, their sacrifice was matched by the reduction of officers' fees and clergy tithes by approximately 25 percent in anticipation of a rise in the price of tobacco.

The Inspection Act did not receive universal approval. Dr. Carroll feared "a kind of South Sea Jobb," something to "answer Onely some particular Interests Different from that of the Tobacco makers." Stephen Bordley, son of Thomas and serving his novitiate in the country party, spoke of the disadvantages to the small planters and the dishonesty of inspectors. The less critical majority believed the act had cleared away the obstacles to economic betterment: the two houses of Assembly met in the council chamber where "all the Loyal Healths, Success to the Tobacco Trade, etc. etc., were Drank." The healths were repeated at the statehouse, while the town battery boomed a ten-gun salute and "the Populace having Punch and Wine distributed amongst them, made loud Acclamations of Joy." The populace judged the accomplishment more correctly than the handful of critics. The first adequate tobacco legislation in twenty-five years of agitation, it served for the next twenty-two years, by triennial renewals.

—2—

The Inspection Act was no panacea. In actual operation inspection did favor larger planters, but proponents had insisted that, without regulation to eliminate the competitive disadvantages of Maryland tobacco, "a great many will be under the unhappy necessity of deserting their habitations, and very few, if any, will come into a country which is on the brink of ruin." Whether the Inspection Act saved the small producer or not as implied in this statement, his type persisted through the Golden Age, making up about half the total population. But the real beneficiaries were merchant-planters and the country gentlemen who remained planters pure and simple.

These families, the squirearchy, inaugurated the building boom associated with the closing decades of colonial dependency and with the Georgian style. Classical and elegant, the Georgian houses commended themselves to the hot summers. Large interior halls with elaborate stair balustrades and high white plaster ceilings gave cool spaciousness to the interiors. Fine mouldings frequently dressed the eaves, cornice, fanlights, stairways, and windows. Like Georgian counterparts in England, Maryland houses were sometimes long in building as owners added wings or other enlargements to the central block. A few of those built in the countryside came to be called manor houses, though the manor had long since disappeared. Others are simply rural mansions, like Montpelier, built in 1752 for Nicholas Snowden in Prince George's County. Snowden's son, Thomas, added the wings in 1770 to complete the design as it stands today.

Builders ordinarily found designs in the plates of such volumes as Robert Morris, *Select Architecture*, published in London in 1757, or an earlier work of Batty Langley, *The City & Country Builder's and Workman's Treasury of Designs* (1740). Contractors could modify the illustrations of these and similar textbooks to suit their client's tastes. Or the client himself could choose his basic pattern and modifications from the manuals and put the actual construction in the hands of local labor. Samuel Galloway followed this latter arrangement for his country place in Anne Arundel County, Tulip Hill (1756), one of the ornaments of the Maryland Georgian style. Still later Governor Horatio Sharpe drew his own design for the elaborate "country lodge," as he called it, Whitehall, just off the bay a few miles northeast of Annapolis. The central block, begun in 1764, became with additions one of the most beautiful houses built in America during colonial times.

By far the heaviest concentration of mansions was in the urban communities and particularly Annapolis. While Chestertown and Oxford on the Eastern Shore each had fine town houses, Annapolis easily stood first in number and distinction of mansions erected by the first fortunes in the province. Since the early 1720s lawyers and public officials had built places for personal accommodation and entertainment during legislative or court sessions in Annapolis even when their main

Tulip Hill, Anne Arundel County, built in 1756 as the residence and office of Samuel Galloway, leading Quaker merchant, reflects the taste of the affluent for the Georgian style in the Golden Age. Courtesy of the Maryland Historical Trust.

residences were in the country. Once they had houses in the city, a few, like Benjamin Tasker, were seduced from their country seats by the convenience of town life. Others, like Thomas Bordley, lawyer and planter, built town houses in Annapolis because the community lay at the center of their business network, or like John Brice, merchant-planter, because he kept a retail store next door to the handsome hipped roof house that he built about 1730. None of these earlier structures compared in size or elegance with the Georgian houses built by the generation after 1740.

The roster of these Annapolis town houses sounds like the social register of the Golden Age. The William Paca House, with a formal garden that was the envy of the province, cost something over £4,000 currency. Charles Carroll, Barrister, son of Dr. Charles Carroll, spent only a trifle less on his town house. The Catholic branch of the Carrolls outdid the Protestant line when Charles Carroll of Carrollton built the most elegant mansion of its time on Spa Creek, on the south side of the corporation, at a cost of nearly £6,500 currency. In time, building became almost a competitive sport as wealthy lawyers and merchants vied in attaining the last degree of luxury and splendor in their houses. Samuel Chase, a rising lawyer, projected a three story structure that called for solid mahogany doors with silver hinges and latches, adorn-ments beyond even his ample means. Before building was completed Chase sold the house to Colonel Edward Lloyd of the powerful Eastern Shore clan. Local gossip, sometimes quite accurate in such estimates, held that Lloyd would need to put an additional £6,000 currency to the £3,000 Chase had spent to complete one of the few three story houses built in the city prior to the War for Independence.

Before war stopped lavish construction, Mathias Hammond built one of the most interesting town houses directly across the street from Colonel Lloyd. An English architect, William Buckland (1734–1774), designed and supervised construction of this admired Georgian house, with its polygonal bays at the end of each wing and its elaborate carved work. Charles Willson Peale's portrait of Buckland, painted in 1773, shows the architect with a drawing bearing the plan and elevation of the Hammond house, which he completed in 1774, the year he died. Thus Buckland, who had begun his American career with George Mason's Gunston Hall in Virginia, ended it as architect of high society in Annapolis by building one of his masterpieces.

The building and furnishing of these places for residence and entertainment had a considerable economic impact on Annapolis. In the decade before the Revolution, the construction costs of only the thirteen largest houses put almost £60,000 currency in circulation.

Outlays for furnishing town mansions further increased the amount of money paid to workmen of other callings. Actually a class of artisans in the city depended on the carriage trade for its very existence. While much of the fine furniture came from England or from Philadelphia, already famous for longcase, or "grandfather," clocks, local cabinet makers supplied many pieces to the wealthiest households. The list of furniture in the great houses seems almost interminable: tables, chairs, waiters, bottle stands, sideboards, looking glass frames, desks, bookcases, writing and reading desks, study tables, escritoires, chests of drawers, secretaries, beds, sofas, settees, highboys, and lowboys. Local cabinet makers advertised for walnut and cherry timber which they turned into articles often quite similar to the best English work. A cabinet maker like Gamaliel Butler could copy Queen Anne furniture from actual pieces or from one of the several illustrated guides. Shortly, a new style offered an alternative to traditional Queen Anne designs. The very year Butler opened his shop in Annapolis, Thomas Chippendale published *The Gentleman's and Cabinet Maker's Directory* (London, 1754), setting a new fashion that quickly caught on in Maryland.

Cabinet makers left more permanent memorials of their work than most other tradespeople who contributed to the elegance of life among the rich in Annapolis. The *Gazette* carried the advertisements of these artisans: William Dixon, staymaker; John Inch, watchmaker; William Prew, hatter from London who sells and cleans all kinds; two peruke makers, Andrew Buchanan and William Elton; not to mention those essential people of the horse and carriage age: Richard Lewis, saddler, and Henry Wright, whipmaker. In time, silversmiths and book sellers joined the ranks of purveyors to the needs of an urban society that continued to consume ever more abundantly.

—3—

One of the most revealing ornaments of the gentleman's house, his library, opens a door on his interests and outlook. For the small planter, literate or not, books were out of the question, a luxury entirely beyond his means. But up the scale of affluence libraries served not only for pleasure but for very practical ends, particularly to persons in the professions: lawyers, doctors, and clergy. Understandably professional men had larger collections, but wealthy planters, who often had a foot in either law or mercantile business, had respectable libraries. After extensive search in the inventories at the Hall of Records, Joseph Towne Wheeler compiled some suggestive statistics on the sizes and composition of personal libraries in eighteenth century Maryland. During the early years of the century about half the inventories of estates, great and small, listed books among the assets. By 1770 the percentage of book owners had climbed to nearly two-thirds, an impressive increase until we learn that one in six of these estates lists the Bible only in the category of books. Furthermore three-fourths of the collections contained fewer than ten books. Yet when all reservations are mentioned, it is still surprising that one-sixth of all households in the province had enough reading matter to comprise a small library. Some, a very few, ran to several hundred volumes. No record has come to light of libraries that compare with the reputed 4,000 volumes owned by Cotton Mather or the 3,600 of William Byrd of Westover.

Fortunately the inventories list books by author and title, a key to reading interests of Marylanders. One is struck by the large numbers of books on religion and morality in every collection of any size, whatever the calling of the owner. Lawyer, merchant, or planter, he always had a few titles—and sometimes a great many—that belong to the devotional literature of the seventeenth and eighteenth centuries. After the Bible the commonest book title in the inventories was that collection of semi-religious lectures on everyday life, *The Whole Duty of Man* (1657), reprinted dozens of times in the century after initial publication, including an edition by William Parks after he moved his press to Williamsburg in the 1730s. Less popular but still frequently represented, Lewis Bayly's *Practice of Piety* (1613, and forty subsequent editions by 1740) provided a similar fare of precepts and practical lessons that could be read aloud in the family circle. Such books had dropped out of fashion in England, but their popularity lasted much longer in the colonies. Others, even more specifically theological, stood beside them on shelves in households that otherwise seem quite secular in this age of rationalism: Dean Sherlock's somber volumes on future judgment, on the immortality of the soul, and on death. In the large

Silver punch ladle and sauceboat by William Faris, Annapolis silversmith. Faris catered to the demand by wealthy customers for custom made silver. After the Revolution his son followed the same trade in Baltimore down into the Federal period. Courtesy, The Henry Francis du Pont Winterthur Museum.

personal library of Daniel Dulany the Elder, almost a fourth of the titles fall under the heading of religion and morality, exactly the same proportion devoted to the combined subjects of history, biography, and travel.

Most planters and professional men had a selection of practical books in their libraries. Such volumes as Jethro Tull's *Horse-Hoing Husbandry* and Henry Bracken's *Farmery Improved, or a Compleat Treatise on the Art of Farmery* introduced new methods and theories to practitioners, who could not yet look to the agricultural journals or extension experts of later years for advice or assistance. Do-it-yourself books had ushered in an age of manuals such as Giles Jacob's *Every Man His Own Lawyer*, and similar titles in medicine, commerce, carpentry, and architecture. These obviously utilitarian works rescued their owners from total dependence on tradition and hearsay and put at their disposal the precise and technical information of a compendium. But the description, "practical," extended beyond the mundane to include history, at least in the eyes of the eighteenth century leadership. How, except by the lamp of history, could men follow a safe pathway as they moved into the obscurity of the future? Leaders read history purposefully for lessons and illustrations, none more seriously than Stephen Bordley.

Son of Thomas, the distinguished lawyer and leader of the country party in its early days, Stephen Bordley (1709–1764) had his essential education in England where he attended the Inns of Court before returning to Annapolis to practice law. Quite naturally Bordley gravitated at first toward the new country party leaders, Philip Hammond and Dr. Charles Carroll. But within a few years he parted company with their brand of politics to spend his mature years in the Lord Proprietor's service, occupying several posts of honor and profit. Club man, bon vivant, and bachelor, Bordley had a serious side that comes out in an extraordinary set of letter books, the only sustained commentary on the life of the mind in Maryland provincial history. Bordley had a splendid collection of books which he constantly enlarged by ordering the old and new from his London correspondent. He sought Pierre Bayle's *Dictionary, Historical and Critical* in five volumes, Alexander Gordon's *Life of Pope Alexander VI and his Son Caesar Borgia*, Harrington's *Oceana*, and so on through a huge assortment of books. In his early letters, particularly those to his bosom friend, Mathias Harris, lawyer and planter in Kent County, Bordley expressed his

Pear shaped tankard, drawing from the William Faris Design Book of Silver. Faris followed the prevailing English style, demanded by his customers, but added touches of his own in handle design and base. Courtesy of the Maryland Historical Society.

critical opinions of the authors themselves and their subjects as well. He found fault with Rapin, popular historian of England: "He seems to me to be an Empty and modifying writer." After reading Rollins's bulky history of Rome, he favored Harris with his critical judgment on Roman statesmen. Already Bordley was refining a style that marked him in his later years as an astute debater and skilled polemicist on his Lordship's Council of State.

—4—

More obvious than literary and scholarly activities in the lifestyle of the elite living near urban centers, the social clubs of the eighteenth century brought members from solitary pursuits into "clubbical concourse," as one put it. The oldest of these, the Ancient South River Club, actually lay in a rural area. Another, the Royalist Club, founded about 1715 by the deported Jacobite, George Neilson, became the parent of the Redhouse Club. Most famous of all, the Tuesday Club, founded in 1745, had its seat in Annapolis.

The Tuesday Club was the brainchild of Dr. Alexander Hamilton (1712–1756), one of the most attractive personalities of the early golden age. Scottish born, Hamilton, "Sandy" to his friends, completed his medical studies at the University of Edinburgh in 1737 and migrated to Maryland the following year to set up in practice. Though successful as a physician, Hamilton found Maryland summers almost beyond endurance. In 1743 he became so ill that Dr. Adam Thomson who came to Annapolis to treat him had the definite impression Hamilton would not live. Hamilton rallied and for his complete recovery in the summer of 1744 made a horseback journey that took him away from the sweltering heat of the bay as far north as Maine. The results were twofold: Hamilton recovered his health and he produced a travel account, the *Itinerarium*, a minor masterpiece that circulated among his friends in manuscript.

Hamilton's forte was his pen, and upon organization of the Tuesday Club in 1745 he became secretary. His full and witty records include not only the minutes of club meetings with pen and ink sketches of members but an elaborate mock epic, *History of the Tuesday Club*, full of irony and satire in the best tradition of eighteenth century prose. Among its members the club included younger members of the first

The Tuesday Club, wash drawing by Dr. Alexander Hamilton, 1749. Sandy Hamilton, shown standing reading the minutes with Charles Cole, merchant, presiding. Above the company, the Club medal and Club seal. Courtesy of the Maryland Historical Society.

families: Walter Dulany, Stephen Bordley, and Edward Dorsey, a promising young attorney. Jonas Green, new owner of the *Maryland Gazette*, the Reverend Mr. John Gordon, and Charles Cole, jolly unmarried merchant, brought other talents and views. Sandy Hamilton's minutes make much of Jamaica rum and the post of Punchmaster-general, an office held by Jonas Green. Actually the pleasure of cultivated wit was the object of the club; drinking and eating were incidental.

Members of the Tuesday Club created their own entertainment. Under their club names, bestowed on them by Hamilton, members made speeches, posed conundrums, and held mock trials that elaborately caricatured the procedure of the law. At meetings they wore badges and carried out none too serious ceremonials for special occasions, such as the presentation of a new cap to Charles Cole the year he was president. Hamilton called the ceremony "The Capation of Cole" and made a comic drawing for the minutes of Cole surrounded by his faithful retainers. The only forbidden subject was politics. At the fourth meeting the club passed the "gelastic" law, which enjoined members to laugh at any discussion or reference "which levels at party matters, or the administration of Government." After one trial the gelastic law effectively eliminated politics from a club with conflicts in political allegiances among its members.

Club high jinx must not obscure the talent of the exuberant members who vented their spirits at meeting. Sandy Hamilton's truly Celtic imagination shone through many of his doings. His *Itinerarium* contains penetrating comments on the literature, pastimes, music, art, and social conditions of the population centers and rural areas he passed through on his travels to the north. He provoked a literary war—the "Annapolis Wits" versus the "Baltimore Bards"—with two Baltimore poets in the *Maryland Gazette* by attacking them in burlesque essays. The same Dr. Hamilton practiced medicine, subscribed to the Edinburgh medical journal, *Physical News*, and published professional essays in his own right. In 1751 Hamilton took up the cudgels in behalf of Dr. Thomson, who had once considered succeeding to his medical practice. Thomson had proceeded to Philadelphia and success in that larger community where he published a pamphlet on his method of preparing patients for smallpox inoculation. When a rival physician, one Dr. John Kearsley, attacked Thomson's method, Hamilton published in his behalf *A Defense of Doctor Thomson's Discourse on the Preparation of the Body for the Smallpox* (Philadelphia, 1751). And in politics Hamilton succeeded in reaching the office of delegate to the Assembly from Annapolis in 1753 through support from powerful family connections. He had married Margaret, daughter of Daniel Dulany the Elder in 1747.

A brother in spirit to Sandy Hamilton, the Reverend Thomas Bacon (c. 1700–1768) brought a different array of talents. Although an honorary member only, Bacon became club musician, with the name Signior Lardini in an atrocious cross-language pun, and composed ceremonial marches and pieces for special occasions. Outside the club, Bacon had an unassailable reputation as a clergyman, with several volumes of sermons to his credit, among them *Two Sermons, Preached to a Congregation of Black Slaves* (London, 1749) and others, published later, addressed to Christian masters and mistresses exhorting them to bring up their slaves in the knowledge and fear of God. In social thought Bacon was somewhat ahead of his time. His last work, *Laws of Maryland at Large* (Annapolis, 1765), a labor that occupied ten years of his life, is a monument of colonial printing, doubtless the best known of Bacon's accomplishments.

A full share of credit for the *Laws of Maryland* belongs to Jonas Green (1712–1767), who was responsible for the typography, one of the beauties of this stately volume. Like Hamilton and Bacon, Green was an immigrant. His grandfather had come to Massachusetts in 1633 and had succeeded the Dayes, first printers in the colonies, as public printer in Cambridge. Timothy, his father, was printing in Boston when Jonas was born, but shortly took his infant son to New London, Connecticut. Jonas grew up and learned his trade in New London, worked for a time in Boston, then in Philadelphia before coming to Maryland in 1738. He was, then, American born but not a native son of Maryland.

For several years Green did job work and the public printing until he established sufficient credit to revive the *Maryland Gazette*, which had expired when William Parks moved to Williamsburg more than a decade before. Green's new *Gazette* infused fresh life into Maryland letters, printing essays, stories, and poems by native authors and, when imperial squabbling began, the polemics of all factions. By this time Green, completely assimilated to Maryland culture and politics, had joined the Tuesday Club where Sandy Hamilton procured for him the title P.P.P.P.P., "purveyor, punster, punchmaker General, printer, and poet." Hamilton even provided a verbal portrait in his *History of the Tuesday Club*:

> This gentleman is of a middle Stature, Inclinable to fat, round-faced, small lively eyes, from which, as from two oriental portals, incessantly dart the dawning rays of wit and humor, with a considerable mixture of the amorous leer, in his countenance he wears a constant smile, having never been once seen to frown; his body is Thick and well-set, and for one of his make and stature he has a good sizeable belly, into which he loves much to convey the best vittles and drink, being a good clean knife and forks man.

Like Hamilton, Green could put on the tongue-in-cheek act, as dozens of entries in the minutes show, including a meeting when Green wrote them up in verse during one of Hamilton's few absences. Nonetheless he took his responsibilities to society as seriously as the squires of ancient pedigree: in 1766 he was elected to the board of alderman of Annapolis.

The Tuesday Club did not long survive its moving spirit, Sandy Hamilton, who died in 1756. But other clubs that followed felt the influence of Hamilton's pioneer society: the Forensic Club organized in 1759 and the Homony Club (1770–1775), which included the governor and the cream of Maryland's elite. Doubtless the clubs reflected the oasis culture of Annapolis, the capital that focused on itself the riches of a country being laid under tribute to man. Never mind that beyond lay the wilderness with untapped resources of nature and the animal energy of toilers turning them to the service of society. Within, society ordered its round of pleasures insulated from the crude and commonplace. All this is true enough, but not the whole picture. Along with the tomfoolery and burlesque, club members were honing their minds to the sharpness that made them masters of expression when they spoke for the country in later years.

—5—

No club ever succeeded in capturing the fancy of all classes, elite and commonalty alike, as did the sport of racing. Since early years private matches between the horses of planters had naturally grown out of banter among neighbors about the speed of their mounts. Planters had kept horses for riding, almost never for draft animals. Consequently a wager between a pair of sporting types broke the tedium of rural life and sometimes attracted a respectable gathering to see a heat or two decide the question of whose horse was better. In the first decade of the eighteenth century Annapolis, as an urban place, institutionalized these occasional contests between the better nags of southern Maryland in the September races.

By mid-century both horses and races had advanced far enough to make earlier matches seem primitive by comparison. As in other fashions, colonists in their racing tastes imitated the mother country, where three imported thoroughbreds from the Middle East introduced new blood into English studs: the Darley Arabian, the Byerly Turk, and the Godolphin Arabian. Sportsmen in Maryland quickly imported foals of these strains, particularly during the time of Governor Ogle and his successor Governor Horatio Sharpe, both of them ardent racing fans. Governor Ogle vied with his brother-in-law, Colonel Benjamin Tasker, in importing blooded horses. Other sporting types emulated them by introducing the strains of fine blood that still, after more than two centuries, flows in the veins of remote Maryland descendants. In 1750 Tasker, always called Colonel to distinguish him from his father Councillor Benjamin Tasker, imported Selima, a mare descended from the Godolphin Arabian. Tasker bred his mare to a son of the Godolphin Arabian, Othello, just brought to Maryland by Governor Sharpe. The horse from this union, Selim, became a turf champion almost immediately and in his prime was sold by Tasker to the merchant Sam Galloway for £1,000.

These were high prices for horses, even for thoroughbreds, but they ran for big stakes. In time the purse for the Annapolis races grew to 100 guineas. But special matches ran to more. In 1752 Captain Butler took his imported mare, Creeping Kate, to a famous encounter with

Alexander Spotswood's Trial at Gloucester, Virginia, where the Maryland mare won a purse of 500 golden guineas. Such stakes were exceptional, to be sure, but occurred as often as a new turf champion emerged to challenge the existing field. The stables of Colonel Edward Lloyd enjoyed high repute among lovers of horseflesh. Lloyd's imported mare, Nancy Bywell, another of the Godolphin strain, ruled as turf queen after the time of Galloway's Selim.

Annapolis became in the Golden Age the racing capital of the Chesapeake and consequently of the seaboard colonies. The Jockey Club, composed of the wealthiest horselovers, made the September races the social event of the year. Alexander Spotswood frequently brought the pride of his stables, in the last years of colonial dependency, his horse Apollo. Colonel George Washington regularly visited Annapolis during the races, with a stopover halfway at the country seat of Ignatius Digges, whose horse, Vendome, figured among the finest in the province. The record does not show Washington racing either horse or mare at Annapolis, but his personal diary gives a novel view of the season as seen by a participant. In 1771 Washington spent eight days in Annapolis and made as many entries in his diary without mentioning a single horse or match. Instead he recorded his dinner engagements with the president of the Jockey Club, Lloyd Dulany, with the governor and other high officials in the administration, and his evenings at the plays or at the coffee house.

Annapolis predominated among other racing centers in Maryland—Chestertown on the Eastern Shore and Marlborough on the Western Shore—simply because social life and accommodations were ampler in the capital. The great town houses harbored the special guests, Washingtons and Spotswoods, and the inns put up those not as well connected. No other community could boast a theatrical season, which for business reasons the impresarios of visiting theatre companies scheduled when possible to coincide with the September races.

When theatrical troupes inaugurated regular visits to Annapolis in the early 1750s, they performed in warehouses or barns fitted up for dramatic productions. The facilities certainly bordered on the primitive in the early years, but the quality of the performances is far from clear. Even the origins of the first companies are obscure. First to make an impression on the colonies, the Murray-Kean Company possibly came from an English troupe disbanded in the West Indies. Two years contending with the hazards of touring the seaboard colonies with indifferent box office returns brought the Murray-Kean Company to dissolution, but not before it had performed a great part of its repertoire in Annapolis in June of 1752. Thomas Kean, noted for his Shakespearian roles, did *Othello* and *Richard III* in the versions of Colley Cibber. The usual fare of forgotten farces made up much of the rest: *The Provoked Husband, The Lying Valet*, and a particular favorite, George Farquhar's *Recruiting Officer*, with the broad jests and obscenities that made it popular in the eighteenth century but spelled its doom in the Victorian Age.

Lovers of the stage in Maryland had their longest association with the Douglass Company, which in the final years of provincial history became known as the American Company. Organized by David Douglass from the wreckage of an English group assembled by William Hallam, the Douglass players included Miss Hallam as their star and her cousin, Lewis Hallam, as a lead. From their first visit to Annapolis, the Douglass Company became a favorite. In 1760 the *Maryland Gazette* announced the building of a new theater, euphemism for remodelling a warehouse that was to serve the Douglass troupe for a dozen years. The season of 1760 has several features of interest to students of the early theatre. First, the sheer length of time the company spent in Annapolis, from the beginning of March to the middle of May, testified to the devotion of the local audience to the theatre. On opening night, 3 March, a double bill included *The Orphan*, a tragedy, and *Lethe*, described in a press notice as a "dramatic satire" but probably more accurately dubbed a farce by England's leading actor, David Garrick. The account of opening night in the *Gazette* is called by one scholar of the early American stage the first piece of theatre criticism in America. It was also the editor's last notice of the spring season, which consisted of double bills until the farewell performance on 12 May.

The first reliable appraisals of the theatre in Annapolis came from William Eddis (1738–1825), a young Englishman who spent eight years in Annapolis as a minor official just before the War for Independence. Neither wealthy nor well connected, Eddis nonetheless played an active part in the social whirl of the capital, in the clubs and the entertainments of well-to-do Maryland families. He had known both the provincial and the London stage before coming to Maryland and in his *Letters from America* gave the American Company high marks

for acting. "My pleasure and surprise were therefore excited in proportion on finding performers in this country equal at least to those
who sustain the best of the first characters in your most celebrated
provincial theatres," Eddis wrote home. Then when Annapolis finally
built a real theater in 1771 he praised the structure for its stage,
scenery, and seating. He predicted that the company would enjoy
public favor and reap "a plenteous harvest."

To observers like Eddis, Annapolis represented all that was most attractive in the province of Maryland: splendid houses, fashionable entertainment, and the newest styles. Indeed, Annapolis resembled English provincial places in life-style of the foremost people, the elite.
And in social organization as well there were similarities, for Maryland
society had the same stratification as the mother country. Lines between
the strata were not, however, as sharply drawn in the province as in
the mother country, and outsiders quickly noted this difference. Eddis
himself wrote that "an idea of equality also seems generally to prevail
and the inferior order of people pay but little external respect to those
who occupy superior stations." He was in fact taking note of a certain
fluidity that permitted vertical mobility in Maryland beyond anything
known in England. Opportunity to rise in the social scale lay open to
talent in the Golden Age as it had in earlier days when indentured
servants could by their own efforts move upward, even to the top of
the ladder. In a more reflective mood, Eddis himself might have
meditated on his own association with the first families in a kind of
intimacy he could never on his limited resources have enjoyed back
home.

Immigration had throughout Maryland history contributed to the
open society. In the closing years of colonial dependency a new immigration of ethnic stocks different from the older tidewater strains
not only transformed the wilderness into populous area but added
variety in husbandry, language, religion, and life-style. Most appreciated of all, the Maryland Germans made a few of the established
families even wealthier by developing the back country where they
settled.

The settlement of the Germans in western Maryland has an almost storybook quality. Through the early decades of the eighteenth century south Germans—the Palatines—had made Philadelphia their port of entry into the colonies and the country west of the city their choice for farmsteads. In time, the line of settlement would have pushed naturally into western Maryland but for the enterprise of the Van Meter brothers, John and Isaac. In 1730 the Van Meters took up a tract of 40,000 acres in the Shenandoah Valley of Virginia on condition that they settle forty families on their grant within two years. One of their first recruits, whose name appears in the records as Joist or Jost Hite, brought with him from Pennsylvania his three sons-in-law and twelve other families. These pioneers broke a trail from Lancaster and York across the Monocacy River through a gap in the Catoctin Mountains into the Antietam and Conococheague valleys to the fords of the Potomac and on into the Shenandoah. Within a short time this trail became a wagon route, known in archaic spelling as the Monocasy Road, and conveyed migrating Germans across Maryland to the Hite-Van Meter settlements in Virginia.

For a few migrants, however, the fat lands of Western Maryland proved too tempting. The Penn sandy loams with clay and loam subsoils in the Monocacy Valley promised bountiful crops and lush pastures. Those who persevered along the route across the Catoctins found the loam three feet deep in the Antietam Valley. And, to compound temptation, an agent, Thomas Cresap, conveniently located on the route stood ready to sell farmsteads on the spot without the necessity of an eighty mile trip through continuous woodland to Annapolis. After the Conojacular War the intrepid Cresap had moved to the west where he set up as a landowner and trader. He had his financial backing from Daniel Dulany, who had taken Cresap's measure and judged him to be an ideal agent for the early wild west of Maryland. Cresap surveyed farms from Dulany's warrants for "Even Mack Daniel" and "Christian Getsitoner" [Getzendanner], spelling the names in his personal orthography but coming close enough to indicate the pedigree of his Scotch-Irish and German customers. For more than half a decade Cresap had sold farms off and on in the Monocacy and Antietam area before Dulany made a business trip to the west in the autumn of 1744. Dulany's first sight of the soil and the migrating Germans convinced him that a fortune awaited a developer of the area, not to mention the reliable pioneer population that would accrue to the province.

Without delay Dulany set in train his development plan. To the consternation of his neighbors, who openly said he had lost his mind, Dulany patented some 20,000 acres of the choicest land that his agent, Cresap, could locate. Then he sold family-sized tracts to immigrants, the majority German, a minority Scotch-Irish, taking mortgages on the property when purchasers had no ready capital, as almost none did. The operation was as simple as it was profitable. Dulany patented the land for £5 sterling per hundred acres plus fees; he turned the land over to buyers in small tracts at £30 sterling per hundred acres. No money changed hands in most transactions: the purchaser simply obligated himself to pay parts of the principal at stated intervals with interest at 6 percent. In a single one hundred acre deal the landlord "created" added value of £25, or five times the original cost, secured against unimpeachable assets, the land itself. Land development or, to give it the usual name, land speculation, was easily the most profitable enterprise in Maryland for those persons who had the initial capital to acquire title to vacant lands in the western part of the province.

The Germans proved ideal settlers for the west country. Their husbandry, based on grain and cattle, required heavier soils than tidewater tobacco lands that could be cultivated with the hoe alone. The loams of the Monocacy and Antietam valleys yielded readily to the plow, but first tillers of the soil had the laborious task of clearing the land by grubbing out stumps after they had felled the trees. The time-honored tidewater practice of simple girdling had no place in the preparation of fields for the plow. German settlers took the same pride in their cleared fields, free of stumps, as in the sturdy barns they built to house their grain and to shelter their livestock. The massive barns with masonry foundations and tight superstructures bore no resemblance to the flimsy curing houses of the tidewater. Indeed, the barn became a characteristic feature of west country architecture, usually larger than the farmhouse itself and frequently decorated with hex signs on gable ends to ward off evil spirits. Like the barns, dwelling houses were solid in construction. Builders customarily made the foundations from fieldstone or from outcroppings easily quarried. The more ambitious constructed the whole house of stone, with walls as much as two feet thick. Obviously the builders were aiming at permanence, and the prevalence of surviving eighteenth century stone houses in Western Maryland witnesses their success.

Baptismal Certificate of Johan Valatin Erhart, born at Deep Run, Frederick county, 1765. These color prints with elaborate ornaments distinguished the German element of western Maryland from their tidewater English neighbors. Courtesy of the Maryland Historical Society.

Insulated from the shipping accessible to dwellers in the tidewater, the landlocked westerners needed market arrangements of a new kind. Their husbandry demanded the services of artisans and processors rather than numerous cheap field hands, and their crops required a market place where producers and consumers met. As chief developer of the west, Daniel Dulany undertook to establish a market town at a convenient location in the Monocacy Valley. In 1745 he had his surveyor lay off a town site near the Monocacy River on a 7,000 acre tract that belonged to him. Obviously intending to reap the maximum return from a market center on his own property, Dulany offered lots of sixty feet frontage and a depth of 350 to 400 feet to artisans and tradesmen at £4 or £5 currency with a ground rent of one shilling a year payable in perpetuity to him and his heirs. Frederick Town, as the community was called, immediately became the center of the western settlements. Artisans and professional men took lots and had their homes and places of business under one roof. Dulany donated lots to both the Lutheran and Reformed congregations to assist them in building churches. When the Reverend Michael Schlatter toured the west in 1747 organizing congregations of the Reformed faith, he found the flock in Frederick Town ahead of him. He preached to the congregation in their "new and yet unfinished church."

As a final touch to insure the success of his city in the wilderness, Dulany obtained a patent from the Lord Proprietor authorizing weekly markets in Frederick Town "for buying and Selling all sorts of Cattle and other provisions of every kind" and two annual fairs, one in May and one in October. The patent also bestowed such ancient seigneurial rights as tolls, stallage and piccage, but the holder wisely exempted all comers from these fees in favor of attracting maximum attendance. From the beginning in October 1747 the Frederick Town fair was a success, not only as a market for fat cattle and provisions but as an agency of cultural fusion. Horse races were feature attractions, at first managed by tidewater settlers who had bought lots and opened stores in the town, but soon joined by Germans who quickly acquired a taste for the planter's sport.

Parallel with the development of the Monocacy settlement focussing on Frederick Town, another center some thirty miles west grew up about the properties of Jonathan Hager. Westphalian by birth, Hager had taken up a grant of two hundred acres on Conococheague Creek

Mrs. Charles Carroll of Annapolis by John Wollaston (ca. 1750–1760). This portrait, one of many painted by Wollaston for the Maryland elite, shows the marked influence of contemporary English portraiture. Owners of the great houses for the first time had spacious rooms to exhibit large canvasses, an expression of their family pride. Courtesy of the Detroit Institute of Arts.

in 1739 when the area was a complete wilderness. By subsequent grants he increased his land to 2500 acres in the middle sixties. Doubtless he took his cue from Frederick Town, for in 1762 Hager laid out a town on his land with lots surrounding a public square. The lots he sold for £5 each with a perpetual ground rent of seven shillings sixpence a year. Hager intended the town's name to be a memorial to his wife, Elizabeth, but popular usage defeated him. From the first the local people called the place Hagerstown.

For many years the Maryland Germans had their closest cultural ties with Philadelphia, where Christopher Sower (Saur) had a printing press that issued a German newspaper and an almanac. But after 1750 Baltimore began to supplant Philadelphia as a port of entry for Palatine immigration. Again Daniel Dulany had a hand in turning the influx toward Baltimore. He opened correspondence with the Rotterdam merchant houses, Dunlop and Company and Rocquette and Vanteylingen, both in the business of transporting Germans emigrating through the lower Rhine. Dulany put his son, Walter, in charge of the incoming Germans, many of whom found their way to the Monocacy properties belonging to the Dulany family.

—7—

A tireless letter writer, William Eddis described and interpreted the Maryland of the Golden Age to his correspondents back home. He arrived in the province in 1769, too late to witness the stimulating effects of the Inspection Act, essential to the prosperity that supported the building boom, personal libraries, club life, and amusements of the elite. Even the settlement of the west figures only briefly in two of his letters. Eddis visited Frederick Town about a year after he had taken up residence in Annapolis. He mentions the industrious habits and the superior husbandry of the new ethnic element that dominated west country population, noting that Frederick Town had passed Annapolis in population. After another trip to the back country a year and a half later Eddis told his correspondent about passing through another German community, Hagerstown, of roughly a hundred houses some thirty miles west of Frederick Town in the Antietam valley. Aside from these infrequent excursions Eddis remained in Annapolis, the focus of his interest, the cultural as well as the political capital.

Among other adornments of the capital city, Eddis counted the "many lovely women." Obviously he speaks of the elite, wives and female kindred of the wealthy whose company he courted. But instead of telling us what we would like to know about the role of women in household management, rearing children, and the like he drifts off into superficial generalities. These "American ladies," he tells us, "assiduously cultivate external accomplishments" though they do not neglect "the more important embellishments of the mind." Accordingly they converse with animation and "deliver their sentiments with affability and propriety." In brief women in capital society, and in the great country houses that were extensions of it, appear as a decorative backdrop for the dominant male sex absorbed, as was Eddis himself, in the games of politics, business, and clubs.

The Golden Age had reached its full splendor by the time of Eddis. He had not personally witnessed its beginnings and early flowering. It is doubtful whether any contemporary observer could have lived through the process of transformation with the detachment to explain what seems so clear in retrospect. In some degree the prosperity associated with an improved staple and galloping economic growth touched all strata of Maryland society. But in the truest sense the beneficiaries were the elite, who rose like rich cream to form a top layer quite different in texture from the mass beneath.

9

CONFLICTING IMPERATIVES

As a province of the British empire Maryland had made the scantiest of contributions to the warfare that succeeded the long peace after Utrecht. King George's War had begun in the frenzy that seized England when Robert Jenkins brought back a pair of ears, claimed as his own, which he avowed the Spanish had cut off in the West Indies. In 1739 Britain declared war on Spain, over the protests of his majesty's chief minister, Robert Walpole, who told his colleagues, "Now they are ringing their bells; soon they will be wringing their hands." Almost at once imperial officers called upon the province for assistance in the expedition led by Admiral Edward Vernon against Cartagena, and the Assembly responded with an appropriation to muster, victual, and pay just over three hundred Marylanders on this ill-fated venture. Five years later, when France joined the war against England, crown officers again requested help in a great expedition against Canada, and once more the Assembly supplied three companies to report for duty at Albany.

But along with these signs of cooperation the Assembly plainly showed an independent streak. More than once the delegates resisted pressure from royal authority. After all the Lord Proprietor, not the crown, stood immediately above the province in the ladder of authority. While the proprietary governor would have been happy to see every crown command met by the Assembly, he could not compel obedience. He had only veto powers over legislation, which he unhesitatingly used to protect any inroads on his Lordship's estate and prerogative. In this first phase of the war for empire, King George's War, the Assembly stood on the verge of making a great discovery: that proprietary and crown interests did not always run parallel, particularly in wartime. Some changes in the proprietary court at home immediately after the close of the war brought the differences into brighter light.

—1—

Alone among the colonies Maryland had a proprietary court resident in England. This unique body, though numerically tiny, played an especially significant role in provincial affairs during the last years of colonial dependency. The proprietary court, or secretariat in modern terminology, dated from 1715, in the days of Thomas Beake and Charles Lowe. But their successor, Sir William Janssen, raised his position as secretary or principal secretary to one of genuine influence. The post carried no constitutional salary. Incumbents received some income from monies allocated to them occasionally by the Lord Proprietor from his Maryland revenues, but their only assured reward came from a curious arrangement of levies—known as "saddles"—on the salaries of provincial officials. In the time of Beake and Janssen the saddle had been small, around £100 a year, and came out of the salary of the deputy secretary, who lived in Maryland and carried out the orders of the principal in England. The arrangement, which placed no real burden on the deputy, was common among officeholders in England and America.

In 1751 the old ways changed significantly with the death of Lord Charles. The accession of his minor son Frederick (1732–1771), sixth and last Lord Baltimore, brought new personages into the entourage known as the proprietary court. Two were temporary, the joint guardians of the young lord: Arthur Onslow, Speaker of the House of Commons, and John Sharpe of Lincoln's Inn, long the family legal adviser. A third, Cecilius Calvert, uncle of the new lord, remained almost a decade and a half as principal secretary. He was the chief author of change.

Cecilius Calvert (1702–1765) had previously served his brother, Lord Charles, as a personal and private secretary. This intimate association with an astute and able older brother gave Cecilius valuable experience if not perfect judgment. A gossipy scandal monger in his youth, Cecilius acquired in mature years an unctuous urbanity which he showered on proprietary officials in Maryland. Over the years he

Charles Calvert in 1761, by John Hesselius. This boy, son of Benedict (Swin-
gate) Calvert of Mt. Airy, Prince George's County, was related to the proprietary family. The artist leaves no doubt about the social position of young
Charles (age five) by including a body servant holding his master's drum.
Courtesy of The Baltimore Museum of Art.

developed considerable insight into men's motives and some skill in managing them by indirect and sometimes devious methods. Earliest among Calvert's crafty schemes, his maneuvers to attach saddles to the chief proprietary offices in the province, succeeded to perfection. Calvert's salary of £450 ran more than four times the payment to previous principal secretaries and had to be spread around among several chief patronage positions. Not only did Calvert carry off his initial objective adroitly, he went further in succeeding years to raise his salary eventually to £650, all by saddling additional sums on subordinates in the proprietary establishment in Maryland.

Calvert became expert at political jobbery in his term as principal secretary. Though he feathered his own nest, he did faithfully attempt to make appointments that would bring into Maryland officialdom persons capable of supporting his nephew, the Lord Proprietor. Calvert modelled his procedure on the current British practice of rewarding friends and paying political debts that Robert Walpole had developed during his long tenure as his majesty's first minister and that the Duke of Newcastle had more recently brought to the status of an art. In one of his letters Calvert explicitly named his model: "The Duke of New Castle is hard run in the Political Warehouse in Britain and in Miniature I in Maryland."

Early in his tenure Calvert began to discover that Maryland ways did not always accord with British. First, he compiled a list of appointive offices in Maryland, from the chief officials down to the smallest clerkships in the counties. In his enthusiasm he concocted a scheme for wholesale political corruption by dangling these plums before the Maryland gentry. Totally enamored of his idea, Calvert seriously proposed the scheme to the proprietary governor, who diplomatically persuaded him to drop it.* The notion that planters of substance would grasp at the tiny stipends attached to county clerkships was ludicrous, and the governor well knew that persons of any stature

---

*Calvert outlined his scheme in a secret letter to Governor Sharpe headed: "General Review of the Constitution and Government of Maryland and of Proper Regulations to prevent Turbulent and Malevolent Spirits . . . And so to Knit and unite the several Branches of Power there, as to form one Grand and Regular Movement, all tending to the Honor and Prosperity of his Lordship and the Happiness and Welfare of the whole Province."

would indignantly refuse such clumsy attempts to buy them off. Provincial families competed unceasingly for the major offices, but they had the keenest self-respect. Calvert never quite grasped the difference between British and American conceptions of political morality. Many British officials who dealt with the colonies shared this myopia either through ignorance of American ways and beliefs or because of their own conditioning in a society sunk to a new low in political morality.

The Lord Proprietor himself was neither a model for Secretary Calvert nor a check on his activities. Last of the Lords Baltimore, Frederick had none of the noble qualities of his distinguished ancestors. Pleasure-loving and self-indulgent, he rarely concerned himself about his province except as a source of revenue to support a style of life that degenerated in the end to viciousness. Provincials came in time to know the tawdriness of their proprietary overlord.

—2—

Ironically the proprietary circle had as its representative in the colony the ablest of governors. Horatio Sharpe (1718–1790) arrived in Maryland in the late summer of 1753 to begin the longest term of any governor in the history of the province. The Sharpe name was already familiar in Maryland. John Sharpe, the new governor's eldest brother, had been legal advisor to Charles, Lord Baltimore, since the 1720s and guardian of Frederick during his minority. Four other brothers, each in his own way, had made their marks: Gregory as a noted orientalist and man of letters, William as clerk in ordinary to the Privy Council, Philip as keeper of the Privy Council records, and Joshua as a successful attorney. Horatio, then, was the youngest and least known of a distinguished family of brothers whose various personalities appear so clearly in the Gowan Hamilton portraits on his large canvas, "The Sharpe Family."*

But if undistinguished in deeds, Horatio Sharpe cut a fine figure as a man, an impression not lost on the gentlemen of Annapolis when they met him at the city dock on an early August morning for the short walk to the statehouse. Tall and erect, Sharpe's appearance betrayed his military background. Doubtless his conversation soon re-

---

*This family piece hangs in Government House in Annapolis.

Horatio Sharpe by John Hesselius, ca. 1760. Sharpe's administration lasted from 1753 to 1769, the longest term in Maryland colonial history and one of the most successful. Hesselius caught his subject's combination of military and social traits that enabled Sharpe to carry out his difficult assignment. Courtesy The Johns Hopkins University.

vealed his sporting instincts, particularly his interest in horses, the passion of Maryland's upper crust. Sharpe carefully sustained this favorable initial impression in social gatherings where his affability, an essential trait of the gentleman, was remarked by those who left records of meetings with him. All the surface characteristics were in Sharpe's favor. Within a few months provincials learned that the not so obvious traits also promised well for his governorship.

Just as Sharpe assumed office the zones of international friction were reheating, threatening a renewal of the periodic warfare between England and France that had gone on since 1689, always involving the colonies. Few living Marylanders actually remembered King William's War (1689–1697) or even Queen Anne's War (1702–1713) but oral tradition had preserved some lore from these conflicts, though actual fighting had not directly touched the province. But King George's War had hardly ended and memories of the ill-fated Cartegena expedition were still fresh. Not only did provincials remember the episodes of the war vividly, they had learned during its course that the position of the province in the imperial order had changed. In the days of King William's and Queen Anne's wars, when a royal governor presided, the colonists responded directly to royal requests or orders about royal concerns. But before King George's War a new element, the proprietary government, had interposed between crown and people. Bickering over proprietary rights had all but prevented Maryland from participating in the war at all. Now, as rumblings in the west augured a renewal of conflict, the new governor faced the future bound to the same policies as his predecessors, Ogle and Bladen. In secret instructions that accompanied his general instructions Sharpe had several positive commands from Secretary Calvert: to permit no "enervation" of either the tonnage duty or the hogshead duty of 1704, to sign no agency bill unless it named Calvert as agent, to pass no act affecting the Lord Proprietor's private rights in land, and to reserve for the proprietor the income from ordinary licenses, which Ogle had once allowed to be appropriated for military use. Under such restrictions Governor Sharpe's administration of the province during the first decade of his incumbency, nearly all of it wartime, called upon all his resources of shrewdness, tact, and firmness.

—3—

The thunder in the west began with a slight rumble. In the summer of 1753 the French governor of Canada dispatched a thousand men into the disputed country of the upper Ohio Basin to occupy and fortify that area, which lay within the bounds of the Virginia charter. Beside the theoretical claim to this wild country, several wealthy Virginians, members of a group of land speculators called the Ohio Company, had a highly practical interest in developing holdings in the west. In the fall, after this "invasion," Governor Robert Dinwiddie dispatched Major George Washington on a winter journey, November to January 1753–1754, to deliver letters to the French commandant warning the Canadian troops away. The French took a course exactly contrary to Dinwiddie's warning. An English fur trader, Captain William Trent, had started to build a fortified trading post at the forks of the Ohio some three weeks after Washington completed his winter journey. Before Trent could make the post defensible the Canadians swooped down, compelled Trent and his companions to withdraw, and constructed a much larger work, which they named Ft. Duquesne, after the governor of Canada.

Until summer of 1754 neither French nor Virginians shed blood. But in July actual fighting began when Dinwiddie dispatched a hastily assembled force under Colonel Joshua Fry and Major Washington to support Trent and dislodge the French. Commanding the advance party, Washington met and defeated a small French force, killing a score of men and taking about the same number prisoner. Then, in the face of a larger French force, he retraced his route back to Great Meadows where he built Ft. Necessity to sustain him against the expected counterattack which occurred on 3 July. Washington's surrender with the honors of war ran up the curtain on the first fighting of a long and bloody war.

News from the west sent a wave of alarm through Maryland. The Assembly met in special session on 17 July; next day the news of the surrender reached Annapolis. Shortly Assemblymen learned that Washington had fallen back to Will's Creek on Maryland soil and had begun constructing Ft. Cumberland. Although no war had been declared, fighting was in progress and the delegates at once voted £6,000 "for

his Majesty's use, towards the defence of the colony of Virginia, attacked by the French and Indians." Unwittingly the Assembly had
given a name to the bloody fighting that was to last for almost nine
years, the French and Indian War. Appropriately the governor commissioned an old western hand with considerable experience with Indians, Thomas Cresap, to raise a company of riflemen for service beyond
the mountains as a shield to the exposed settlements from Frederick
Town on westward to Hagerstown.

England, too, took cognizance of the fighting in the west. While
maintaining the pretense of peace, his Majesty's government decided
to support its western claims with an adequate force under a commander
said to be one of the bravest and most accomplished officers in the
empire, General Edward Braddock. Actually Governor Sharpe showed
more enterprise initially than Braddock: in January 1755 Sharpe personally set out to reconnoitre the future area of operations about Will's
Creek and made the return journey of two hundred fifty miles back
down the Potomac by canoe in mid-winter, purchasing supplies and
forage for future use of troops and animals as he came. Braddock,
himself, did not arrive until late February and then "stormed like a
lion rampant" attempting to impress wagons, horses, and teamsters
for transporting supplies and equipment.

Braddock's command was the largest assembled in the southern
colonies to that time. Altogether his effective men numbered more
than two thousand, including two regiments of British regulars augmented by volunteers who were mainly indentured servants from southern and western Maryland, rangers from New York, pioneer companies
from Virginia, and other ranger companies from Maryland and North
Carolina. For logistical support Braddock had Governor Sharpe, who
went to Frederick Town as expediter, Benjamin Franklin, who came
from Philadelphia to Frederick Town to concert plans for forwarding
dispatches and supplies from Pennsylvania, and finally George Washington, who joined his staff as aide-de-camp, familiar with the region
and with Americans in the expedition. Franklin warned Braddock of
the wiles and stratagems common in Indian warfare only to be brushed
aside.

Duquesne [Braddock replied] can hardly detain me three or
four days; and then I can see nothing that can obstruct my

march to Niagara. . . . These savages may indeed, be a formidable enemy to your raw American militia; but upon the
king's regular and disciplined troops, sir, it is impossible they
should make any impression.

In this frame of mind Braddock marched to the most disastrous
defeat in the annals of contemporary warfare. On 9 July within ten
miles of Ft. Duquesne he lost 877 killed or wounded out of a total
forward force of 1460 officers and men before withdrawing the shattered
remnant back to Great Meadows, where he died of a wound received
earlier in the fighting.

Shocked disbelief perhaps best describes the initial reaction to the
disaster. Even a military man like Sharpe accustomed to the fortunes
of war remarked, "It is as surprising a defeat, I think, as has been
heard of." But immediately thereafter the full implications of a frontier
practically denuded of effective troops occurred to westerners. Colonel
Thomas Dunbar, commander of one of the regiments of regulars, left
Ft. Cumberland for Philadelphia on 2 August with the whole contin-
gent of British troops and the independent companies. Even Thomas
Cresap moved back east to the plantation of his son, Michael, on the
Conococheague, to help fortify the house against attack by Indians.
Young Cresap's stockade and Ft. Cumberland, held after Dunbar's
departure by a mere handful of Maryland militia, were the two refuges
for westerners when invasions, which were rumored weekly, did in fact
occur though somewhat less frequently.

Another consequence of Braddock's defeat is more difficult to assess.
Colonials had inclined to take British military prowess at British evaluation. More than one American found cause for disillusionment in
the conduct of the confused and terror-stricken regulars that had been
Braddock's boast. Washington described them as "dastardly." Other
critics used equally harsh adjectives: stupid, cowardly, and pusillani-
mous. The legend of redcoat invincibility vanished in 1755.

—4—

Fighting in the west revived the ancient fears of Catholics and the
association of the French with catholicism. Imperial authorities could
scarcely have chosen a less opportune time to deport thousands of

French-speaking Catholics from Acadia (Nova Scotia) for refusing to take the oath of allegiance to George II. Periodically, since Britain had acquired Nova Scotia during Queen Anne's War, crown officers had threatened deportation unless the Acadians took the oath, and each time had relented until the rural population came to expect last minute reprieves. Now with fighting already under way and declared war obviously not far distant the long-threatened expulsion occurred, carried out with a harsh hand. Altogether, British authorities sent about five thousand exiles to the seaboard colonies from New Hampshire south to Georgia.

On the first day of December, 1755, five vessels arrived at Annapolis with nine hundred Acadians aboard. Five months to a day had passed since the lower house of Assembly had petitioned the governor to order all magistrates in the province to execute the penal statutes against Roman Catholics. In the hostile and tense atmosphere the provincial council decided to allow only one ship to disembark passengers at Annapolis and to send the remaining four to other ports in the province. Provincials quickly learned that the Acadians were more wretched than dangerous. Even so the hostility toward them resulted in shameful neglect during an unusually harsh winter.* Only the groups that went to Baltimore and to Oxford on the Eastern Shore had genuinely sympathetic treatment. The sufferings of the Acadians were an omen of things to come in the long war ahead.

—5—

Officially war began in May 1756. European historians, with eyes on the protocol of European chancelleries, have called this conflict the Seven Years War. For Europe proper the name is correct. Actually hostilities in America throughout the two years since Washington's surrender at Ft. Necessity had finally compelled England and France

---

*On 25 December 1755 Henry Callister at Oxford wrote Anthony Bacon, the London merchant prince:

"Particularly, Mr. Lowes sent up this way to inquire what was done in behalf of those sent hither, and made a dismal representation of the condition they were in in Somerset, where they were obliged to betake themselves for shelter to the swamps, now and a long time full of snow, where they sicken and die."

to square off, to recognize the fighting in disputed parts of their empires. In the two years of preliminary combat and in the first years of declared war the advantage had been clearly with France. Braddock's defeat, the capture of Oswego in New York by French troops, the loss of Minorca in the Mediterranean—each of these contests had meant the loss not only of men and materiel but of prestige as well. Formal rupture with France and the acknowledged state of war changed English fortunes not one whit. Disasters continued to plague British arms throughout the first years.

Though war had come haltingly, the crown had been forehanded in military preparedness. Sharpe had been in Maryland less than two months when he submitted the royal call for cooperation to the session of Assembly in October 1753. The delegates delayed enacting a supply bill until the following year when they passed the first and smaller of Maryland's two war-tax laws. Even this measure the delegates agreed to only on condition that income from the ordinary licenses be appropriated, as they had been during King George's War. Sharpe reluctantly violated his instructions in consenting to the act, but he did so with the support of the council and of Daniel Dulany the Younger, the legal oracle. At the very outset Sharpe saw his predicament clearly: in order to serve the crown he had to put the proprietary interest in jeopardy. He explained to Secretary Calvert that he was "reduced to great streights, by the people's determined resolution to make his majesty's service and his lordship's interest clash."

The governor could hardly have made a more succinct statement. At every subsequent stage of the conflict the House of Delegates used the war demands of the crown as a fulcrum to pry the Lord Proprietor from his revenues. The members had fumbled toward these tactics in King George's War. Now having discovered a promising line, they followed it rigorously throughout the French and Indian War. Nevertheless only once more, in 1756, did the lower house extract concessions from the proprietary circle; thereafter province and proprietor stood at impasse.

There were excellent reasons why the £40,000 Act of 1756 finally passed. The European phase of the war was about to begin, and the crown had increased the pressure on colonial governors to put their provinces in better postures of defense. Clearly, too, the military hazards in the western areas had convinced all elements in Maryland of the need to pass a supply bill. Even so the Assembly wrangled for a record twelve weeks before producing the act.

The act of 1756 was a two-fold victory for anti-proprietary forces. First the delegates wrote into the law two taxes explicitly forbidden by the governor's instructions: a levy of twelve pence per hundred acres on all land including the proprietary manors and a double tax on Roman Catholic landholders. The first violated the instruction forbidding any impairment of the proprietor's rights in land, the second violated the instruction on religious equality. The other victory was the projection of lower house authority into new fields of financial and military control hitherto considered to be the sole province of the governor. The legislation spelled out in detail how the money appropriated should be spent, named commissioners who were to share with the governor the administration of provincial defense and of Indian relations, and even specified how and where forts were to be built. In short the House of Delegates had succeeded as never before in increasing its own power and tapping proprietary revenues.

Governor Sharpe took unusual pains in justifying these objectionable provisions to the proprietary court. He regretted, he told Secretary Calvert, the double tax on Catholics, but withholding approval would have identified the proprietary interest with the Catholic interest, a disaster not to be risked in the high feelings of the moment. As to the land tax, Sharpe pointed out that the levy applied only to the leased and productive lands, not the unproductive reserves. He estimated the cost at £400 a year for the five-year life of the act, or just over half the normal income from the manors. Sharpe thought this concession ought to be compared to the £1600 in western quitrents the proprietor lost when settlers fled the area. Finally he pointed out that the law was enacted for five years and in no way compromised the proprietor's permanent rights.

The Lord Proprietor allowed the Act of 1756 to stand. Disallowance would have invited unwelcome publicity in the British press for obstructing the welfare of the realm in a moment of crisis. But the Calverts steeled their governor against any further inroads on proprietary revenues or prerogative. Both governor and councillors received orders to stand firm against future encroachments.

Accordingly, when the delegates went the next step in the futile session of 1757 the upper house was ready with a negative. Obviously the handiwork of the most radical group of delegates—Hammond, Carroll, and the Tilghmans—the proposed act placed a 5 percent tax on quitrents and on the incomes of all proprietary officeholders. Though stymied by supporters of the proprietor in the upper house, leaders of the country party had other resources in the battle against the establishment and they immediately turned to the most promising: the press.

Printing of Assembly proceedings was nothing new in Maryland. In early years the nascent country party had used William Parks to publicize their program as long as he remained in Maryland. Jonas Green had revived the *Maryland Gazette* in 1744, but while he was establishing his press in the later years of King George's War he had cautiously restricted his printing to proclamations, addresses opening the formal sessions of Assembly, and the usual acts passed at the end. But once firmly established, his paper carried an unprecedented amount of political material, notably after 1752 when he printed the journals of the House of Delegates for all to see the votes of individual members and the shape of Assembly battles. Thus Green had set the stage for the extramural politics of the French and Indian War. The delegates now ordered a special printing of the defeated bill of 1757, along with the proceedings related to it, for distribution to all members of the lower house and to the county clerks who were to keep copies for people in the counties to read. The special printing under the title, *An Act for Granting a Supply of Twenty Thousand Pounds for His Majesty's Service* (Annapolis, 1758), was in effect a political pamphlet, the first of many that were to issue from Green's press over the next decade and a half.

To the satisfaction of the popular element in Maryland the pamphlet provoked an open newspaper debate in England over the rights and wrongs of Maryland's poor showing in the war effort. A sympathetic writer in the *London Chronicle* took the side of the lower house and posed a series of twenty-nine questions, each one a barb aimed at the Lord Proprietor. Did not the proprietor receive "very large incomes or revenues from the province?" Did he pay "a penny, a farthing, or even half a farthing per pound . . . on those revenues?" Did the bill not receive all the opposition the government could muster "both within and without doors" and yet pass in the lower house by a vote of 40

to 10? Did not the conflicts in the proprietary colonies call for investigation and corrective action "to put them on a better footing?"*

Whether anticipated or not, the pamphlet took the discussion outside the Assembly halls. And this extramural debate plagued the proprietary establishment within the province and in the capital of the
empire where policy makers could not fail to note the failure of Maryland to contribute to the war effort and to ask embarrassing questions
about the reasons for failure. Once they had established their line, the
delegates stuck to it. The printed supply bill with the supporting
constitutional arguments offered by the lower house became the standard reply to every request by the governor for wartime revenues. The
argumentative statements, sweetly reasoned and widely publicized by
publication, drove home one of the most keenly felt convictions of
Maryland political thought: "That the free born subjects of England,
and consequently their representatives, have a right to grant their own
money in their own way." The anti-proprietary rhetoric acquired the
ring of popular government. Such basic premises could, of course, have
implications beyond opposition to the proprietary incubus, but these
became apparent only after the war. As long as the war continued,
Maryland's representatives linked the failure of supply bills to Baltimore's adamant refusal to bear his share of the common burden. Years
afterward, when Benjamin Franklin was asked by Parliament whether
he had heard "that Maryland, during the last war, had refused to
furnish a quota toward the common defense," he replied: "It is true,
Maryland did not then contribute its proportion, but it was, in my
opinion, the fault of the Government, and not of the people."

Maryland resistance to the wartime calls of an embattled empire was
neither capricious nor unpatriotic. As sincerely as the citizenry of
Virginia or New York, Marylanders spoke and thought of Britain as
"home." Like other colonies Maryland, too, had a western exposure
to French and Indian incursions. More than once settlers in the outer
reaches—the Conococheague valley and the Ft. Cumberland area—fled

---

*This polemic, in the *London Chronicle*, 16–19 September 1758, had a style that
suggested Benjamin Franklin as the author.

eastward leaving their houses in flames and members of their families prisoners or dead. Even the bands of rangers in the western parts proved ineffective in deterring raids or in punishing the offenders. The immense primeval wilderness favored the hit and run tactics of the Indians, who managed to elude pursuit parties without exception. A special problem, unique to Maryland, blocked contributions to the war effort in spite of the bonds of affection and the common danger.

Alone among the seaboard colonies Maryland labored under a burden of three privileged elements over which provincials had exercised no real control since Lord Baltimore's constitutional coup of 1733. All three elements—the Lord Proprietor, the proprietary government, and the clergy—cost provincials dearly in both direct and indirect ways. When compared with the total value of export trade of the colony, the support of these three elements amounted to something like one sixth of the whole. When the Assembly proposed a 5 percent tax on the salaries of proprietary officials to support the war effort, the negative reaction was sharp and instantaneous. The governor as well as the council members who comprised the upper house saw their privileged positions threatened and, however good the cause for which the tax was designed, categorically refused their assent. Insistent that the burden of war supplies be borne by all, the lower house refused to pass tax bills that would exempt officials. The province by stages reached the politics of irreconcilables.

The emotional attachment to their conflicting positions by both the popular majority on the one hand and the proprietary establishment on the other rested in part on the financial stakes at issue. At the time no one outside a small circle within the establishment knew in exact figures what the costs of proprietary government came to. Such matters were carefully guarded secrets. Provincials made rough guesses, surmises that came uncomfortably close to the truth. Later scholars with access to the records have untangled the complexities of tax returns and agents' accounts to compile an accurate picture of the costs to the province arising from funds channelled into support of the privileged elements.*

---

*Charles A. Barker, *The Background of the Revolution in Maryland* (New Haven, 1940), made a thorough and exact analysis of a) proprietary income, b) the officers' salaries, and c) incomes of the clergy. The following pages summarize his findings.

The share of the Lord Proprietor was the largest. His personal income derived from land revenues, export duties on tobacco, and minor perquisites claimed from such sources as ordinary licenses and permits to keep ferries. This palatine income had mounted steadily for forty years, as the elder Dulany had predicted.

ANNUAL PROPRIETARY INCOME
FROM ALL SOURCES
(Pounds Sterling)

	Gross Income	Net Income
1731	£ 6,620	£ 5,055
1733	8,091	5,969
1748	11,652	9,880
1754	16,440	14,960
1760	17,422	14,828
1761	18,994	15,976

The only debits of any consequence were the governor's salary (£1,000) and the petty commission to the rent roll keepers. Occasionally the Lord Proprietor made a gift of a few pounds to a school. The remainder, his net income, was remitted in sterling exchange payable in London.

This transfer of funds to a privy pocket on so large a scale in war and peace, whatever the condition of prosperity or poverty in the colony, had real economic impact on the province. The province depended on the value of its exports for purchase of all goods and services from abroad such as imported manufactures, education in England, and luxuries. For the closing decades of the proprietary period total exports from Maryland came to roughly £200,000 a year. By just so much as the Lord Proprietor diverted a fraction of this total to his private use, the purchasing power of provincials was reduced. Thus the diversion of funds to Lord Baltimore's privy purse represented a levy of between 6 and 7 percent annually on the total purchasing power of the province arising from the export trade.

The Lord Proprietor was but one of three elements that enjoyed a privileged position economically. Proprietary officials—the Maryland proprietary establishment—stood in a position at once like and unlike

Lord Baltimore. Their share of the financial benefits of the system were, like his, considerable. But their incomes, deriving from different sources or from the same sources before they were transmitted by the agent and receiver general, present a more difficult task of computation. Provincial officers' incomes flowed from one or more of three sources: first, commissions on monies collected (naval officers and rent roll keepers); second, fees for individual services (the chancellor, deputy, secretary, commissary general, county clerks, sheriffs and others); and third, the receipt of an annual sum from a principal officer by his deputy who actually did the work. None of these came under a general accounting because the recipients considered them private matters.

Three times during the Golden Age reliable estimates were made giving systematic valuations of the proprietary offices. These, taken together with other figures, supply a reasonably close approximation of the property interest represented by provincial offices. The ten higher officials (chancellor, surveyor general, commissary general, judges of the land office, and naval officers) and some seventy lesser officers (of the county clerk rank and slightly above) received a combined total of £12,000 to £14,000 sterling. Some officers had quite handsome incomes, the commissary general and provincial secretary heading the list with above £1,000 each. Lesser ranks, sheriffs and county clerks, received between £80 and £200, or in practical terms a meagre to a good living. Nearly all, however, were planters who had returns from their crops and who regarded official income as something additional, a perquisite. But whether well or poorly paid, some eighty members of the establishment levied almost as much on the economy as the Lord Proprietor. The Assembly questioned the amount of genuine service returned by these officers.

A third element, the clergy, did not have the character of shared political authority. Nevertheless the proprietor had in his gift some of the best church livings in America through his prerogative of presenting clergymen to their benefices. In neighboring Virginia, parish vestries controlled appointments to the exclusion of the royal governor, who had merely perfunctory duties in the established church. But Maryland clergymen enjoyed security in their posts and guaranteed salaries, "livings" in contemporary phraseology. From 1702, the date of the permanent establishment, to the Inspection Act of 1747 each clergyman was entitled to forty pounds of tobacco per taxable within his parish. The Inspection Act lowered the amount to thirty pounds per poll, as the expression went, in expectation of the rise in value of the higher quality inspected tobacco. As population grew the value of the livings increased, in some of the more populous parishes to over £300 sterling. Governor Sharpe reported in 1766 that the forty-odd clergymen of the Church of England received 1,920,930 pounds of tobacco, which he valued at £8,173. "This situation," observed Professor Barker, "makes understandable the appearance of favorites in the church, men more distinguished for their association with the proprietor than for their piety in the Anglican faith."

The clergy, with a few notorious exceptions, did render service for value received. Dissenters—Quakers, Baptists, Presbyterians, and the Germans—did not entirely agree, but at least the established church escaped real opposition until the proprietary regime began to falter. It is therefore technically inaccurate to say that the £8,000 for the Anglican Church represented a levy on the economy, as did the Lord Proprietor's personal income, but in the eyes of provincials it formed a part of an expensive establishment. Taken with the other elements and expressed in round numbers the resultant costs appear as follows:

Lord Proprietor	£ 12,500
Administration	12,000
Church of England	8,000

or a total of £32,500. This figure is not far from an "exact estimate" made by Governor Sharpe at the request of Lord Shelburne in 1767. In the popular view the £20,000 received by patronage officers and clergy was as much a levy—about 10 percent of the £200,000 generated by export trade—as the percentage credited to Lord Baltimore.

Costs of the official establishment numbering roughly one hundred twenty persons—eighty officers and forty clergy—were probably the heaviest of any American colony. By the beginning of the French and Indian war these costs had pitted provincial interest against proprietary establishment in permanent tension. The proprietary policy of securing every possible monetary advantage, often by prerogative action, was in complete accord with legalities as defined by a charter already archaic when issued more than a century previously. But in the Assembly elected delegates had begun to raise embarrassing questions that went beyond mere legalism. Should not the proprietary element bear its share of the common burden in times of crisis? Gradually through the course of the Great War for Empire, as the conflict has been called, Assembly leadership gave answer by formulating tactics and rhetoric to achieve their goal. Both tactics and rhetoric were to serve well in the future.

—7—

The financial burdens of wartime merely sharpened the sense of difference between the proprietary interest and the "country interest." Most obvious, and most easily dramatized, was the considerable difference in cost. The proprietary establishment, including the clergy, received about twice the sum appropriated for purely provincial officers and public services combined. Yet these officials in the judicial and legislative branches numbered more than 260 altogether,* over twice as many as proprietary officials and clergy. Moreover provincial officers of all descriptions performed services in rough proportion to their pay. None held a sinecure. Finally provincial officialdom was both responsive and responsible to its constituency: salaries depended on annual legislative appropriation. The prolonged tussle between proprietor and province throughout the war helped to distinguish officials responsible and loyal to each. As time went on these differences heightened.

Structurally the provincial establishment had stood almost without change since the royal period. Simple in pattern (a legislative branch and a judicial branch), the workings of provincial offices and officers were complex, and they touched the people of Maryland closely, season in and season out. The legislature still had its tiny upper house—the proprietary council out of session time—with a dozen members or fewer. And as always the lower house consisted of four elected delegates from each county and two from Annapolis. Together these houses battled or cooperated in legislation, but the proceedings left no doubt that the councillors in the upper house were in the debt of the proprietor and guarded his rights and privileges. The lower house continued to voice the sentiments of provincials and, since the end of the royal government, had stood as the popular champion. Through its com-

---

*The provincial, as contrasted with the proprietary, officers included chiefly county justices (168), constables (40), and delegates to the lower house (56).

mittee infrastructure, and particularly the Committee on Aggrievances, the Assembly felt the political pulse of the province and expressed its imperatives. Yet the cost of the legislative branch was modest. Using 1766 as his sample year, Governor Sharpe put the annual expense of the Assembly at £1,750.

Understandably the court system came to a considerably higher figure. Yet when the numbers of officers and the scope of services are considered, the reckoning cannot be counted dear. Since the days when Governor Seymour had tried to improve the quality of local justice by his assizes, the county courts had remained the same in size: twelve justices of the peace who assembled quarterly to make up the county bench. And, as in an older day, the menfolk of the county converged on the place when the court met. At the beginning of the century both Governor Seymour and the poet, Ebenezer Cook, could with truth speak satirically of the county judges. However great their practical knowledge and experience, judges had the bare minimum legal training for carrying out their official duties, and the courthouses where they sat were rather primitive affairs.* But increased opportunities for legal training brought more qualified men to the county benches, and broader tax bases provided funds for more adequate courthouses. Time and growth took care of many criticisms levelled at local courts half a century previously. At mid-century the most substantial and best educated planters of the county presided at the quarterly sessions.

More than any other secular institution the county courts were bound up with the lives of provincials. A student who wishes to get the feel of rural life in eighteenth-century Maryland, its texture and color, could hardly find a more informative source than a volume of county court records. To be sure the entries tend to stiff formality, neither easy nor exciting reading. Yet through them one may view the social, economic, political, and moral condition of planters, their families, their servants, and their slaves. In no other source are the materials so plentiful for reconstructing a past that lies back of the age of rapid transportation and instant communication. From no other pages do

---

*When new counties were formed, their first court sessions were frequently held in a tavern or ordinary. But justices invariably made provision for letting a contract to erect a building of some sort, as well as stocks, a cage, and pillories, the other indispensable furnishings of a proper court.

the insights and understandings of a rural society so vividly flash into consciousness. A history of the eighteenth century which does not place the county court and its presiding justices in the very foreground of the picture would be a caricature. From their courtrooms the Shallows and Silences of real life, in F. W. Maitland's felicitous phrase, gave the county its government.

Over the fifty years since Seymour's time the structure of court sessions had changed little. The docket still began with criminal suits brought by the public prosecutor. Then followed the dozens of private suits, almost exclusively for debt. The notion that land titles were the chief issues in the massive litigation of Maryland courts doubtless comes from the cases included by Thomas Harris and John McHenry in their *Maryland Reports*, most of which are precedents in land law. But an examination of the court proceedings leaves no doubt that the action "trespass on the case" for collecting debts comprised more than 90 percent of the civil suits. In a society that rested on a tissue of debt these consequences were inevitable.

With litigation finished, the justices turned to business today largely in the hands of boards and commissions, namely county government. Their responsibilities included maintainance of the poor, repair of churches, roads, and bridges, and various regulatory functions. For major tasks the court had the sheriff as its executive officer, but the justices also appointed a panel of subordinate officials, the constables of the hundreds. Though subordinate, constables performed important services: they prepared the list of taxables, they gave information to the grand jury, and they raised the hue and cry for the pursuit of criminals and fugitive servants. But ultimate responsibility always rested with the justices for binding out orphans as apprentices, engaging physicians for sick paupers, and sometimes selling insolvent debtors into servitude. They awarded contracts for repairing public buildings and acted on petitions to lay out new highways and build bridges. Finally, from time to time the justices took under consideration prices charged by taverns and inns in order to revise rates for services.* In the age of mercantilism no one dreamed of permitting these businesses affected with a public character to go unregulated.

---

* Regulation extended to the most minute details. Rates established by the Anne Arundel County Court (1723) for ordinaries (inns) within its jurisdiction illustrate the attention to the price of drink:

Somehow the justices managed to discharge this load of work in sessions that lasted between two and five days. At the end, as a final act, the court "apportioned the county levy," as the authorizing Act of 1704 read, to defray "the several and respective county charges." Apportioning the county levy was, of course, in plain language taxation for the support of local government. For his sample year, 1766, Governor Sharpe put the total for all fourteen Maryland counties at £14,695, certainly a reasonable sum for the services rendered.

Nevertheless provincials eyed these annual levies narrowly and refused to let any levy at all out of the ordinary go unchallenged. In 1747 the Prince George's County court passed an order for 100,000 pounds of tobacco to cover extensive repairs on the courthouse. For half a year thereafter essayists in the *Maryland Gazette* muttered protests that the Act of 1704 envisioned nothing more than levies for small charges, that execution of an order of this size would soon result in taxation without representation. Shortly afterwards the Assembly passed a supplementary act limiting court levies to the "ordinary, usual, and necessary charges annually arising." By law, therefore, any

	£	s	d		£	s	d
Rum per quart	0	3	0	French brandy			
Flip per gallon				per quart	0	5	0
(with a quart				English brandy			
of rum)	0	4	0	per quart	0	3	0
Punch per				Cider per quart	0	0	6
gallon (with				Double strong			
a quart of				beer per			
rum, lime				quart	0	1	0
juice, and				Single beer per			
sugar)	0	4	0	quart	0	0	6
Madeira per				English stout			
quart	0	2	0	and other			
Canary per quart	0	5	0	English			
Claret per quart	0	4	0	strong beer	0	1	6
Sherry per quart	0	4	0	Small beer per			
Rhenish per				gallon	0	1	0
quart	0	4	0	Night's lodging			
Punch (with one				in a bed	0	0	6
quart French							
brandy,							
wine, juice							
and white							
sugar)	0	6	0				

special expenditure had to come before elected representatives of the people in the Assembly.

Beyond the charges incurred by the Assembly and the costs of county courts, provincials were called on to lay out money for only three other purposes. For education, some minor special duties yielded £419 by Sharpe's estimate, divided among King William's School in Annapolis and the few counties that had a public school. Another duty brought in about £819 annually into a reserve fund for compensatory payments to masters of slaves executed under the law. The last outlay, for the provincial court, the province made by legislative appropriation annually or biennially. The nine justices of the provincial court, the capstone of the common law courts, had both original and appellate jurisdiction. Accordingly the court occupied a rather special and, as later events proved, a somewhat controversial position in the Maryland judicial system. The justices of the provincial court heard appeals from the county courts and acted as court of first resort in three types of cases: actions for determining titles to land, felonies extending to life or member, and suits for debt or damages exceeding £30 sterling or 7,500 pounds of tobacco. On a court of this importance the Assembly preferred to have the leverage of periodic appropriation. Sharpe estimated the annual amount at £637.

Altogether, then, the entire cost of the Assembly (£1,750), county and parochial charges (£14,695), education (£419), compensatory payments (£819), and the provincial court (£637) came to a grand total of £18,320, mostly payable in tobacco. For each category of expense provincials could see returns in actual services.

The contrast between these outlays and the amounts—even if imperfectly known—that went to support the privileged proprietary establishment was disturbing. For his "exact estimate" Governor Sharpe had access to sources closed to provincials. But delegates in the Assembly performed their own calculations and, when dependable documentation was unavailable, made guesses not too wide of the mark. They could not say with Sharpe's certainty exactly what the proprietary establishment cost, but they made a close approximation. The figure that both arrived at was £32,500 per annum. In a nutshell the proprietary interest cost considerably more money and returned far less in service than the provincial establishment. The contrast deepened discontent and disillusion.

—8—

One privileged element, the church establishment, was destined to play an unusual role during the administration of Governor Sharpe and indeed that of his successor. Since the restoration of their governmental rights in 1715 the Lords Baltimore had exercised their charter right of presenting clergymen of the Anglican Church to their livings. Parish vestries had no authority whatsoever in naming their rectors or in bringing them under discipline once they were appointed. Consequently the potential existed for tension among three parties who touched the clergy: the Lord Proprietor who appointed them, the Bishop of London who was the diocesan of all Anglican clergymen in the colonies, and the parishioners who paid them and looked to them for pastoral care. Shortly after the restoration of 1715 the Bishop of London had appointed a commissary or deputy, the Reverend Jacob Henderson, who for many years exercised some disciplinary authority in the bishop's name over the Maryland clergy. Henderson had struck at the immorality and corruption of a few clergymen who had given the whole body a bad reputation. But his powers were limited and in one of the most flagrant cases he found himself unable to remedy the evil complained of. In 1731 the vestrymen of St. Paul's Parish in Baltimore County complained that their rector, the Reverend William Tibbs, had actually moved out of the parish, installing as his clerk a convicted felon who read the service including the final absolution which could be pronounced only by an ordained priest. Tibbs refused burial to several parishioners and seldom came to the church to administer the Lord's Supper. Apprised of these "enormities," Henderson could do no more than write the Bishop of London underscoring the vestry's complaint, with the added observation that in forty years Tibbs had "lived to Scandal to the holy Function in Drunkenness, cursing and swearing, Fighting and quarrelling."

After Henderson's time the office of commissary lay vacant for twenty years. An unresolved dispute between Lord Baltimore and the Bishop of London prevented appointment of a successor. Accordingly the clergy of Maryland had no local head and held no provincial assemblies to discuss church affairs until the arrival of Sharpe. Against this background the "self-moved" meeting of fifteen churchmen less than a fortnight after Governor Sharpe's arrival is of special interest.

The gathering at Annapolis on 22 and 23 August 1753 included fewer than half the incumbent rectors of the province. Precisely who took the lead in assembling even this number of Maryland divines is not clear, but the act itself attracted some unfavorable comment from the provincial secretary, Edmund Jenings, who expostulated with Thomas Bacon, duly elected clerk and recorder of proceedings. Such unauthorized assemblies looked ominous to proprietary officialdom. Actually the chief business transacted was innocent enough: formal addresses to the Lord Proprietor and the new governor. To his Lordship the clergy promised their utmost endeavors to promote "Piety and good Morals and to cultivate a firm and lasting Harmony between the numerous Inhabitants of this flourishing Colony, and those to whom your Lordship shall think proper to commit the Administration of the Government." A congratulatory address to Governor Sharpe followed the same flowery rhetoric. Then the assembled clergy moved to other ground, an area always feared by officials like Jenings. The clergy petitioned the governor against a "certain Person, in holy Orders"— lately arrived in the province—who "labours under a most vile and scandalous Report" and begged that the governor defer inducting him into a living until his reputation could be cleared. Finally, before adjourning the clergy arranged to meet again in October to discuss church affairs.

A few days after the August meeting two leading divines, both men of exemplary lives, wrote a joint letter to the Bishop of London. Their tone was serious and doubtless an indication of the direction some of the clergy were prepared to go. Hugh Jones of St. Stephen's Parish, Cecil County, and Henry Addison of St. John's Parish, Prince George's County, reminded the bishop that Lord Charles, father of the present proprietor, had inducted unworthy clerics in the past with dire consequences to the reputation of the established church. The Roman Catholics had made inroads among provincials, and "the Enthusiasts and Schismaticks, rambling up and down the Provinces have too much prevailed on the wavering & ignorant." Jones and Addison thought the remedy a commissary with "coercive power over the profligate and refractory Brethren, so we may be no longer a Body without a head." They urged the bishop to take steps in this direction.

The October meeting attracted an even scantier attendance. On the Sunday preceding the session the Reverend Thomas Cradock (1718–1770) of St. Thomas Parish, Baltimore County, preached in Annapolis one of the most courageous sermons of prerevolutionary Maryland. Cradock opened by telling his audience that he could remain silent no longer. He recalled to his audience the lives of two notorious ministers, "monsters of wickedness," in the Maryland church. One had fallen into the fire when drunk and burned to death; the other had almost certainly been guilty of murdering his wife, though he had gone unpunished. Many of the profligate clergy were now dead and he prayed that their likes would never be given parishes again. The only security against repetition, Cradock continued, lay in some form of discipline. He declined to specify a form of discipline, but he did speak at some length of the movement to establish an American bishopric. Turning to the condition of religion among the people, Cradock pointed out the gains made by Catholics and dissenters. But the real enemies, he claimed, were those who "make a jest of the Christian scheme" and who "*laugh* at the *Bible* as fit only for the amusement of old women and children." Only godly men could deliver the necessary counterstroke: "I dare say there are but *few* in this audience but must have observed, that the people, especially the lower classes of them, have been better or worse, more or less religious, according to the conduct of the pastor they had."

Cradock's sermon created consternation in proprietary circles. It put responsibility for irreligion squarely on unsound clerical appointments of the Lord Proprietary. Thomas Bacon, surely one of the most responsible of Maryland clergymen, expressed shock as he described Cradock's performance for the information of the proprietary court: "A Sermon of a very extraordinary Nature, tending to prove, from known Facts, the absolute Necessity of an Ecclesiastical Jurisdiction over the Clergy here, and recommending the same to the Consideration of the Legislature." Without actually saying as much, Cradock clearly had in mind some sort of representation to the Assembly by the meeting of clergymen. But his brethren proved less bold, particularly Bacon, who kept the meeting from organizing formally and consequently prevented any action by the clergy as a body. After nearly two days of maneuvering, about half the clergymen present took their case to the Committee of Aggrievances, while the remainder presented a memorial to Governor Sharpe. No one dared rise to the level of Thomas Cradock in condemning evils in the church and pushing for their elimination.

To his credit Sharpe was sufficiently impressed to suggest some measure of discipline to the proprietary court. Secretary Calvert evasively replied that Lord Baltimore had in mind a plan to be elaborated at another time. In fact proprietary authority did nothing at all; Lord Baltimore and Secretary Calvert had no intention whatsoever of abridging their authority in clerical affairs. But without doubt the proprietary court disliked voluntary and unauthorized meetings of the clergy, and there were no more formal ones until the brief session in 1769 for the specific purpose of addressing Governor Sharpe on the occasion of his retirement.

An incident that occurred after Sharpe had been in office several years illustrated both the determination of the proprietary court to hold on to every shred of the prerogative and Sharpe's tenacity in carrying out proprietary orders, however distasteful. Sharpe had been familiar with scandal and difficulties in Coventry Parish, Somerset County, since his first year in the province. Even then the parish had long suffered from the ministry of one Nathaniel Whitaker, who, in Sharpe's words, "by his Sottishness and immoral behaviour had long been considered an intolerable Burden by his Parishioners." Sharpe told the Proprietor that Whitaker should be removed, but that there was no way to force him out. Consequently the fire smouldered until 1766 when Whitaker died. The vestry immediately invited Dr. Thomas Bradbury Chandler, a New Jersey clergyman, to come and preach for a trial period. Much impressed by Chandler's performance the vestry petitioned the governor to induct him. With a single eye for his instructions Sharpe refused and inducted instead the rector of a neighboring church, a man much like Whitaker in character.

The explosion that occurred in Coventry Parish sufficiently alarmed the rector Sharpe had named that he decided to remain in his present living. Thereupon Sharpe turned to the Reverend Thomas Hughes, whose reputation was almost as unsavory as the other two. When Hughes arrived revolt occurred: parishioners bolted and nailed the church against him and declared they would resort to force to disbar the unwanted cleric, justified "as we presume by the laws of God, nature, and man." The people of Coventry had moved to fundamental law in defense of what they considered their rights and from Anglican tradition to radical congregational church policy. Nevertheless they lost the day. According to Dr. Hughes's account, the opposition came from "the vestry men and church wardens in arms, (to the terror of some honest men and families,) with swamp men and shingle makers and the rest of their banditti, which they had been collecting for two days and nights." He had little trouble in persuading the council to authorize the attorney general to proceed against the leaders in the courts as violators of the public peace. Opposition quickly collapsed in the face of legal action. But the religious convictions, spontaneously declared and widely entertained, left their mark in the thought of the anti-proprietary forces.

—9—

It is one of the ironies of provincial history that Maryland hardly participated in the Great War for Empire during the term of the only governor with demonstrated military skill. Horatio Sharpe had served to the rank of captain in his Majesty's Twentieth Regiment, long enough to learn army traditions and more than a little of actual operations. For a brief interval in the early part of the war Sharpe had been commander-in-chief of British forces in the colonies, an honor that pleased him no end but that worked no magic on the Maryland House of Delegates. After two supply bills for the war, one in 1754 and the other in 1756, the Assembly steadfastly refused to vote funds for the war effort unless the Lord Proprietor paid his share. For protection of frontiersmen two tiny ranger companies, authorized for duty in the western parts, could do little enough in the vast area they tried to patrol. By law these soldiers could not leave the province. Thus even in the dark early years of war Maryland supplied neither troops nor money, despite the calls of desperation by imperial authorities in London and nearer at hand by Governor Sharpe.

In 1758 the fortunes of war changed dramatically. William Pitt, called to be his Majesty's first minister, infused Whitehall with some of his demonic energy and will to win. With a rough hand Pitt pushed aside incompetent seniors and in their places put talented achievers, young and hungry for battle and fame. Achievements of the two years following bordered on miracles as Pitt's handpicked leaders overcame the French around the globe: General Wolfe at Quebec, Jeffery Amherst at Montreal, Robert Clive and Admiral Pocock in India, Admiral Rodney in the West Indies. When George II died on 25 October 1760, Pitt was at the zenith of his power. No British statesman, not even the great Marlborough, had carried Englishmen as dramatically from humiliation to victory in all parts of the world. Maryland rejoiced and celebrated with the rest of the empire. Pitt was the idol of the day.

It remained for the new monarch, George III, to appoint the ministry that negotiated the peace. Haughty, imperious, brooking no contradiction, Pitt refused to share either warmaking or peacemaking powers with colleagues, and particularly with a new minister, Lord Bute, the king's favorite and advisor. Within a year Pitt resigned, but his hand was everywhere felt and his influence feared. And when England and France ended the long contest with the Treaty of Paris (1763), Canada and the trans-Appalachian west became part of the British empire, one of Pitt's war aims.

For Maryland peace meant respite from the incessant demands for wartime subsidies. More important it meant safe shipping lanes for tobacco, free of enemy privateers that had cost provincials dearly in captured merchantmen carrying home their staple crop. But the coming peace did not signal the end of controversy between province and Proprietor. The struggle continued with some surprising variations.

10

A SEARCH FOR DIRECTION

On Friday, 11 February 1763, Governor Sharpe called the Council of State into session to hear a dispatch from Whitehall announcing the signing of preliminary articles of peace. Only sixty-six days had elapsed since the ministry had made the same proclamation in London. News had traveled at a normal pace. The preliminary articles themselves witnessed to the realities of distance and contemporary communications by setting clear limits within which warlike acts would be recognized as legitimate: all vessels seized in the North Sea and English Channel more than twelve days after the proclamation would be restored; all seizures between those waters adjacent to Britain and the Canary Islands after more than six weeks would be restored; between the Canaries and the equator the time limit was three months, and beyond the equator six months. Ending global war in the day of sailing ships could be complicated and uncertain at best. Sharpe and the councillors immediately prepared the customary congratulatory address to the king before adjourning to drink the mandatory toasts to the king, to Pitt, Lord Jeffery Amherst, and others.

Five weeks later, in the seat of empire, two sons of Maryland met with somewhat less fellowship on the day church bells rang the tidings of the definitive peace, the Treaty of Paris. Both were to be leading figures in the next decades of provincial history. Daniel Dulany the Younger, recently appointed deputy secretary, was ending a two year visit to England for recovery of his health and more than incidentally to cement relations with his superior, the aging Cecilius Calvert, secretary of Maryland. Charles Carroll of Carrollton (1737–1832) was completing a longer European tour, a course of study at St. Omer's in France topped off with informal attendance at the Inns of Court in London as the capstone of his legal training. Dulany, aged forty-one, was returning several calls twenty-six year old Carroll had made without finding his elder at home. What happened during the encounter is known from a single source, a vague letter the younger man wrote that evening to his father in Annapolis, with one point, however, crystal clear: Carroll took an instant dislike to Dulany. *"C'est un homme bizarre,"* he told his father. The chill followed both back to Maryland and lasted the rest of their days.

—1—

At the war's end the Maryland Assembly was not in session. Consequently one vital actor on the provincial stage had for the moment no voice. Councillors, in one aspect of their dual roles as advisers to the governor and as upper house of the Assembly in session time, could make pronouncements, issue manifestoes, and make themselves heard as they had done when they sent their congratulatory message to the king. But the elected House of Delegates—the "grand inquest" of the province—had a constitutional life and a voice only in those brief periods between the governor's summons to a session and his prorogation of a meeting.

During the war the lower house had successfully broadened its powers a trifle and had attempted an even larger role. One such effort, unexciting to follow in detail but important equally to the proprietary establishment and country party, brought the treasurers of the Eastern and Western Shores into a position of accountability to the lower house, specifically to its Committee of Accounts. The treasurers owed their appointments to the Lord Proprietor and accounted to him. But they also received certain funds for public use under the two early wartime acts which had appropriated for military purposes monies arising from the disputed fines and forfeitures and from the land tax. Under pressure Governor Sharpe had violated his instructions to pass these bills, but after 1756 he refused, with council backing, to accept other bills that went further in the direction of touching any prerogative matter. Nine times between 1756 and 1762 the lower house sent up supply bills, as regularly as Sharpe requested funds for the military, each bill levying on the incomes, either fees or salaries, of officials. Each time the upper

house, at Sharpe's behest, refused to acquiesce. Toward the end of the
war even Whitehall had become impatient with Maryland for continual
foot dragging. In 1762 the Earl of Egremont, secretary of state charged
with responsibility for the colonies, made the final demand on Sharpe
for military supplies with the blunt statement that his Majesty expected
"your Province will not Obstinately persist in refusing to comply with
their Duty to the King." Understandably delegates in the lower house
took umbrage at this passage when Sharpe used the letter to buttress
his oft repeated request for funds. But they stood their ground and for
the last time replied with exactly the same bill they had sent up so
many times before to meet exactly the same fate.

With the Assembly of 1762, Sharpe's schooling in Maryland politics
was complete. Doubtless the governor had hoped for a better issue
from the meeting. He had dissolved the preceding house in 1761 after
repeated failures to obtain supplies and had ordered new elections in
the late fall. As soon as he learned the results of the balloting he
observed optimistically that the country party had lost a little strength.
But the key popular leaders had returned, seasoned veterans after years
of opposition to proprietary authority: James Tilghman of Talbot
County, Edward Tilghman and Robert Lloyd of Queen Anne's County,
and Thomas Ringgold of Kent. In their own right these delegates had
estates that put them in the top bracket of wealth. Moreover they came
to the lower house with the votes of their compatriots, great and small,
solidly behind them. Accordingly they spoke with authority not easy
to gainsay when they interpreted the will of their constituencies, and
they did not hesitate to push the battle against the Proprietor and his
most august officers. When the usual military supply bill failed, the
leadership moved on two other fronts. First they offered measures
allocating to various public purposes the fines and forfeitures claimed
by the Proprietor as part of his prerogative and by the country party
as a proper object for legislative appropriation. Indeed some years
previously the House of Delegates had condemned proprietary collection of these monies as illegal, an infringement of the right that British
citizens have "of not being subject to any payments, whether they be
taxes, duties, imposts, fees, or under any other denomination whatsoever; but what shall be raised, settled, and appointed by laws to
which . . . they give their assent." Between this Lockeian assumption
and the authoritarian position of the proprietary element no compro-

mise was possible. The upper house rejected every proposal to allocate the fines and forfeitures to any public use whatsoever.

On the second front also the delegates had no success. Responding to instructions from their constituencies in the counties, the House of Delegates attempted to extend the jurisdiction of the county courts. For years, small planters had complained that creditors put them to enormous expense by hailing them into the provincial court for suits that could have been settled at half the cost in a county court. By their commissions county justices could try civil cases in which the value did not exceed 30,000 pounds of tobacco or £100 sterling.* But the provincial court had original jurisdiction in cases where the debt or damage was not less than 5,000 pounds of tobacco or £20 sterling. In practice creditors preferred the provincial court when the value under litigation came to £20 sterling or more, because, they argued, county courts displayed a notorious prejudice in favor of debtors, the decisions of county judges were often in error, and the attorneys practicing in the counties were undependable. The chief creditors of the province were merchants, the largest of them seated in Annapolis or surrounding Anne Arundel County very close to the provincial court. Proposals to raise the minimum value of debts or damages under the original jurisdiction of the provincial court even to £30, much less £50 or even £100 as some extremists proposed, would force large creditors to retain an attorney in each county where they had debts to collect. When their cases were heard at the provincial court they needed to employ only one, usually a leading member of the bar with a record of continual success.

The fundamental issue was centralization versus local justice. Delegates in the lower house, many of them county court justices, had every incentive to oppose centralization, all too apparent in the proprietary scheme of things from land revenues to the administration of justice. Session after session the lower house sent up bills innocently titled An Act For the Better Administration of Justice. Just as often the upper house refused its assent.

The end of the war took away the leverage of supply bills. At the meeting of 1762 Sharpe made his last fruitless annual appeal. Thereafter

---

*Considerably above the upper limit of Governor Seymour's day.

the lower house had to find another fulcrum for its effort to divert fines and forfeitures from the privy purse of Lord Baltimore to public use. The land tax, possibly the most unpalatable wartime measure to Baltimore, had expired by limitation in 1761. Accordingly, at the war's end the Lord Proprietor retained intact all of the rights he claimed.

On its side the lower house as the grand inquest of the province had not forsworn any of its objectives. During the war, unyielding opposition between upper and lower houses had prevented the passage of any legislation whatsoever, thus making several of these sessions technically "conventions" in contemporary parlance. Four of the ten meetings during war years had been conventions, fruitless but expensive to taxpayers. But some legislation was imperative, however great the hostility between country and proprietary. Even the tense session of 1762 passed thirty-four acts in response to provincial needs, many of them parochial: acts for the destruction of crows and squirrels in Baltimore county, for establishing a market at Chestertown on the Eastern Shore, for chapels of ease in several parishes, and such private bills as one for naturalization of Colonel Henry Bouquet, a Swiss commanding his Majesty's Royal American Regiment. All practical and needful, but no important principle was at stake. The time for fresh assertion of principle lay ahead.

—2—

The promise of peace after nine years of war proved chimerical. In May 1763 the first blows fell on British forts to the west in peculiarly savage warfare that quickly acquired the name Pontiac's Conspiracy. The Ottowa chieftain, Pontiac, had organized the western tribes in massive resistance to white encroachment and in retaliation for the abrupt termination of annual gifts, including powder and shot. Jeffery Amherst, his Majesty's commander-in-chief, had ordered these economies in spite of warnings from persons more familiar with Indian needs and feelings. Nevertheless he and his command had not expected either the violence or the efficiency of the Indian reaction. By July Pontiac's confederated tribes had seized all but the strongest western forts and threatened settlements as far east as central Pennsylvania. Fort Pitt, at the doorstep of western Maryland, was under attack.

Thomas Cresap sent back to the capital periodic reports of the new troubles. Cresap had become something of a personage in the west over the years, serving as a justice of the county court and more recently as delegate to the Assembly from Frederick County. He had unusually good sources of information from friendly Indians who stopped at his stockade for food in their marches to and from hunting grounds and when on the warpath. As often as he dispatched intelligence of Indians, Cresap sent bills for "entertaining" them on the ground that as host he spared other frontiersmen from spoliation. Even more sober than Cresap's reports, letters from observers in Frederick Town that were published in the *Gazette* painted a picture of horror and distress.

> Numbers of those who have betaken themselves to forts, as well as those who have actually fled, have entirely lost their crops, or turned in their cattle and hogs to devour the produce, in hopes of finding them again in better condition. . . . Many who had expected to have sold and supplied the necessities of others . . . now . . . see the fruits of their honest industry snatched from them by the merciless attacks of these blood-thirsty barbarians.

Not until mid-August was Fort Pitt out of danger and some of the pressure on western Maryland relieved. Colonel Henry Bouquet, now a citizen of Maryland, led his command from central Pennsylvania to the forks of the Ohio, narrowly escaping massacre at Bushy Run almost within sight of his goal. Once at Fort Pitt, Bouquet invited reinforcements to help him pursue the enemy beyond the Ohio. In response, Captain William McClellan organized a body of "forty-three brave woodsmen, besides officers, all of them well equipped with good rifles, and most of them born and bred on the frontiers of Frederick County" and marched them from Frederick Town on 3 October to Fort Pitt, to serve without pay. Nine days later, at the gates of Detroit, Pontiac asked for terms.

Pontiac's Conspiracy was more than a lurid episode that set the frontiers of Maryland and colonies to the north aflame. Amherst had sparked the burning and killing by his haughty refusal to pamper "pernicious vermin," as he called the Indians, with further gifts. His ill-timed decision grew out of the economic retrenchment that followed the coming of peace. England emerged from the war with the greatest trade empire in history. But at a price: the national debt had doubled since the beginning of the war. Annual budgets in the last years of conflict had reached nearly £20 million, a staggering amount to dazed taxpayers in Britain. Only by rigorous economy was the budget reduced to £13½ million in 1763. Then beyond economic problems, troublesome as these appeared, other concerns faced the king and Parliament: organization of the new American conquests—Canada, Florida, and the Mississippi valley—and the general defense of the empire.

There were those in Parliament willing to undertake the formidable tasks of organization and financing this unprecedented accumulation of territories and trade areas. A few voices had even before the war called for more rational policies, for reforms in the antiquated mechanisms of control. History has called them the imperial reformers, perhaps suggesting too cohesive a group and too much consensus. In actuality the reformers had no well-conceived program nor did they owe allegiance to a single chieftain. They were individual voices in and out of the ministries in a period notorious for political instability and for swift, sometimes unpredictable, changes in the cabinet. Any reformer attempting to bring rational solutions to the very real problems of empire after 1763 labored under an insuperable handicap.

Nevertheless plans were imperative, and in June of 1763 the Board of Trade under the presidency of the Earl of Shelburne made a report that became the basis for postwar organization and policy for the continental colonies of North America. A loyal follower of William Pitt, the Earl of Shelburne had considerable expertise in American affairs. He and the Board of Trade recommended the total cessation, for a time, of white settlement west of a line drawn along the crest of the Appalachian Mountains. Pontiac's Conspiracy gave point to the policy of keeping whites and Indians apart, and the king embodied the recommendation in the Proclamation of 1763 issued in October, just as the fighting ceased. As it happened, then, the first measure of the imperial reformers scarcely touched Maryland at all. The Proclamation line ran approximately thirty miles west of Fort Cumberland, the outermost defense post, and forty-five miles west of Cresap's stockade, the most remote settlement. Governor Sharpe and the land officers proceeded cautiously in approving grants to the west of Thomas Cresap's place. In the imperfect knowledge of western Maryland geography no one could be quite certain where the line ran. At the moment, however, few settlers cared to risk their scalps in the dangerous zone between Cresap's and the line.

In this posture of provincial and imperial affairs the provincial Assembly met on 4 October at the call of the governor. The immediate business in hand was renewal of the Tobacco Inspection Act now about to expire by limitation, but the country party used the session to test new tactics and strategy appropriate to peacetime conditions. From the opening day delegates in the lower house groped toward new formulae in the quest for initiative. By a sound instinct they chose to thrust toward a weak place in the proprietary armor, the license monies from ordinaries. During the war the lower house had appropriated these to public purposes, and Sharpe had acquiesced even though he had violated his instructions. At least there had been precedent for appropriating these funds, which a lower house committee estimated at £600, for popular causes. And a cause that public sentiment would support stood ready at hand: education. Early in the session the lower house readied a "College Bill" and promptly sent it upstairs. In two particulars the bill was exceptionable. First it converted to a college building the unfinished structure a few hundred yards northeast of State Circle, "Bladen's Folly," which Lord Baltimore had positively charged Sharpe to have completed as the governor's residence, its original purpose. Secondly, the bill appropriated the ordinary license monies to the support of the "seminary of learning" to be housed in the finished structure. To the surprise, no doubt, of Governor Sharpe the councillors sitting as the upper house split, three of them led by Daniel Dulany favoring the "College Bill." But the majority stood firm and declined to pass the measure.

Undaunted, the lower house had still another try. Early in the session Thomas Cresap left his seat as delegate from Frederick County to hurry west where new Indian trouble was brewing. Shortly, his express messenger brought back the disheartening news that "a party of Indians and Some Mischief they had lately done . . . hath thrown our frontier Inhabitants into the greatest Consternation." Furthermore, Cresap alleged, "Unless an Armed force be Speedily sent to their Relief Numbers of them will desert their Habitations and the frontier Settlement again become a Scene of Distress and Desolation." Immediately the lower house framed a "Frontier Bill" appropriating the license money. And again the upper house divided, but this time after an amazing pronouncement from Dulany. He flatly told his colleagues that "He had no Idea of a Right without a Remedy," adding that "he could not see how His Lordship could support any Claim or Pretensions to [the ordinary license money]." For all this display of legal argument from the foremost lawyer in the province, the upper house defeated the "Frontier Bill." In reporting Dulany's stand to the proprietary court in London, Sharpe penned an aphorism that contained a grain of truth:

> That he is fond of being thought a Patriot Councillor and rather inclined to serve the People than the Proprietary is evident to everyone.

In these first months of peace there were many uncertainties and ambiguities. The signs were not easy to read. If leading councillors took unpredictable stands, popular leaders of the country party eased away from the politics of irreconcilables. At the end of the session several pieces of legislation lay before the governor awaiting the great seal and his accompanying formula: "On behalf of the Right Honourable the Lord Proprietary of this Province I will this be a Law." The only really important one, the Tobacco Inspection Act, had passed after weeks of wrangling; the remaining thirty-three laws served useful purposes without touching major principles. Clearly the country party intended in the future to move further on matters that the Proprietor regarded as rights such as the ordinary licenses, and perhaps after that the fines and forfeitures. This appeared to be the direction of the anti-proprietary movement in the first year of peace.

For the literate planters of Maryland, political news came from two sources. The *Gazette*, published every Thursday at Annapolis by Jonas Green, carried columns of the "proceedings" of the Assembly and occasional essays or letters from local contributors. For doings outside Maryland, provincials depended on the *Gentlemen's Magazine* or other London journals and on political pamphlets that dropped from British presses by the score. Merchants and planters frequently asked their London correspondents to make a selection among the current pamphlets for inclusion with their orders of other goods. Not surprisingly

Maryland readers had fuller knowledge of affairs in Britain than they did of sister provinces to the north and south. To be sure colonial printers exchanged journals and occasionally Green picked up a newsworthy item from Pennsylvania or an even more remote province but without any system beyond personal fancy.

Understandably some of the early acts of Parliament directed toward reforming the machinery of the Old Empire passed almost unnoticed in Maryland. The impact, keenly felt in other colonies, had little effect on the province. Even earlier than the reform acts, such political explosions as the issuance of general search warrants, the writs of assistance, passionately opposed by James Otis in Boston, awakened no echoes in Maryland. The Sugar Act of 1764 which created a furor in New England, where smuggling was an integral part of commerce, made few waves in the Chesapeake. The Currency Act of the same year restricting unsecured paper money posed no problem in Maryland where the bills rested on the security of Bank of England stock.

But when Jonas Green announced the passage of the Stamp Act in the *Gazette* of 18 April 1765 he dramatized its threat with heavy black bars of mourning. Through the summer he kept up the sense of menace by weekly notices of the act, emphasizing the speeches against it and printing contributions from "Cato" and "Lycurgus," who branded it as impolitic and unconstitutional. Green's concern was real. The Stamp Act placed duties on newspapers, pamphlets, and legal documents of almost every description. Naturally these bore hardest on publishers and lawyers, who could not carry on business without paying a duty, even if they passed it on to their customers. As the summer went on the editor found excellent copy for the *Gazette*. Zachariah Hood, a small-time Annapolis merchant, had, it seemed, accepted the office of stamp distributor while on a business trip to London. Green printed the news in the form of a letter from a "Gentleman in London," who reported Hood as remarking that if his country was to be stamped, it might as well be done by a native. The incendiary letter touched off a demonstration led by Samuel Chase, a young lawyer recently elected to the House of Delegates. Chase and other "assertors of British American privileges" made an effigy of Hood, paraded it noisily through the streets of Annapolis to the executioner's lot just outside the city gates, where they hanged and burned it. According to the *Gazette* the dummy nodded penitently all the way to the gallows.

A few days later another demonstration with nothing of high jinx or comedy occurred, just after Hood returned from Britain. Under cover of darkness a mob of between three and four hundred rowdies descended on a small warehouse Hood had rented for storing and distributing the stamps and razed it to the ground. Feeling that his own hide was not safe, the frightened distributor hid for a few days before escaping to haven in New York.

Far the most telling blow against the Stamp Act came from the pen of Daniel Dulany the Younger, who like his father before him wrote a pamphlet at a critical stage of affairs. The Stamp Act was to take effect 1 November. On 10 October Jonas Green got out a spectacular issue of his paper headlined:

THE MARYLAND GAZETTE, EXPIRING
IN UNCERTAIN HOPES
of a Resurrection to Life again

He also advertised Dulany's pamphlet, without reference to authorship, under the resounding title, *Considerations on the Propriety of Imposing Taxes in the British Colonies, For the Purpose of Raising a Revenue, By Act of Parliament*. Known then, as today, under the more manageable title, *Considerations*, it was an instant success.

Dulany argued on ground he had long since mastered in studies at Cambridge and the Inns of Court prior to his call to the bar of the Middle Temple, the British constitution. "It is an essential principle of the *English* constitution," he began, "that the subject shall not be taxed without his consent." This proposition granted, the Stamp Act could proceed only on the assumption that in some way Americans had consented to the levy, presumably by "a *virtual*, or *implied representation*" in the House of Commons that had levied the tax. It followed, then, that whether or not the imposition of the stamp duty was a proper exercise of constitutional authority depended on the answer to a single question: were "the commons of *Great Britain . . . virtually* the representatives of the commons of *America*, or not?" Once his logic was established Dulany turned to experience. In a few pages he demolished the sophistry that Americans could be represented in Parliament. "The notion of a *virtual representation* . . . is a mere cobweb spread to catch the unwary, and to entangle the weak."

Here with a suitable flourish in conclusion Dulany might have rested his case. But the gravity of the crisis prompted him to a fuller exposition of the imperial constitution. Two further questions required answers. Where were the colonies represented for tax purposes, if not in Parliament? And, what were the relations of the colonies to the mother country and her legislature? Dulany supplied answers to both. "The colonies have a complete and adequate legislative authority, and are not only represented in their assemblies, but in *no other manner.*" To those who argued that the assemblies were no more than corporations he retorted, "It is as absurd and insensible to call a colony a common corporation, because not an independent nation . . . as it would be to call Lake Erie, a *duck-puddle*, because not the Atlantic Ocean." Addressing the second question, Dulany explicitly denied that his doctrine freed the colonies of dependence upon England: "The subordination of the colonies, and the authority of parliament to preserve it, hath been fully acknowledged." But taxation of the colonies was not a proper exercise of that authority.

Finally Dulany had a recommendation to offer. To hasten the day of relief from an unconstitutional tax levied by an all-powerful Parliament he recommended constant but orderly protest and economic pressure. "We ought with spirit, and vigour, and charity, to bid defiance to tyranny, by exposing its impotence. . . . By a vigorous application to manufactures, the consequence of oppression in the colonies to the inhabitants of *Great Britain*, would strike home, and immediately."

The *Considerations* was an immediate success and Green announced a second edition three weeks after initial publication. Enterprising publishers to the north recognized a good thing when they saw it: John Holt printed an edition in New York and an unnamed Boston publisher another before the end of the year. Far the most flattering notice came from London where John Almon, dean of Grub Street, brought out two editions. Members of Parliament who opposed the Stamp Act quickly made Dulany's argument their own. William Pitt, in his famous speech for repeal in the House of Commons in January 1766, repeated the reasoning, and some of the language, of the *Considerations*. Lord Chief Justice Camden followed Pitt's example in a speech to the House of Lords. The proprietary court took notice that Camden's speech for repeal was based on the *Considerations*, which had appeared in London under Dulany's name.

In Maryland it appeared that provincials had accepted Dulany's counsel to keep opposition within lawful bounds. After the September riots cooler heads prevailed. The council and members of the bar prevailed upon Sharpe to convene the Assembly, which immediately appointed delegates to the Stamp Act Congress meeting in New York in early October to protest parliamentary taxation. For a time thereafter quiet prevailed. On 1 November, the effective date of the Stamp Act, business in the courts and proprietary offices came to a halt, and the *Maryland Gazette* ceased publication. No stamped paper for use in Maryland had arrived, and without it neither printing nor legal processes could proceed.

Late January, however, brought a certain restlessness. News came to Maryland that courts in the northern colonies had reopened without stamped paper. In Frederick County the clerk of the county court had begun issuing writs without stamped paper at the order of the justices. Then on 30 January Jonas Green ventured an issue of his paper headed *The Maryland Gazette Reviving*. Three weeks later he resumed regular Thursday publication. A few days after Green began printing again the "principal gentlemen" of Baltimore County met to form a "Society for the Maintainance of Order and Protection of American Liberty" whose members called themselves "Sons of Liberty." At the meeting the Sons issued an open invitation to other counties to form similar associations and to send delegates to a provincial congress for the purpose of requesting the opening of all governmental offices. Then without waiting for counties to organize, the Baltimore Sons resolved to assemble at Annapolis on Friday, 28 February, to demand opening of the courts. Before they arrived Samuel Chase and another active young politician, William Paca, frequently mentioned as a rising star, had organized the Sons of Liberty in Anne Arundel County. Together the Baltimore and Annapolis Sons confronted Dulany, the provincial secretary, and other officials demanding replies in writing to their resolutions calling for the resumption of public business. Though the Sons of Liberty were not fully satisfied with the responses, they published them in the *Gazette* and saw to it that all the counties received copies.

Out-of-doors politics as practiced by the Sons of Liberty did not go down easily with everybody. Young Charles Carroll of Carrollton, recently arrived home from the Inns of Court, observed caustically that the doings of the Sons grew out of "ignorance, prejudice, and passion."

Clearly, he thought, "The scheme of opening the offices seemed to the most thinking men of the town, improper at this juncture." Dulany had said to his colleagues on the council: "In Proceeding to Business at this Time I should act against my own Sentiments." He had, nevertheless, given the Sons a diplomatic answer. But the Sons gathered strength as their numbers increased during March, and on 1 April they demonstrated in Annapolis to persuade the justices of the provincial court to proceed to business. The *Gazette* told readers that the meeting went off with "utmost decency." The further statement that the Sons acted with "united hearts and voices" gauged the determination and force of a new factor in Maryland politics. Four days later news that Parliament had repealed the Stamp Act reached Annapolis.

—4—

Repeal of the obnoxious stamp duty brought a season of rejoicing in Maryland. In the counties, celebrating provincials gathered to drink the health of George III and the Protestant House of Hanover and to propose patriotic toasts: perpetual union between England and the colonies, "May the Submission of America to the Mother Country be ever Compatible with her Constitutional Liberty," and similar aphorisms. Someone started a subscription to erect a monument to William Pitt for "service done to this province and continent, and the lovers of liberty in general." The Assembly proposed to erect a marble statue of Pitt at Annapolis and to commission a portrait of Lord Camden for the provincial court.

Thoughtful men, however, recalled with some concern the brash behavior of a radical element that had tasted success during the brief paralysis when offices had closed. Daniel Dulany, now at the height of popularity for his contribution to repeal of the Stamp Act, had cautioned moderation and prudent behavior within the constitution. Charles Carroll of Carrollton said outright that suspension of public business had been burdensome but not unbearable and judged the desperate actions of the mob unnecessary. Across the water British merchants left no doubt about their convictions: "intemperate proceedings of the Sons of Liberty in Maryland" had embarrassed their efforts to persuade Parliament to repeal the stamp duties. The *Gazette* published their letter. Now that the Stamp Act crisis had passed, the time was obviously ripe to settle some of the issues that had embroiled provincial politics for decades.

At bottom the question that had split provincials into court and country grew out of the settlement of 1733. Lord Baltimore's coup had been a naked exercise of the prerogative, an assertion of his charter rights as he saw them. His physical presence in the province with all the palatine regalia had for the moment silenced, perhaps overawed, effective opposition, particularly after the understanding that brought Daniel Dulany the Elder into his camp. When the country party revived on the threshold of King George's War, the new leaders questioned every article of Baltimore's settlement: his authority to establish officers' fees unilaterally and his appropriation of the tonnage duties, the export duty on tobacco, the fines and forfeitures, and the license money from ordinaries. Through two wars, beginning in 1739 and ending with the Peace of Paris in 1763, the country party had questioned the settlement of 1733 chiefly by making "his majesty's service and his lordship's interest clash," in Sharpe's astute formulation. Neither side gave way in the politics of irreconcilables, the stalemate that had frustrated military supply bills throughout two wars, the "College Bill," and the "Frontier Bill."

As yet no one had commented—at least publicly—on the curious resemblance between the proprietary revenues imposed by Baltimore's fiat in the settlement of 1733 and the taxes Parliament laid on Maryland and the other colonies by the Stamp Act. But the similarities were there, including the resort to out-of-door politics, those violent gatherings unsettling to conservative minds of the elite who had prospered under the status quo. A disturbing incident, reminiscent of mob action against the Stamp Act, had in fact occurred during the tense winter of 1765–1766 while sensibilities were inflamed by the menace of parliamentary taxation. Men from the western parts of the province had actually threatened an armed march on Annapolis to put an end to the impasse that had long held up public business. At least so the rumor went.

The problem that had halted legislation was at once simple and severe. For years the "Journal of Accounts" with payments to all public creditors had failed to pass because at each session the lower house had refused to include the salary of a single man, John Ross, clerk of the council. Country party leaders argued that the clerk was an instrument of the prerogative and consequently not entitled to public funds. They had used the same argument back in 1756, when they had deprived council members of pay for their services while meeting as his Lordship's Council of State, as distinguished from the days spent as legislators in the upper house during sessions of Assembly. With the councillors' pay disposed of, they had turned to eradicate the clerk's salary, the last vestige of public payment to "instruments of the prerogative," as they put it. Meanwhile every public creditor had suffered, the rich who could bear the burden as well as the poor who could not. One Bayard Veasey was still, ten years later, waiting payment of £30-3-3 due him for messenger service in November 1755 during an Indian alarm in Lancaster, Pennsylvania, and Baltimore County.

To this colorless controversy, the kind that usually dragged out endlessly, irascible old Thomas Cresap brought his special brand of political science. Openly talking about direct action, Cresap saluted the lower house as that "renowned ancient true" Roman Senate, the guardian of liberty. Captain Evan Shelby of Frederick County testified under oath that between three and four hundred westerners with guns and tomahawks had gathered at Frederick Town to elect officers and "march down in Companies to Annapolis in Order to settle the Disputes betwixt the two Houses of Assembly in Relation to passing the Journal." Imaginations ran riot in the capital as the citizenry and the Assembly awaited invasion. But in the showdown a mere handful of peaceable citizens from the "upper parts" drifted in to petition rather than intimidate. Provincials breathed easier.

The potential nevertheless existed for the intrusion of out-of-doors politics into the continuing antagonism between country party and Proprietor. The self-appointed agent to prevent such a contretemps was Daniel Dulany, whose laurels from his role as champion of America in the Stamp Act were still fresh. And he turned in an extraordinary performance. Just ten days before the Assembly met in May of 1766 Dulany published his second pamphlet, *The Right to the Tonnage*, forty pages of massive prose. Without so much as a side glance at other issues, Dulany focused solely on the revenue question. He proposed to show, he told his readers, that Lord Baltimore had an "undeniable right" to the duty of one shilling per hogshead on all exported tobacco, that the tonnage duty had always belonged to him, and that his claim to the fines and forfeitures was consonant with English practice and the common law. In format *The Right to the Tonnage* followed the lines of the lawyer's brief, copious extracts from the statutes cemented together with explanatory remarks, wholly lacking in the sparkle and bright rhetoric of his earlier pamphlet.

Dulany's legal reasoning led to a distasteful but incontrovertible result, namely that Baltimore did indeed have a right to the revenues he claimed. Not many provincials outside the proprietary establishment applauded the pamphlet, but the lower house of the Assembly for the first time in years refrained from the usual rhetoric attacking proprietary claims to these monies. The quiet took on an ominous tone, however, when the delegates named a committee "to consider and report by what Law or Custom" the Lord Proprietor received his revenues; in other words, to critique Dulany's pamphlet.

While provincials were negatively impressed with *The Right to the Tonnage*, the proprietary court was delighted to have such a champion. It was also softened up for an argument the author was to make in the upper house: to permit appropriation of the license monies for public purposes. Dulany chaired a special committee of the upper house to draw up an argumentative address to Lord Baltimore requesting him to relinquish his claim to these funds. At long last Baltimore yielded after confessing that he had never really understood the matter at all. Thus an issue that had kept upper and lower houses at loggerheads for years disappeared.

Almost simultaneously an agreement by upper and lower houses on the clerk's salary paved the way for passing the long-delayed Journal of Accounts. The houses agreed to submit the question to the king-in-council for a decision that would be binding. Meanwhile the lower house prepared the Journal and drew up an act for paying public claims by issuing bills of credit. The public debt stood at 5,623,499 pounds of tobacco and £19,841–1–2 currency, which together equalled £32,992–15–2 sterling, according to lower house estimates. For the first time the Assembly assigned a new monetary unit to the new currency, the dollar, at the rate of four shillings sixpence per dollar. The act provided for a total emission of 173,733 dollars in bills of various denominations, all secured by Bank of England stock in the hands of the trustees in London. Within less than two months the paper money office had disbursed 145,801 dollars to hungry claimants, some of them unpaid creditors of ten years standing.

For the moment appearances seemed more promising for rational methods of settling questions at issue between province and Proprietor. The two sides had made a beginning by disposing of two sources of friction: the ordinary license monies were now in principle adjudged public funds for appropriation by the Assembly in the future, and the Journal of Accounts had passed once the clerk's salary was removed for ultimate decision by the crown. Moreover the new paper money had speedily liquidated the hitherto frozen assets of public creditors and put fresh bills in circulation to ease the shortage of specie hitherto pinching commercial transactions. On the negative side the larger issues of the tonnage, the export duty on tobacco, and the fines and forfeitures remained, at least in Dulany's adroit analysis, the right of the Lord Proprietor but of doubtful legality to the lower house committee now ready to begin its work. But the signs pointed to negotiation in camera rather than demonstrations out-of-doors.

—5—

A young Virginian visiting Annapolis during the spring of 1766 left a unique account of a lower house session during these months of transition when the Assembly was developing the new method of settling formerly irreconcilable differences. Aged twenty-three, Thomas Jefferson saw nothing impressive about the lower house "sitting in an old courthouse, which, judging from its form and appearance, was built in the year one." As he approached he was astonished "to hear as great a noise and hubbub as you will usually observe at a publick meeting of planters in Virginia." Surprises were only beginning.

> The first object which struck me after my entrance was the figure of a little old man dressed but indifferently, with a yellow queue wig on, and mounted in the judge's chair. This the gentleman who walked with me informed me was the speaker, a man of very fair character, but who by the bye has very little the air of a speaker. At one of the justices' bench stood a man whom in another place I should from his dress and phis have taken for Goodall the lawyer in Williamsburg, reading a bill before the house with a schoolboy tone and an abrupt pause at every half dozen words. This I found to be

the clerk of the Assembly. The speaker was Robert Lloyd of Queen Anne's county, a leader of the country party.

But the membership genuinely astounded Jefferson.

> The mob (for such was their appearance) sat covered on the justices' and lawyers' benches, and were divided into little clubs amusing themselves in the common chit chat way. I was surprised to see them address the speaker without rising from their seats, and three, four, and five at a time without being checked. When a motion was made, the speaker instead of putting the question in the usual form, only asked the gentlemen whether they chose that such or such a thing be done, and was answered by a yes, sir or no, sir.

Nurtured on the decorum of the Virginia Burgesses, Jefferson found nothing to admire about the informality and lax procedure of the House of Delegates. But even in their unsatisfactory housing, which was to be rectified a few years later by a handsome new statehouse, the delegates could rise to heights of punctilio when occasion demanded.

—6—

At the very time when proprietary establishment and country party seemed ready for more harmonious relations, the Lord Proprietor chose to exhibit a callous side, offensive to provincials. In late 1766 Baltimore's crony, Bennet Allen, an Oxford graduate in holy orders, appeared in Maryland with a letter directing his induction into the best vacant living available until a really choice pulpit opened up in one of the rich parishes. Baltimore's orders had been explicit enough and the new principal secretary, Hugh Hamersley, who had succeeded to the post on the death of Uncle Cecilius in 1765, confirmed them, attributing the intimacy between Allen and the Proprietor to "a Similitude of their studys." In fact Allen had made his living "by pandering in the press to fashionable vices" and the sum total of his so-called studies consisted of a slender book of verse that reviewers appraised as "vile, fawning, and slavish flattery," "gross and unmanly," and "low and contemptible."

Allen chose St. Anne's church, not two hundred yards from State Circle, as a stopgap while he waited for the incumbent of a wealthy parish in Prince George's County to die. Parishioners of St. Anne's shortly discovered to their dismay the real Bennet Allen. He drank to excess. Word went around that his sister, who had accompanied him to Maryland, was "a Sister to Him as Sarah was to Abraham." A variant view, contained in a crude satire that circulated in manuscript, attributed to him several conquests among "sweet pretty mulattoes, the yellow Damsels of An--p--s." The climax came when Allen challenged Sammy Chew, son of a wealthy merchant and stepson of Daniel Dulany the Elder, to a duel. Chew accepted in a quaint note that warned Allen, "I am determined that only one of us shall live to tell the tail." Allen's taste for physical combat disappeared when he heard that Chew—good as his word—had proceeded to the field of honor armed to the teeth. Allen hurriedly scribbled a note calling off the meeting because of bad weather and "the informality of the arrangements."

Even before this fiasco Allen was by common fame a freak. Now he made himself ridiculous by turning to the newspapers. Not only had he alienated the numerous and wealthy Chews, but he had come to blows with the powerful Dulany clan, who had at first treated him with lavish hospitality as a friend of Baltimore. The Dulanys had for months hoped that Allen would find his lucrative vacancy and open the way for appointment at St. Anne's of a rector who could also conduct a school for the boys of Annapolis, including their own sons. Walter Dulany, a vestryman of St. Anne's, had even found a candidate in the Reverend Jonathan Boucher, who ran a school in his parish in Caroline County, Virginia. Under the pseudonym, "Bystander," Allen lashed out in verse against the Dulanys and Chews with a quatrain that anticipated his Lordship's rebuke to these presumptious provincials.

> Too well, methought, you knew me, War to wage
> Raise my resentment, and defy my Rage;
> Whom Phoebus favours, Baltimore commends,
> The noblest Patron and the best of Friends.

Unabashed, a versifier for the Chews and Dulanys rejoined:

But, say not, Baltimore commends thy crimes,
Or weighs Men's Merits by their jingling Rhymes:
Strict Virtue oft, to others' Vice is Blind.
Suspicion dwells not in the noble Mind.

Through several issues of the *Gazette*, Walter Dulany's sympathizers, writing as "Querist," "A Plain Dealer," and "Tom Fun," published hilarious bits ridiculing "Bystander" before the exchanges descended to common mud-throwing. Then abruptly the feud ended when the death of the Reverend Thomas Bacon left vacant the immense western parish, All Saints, in Frederick Town, said to be the most lucrative in the entire province. Allen asked Governor Sharpe for the living and departed without delay, letter of induction in hand.

Allen's conduct in Frederick County surpassed anything provincials had ever witnessed and carried his infamy all over Maryland. In his haste Allen arrived on the day of Bacon's funeral. Advised that the parishioners planned to petition for a division of the huge parish, he wheedled the church keys from the sexton's serving maid, entered the sanctuary, and performed the whole ceremony of induction—reading the Thirty-nine Articles and his letter of appointment—to an empty church. When the outraged vestry ordered the church doors bolted before Sunday service Allen rose before sunrise and, with the aid of a ladder, entered through a window. At the hour for services a delegation of parishioners entered and attempted to drag him from the pulpit. At this point, Allen later recollected, he shouted, "By God I would shoot him." The committee withdrew and joined the crowd outside to await Allen's exit with rocks in their hands. Allen's retreat did not end until he reached the safety of Philadelphia.

From Philadelphia, Allen replied to his critics in the *Pennsylvania Chronicle*. Specifically, he accused his opponents in Annapolis of raising the rabble in Frederick Town and of inciting them to violence. Walter took up the cudgels for his kinsmen, not in the public prints but in a vigorous letter to Hamersley, who was certain to share the contents with the Lord Proprietor. Walter's anger was still hot when one Sunday afternoon he encountered Allen, who had rashly returned to Annapolis. Walter quickly deprived Allen of his sword stick and caned him unmercifully before a crowd that quickly gathered, "staring, as well they might, at such a striking Novelty." Once separated by onlookers, Allen offered to prolong the contest by shedding his coat and shouting, "By God, I will box you," before his sister dragged him away.

News of Allen's misconduct finally destroyed every shred of respect for him in Maryland. His bizarre behavior in Annapolis and Frederick toward the humble and the highly placed left the Lord Proprietor no room for further countenancing his antics. Moreover Frederick, Lord Baltimore, was in no position to offend his faithful tenants. At the moment he had himself either gone into hiding or fled to the continent, no one knew certainly, to escape the consequence of the most disgraceful act of his tawdry career. He had, it seems, brutally raped a seamstress, a certain Miss Woodcock, "a beautiful young girl who upon examination proves to be of a creditable Family and unimpeach'd Character." The Woodcock family had scorned Baltimore's offer of a huge money settlement and his Lordship stood in jeopardy of criminal prosecution.

From his hideaway Baltimore gave provincials the word through his highly respectable principal secretary, Hugh Hamersley. According to Hamersley, Baltimore had once held Allen in esteem but "all his measures . . . particularly in Attacking his Lordship's best friends . . . his . . . Indecent outragious behaviour . . . at Frederick . . . have been ill calculated to encrease it." Baltimore had ordered Allen to retire to Frederick and keep his peace. With relief the people of Annapolis welcomed Jonathan Boucher as rector of St. Anne's and master of the school for boys.

The Bennet Allen sideshow had certainly reflected no credit on the Lord Proprietor, sponsor of the notorious parson. Provincials and their representatives felt strongly enough to set afoot a plan for regulating the clergy by a commission composed of laymen and divines, but the legislation was set aside by the Assembly temporarily for far more serious matters that threatened a second imperial crisis.

—7—

For the second time in as many years Parliament had ventured on the treacherous path of colonial taxation. Still hard pressed for funds to defray costs of the imperial establishment in America, particularly troops for protection against Indians and possible strikes by France, Parliament listened with interest to a scheme worked out by Charles

Townshend, Chancellor of the Exchequer. Townshend's idea was to raise a revenue without resort to the internal taxation of the Stamp Act. Briefly he proposed a duty on glass, lead, painters' colors, paper, and tea, to be collected at the water's edge in America for the specific purpose of supporting the American civil list. Such duties, Townshend explained, were by definition not internal and American colonists could not object to them. Parliament responded to his sophistry by passing this measure and two related acts, one reorganizing the American customs service and another giving admiralty courts greater flexibility. Altogether this legislation acquired the name, Townshend Acts, although Charles Townshend had actually died before passage of the last of the acts.

Reaction in Maryland paralleled the responses of provinces to the north and south. Opposition of the seaboard colonies came in two waves, first in petitions to the king asking relief from unconstitutional taxation, and later in the organization of associations to supervise a boycott of the taxed commodities. Communication among the colonies prefacing each swell was remarkable and gave considerable concern to British authorities, who exerted themselves to prevent concerted action in America. Threatened beyond all others by the Townshend taxes that fell heavily on trade, Massachusetts took the lead in both petitioning and forming associations. In June 1768 the Maryland House of Delegates took under consideration a letter from the speaker of the popularly elected house in Massachusetts. In defiance of Governor Sharpe's plea to disregard the letter, the lower house endorsed the Massachusetts communique calling it "expressive of duty and loyalty to the Sovereign" and "replete with just principles of liberty." Immediately afterwards delegates adopted their own remonstrance to the king against imposition of duties by Parliament. Sharpe, of course, prorogued the Assembly for its audacity after making a caustic comment on its contumacious behavior. His own face was red because he had written complacently to the Earl of Hillsborough that Maryland had not followed the example of the clamorous New England colony and that he expected no trouble from the Assembly.

As yet differences were confined to a war of words expressed in petitions and remonstrances, verbal thrust and riposte. The *Gazette* made the most of expresses from the north as well as local news. Jonas Green had died unexpectedly in April 1767, but his widow, Anne

Catherine, and her sons continued the press, which thereafter seemed even more identified with the country interest. Anne Catherine reprinted, as they appeared in the northern press, all installments of the *Letters of a Pennsylvania Farmer*, John Dickinson's contribution to refuting the constitutionality of taxes for the purpose of a revenue. Dickinson included some artful propaganda for those who wished to promote a community of interest among the American provinces: "They form *one* political body, of which *each colony* is a *member.*" The *Gazette* also had full coverage of Thomas Hancock's sloop *Liberty*, condemned in Boston admiralty court for smuggling.

Confiscation of the *Liberty* brought on the second and more ominous phase of opposition to the Townshend Acts. Within weeks Boston had formed a non-importation association, pledged to boycott dutied goods, and shortly New York, Philadelphia, and smaller ports had similar associations. The sense of alarm in Maryland and the warmth of provincial feeling found expression in the Poet's Corner of the *Gazette* which printed an effusion, beginning

"Come, join Hand in Hand, brave Americans all."

But the retaliatory boycott, though discussed in Annapolis and at county court sessions, did not come easily in a province so completely rural as Maryland. Not till 20 March 1769 did Baltimore merchants, under pressure from their Philadelphia rivals, sign an agreement. The Baltimore Association broke the ice. On 19 May the "merchants, traders, and gentlemen" of Anne Arundel County met at the courthouse and adopted a non-importation convenant that established a pattern for the other counties, which followed suit in subsequent weeks.

On 20 June a general meeting of forty-three "merchants, traders, freeholders, mechanics, and other inhabitants" from all the counties put the capstone on the structure. On behalf of the Anne Arundel County associators, Brice Worthington of the House of Delegates, James Dick of the mercantile firm of Dick and Stewart, and two prominent lawyers, John Dorsey and Charles Carroll, Barrister, invited the counties to send representatives to Annapolis for the purpose of drafting a province-wide association. During three days of vehement debate the members hammered out an elaborate document, a preamble and nine articles spelling out details of a pact binding on every citizen.

After voicing the common feeling that the Townshend duties con-travened "the spirit of our constitution" and manifested a tendency to "deprive us in the end of all political freedom," the agreement went on to ban not only the taxed articles but, for stronger economic pres-sure, some 125 additional commodities ranging from textiles to hard-ware. The signers pledged themselves and their constituents to boycott any person who imported the forbidden goods or who raised prices above current levels on those in stock. Persons violating the agreement, whether signers or not, were to be considered "as enemies to the liberties of America . . . and treated with the contempt they deserve."

Printers of the *Gazette* joyfully hailed "that Bond of Union, The Association." Maryland had lagged behind provinces to the north in setting up machinery to enforce a boycott. But once under way in late March 1769 provincials had formed associations in the counties and finally the master association within twelve weeks. A participant later attributed this speed to the *Farmer's Letters*, which had opened Maryland eyes to dangers inherent in the Townshend Acts. Nearly two centuries later a careful scholar denied that Dickinson's *Letters* attracted much attention in Maryland and cited opinions expressed in other colonies that Marylanders were asleep. Actually provincial leaders had been slow to move for another reason. Their target had been the Lord Proprietor, the crown their hope for relief. Once awakened to impli-cations of the Townshend Acts, leading lawyers, merchants, and plant-ers quickly put their hands to the task of organizing effective oppo-sition. The Association was fathered by the elite: twenty-two of the forty-three signers were delegates to the Assembly. To be sure, the forty-three included freeholders and mechanics, less affluent and less prominent, but Assemblymen and merchants dominated proceedings and staffed the local committees. In effect, for purposes of managing the boycott, Maryland had formed an extra-legal government paral-leling the established government.

—8—

Enforcement of the Association proved both effective and smooth. The meetings of the "inhabitants," as the *Gazette* usually put it, elected to local committees the heads of leading county families, persons already accustomed to public business as justices, vestrymen, merchants, lawyers. Instances of enforcement came from every corner of the province and through the summer and fall were systematically reported in the pages of the *Gazette*. The capital city itself had an early case when the prominent mercantile firm of James Dick and Anthony Stewart bought some parcels of goods imported in the *Betsy*. Finding prohibited commodities among the bales they had purchased, Dick and Stewart proposed storing them in the warehouses of other merchants—their competitors—as custodians until repeal of the Townshend duties. The Anne Arundel committee approved. Other counties such as Charles, St. Mary's, and Talbot took tougher stands. In these counties local committees compelled consignees of prohibited articles to return them to Great Britain.

The crucial test of the Association and supporting public sentiment came in early February 1770. Later referred to as "The Case of *Good Intent*" the episode came to public attention when the brigantine, *Good Intent*, docked at Annapolis with a cargo valued at about £10,000 sterling consigned to some of the most prominent merchants on the Western Shore: Dick and Stewart, the partners Charles Ridgely and William Goodwin, William M'Gachin of Baltimore, another partnership of John Read Magruder and John Hepburn, and several others. All the merchants were located in three adjoining counties: Anne Arundel, Baltimore to the north, and Prince George's to the west. After discovering that the cargo contained prohibited goods, Messrs. Dick and Stewart, among the biggest consignees, requested a joint committee of representatives from each of the three counties to examine the matter.

If Dick and Stewart, or any of the others concerned, thought that some simple solution such as storing the prohibited goods would come out of the examination, they soon discovered their error. The committee of twelve, four from each county, proceeded as a true judicial tribunal: summoning witnesses, calling for documents, and cross-examining those who gave testimony. The merchants made no attempt to conceal their interests in the cargo. They entered the plea of extenuating circumstances, namely that they had ordered the prohibited goods before the formation of the Association. Unfortunately for their case the merchants, and particularly Dick and Stewart, gave less than candid testimony and finally found themselves caught in downright misrepresentation when the committee members compelled Dick to produce a letter that clearly contradicted his oral replies to questions already put to him. By the end of the examination a majority of the committee had concluded that the bulk of the importations violated the letter and spirit of the Association. By a vote eight to four the *Good Intent* was sentenced to return to England without breaking cargo. The merchants asked to store the goods as they had done once before. Even the governor intervened to the extent of showing a letter from Hillsborough promising early repeal of the Townshend Acts. But the committee held firm and on 27 February the *Good Intent* sailed for London, exposed to possible confiscation for not unloading and the certain monetary loss to her owners for a profitless voyage.

Originally the committee had proposed to publish its proceedings in the *Gazette* but after compiling the record with supporting documents found it too long for the newspaper. Instead Anne Catherine Green printed an abstract only in the *Gazette* and published separately as a fat pamphlet *The Proceedings of the Committee Appointed to Examine into the Importation of Goods by the Brigantine* Good Intent . . . *from London, in February 1770.* Distributed to all the counties, this full account familiarized provincials with procedures of the extralegal body that had carried out the will of the people when established agencies were unable to act. Equally important, the text included a philosophical justification for the resort to extra-governmental machinery to express the popular will. Though widely applauded, this doctrine profoundly troubled conservative minds. Without fiery rhetoric the author, or authors, of the pamphlet had taken a line of argument that, followed through all its implications, smacked of revolution.

Marylanders had lagged behind colonies to the north in forming the Association. But once they adopted the boycott and set up enforcement machinery they clung to their handiwork even after their northern neighbors dropped theirs. In 1770 Parliament did, as Hillsborough had promised, repeal the Townshend duties with the single exception of the tax on tea. Baltimore merchants had taken the lead in the boycott; now in the autumn they moved to trade freely with Great Britain again as the colonies to the north were doing, except of course in tea which was still dutied. After some protest other counties followed suit and by the year's end provincials had reverted to former commercial habits. But the Association had marked new levels of political consciousness and opened to speculative minds new dimensions of thought and protest.

—9—

Twice after the end of the French and Indian War imperial crises had diverted provincial attention and energies from purely local concerns, though never completely. Every legislative session had called for commonplace acts to relieve languishing prisoners for debt, to establish chapels of ease, to naturalize foreign born, or to make good some deficiency in a will or contract. Even the antagonism between Lord Proprietor and country party over larger issues had surfaced in every session of Assembly without, however, noticeable progress toward reconciling opposing views. With the easing of the Townshend crisis, provincial affairs, economic and political, again moved into the mainstream of thought and action.

The province entered the post-Townshend era with not only new and heightened perceptions but with important changes in leadership. On the proprietary side Governor Horatio Sharpe, who had presided sixteen years as chief magistrate, stepped aside to make a place for Robert Eden (1741–1784), brother-in-law of Frederick, Lord Baltimore. Throughout his long and difficult tenure during the war and two imperial crises Sharpe had at once served the Proprietor faithfully and maintained the respect of even his sworn opponents. On 5 June 1769 he turned over the great seal to Eden and retired to his country seat, Whitehall, an hour's sail from the capital, where he remained until 1773 before returning permanently to England.

Within provincial ranks as well new leaders were emerging. Elections in December 1767 had brought twenty-six new delegates, almost half the total membership, into the lower house. Stalwarts of the country party such as John Hanson, Thomas Johnson, Samuel Chase, and their likes held their seats and gained fresh voting strength from the new faces, many of them committed beforehand to anti-proprietary policies. Among the new recruits William Paca of Annapolis and Matthew Tilghman* of Talbot, both with brilliant futures ahead, had already shown the direction of their thought. Tilghman had explicitly

---

*Tilghman had served as delegate some years before but had not been a member of the Assembly immediately preceding the election.

told a correspondent that he constantly ruminated on the question of freedom or slavery for America. "I revere," he wrote, "the spirit of the northern people, and am clearly of opinion that they are right in their warm and unrelaxing opposition" to oppression from overseas. The outlook of such provincial spokesmen promised no easy road to Governer Eden and his superiors.

In search for direction after the war provincials and their leaders made important discoveries. They found new issues. They also found new and potent weapons: out-of-doors politics and extralegal organizations responsive to popular will.

11

THE CONTOURS OF FREEDOM

The last half decade of provincial history, the years 1770–1775, surprises anyone who expects to find the steady growth of a revolutionary
spirit. An internal crisis—the "fee controversy"—in 1770 reemphasized
to provincials who really needed no reminder the inequity and perhaps
the iniquity of the proprietary regime. But though sharp, the crisis
passed and was succeeded by a calm so profound, on the surface at
least, that one lively provincial complained to an English friend: "This
is a dead time with us. Politics are scarce talked of." Charles Carroll
of Carrollton had a reasonably good sense of the public pulse, but he
fell short of infallibility. Surface excitement he would have noticed;
deep running currents he sometimes missed or ignored. Certainly newcomer William Eddis sensed nothing unusual until almost mid-decade
when the sudden vehemence of public protest astounded him. Between
1770 and 1774 Eddis wrote pleasant descriptions of the Maryland scene
to his friends in England, hardly suggesting the wrath to come.

—1—

The fee controversy, as it came to be called, initiated Governor Robert
Eden into Maryland politics. When Eden received the Great Seal of
Maryland from Sharpe in 1769 he was just short of his twenty-eighth
birthday, and his entire political career lay ahead. Second son and
namesake of Sir Robert Eden of Durham, Eden had held a captaincy
in the Coldstream Guards and had seen service in Germany during the
Seven Years War. After the war he had married Caroline Calvert, sister
of the Lord Proprietor, in a ceremony performed by Dr. Gregory

Sharpe, Governor Sharpe's elder brother. As a member of the proprietary family with claims for support, Eden received the governorship, the most lucrative post in the Lord Proprietor's gift, almost as
a matter of course. Though youthful, he had good common sense and
uncommon personal charm that went straight to the hearts of the elite
of Maryland, who became his closest associates.

It is hardly likely that the new governor misunderstood the stakes
as the date for the expiration of the Tobacco Inspection Act drew near.
The act had been in force since 1747, periodically renewed by the
Assembly, and the principle of inspection had become an accepted,
even necessary, part of Maryland economic life. But inspection was
only a part of this omnibus act, which also regulated clerical incomes
and established officers' fees. The important question for the country
party had come to be the incomes of clergy and officers. Walter Dulany
had written as much to Hamersley, Baltimore's right hand man. "Great
reductions are talk'd of both with respect to the fees of the officers and
the revenues of the clergy, which they say must take place or the
inspecting act fall to the ground, which indeed, wou'd be attended
with terrible consequences to the whole province." Dulany had read
the cards right.

The Tobacco Inspection Act expired on 20 October 1770 while the
Assembly was discussing the terms of new legislation. Immediately
the question of collecting fees arose, now that the statutory right had
vanished. The lower house decided to make a test case when its Committee of Grievances learned that the clerk of the land office, one
William Stewart, had collected fees after the expiration of the act. The
house resolved that Stewart had violated the British constitution. The
right to enact taxes and fees lay entirely with the Assembly, and fixing
them by prerogative action—as Stewart had done implicitly by accepting the fee—was an oppressive act. In its most parliamentary
manner, the house directed its sergeant-at-arms to take Stewart into
custody and lodge him in the county jail until discharged by future
order.

The jailing, an act of deliberate political aggression, provoked immediate response. With the advice of the council Governor Eden prorogued the Assembly as a way of releasing Stewart, then reconvened
it directly afterward to continue necessary legislative business. When
the house complained that the interruption had been an extravagance,

a waste of public money, Eden retorted that the house had invited his action by jailing an innocent man. But clearly, constructive business had ended, and the governor dissolved the Assembly when the house ordered printed a committee report that showed the size of several major officers' incomes from fees: the secretary, between £1,000 and £1,500 a year, the clerk of the land office, upward of £1,800.

Immediately after the dissolution, Eden issued his fee proclamation of 26 November 1770. A brief document, the proclamation took the lofty position of defending the people against exorbitant exactions by officers: it simply ordered all officers to take no other or greater fees than those provided in the act just expired. Consequently the proclamation had exactly the same standing constitutionally as Lord Baltimore's original proclamation of 1733, which had been an exercise of the prerogative. Far from satisfying the delegates, the fee proclamation confirmed their dim view of proprietary government. But once dissolved, they had no further leverage.

—2—

Expiration of inspection provoked grumbling, and the fee proclamation brought acid comments about the cupidity of officers in pursuing fees. But provincials looked about for a practical solution to the real problem they faced. No one needed to read homilies to planters on the benefits that tobacco inspection had conferred on the economy over the past twenty-three years. In the first years of the act, Henry Callister, Eastern Shore factor of Foster Cunliffe and Company of Liverpool, had pointedly told his principal that inspection had been the "one grand cause of the rise and support of the Credit of Tobacco" and fully accounted "for the great prices given in Maryland and which appear so incredible to you." Once the lesson of good prices for quality tobacco had sunk in, Maryland planters had adjusted to the routine of inspection that culled out the trash so disastrous to prices in earlier years. Faced with losing the benefits of inspection, particularly the stable prices, planters and merchants fell back on reason and experience for a solution to their predicament.

Immediately after the close of the session, merchants and planters at the shipping centers, already accustomed to voluntary organization in restraint of trade, set up extralegal inspection. With applause from the *Maryland Gazette*, twenty-five "buyers of tobacco" at Port Tobacco agreed among themselves to maintain quality standards established under the recently expired act by purchasing only at stated times and only such tobacco as one of their number had inspected and approved. Planters along the Patuxent made a similar agreement, at Queen Anne's Town, at Upper Marlborough, and at Indian Landing. During the winter, shipping centers on both sides of the bay followed suit until a network of voluntary committees covered the prime tobacco counties. Since these committees left no records, the effectiveness of this popular participation in public affairs cannot be accurately determined, but the spirit impressed local observers, who made their views known through approving letters to the press. Only one writer distinguished himself by dissent and in support of his disapproval quoted Voltaire: "frequent associations of individuals are critical symbols of a sick commonwealth." He feared that extralegal inspection would lead to government by faction and would produce a "monster." Majority sentiment, however, heavily favored the voluntary associations. Provincials were gradually becoming accustomed to extralegal institutions running their affairs.

—3—

The continuing prosperity of the early 1770s appears most clearly in the business records of a new Maryland firm, Wallace, Davidson, and Johnson of Annapolis. All three partners had been in business separately in the city before concluding on 22 March 1771 an agreement that created the new firm. Charles Wallace (1727–1812), wealthy landowner and entrepreneur, had important connections that won him the contract for building the new Maryland State House, with the credit that went with this profitable project. John Davidson (1738–1794), also a merchant, supplied accounting expertise as bookkeeper for the trio. Youngest of the partners, Joshua Johnson (1742–1802) was descended from an established planting family in Calvert County, heart of the tobacco country. His older brother, Thomas Johnson, practiced law in Annapolis and was a leader in the country party.

Of the three, Joshua Johnson had the adventuresome career. It began soon after the partnership agreement merged all three businesses into one. According to plan, Joshua left for London in the spring of 1771 to represent the firm in its novel enterprise, nothing less than circumventing the British merchant houses that had traditionally supplied manufactured goods to Maryland. Johnson was to deal directly with manufacturers themselves, eliminating the London middlemen. His mission included purchasing goods for export to Annapolis, arranging freight, making payments for the firm's purchases, and in general securing to the partnership the advantages of independence from British correspondents, who of course exacted commissions for all these services. Johnson, then, acted only as London purchasing agent; the firm did not intend to consign tobacco to him for sale on the British market. Instead he took some £3,000 in bills of exchange drawn on Osgood Hanbury and Company as working capital of the London branch.

As the partners had hoped, Joshua Johnson received help from the influential Hanburys, who introduced him to the tradesmen-suppliers of hardware, woolens, and linens for American bound cargoes. With these introductions and his ready cash Johnson shipped goods valued at over £10,000 sterling the first year. Avoiding goods of inferior workmanship and shabby condition which had long plagued Maryland merchants unable to inspect the merchandise in advance, Johnson dispatched handpicked cargoes so pleasing in Annapolis that in the first six months of 1772 he expanded shipping operations to £16,000. He found British tradesmen and suppliers eager to do business with a buyer who had sound credit, and he discovered the mysteries of the trade much exaggerated.

The partners' Annapolis store, nevertheless, fell on hard days in late 1772, when the effects of bumper crops produced in successive years after 1770 made themselves felt. Several of the largest British houses, by extending too much credit to Maryland planters, brought on a "credit crisis" that continued on into 1773. Wallace and Davidson found sales slow and payments to their London partner difficult. Johnson wrote, to their dismay, that he fully expected to be arrested for debt and held "fast in some Damd Dungeon living on musty Mutton Chops." Moreover the Hanburys had cooled as the American firm's export business cut into commissions that the London house had enjoyed from shipping merchandise to Maryland for half a century. Accordingly the partnership decided, albeit with some misgivings, to embark on tobacco consignments to Joshua Johnson, even at the risk of antagonizing all the London merchants trading to Maryland. This change of policy created some new hazards for the firm. The partners lacked capital to extend credit to planters, who wished to draw bills of exchange as soon as their tobacco was shipped and, consequently, before the firm could realize any return from its sale. Moreover the two Annapolis-based partners had reasonable doubts that Joshua Johnson could compete with the wizards of tobacco marketing long established in London, though Johnson's letters contained reassurances. As he put it, "The great mystery made of the management and sale of tobacco has only been held up as a scarecrow to our countrymen to deter them from entering into the business."

The practical problem of capital the Annapolis partners solved by local borrowing. Over succeeding months they found a dozen lenders willing to advance £500 or more: Margaret Murdock, widow of a doctor in Prince George's County, £543; Mary Howard, Annapolis innkeeper, £785; Ann Tasker, widow of the late senior councillor, £6,308, almost half of what they borrowed. By mobilizing local money the firm tapped a rich vein, one that enabled them to borrow funds from, among others, rich widows unaccustomed to investing the wealth left them. The partners overlooked no source of capital: they borrowed £1,000 from the commissioners to build the church in Annapolis. Beyond this working capital the firm also enjoyed the boon of public credit, nearly £5,000, most of it through Wallace, who had advances from the state on his contract for building the new State House.*

Maryland capital and careful management of the company's business made a success of tobacco consignment. Between the fall of 1773, when they inaugurated the new policy, and the autumn of 1775, when Maryland adopted Nonexportation, the firm handled 4,475 hogsheads of tobacco, approximately 7 percent of the Maryland crop. Joshua Johnson reckoned the profit at £1 per hogshead. As business flourished, the partners opened stores at Nottingham and Queen Anne's Town in the Patuxent basin. The new stores yielded double profits: from com-

---

*Among other purchases, Joshua Johnson bought copper roofing for this imposing structure and forwarded it to Annapolis.

missions on planters' tobacco and from markups on store goods sold them, for planters in the countryside usually took their returns from tobacco in imported hardware, fabrics, and other commodities sold at the customary high advances over wholesale prices.

The Wallace, Davidson, and Johnson partnership was not unique. At least two other firms followed their example of sending a purchasing agent to London. It appeared as though a reversal of traditional arrangements might be in the making, a step toward commercial independence that had occurred to provincial minds as early as the hard times of the late 1720s. But one of the firms, Barnes and Ridgate in Charles County, could not weather the financial crisis of 1772–1773. The other, West and Hobson of Prince George's County, survived but never equalled the performance of Wallace, Davidson, and Johnson. Neither firm had the advantages of location in the capital city, a heavy consumer of the goods so carefully selected by Joshua Johnson for shipment home. Moreover the Annapolis partners enjoyed the patronage of such discriminating customers as Charles Carroll of Carrollton, reputedly the wealthiest man in the province. Carroll demanded—and received—personal attention to his tobacco crop and his needs for imported luxuries to adorn his family and his houses. "The attention you discover to my business," Carroll told the partners, "your readiness to oblige and the punctuality of your correspondence deserve my thanks."

Personal accommodation did not end with the rich. Lesser planters received a kind of attention they had not previously known from established London merchants, who knew them only as names on their books. The personal touch had meaning to many elements of a Maryland social order that had been evolving for generations. Johnson not only knew this society as a native son, he was prepared to indulge its tastes.

—4—

By the 1770s Maryland population had lost its almost uniformly British character. Besides the English, Irish, and Scots—ethnically different enough—who made up the predominant British element, extensive German immigration into the western parts had given that area a distinctive character. If not polyglot in the manner of New York, the population had considerable ethnic variety and, increasingly since about the year 1700, racial variety also, as importation of slave labor enlarged the percentage of Blacks in the total population.

But the most impressive aspect of the Maryland population was its growth since 1700*. In 1770 an estimated 200,000 persons, free and bond, inhabited Eastern and Western Shores, a sixfold increase during seven decades. Yet within this mass the social structure retained essentially the pattern already established at the turn of the century.

The most visible element, an elite of wealth, had traditionally provided leadership in politics and in business. Though never exclusive in the sense of disbarring new recruits from advancing upward to the top of the ladder, the community of wealth and talent had a strong sense of identity strengthened by common interests and reinforced by intermarriage among families within the charmed circle. The Lloyd family of the Eastern Shore, distinguished in politics since the days of Major General Edward Lloyd, the chief magistrate after the death of Governor Seymour in 1709, was related by marriage to the Tilghmans, the Chews, and the Pacas. Elder statesman Benjamin Tasker married his four daughters into prominent Chesapeake families: the eldest to Governor Samuel Ogle, and her sisters to Daniel Dulany the Younger, Christopher Lowndes of Bladensburg, and Robert Carter of Nomini Hall just across the Potomac in Virginia. Each daughter in turn founded a dynasty in her husband's name. The fact that Dulany's father had arrived in the province in 1703 as an indentured servant before success brought him riches created no obstacle to his son's alliance with the Taskers, among the oldest and wealthiest families in Maryland. After all, the elder Dulany had succeeded brilliantly as a lawyer, merchant, land-speculator, and iron manufacturer, but above

---

* Estimated Total Population

1700 — 31,000	1740 — 105,000
1710 — 43,000	1750 — 137,000
1720 — 62,000	1760 — 162,000
1730 — 82,000	1770 — 220,000

(Source: J. Potter, "The Growth of Population in America, 1700–1860," in D. V. Glass and D.E.C. Eversley, *Population in History* (London, 1965), pp. 631–679.)

The Edward Lloyd Family by Charles Willson Peale, 1771. Maryland born, Peale painted this canvas at age thirty shortly after returning from two years of study in London with Benjamin West, whose style is in evidence here. An early convert to the Revolutionary movement, Peale appropriately has as his subject in this earliest of his "family pictures," so popular in that age, a powerful Eastern Shore family that furnished leadership from the royal period through the Revolution. Courtesy, The Henry Francis du Pont Winterthur Museum.

all as a public official. He arranged marriages for his numerous children with leading men of the region: his son Walter to a daughter of the Graftons of Delaware, his daughter Rebecca into the Heath family of Cecil County, and Margaret to Dr. Alexander Hamilton, physician and wit of the Tuesday Club. A kinship chart of the first families has the appearance of a tangled net, with filiations that baffle the eye. The extreme case occurred in the second decade of the century when one of the prominent Addisons of Prince George's County became by marriage both brother-in-law and father-in-law to Richard, one of the leading Smiths of neighboring Calvert County.* Brice, Beale, and Worthington intermarriages resulted in a uniquely named descendant, Brice Thomas Beale Worthington.

Provincials had their own ways of designating status. Readers of marriage notices in the *Maryland Gazette* still found as of old some indication of dowries brought by brides as their portions in the suggestive phrases, "a handsome fortune," or "a plentiful fortune," and on occasion "a very plentiful fortune." But of course dowries—money or its equivalent in land and slaves—did not tell the whole story. Marriage alliances to highly placed provincials with patronage to provide places for other members of the family counted for something, however difficult to measure. Few were surprised when a bride's younger brother came into a lucrative clerkship or collectorship following her marriage to a leading provincial officer. Indeed among the first families the quest for place, preferably for a sinecure, never ended.

Loose phrases such as "ruling class" or "gentry," and certainly "aristocracy" do not properly describe the provincial elite. A noted scholar, Louis B. Wright, has styled it the "agrarian leadership," a more functional and accurate designation. Those who rose to distinction resemble textbook models of the work ethic, unremitting in their attention to planting and to enterprise, whether commercial or industrial. In their later years of affluence they did not lose touch with their less fortunate neighbors, whom they understood as planters because they themselves were not far removed from the realities and the vagaries of weather,

---

*Colonel Thomas Addison married Eleanor Smith, sister of Richard, and gave his daughter by an earlier marriage to Richard.

pests, and prices. In the ordinary round of duties the affluent, many of them lawyers, moved in the concourse of small planters at county court sessions where they heard local gossip and swapped ideas with all and sundry. Doubtless this common touch and a strong sense of responsibility to their constituents, who were mostly poorer freeholders, combined to win them the respect that tempts one to describe provincial Maryland as a deferential society. In sum the elite element of late provincial times remained, as it had been at the turn of the century, something less than a sharply defined class. Always a small fraction of the total planting families—about one in twenty or twenty-five—wealth alone did not define the elite.* Political leadership, social position, kinship, education, dress, and housing all figured in a complex equation perfectly understandable in a community accustomed to recognizing the earmarks of quality. These favored few were leavening in a population that had multiplied itself six times over in the seven decades of the eighteenth century.

—5—

The really massive growth in numbers, however, had occurred in those layers of population below the affluent elite. Economically the spectrum was broad, the bands ranging from the comfortably well-to-do with estates just below £1,000 down to marginal planters at the bottom worth no more than a few pounds. Their numbers created an immense market for consumer goods, their crops freighted outbound cargo ships,

---

* The one commensurable in determining status is wealth. The percentages below show both gross and net personal estates. Net personal estates, that is estates after the settlement of all debts and charges, represent real wealth. Gross estates obviously ran higher.

Estates Above £1000 (currency), Expressed as
Percentages of all Personal Estates Recorded

	Gross Estates	Net Estates
1710–1719	2.3	1.6
1730–1739	3.4	2.6
1750–1759	7.2	4.4

(Source: Inventories and Accounts, Maryland Hall of Records)

and in elections their votes decided the outcome. On their well-being and their imperatives rested the economic health and the political direction of Maryland in the Golden Age.

A natural division of this huge segment of planting families below the elite occurs at the line where estates were valued at £100. Most of the estates above £100 show one or more slaves.* In almost none of the inventories below £100 do slaves appear among the assets. These small planters, or yeomen as they are sometimes called, persisted into the Golden Age as an important factor in the economy as producers and in politics as voters.** As a fraction of the total planting families, non-slaveholders decreased from over two-thirds in the early years of the century down to well under half by the 1760s. This percentage decline can, however, be seriously misleading unless taken with general population growth. In absolute numbers households of petty planters—those with estates below £100—multiplied considerably.

In lifestyle the poorer planters closely resembled their counterparts of the late seventeenth and early eighteenth centuries. They lived in the same primitive houses, furnished with the barest necessities. Merely to say that these families had gross personal estates less than £100 does not clearly indicate how close to the margin most of them lived. In the decade 1750–1759 exactly 1,002 estates below £100 came to probate. Fewer than half had livestock, tools, and furniture worth

---

* There are of course exceptions. For example, by the 1750s few Quakers, even the richest, held slaves.

** The trend over the preceding half century appears in the following tabulation:

Gross Estates Below £1000 (currency), Expressed as
Percentages of all Personal Estates Recorded

	£100 and Below	Total	£101–1,000	
			£100–500	£501–1,000
1710–1719	69.5	28.3	23.9	4.4
1730–1739	54.8	41.8	36.0	5.8
1750–1759	41.4	51.5	40.1	11.4

(Source: Inventories and Accounts, Maryland Hall of Records)

above £50.* The distribution suggests that have-nots found rising in the economic scale far from easy. Freed indentured servants and sons of planters without patrimony often ended their days without accumulating worldly goods to the value of £75 or above. Fewer than one fifth of small planter decedents in the decade 1750–59 had attained even this modest competence.

—6—

Yet opportunities for personal advancement had by no means disappeared at midcentury and later. The spectacular successes of Bordley, Dulany, and the first Carrolls were not repeated in quite the same way. But the mechanisms of their advancement were still at hand for talent and ambition. In the bracket of planters whose estates fell between £100 and £1,000 the limitations on social mobility appear most clearly.

It would be erroneous to describe the assortment of types in this broad band as a "class," certainly not a middle class in the usual sense of the term, even though they stood above the poorest planters in the lowest bracket of wealth and below the affluent elite. Households within this middle band show bewildering variety in sumptuary circumstances and behavior, almost kaleidoscopic in appearance. Two aspects are immediately striking. Most remarkable is the growth of this component among Maryland households from just over a quarter to more than half the total population during a fifty year period.** Taking these percentages with the increase of population in absolute numbers gives a fair idea of the market power wielded by planting

	* Gross Estates Below £100 Currency, 1750–1759	
Size of Estate	Number of Estates	Percentages
£ 0–25	262	26
26–50	298	30
51–75	259	26
76–100	183	18
Total	1,002	100

(Source: Inventories and Accounts, Maryland Hall of Records)
**See table on page 278.

families in this middle bracket of wealth. As consumers they kept the stream of commerce flowing by purchases of goods of every description: household furnishings, tools, utensils, and articles of personal adorn- ment. Merchants reflected this demand in their accounts and catered to their desire to accumulate goods, both imported and locally man- ufactured. While imparting new graces and comforts to life, this flour- ishing trade also swelled inventories and enhanced the incomes of wealthy merchant-planters.

Not as immediately arresting is the distribution of estates within this important bracket of wealth. Far greater numbers stand near the bottom of the scale, in the dimensions, £101–200 and £201–300, not far above the small planter level.* Thereafter in successive steps up- ward the numbers decline noticeably: the £901–1,000 step included only 23 estates in the decade 1750–59.

The analysis of these statistics suggests that the noteworthy growth of estates in the £101–1,000 bracket represents a movement of small planters from the lowest economic stratum into more affluent circum- stances. The percentage decrease of estates below £100 during the eighteenth century coincides very closely with the percentage increase in the £101–1,000 range. The higher bracket of wealth grew at the expense of the lower. In part the dynamics of this upward movement can be accounted for by the staple market, the steady increase in European demand for tobacco that maintained a generally favorable

---

*This tabulation presents estates as they appeared to an outside observer, before settlement of charges against the decedent.

Gross Estates Valued at £101–1000
Currency, 1750–1759

Size of Estate	Number of Estates	Size of Estate	Number of Estates
£101–200	448	£601–700	69
201–300	249	701–800	57
301–400	154	801–900	37
401–500	119	901–1000	23
501–600	89		
		Total	1,245

(Source: Inventories and Accounts, Maryland Hall of Records)

price level after 1750. Small producers could not expect instant riches even in this seller's market, but those who could expand production stood to increase their disposable incomes. For most producers, enlarging their tobacco fields meant adding an extra hand or two.

Since the first decade of the eighteenth century the term "extra hands" had become almost synonymous with slaves. The stream of indentured servants had in earliest decades provided field labor. After freedom they had added increments to the free white population. But servants did not keep pace with the increasing flow of Blacks into the province after 1715. The indentured servant represented a short term investment, four to six years depending on the contract, at high cost. By investing 50 percent more money, the planter could acquire a slave who served for life. More and more indentured servants came to be identified with one of the skills useful in a planting community: a clerk, an artisan such as a carpenter or mason, a housekeeper, and on occasion a tutor for the children in affluent households. The movement of artisans, bond and free, to Maryland continued and perhaps even increased during the Golden Age, spurred by the demand for special skills in building and services to the affluent. But for field work planters preferred Blacks.

Many small planters, possibly most, bought their first slave on credit. Purchase of a Black field hand at a price between £40 and £75 currency almost automatically pushed the value of the owner's visible property above £100, though not very far beyond. It mattered little that the estate was indebted by about the same amount as the value of the slave, frequently a debt secured by a chattel mortgage on the very same slave. An owner could look forward to recovering his capital investment, paying off the debt with profits from larger tobacco crops, and thus opening the way to purchase of a second slave. Such dreams of escalating wealth became reality for only a few. The inventories are clear on this point. In the year 1760 the commissary general entered on his record 118 estates with slaves. Twenty-eight inventories listed only one slave, sixteen listed two, and ten listed three slaves. That is to say, almost half the estates probated that year had three slaves or fewer; a quarter had only one. These were planters who had come to the end of their earthly days, not vigorous young men with their futures ahead of them. Obviously for most households the first slave purchase had not led to endless enlargement of their labor force.

Nevertheless some planters did prosper handsomely in worldly estate, not beyond the dreams of petty slaveholders but certainly beyond their performance. Those who forged ahead usually grasped opportunities for enrichment outside the routine of the staple crop that bound so many hands to the cycle of planting, tilling, and curing tobacco. In every region of the province, including the richest tobacco counties of the lower Western Shore, planters had at hand additional products for cash income. Every planting household required cooperage, the barrel staves and headings for hogsheads that contained exported tobacco. Planters either produced their own or purchased their supply locally from a neighbor with the skill and labor to make them. Beside the steady neighborhood demand for cooperage, merchants like Dr. Charles Carroll bought enormous quantities for export to the sugar islands of the West Indies and the Wine Islands, especially Madeira. Any planter with an expert cooper, either indentured servant or slave, could count on selling as many staves as he could manufacture during winter months, the offseason for tobacco. By the same token, cooperage kept many poorer families from actual want.

Woodland industry also included rough lumber—oak, poplar, and pine—for export or for local building. Smaller quantities of fine hardwoods, particularly walnut, supplied cabinet makers who plied their trade in Annapolis to meet the demands of their wealthy clientele for highboys, chests, and other cabinet work. Even in the more settled districts, woodlands still covered more acres than cleared land. Costs of production included only tools and, more important, labor. Planters with hands for felling and sawing had ready access to income from forest products. Money returns were hardly bonanzas, but the cash income helped offset drought years or seasons when tobacco prices temporarily sagged.

Even the ordinary husbandry of the plantation contributed trickles of cash into the purses of the enterprising. Barrelled pork and pickled beef in casks found ready sale either to merchants making up miscellaneous cargoes to the West Indies or to ship captains provisioning their vessels for the voyage home. Native merchant shippers continually sought beans, corn, and wheat. After the French war, parts of the Eastern Shore turned from tobacco to grain crops in response to this demand. To be sure, the tidewater remained essentially a tobacco province, but a significant part of provincial income derived from other agricultural products. Perceptive planters quickly adjusted to these opportunities for cash income.

Such modest but important additions to personal income from cooperage, lumber, and foodstuffs enabled some small producers to move up into the class of petty slaveholders. But these avenues to personal advancement paled beside the lucrative trio of commerce, industry, and land speculation. Small producers and petty slaveholders had far too little capital and credit to assemble a cargo or to erect a smelting furnace. Such undertakings required not only funds but knowledge and experience. Nevertheless opportunities still remained for those who would emulate the bold spirits of an earlier day—Taskers, Carrolls, Dulanys, Bennetts, and Lloyds—who had moved into the elite on their profits from iron, land dealing, and merchandising. Candidates for these giant strides upward were planters whose estates put them in the upper reaches of the wide £101–1,000 bracket of wealth. Individually and in partnerships, planters with personal assets of the magnitude £700 or £800 were in a position to take the risks of larger and more profitable enterprises.

An appreciable number succeeded. In iron making three families joined the pioneers who had earlier built the Baltimore Iron Works into the foremost single manufacturing plant in the province. The Snowden, Dorsey, and Onion families prospered from their operations, particularly in wartime. Before 1776 Maryland had eight blast furnaces casting pig and ten forges working these raw castings into wrought iron for blacksmiths and farriers. Yet a larger number put their hands to commerce. Richard West of Anne Arundel County, James Dick and Anthony Stewart of Annapolis, and the cinderella firm of Wallace, Davidson, and Johnson made fortunes in the vicinity of the capital. A census of the Annapolis merchant community in 1774 lists twenty-one firms ranging in size from newcomers with limited capital up to houses that commanded resources in the tens of thousands of pounds.*

Baltimore had not fully come into its own. Iron works in the neighborhood had brought initial prosperity to the tiny but growing community on the Patapsco. A superb harbor promised a commercial future. Christopher Johnson had seen the possibilities and had done

---

*The tabulation appears on page 33 of Edward C. Papenfuse, *In Pursuit of Profits: The Annapolis Merchants in the Era of the American Revolution, 1783–1805* (Baltimore, 1975).

Baltimore in 1752, from a contemporary sketch made by John Moale, engraved in 1817 by William Strickland. The single masted sloop *Baltimore* near the shoreline belonged to the Baltimore Iron Works. Directly to its front lay the tobacco inspection warehouse on Charles Street. Directly above the puffy tree at the waterline in front of the sloop was the residence and warehouse of Darby Lux, prominent merchant. Atop the hill near the center was old St. Paul's Church. Courtesy of the Maryland Historical Society.

well as a local merchant. But as the back country around Frederick settled up with an economy based on grain and forage a nucleus of merchants began to fatten on the overseas demand for cereals. The local organization of this trade called into existence nineteen mercantile firms, some small but others, such as those of William Lux and Archibald Buchanan, quite respectable in size.

Finally, in every county of the province land dealers drove profitable bargains. Even in Prince George's County, one of the most settled and stable of the tobacco regions, the debt books show an astonishing number of tracts changing hands. But in the huge block of the west that comprised Frederick County the wild lands were a speculator's paradise.*

Enterprising planters who advanced through this huge middle bracket of estates between £100 and £1,000 had an increasing stake in society. Typically they were somewhat conservative in outlook, not revolutionaries ready to man the barricades mindlessly. Many of them opposed the Lord Proprietor's palatine regalia: his officers' fees established by proclamation, the land office fees, and the clerical tithes. Consequently they gravitated toward the country party, supported their delegates' stand against the proprietary court, and voiced sentiments that often had an inflammatory ring. But they neither sought social revolution nor encouraged have-nots to entertain levelling tendencies.

—7—

One element alone of the provincial population stood outside the pattern of mobility, the Blacks. Bondsmen for life, Blacks remained the mudsill, the bottom of the social order. Yet these unwilling immigrants formed an increasing percentage of the population during the eigh-

---

*Not all those called "speculators" deserve the stigma that sometimes attaches to the term. All, of course, sought to make money from their operations, but not all were greedy engrossers who connived to acquire wild lands for a song to hold them for higher prices. Some, notably Daniel Dulany the Elder, were instrumental in opening the west to settlement by establishing market towns, surveying suitable farmsteads, lending to penniless buyers, and even pushing for local self-government. Dulany and a few others like him might just as properly be called developers, though their object was understandably profit.

teenth century and contributed in unsung ways to the economic well-being of the province. The census of 1704 shows them as just under 13 percent of the total population, most thickly concentrated in the prime tobacco counties of Calvert, Prince George's, Anne Arundel, and Charles on the lower Western Shore. By 1762 Blacks made up slightly more than 30 percent of the population, still concentrated largely in the same counties but now also in appreciable numbers in all other Eastern and Western Shore counties except Cecil at the head of the bay on the Pennsylvania border and Frederick in the west. During these years of rapid population growth Blacks increased twelve fold while the white element increased four fold. Almost all Blacks—99.1 percent to be precise—were slaves, incapable of owning property and helpless before law.

Only within the past decade has significant study brought to light the social and cultural life of the Black community of provincial Maryland.* We now know that male Blacks outnumbered females in the last decades of the seventeenth century, seriously handicapping the establishment of families and the natural increase of the Black population. But early in the eighteenth century females came in greater numbers on the slave ships, and planters bought them eagerly. Once the sexes came into more even balance, male slaves had fuller opportunities to find wives and to establish families. In the 1720s and 1730s the increase in native born slaves more than offset the death rate. Children of slave unions, added to the continued importation, account for the striking growth of the Black population.

To planters who bought them, slaves meant extra hands for plantation work, at first mainly field hands. To the helpless Blacks sold by auction or private treaty the uprooting resulted in trauma. Bereft of familiar kinship ties, tribal culture, and the slightest vestige of freedom, Blacks had to contrive social relations to make the harsh conditions of chattel bondage tolerable. Their adjustment must be accounted a great creative act in the face of enormous handicaps.

Family life, the very basis of natural increase and the sustaining social web, came most easily to slaves on sizable plantations (ten or

---

*Russell Menard and Allan Kulikoff have both done basic demographic and social studies, some still unpublished. Their works are noted in the bibliography.

more slaves). Approximately half the slaves in Maryland lived on such plantations, sometimes dispersed in "quarters" about the vast acreage. Not only could men find wives more readily among the young women on the great plantation but the chances of maintaining a household with husband, wife, and children living under the same roof improved considerably. On the lands of James Wardrop (32 slaves), Thomas Addison (3 plantations, 109 slaves), and Charles Carroll (13 quarters, 385 slaves) almost half the slaves lived in husband-wife-children families. The next largest number were in mother-children households, either because the father had died or more likely had been assigned to work at a different quarter or even sold. By far the largest slaveholder in Maryland, Carroll showed considerable concern for the family life of his "people," though never to his serious personal detriment. Daniel Dulany the Younger found the distress of selling slaves on the Tasker estate "intolerable" and, rather than separate husbands and wives, compelled the heirs to take lower prices for the slaves he sold. By contrast, full family life on plantations of small slaveholders (1–9 slaves) was less common. Fewer than a fifth of slave families on these plantations had husband, wife, and children under one roof. More than a third of the slave households consisted of mother and children, the husband and father residing at best on a neighboring plantation, at worst far enough away that he could visit his family no oftener than once a week. But extreme cases gauged the iniquities inherent in chattel bondage and the devotion of bondsmen to family ties. A slave by the name of Will travelled over a hundred miles, from Charles County to Frederick County, to visit his wife because her master had taken her from Will's neighborhood to a distant quarter.

Slave society, then, was not as fragile as it was vulnerable. Once family life insured the increase of native Blacks, a host of kinship relations developed in patterns that only recently have become clear. Obviously slave mothers had a key role in rearing young children and preparing them for the harsh life to come when they went to the fields between the ages of seven and ten. But fathers, too, contributed in practical ways, especially artisans such as Charles Carroll's Cooper Joe, who instructed one of his thirteen children, also named Joe, in the mysteries of cooperage, a prized skill in Maryland. Young Joe in turn had his apprentices, two of his near kin from neighboring quarters. Thus was knit a web of kinship and consociation that gained further strength from gatherings about the slave cabins in evenings and on special days for dancing, singing, storytelling, and drinking the scanty issues of rum.

If some later historians have presented a "Sambo" conception of the simple, guileless Black, happy in his ignorance, Maryland whites who lived in daily contact with the slave population entertained no such delusions. They imposed an iron discipline on transgressors of the master's code. One planter in fury had a sound whipping administered to his slave, Manuel, on suspicion that he had broken open the door of the plantation lock-up to release his daughter Sarah, who was being punished for running away for several days. Few slaveholders could have fancied that Blacks enjoyed bondage. If they needed a reminder of smouldering Black resentment, the abortive revolt on the lower Western Shore in the winter of 1739–1740 supplied it. When that conspiracy came to light the white community reacted at once by mustering foot and horse for duty at an hour's notice and by establishing security watches about the provincial powder magazine and public buildings in Annapolis.

—8—

Human bondage was merely one layer of the foundation that supported the elite at the very top of the social pyramid. Field hands under overseers and domestic slaves under the eye of either the housekeeper or the master himself have been highly visible in accounts of the planting scene. But Maryland had attractions for other, more willing immigrants, perhaps lured by the baronial splendor of the great planters and possibly the hope that they too might ride fortune's wheel to the top, as the Dulany dynasty had earlier in the century. The Chesapeake seemed a land of opportunity, Maryland in particular. Whatever the reason, British immigrants poured into Maryland in the years following the French War, some 2,603 in the years 1774 and 1775 alone. The overwhelming number (83 percent) came from England, over half of them from London alone. Typically, they were unattached males rather than families, and only a fraction listed agriculture as their occupation. Over half were skilled craftsmen or tradesmen. Whatever the urge to get to Maryland, it was powerful enough to lure many of them to

indenture themselves for a period of servitude as the price of passage.*
The notion that indentured servants no longer figured in the immigrant
flow to Maryland once slavery had taken firm root cannot be supported.

The key that unlocks the puzzle of high demand for craftsmen and
tradesmen as well as slaves is the abundant prosperity in the decade
of the seventies. Credit had assumed new dimensions with the entry
of Scottish factors, bankrolled by the financial wizards of Glasgow.
But even more important, Chesapeake natives had discovered ways of
mobilizing local credit resources. The firm of Wallace, Davidson, and
Johnson pioneered in tapping Maryland capital for their export-import
business. For decades individuals here and there had sustained smaller
operations on neighborhood credit. Merchants, petty manufacturers
(and some larger ones, particularly ironmasters) and land speculators
created loans for their clients. That is, they sold on credit. Some met
disaster in bankruptcy, others became wealthy; but boom or bust they
floated on a tissue of debts: mortgages, book debts, and specialties.
Every estate that came to probate had debts to be paid before heirs
received their inheritances.

Although all were indebted in some degree, the number of insolvent
estates dropped surprisingly after the turn of the century. Around
1700, nearly one third of all Maryland planters were bankrupt at the
end of their days: personal assets did not cover their outstanding debts.
Over the century this fraction dropped to one fifth and finally to just
over one tenth by the 1770s. Creditors stood on an increasingly sound
footing as the decades passed. But even bankrupt estates dealt far less
serious blows to creditors than might be imagined. Cautious merchants
rarely allowed their patrons to pile up debts too far beyond their means.
In the entire decade 1750–1759 insolvent estates numbered only 351.
But only thirty had debts of more than £25 sterling that could not
be satisfied by assets. The remaining 321 were in the red by a few
pennies up to £25, not a crushing loss to creditors when the deficit
was prorated among several persons with claims against the estate. To
be sure, business hazards had not disappeared, but they had signifi-

---

*I owe these figures to Professor Bernard Bailyn whose quantitative study of im-
migration is yet unpublished.

cantly decreased to the decided improvement of business confidence and security.

Much has been made of debts owed to British merchant houses in the closing years of colonial dependency. Certainly in those areas where the Scottish factors had established their branches, small planters particularly had allowed themselves to be caught in the toils. Some larger planters who still directly consigned their crops to London houses also overspent, and a few had given mortgages on their plantations to secure cumulative deficits. But alongside the improvident, other planters maintained sterling balances with their London correspondents; their accounts were in the black. Kensey Johns of Calvert County consigned a part of his tobacco to the London firm of John Philpot, who sent back quarterly statements still in the family papers, each showing a sterling balance. A neighbor, Thomas Davis of Anne Arundel County, had sterling balances with all six of his London correspondents: £3 or £4 each with William Black, Joseph Adams, William Perkins, and Richard Molineaux, but £36 with John Hanbury and £388 with William Hunt. Most revealing of all, James Marshall of Calvert County, not among the wealthiest but certainly comfortably well-to-do, had sterling balances with three London merchants totalling just over £120. Moreover Marshall had debts due him from neighboring planters, forty-one in all, in the amount of £470 current money of Maryland, equivalent to £13 sterling. To Marshall and his kind, Maryland planters owed debts many times larger than the sums due British houses. Amos Garrett, who owned one of the great fortunes of the province, had hundreds of debtors. When Garrett died his executors reported several batches of collections: at one time 113 debts in all three kinds of money (sterling, currency, and tobacco); later twenty others in sterling and currency and so on periodically until after half a decade they had collected all his good debts for his heirs.

As a solid element diffused through all counties of Maryland, the business community made common cause with planters in provincial politics. In imperial concerns they watched the parliamentary measures and, in British eyes, tended to take a liberal position, demanding exemption from laws that put colonials at a disadvantage alongside Britons. Similarly, they chafed at the exactions of the proprietary establishment beyond their control and even beyond their influence. Many sympathized with country party sentiments. All scrutinized the doings of governor and legislature when either impinged upon their interests. In mid-winter of 1773 they unexpectedly found a target for their discontent.

—9—

On 7 January the *Maryland Gazette* published a piece under the innocuous title, "A Dialogue Between Two Citizens." Pretending to report a debate between two friends, the First Citizen and the Second Citizen, the anonymous author focused on a matter that had troubled provincials for more than two years: the Fee Proclamation of 1770. In their dialogue, the First Citizen, an opponent of the proclamation, found his position demolished by the Second Citizen. Somehow, the Second Citizen argued, "politicians . . . without remorse" had in their electioneering seduced a part of the public to the belief that supporters of the proclamation were enemies to liberty and good government. After several exchanges between the two of them, the First Citizen confessed that he had been misled and promised in the future to let reason, rather than the invective of candidates opposing the proclamation, guide his decisions. Obviously the *Dialogue* was directed against the country party.

Quite clearly this homily in dialogue form that had converted the First Citizen intended a similar impact on Maryland voters in the upcoming elections. The Proprietor, Frederick, last Lord Baltimore, had died in September of 1771 without legitimate heirs. In his will he bequeathed the province to his bastard son, Henry Harford, still an infant. With Baltimore's death, all commissions expired, as well as the terms of elected representatives. Already new commissions issued to proprietary officers by Henry Harford's guardians had evoked new grumbling about fees, their size and legal standing. Elections promised a politically exciting spring.

In this atmosphere the *Dialogue* created something of a stir. The authorship was an open secret: the literary style and political position of Daniel Dulany the Younger were too well known for concealment. For more than a month no rejoinder other than a short protest signed "Independent Freeman" appeared in the *Gazette*.

Then early in February another anonymous author took up the cudgels. Signing himself "First Citizen," he alleged that his arguments had been falsely reported in the *Dialogue* and proceeded to set the record straight. In his version "First Citizen" took his opponent to task for abandoning sound principles and engaging in the very tactics he professed to abhor, particularly of attaching himself to party, the court party dominated by *"one family."* Readers, of course, understood this innuendo as directed at the Dulany family and at Daniel in particular. "First Citizen" went on to quote the "justly admired author" of the *Considerations* for the admirable doctrine laid down against arbitrary proceedings. But, he continued, "A wicked minister has endeavoured to and is now endeavouring in this *free government*, to set the power of the supreme magistrate above the laws." Then came the obvious analogies to those advisers of Charles I whose counsel finally brought him to the block. In short "First Citizen" turned the table on his opponent and left him to ponder some "disagreeable truths" frankly spoken in this saucy reply.

Provincials immediately recognized the rejoinder as the handiwork of Charles Carroll of Carrollton, long at odds with the whole Dulany family and especially with Daniel. Carroll undoubtedly voiced the sentiments of the country party and of a majority of the voters. Several of them publicly thanked the "First Citizen" in the columns of the *Gazette* under the pseudonym, "Independent Whigs," for speaking out against arbitrary government. The "First Citizen," still technically anonymous, became the toast of Annapolis.

Obviously a reply was in order. Carroll's letter not only joined the issue but contained several personal barbs which provincials understood perfectly and chuckled about as they read. Carroll had preempted the title "First Citizen," leaving his opponent to find some other, less attractive pen name. Dulany chose "Antilon" for his rejoinder, and over this signature wrote a learned refutation, spiced with choice invectives, for publication in the *Gazette* on 18 February. The battle was on, to the delight of all readers who relished a good fight. The exchanges between "Antilon" and "First Citizen" continued into July, weeks after elections to the Assembly. Neither Dulany nor Carroll gave ground. Dulany spoke as a constitutional lawyer, elaborating a position that was unassailable by legal tenets of his day. Carroll voiced the doctrine of natural rights, the platform of the discontented, and he carried off the laurels as intellectual leader of the country party. Once his identity as "First Citizen" was acknowledged he received thanks from legislative delegations and in letters to the *Gazette* praising his achievement. "It is the *public voice*, Sir," exclaimed one admirer.

With public discussion at such a pitch, the new House of Delegates acted with surprising moderation. Country party delegates, though in a clear majority, did not descend to the politics of irreconcilables. Instead through two short sessions in the summer and early fall the lower house acted calmly as its members took stock of alternatives to impasse. Then in a noteworthy session that lasted through November and December of 1773 the two houses found a simple formula for putting major legislation on the books. They separated the issues. Instead of an omnibus bill that provided for tobacco inspection, support of the clergy, and regulation of officers' fees, the Assembly took up each in turn. Early in the session a new inspection act, similar in essentials to the law that had expired exactly three years previously, passed both houses without extraneous provisions affecting clergy and officers. The lower house had thus deliberately sacrificed its chief source of bargaining power, at least for the life of the act. In part, this unexpected action of self-denial resulted from the influence exerted in the lower house by wealthy planter delegates who held voluntary inspection unsatisfactory as a long term substitute for positive law. Delegates also seemed weary of the politics of irreconcilability when the economy was in a boom stage.

Next the Assembly turned to the "vestry question," as it had come to be called in newspaper polemics during recent months. When the Inspection Act of 1747 expired in 1770—and with it the limitation of thirty pounds of tobacco from each taxable toward support of rectors in each parish—the clergy claimed the larger amount of "forty pounds per poll" provided in the act of establishment of 1702. Opposition began instantly. No such giants as Dulany and Carroll took up pens in the literary encounters over the vexed question of payment to clergy of the established church, but lesser polemicists took a hand in the dispute. In a widely circulated handbill, a writer signing himself "The Church of England Planter" claimed that the clergy rode him "like an ass" and proposed cutting their salaries to ten pounds of tobacco per poll and, for good measure, putting them under their parish vestries for discipline. Remembering the antics of Bennet Allen, many communicants agreed that the time had come for some measure of control over "High Church (or rather No-Church) Ruffians." Two leaders of

William Paca by Charles Willson Peale. One of Peale's 1,100 portraits, this likeness shows in the background to the right Paca's famous gardens with a garden house and bridge over the tiny stream that threads through the grounds. Courtesy of the Maryland Historical Society.

the country party, Samuel Chase and William Paca, fell in behind "The Church of England Planter" with supporting polemics alleging that the basic establishment act of 1702 was invalid on a constitutional technicality: "That, therefore, no obligation can result from the said forty per poll act as a law." Following this theory Joseph Harrison, a delegate from Charles County, refused to pay his church tax and was promptly jailed by the sheriff, Richard Lee, also a member of the council and, by association, the court party. Harrison made his incarceration a test case, brought suit for damages against Lee, and won judgment of £60 sterling, according to the *Gazette*.* As in the celebrated Parson's Cause argued by Patrick Henry in the Virginia courts, the law, not the defendant, had been on trial.

In this atmosphere the Assembly considered various positions and proposals before settling on a simple solution. During November an act passed setting the poll tax for the church at the same thirty pounds of tobacco per taxable that provincials had paid while the Inspection Act was in force. Churchmen expressed disappointment, but provincials accepted the law as fair and tolerable. On the fee question for officers of the establishment, the Assembly did nothing at all. By the governor's fiat—the Proclamation of 1770—these were already fixed at the same rate paid under the Inspection Act of 1747. The Assembly let the arrangement stand.

This legislation represented important policy decisions by the provincial Assembly and they proved to be the last genuine deliberations of that body. A final session in March 1774 dealt with routine matters. For a hundred thirty-eight years this "grand inquest" of Maryland had met, sometimes in harmony with Proprietor or crown, sometimes locked in strenuous combat, but always championing the provincial way as delegates saw it. The settlement of 1773 marked some relaxing of tensions but no real advance beyond the position of court and country beyond the lines of 1770, when the Inspection Act had expired.

---

*A search of the Charles County court records for this period has turned up no record of this case. Provincials accepted the *Gazette* report and many agreed with the reported verdict.

—10—

During the last quarter of 1773 the attention of the citizenry had centered chiefly on provincial issues. But distracting news of Parliament's activities did not go entirely unnoticed. Specifically the Tea Act had raised again the old question of parliamentary taxation. Shortly after the autumn meeting of the Assembly began, the House of Delegates accepted an invitation from speakers of the legislatures in Virginia and Massachusetts to set up a Committee of Correspondence for obtaining "the most early and authentic intelligence of all such Acts and Resolutions of the British Parliament or proceedings of administration, as may relate to, or effect the British Colonies in America." The eleven man committee reads like a roster of country party stalwarts: Matthew Tilghman, William Paca, Thomas Johnson, Samuel Chase, Edward Lloyd, Matthias Hammond, John Hall, James Lloyd Chamberlain, Brice Thomas Beale Worthington, and Joseph Sim. Actually the committee did next to no corresponding, at least while the Assembly sat working out legislation on tobacco inspection and on fees for both clergy and officers. Like other provincials, they read newspaper notices that the tea ships had arrived in ports to the north and also of the colorful story of the Boston Tea Party in December of 1773. Both the *Maryland Gazette* and a new weekly paper recently established in Baltimore, the *Maryland Journal and Baltimore Advertiser*, printed full accounts of the Tea Party, which was talked about without creating real excitement.

But the calm abruptly ended in May 1774. On the twenty-fourth, a circular letter from Massachusetts reached the province with news that Parliament had closed the port of Boston until the destroyed tea had been paid for. The letter asked support for the beleaguered city against this act of tyranny. Next day Annapolis residents assembled to consider the request. Without a dissenting vote the meeting passed three resolutions: "that the town of *Boston* is now suffering in the common cause of *America*," that a trade embargo would best preserve the "liberties of North America," and that Annapolis residents stood ready to join the counties in a non-importation association, "such Association to be on oath." Unanimity broke down on the fourth resolution binding lawyers to refuse to bring suits for any debt due

Chippendale arm chair belonging to William Paca, maker unidentified. Typical of the elegant furnishings of Paca House.

Tea Service belonging to Charles Carroll, Barrister. The pair of cannisters and sugar bowl were made by Samuel Taylor of London; the chest of Chinese lacquer was imported. Courtesy of the Maryland Historical Society.

an inhabitant of Britain. About two dozen citizens, including some of the wealthiest men in the city, dissented with a warning that American credit would expire from the wound. Nevertheless the fourth resolution carried by a clear majority and the meeting adjourned after appointing a committee composed of Samuel Chase, William Paca, Charles Carroll, Barrister,* John Hall and Matthias Hammond—every one of them a country party man—to engage Baltimore and the counties in an association for securing American liberty.

The Annapolis meeting galvanized the counties into action. Crises had twice previously evoked such associations, and the counties now responded within two weeks to the call for organized resistance. Many simply chose their representatives to the House of Delegates to act for them and, as further bad news arrived, demanded a provincial congress of all their committeemen at an early date in Annapolis. The Boston Port Act shocked the province, but Parliament had under consideration other legislation even more threatening: the Massachusetts Government Bill, which virtually prohibited town meetings and gave the selection of jurors to sheriffs; and the Administration of Justice Bill, which permitted crown officers to remove trials of British officials from the courts of the vicinity, which were presumed to be hostile, to another colony or to England. Maryland county meetings sniffed tyranny, subversion of the constitution, and the death of American liberty in these acts. The rhetoric of speakers reflected their fears.

Excitement rose as the date of the provincial congress approached. Yet although the rhetoric blared, public meetings in the counties had gone off without disorder and without a trace of violence. Even the

---

* The Maryland Carrolls can be confusing unless identified with the cognomens that were attached to them in their day. Three Charles Carrolls were active during the War for Independence. This genealogical table may clear up confusion.

Protestant Branch	Catholic Branch
Dr. Charles Carroll (ca. 1691–1755)	Charles Carroll, the Settler (1660–1720)
Charles Carroll, Barrister (1723–1783)	Charles Carroll of Annapolis (1702–1782)
	Charles Carroll of Carrollton (1737–1832)

Chippendale highboy, unidentified American maker, ca. 1760–1770. A ubiquitous piece in wealthy households. Courtesy of the Baltimore Museum of Art.

governor concluded that he could continue his plans for a four month business trip to England and sailed shortly after the impromptu public meeting in Annapolis that set off the movement for a provincial congress. Governor Eden had some reason to believe that his absence would not be a catastrophe. Earlier in the spring he had called the Assembly into a session that lasted just over three weeks, 23 March to 19 April, and produced twenty-eight acts, none of them controversial but all necessary for such provincial housekeeping matters as roads, schools, and debtor relief. As it turned out the meeting proved to be the last official session of the institution that dated back to 1635. Its end came not with a bang but with dull routine.

By contrast the provincial congress, unprecedented and without constitutional basis, acted with the energy and self-reliance of a long-established body when it met on 22 June 1774. In fact all the ninety-two delegates were experienced politically, a majority of them as former delegates to the general Assembly. They called Matthew Tilghman to the chair and proceeded to business in the most parliamentary way. First they adopted the style, "convention," for the assemblage, then moved forthwith to state a position and to lay out a plan of action. In measured language the convention condemned the Boston Port Act as "cruel and oppressive invasions of the natural rights of the people of Massachusetts Bay . . . now suffering in the common cause of America." Next the convention went on record as favoring commercial non-intercourse with England, called for a general congress of all colonies to meet at Philadelphia in September to concert policy, and resolved to open subscriptions in all counties for the relief of the distressed inhabitants of Boston. As their delegates to the proposed Philadelphia congress the convention chose tested leaders, their chairman, Matthew Tilghman, his Eastern Shore neighbor, Robert Goldsborough, and three stalwarts from the Western Shore: Thomas Johnson, William Paca, and Samuel Chase. These "deputies" were, on their return, to "call together the committees of the several counties, and lay before them the measures adopted by the general congress." After four days of dawn-to-dusk sitting the convention adjourned.

Conservatives shook their heads, dreading consequences. The convention had enacted no "laws" but had clearly indicated a direction and an intent in their resolutions. Henceforth successor conventions, out-of-doors politics with popular support, were to guide the province through the uncertainties of the months ahead.

—11—

While the deputies to the Continental Congress were still sitting in Philadelphia, Maryland had a tea party, less celebrated but even more dramatic than the Boston frolic nearly a year previous. On 15 October 1774 the brig *Peggy Stewart* made port at Annapolis with an assorted cargo that included seventeen packages of tea weighing about 2,320 pounds. Anthony Stewart, owner of the vessel, was caught in a trap. Some months earlier he had chartered his brig to an Annapolis firm for the voyage to England with instructions to his London correspondent, James Russell, to sell the ship there for £550 sterling if possible. When no buyer at Stewart's valuation appeared, Russell committed the act of folly that trapped Stewart: he chartered the *Peggy Stewart* for the return voyage to the Annapolis firm of Williams and Company and put the tea on board by stealth. When Anthony Stewart paid the customs at Annapolis, keen-eyed officials discovered the deception. Already suspect as one of the culprits in the *Good Intent* episode a few years previously, Stewart was caught red-handed.

Alert committeemen sounded the alarm and called a meeting of delegates from the counties for Wednesday, 19 October. Stewart himself went into a frenzy of action as soon as he realized the possible outcome of a confrontation with the same men who had guided recent convention proceedings. He first requested a meeting of Annapolis citizens on Monday hoping that his fellow townsmen might permit him to land the tea and burn it publicly as an act of contrition before the more restless spirits from the counties arrived. But a highly vocal element at the Monday Assembly insisted on delaying proceedings until the general meeting. An apologetic handbill, hastily printed at Stewart's expense, did nothing to win him favor. By Wednesday resentment had mounted to an alarming pitch, thoroughly unnerving to Stewart and to the luckless Williams brothers, guilty of ordering the tea in the first place. At the meeting Stewart read with bared head an abject apology on behalf of Williams for "*importing the tea*" and for himself for "paying the duty thereon." Over their signatures all three

1. Front View of the State-House &c. *at* ANNAPOLIS *the Capital of* MARYLAND.

The Statehouse at Annapolis. Engraving from the *Columbian Magazine*. The two buildings nearest the statehouse have been removed; the small building, known as the old Treasury Building, still stands. The main structure has been in continuous use by the upper and lower chambers of the Assembly since Revolutionary times. The cornerstone was laid 17 April 1772. Courtesy of the Maryland Historical Society.

humbly asked pardon, promised never to violate the non-importation agreement, and requested all present to witness the burning of the tea "at any place where the people shall appoint."

An adroit gesture, the paper of apology failed. Sentiment at the meeting divided. A few "frantic zealots . . . warmly proposed the American discipline of tarring and feathering." Others clamored for the destruction of the brig that held the tea. But a majority held the apology and "unextorted consent to burn the tea" a sufficient punishment and satisfaction. When the question was put "Whether the vessel should be destroyed," a majority answered in the negative. Unappeased, the minority promised to return as soon as they could assemble their supporters "to proceed to the utmost extremities."

Stewart waited no longer. "From an anxious desire to preserve the public tranquility, as well as to ensure his own personal safety"—as an eye-witness wrote with unconscious humor—Stewart proposed to fire the vessel himself. Accompanied by witnesses he went on board, directed the crew to run the brig aground at Windmill Point in full view of the city, and applied the torch with his own hand. In a few hours the *Peggy Stewart* burned to the water's edge.

—12—

The burning of the *Peggy Stewart* was the first spectacular auto-da-fé in these troubled weeks, and the last. When a second convention met in Annapolis on 21 November the membership again closely corresponded to the roster of country party delegates to the now defunct Assembly. All were men of substance, prominent in their home counties, schooled in local or provincial office. No populist groundswell brought untried poorer freeholders into the higher councils of the province. And for good reason: the county organizations, themselves miniconventions, were dominated by well-to-do, solid planters and merchants. Clearly the foremost men in Maryland were not abdicating in favor of Tom, Dick, and Harry.

Proceedings at the second convention were as sedate as those of any meeting of the Assembly. Members heard a report from the delegates to the Continental Congress recommending strict cessation of trade with Britain and approved it unanimously. Then, again unanimously, the convention "recommended" recruiting and arming a militia, one unit for each county. Ever so slightly, this decision began moving the convention toward a legislative body. Its decisions were still framed as "recommendations" and not laws, but by whatever name they had binding force. The movement continued with resolutions to establish a Committee of Correspondence for the province and to appoint delegates to the next Continental Congress. Finally, before adjourning the convention provided for its successor, "a provincial meeting of deputies," chosen by the several counties to meet in April of 1775. The convention was institutionalized.

In succeeding months Maryland had a taste of dual government. Governor Eden returned to Annapolis refreshed by his voyage shortly before the second convention met. Under his eye the proprietary machinery continued to function: the land office issued warrants, courts held their accustomed sessions, and minor officers in the counties went about their duties as usual. But alongside the established administration, with its constitutional and legal sanctions, an extralegal order backed by public sentiment gradually took shape. County committees, huge in numbers, undertook to enforce the non-importation agreement and to raise the militia. In Frederick County the committee had a membership of one hundred fourteen, though any five had power to act. Older but smaller Charles County had a committee of ninety, any seven empowered to act. Virtually all the justices of the county courts, constables, and deputy surveyors of the land office were also members of county committees. Yet, though many provincials wore two hats, they exchanged them without apparent conflict of interest. In part Governor Eden's deportment accounts for the lack of friction. Even his intimate friends said that he would have to call on his every resource to "stem the popular torrent." Actually he calmly ignored the meeting of the third convention in April of 1775, at least outwardly, while writing astute appreciations of American attitudes and actions to his superiors in England. On its side the convention was hardly truculent. Its longest resolution called for "a happy reconciliation of the differences between the mother country and the British colonies in North America, upon a firm basis of constitutional freedom."

The one potentially inflammatory piece of intelligence that could have set off a blaze miraculously created no popular fury. Shortly before noon on 28 April, while the convention was still in session, news of the shooting at Lexington and Concord reached Annapolis by relay rider. A thrill of excitement ran through the town, but no popular outburst followed. The previous day a committee of six gentlemen had waited on the governor to request that the firearms in the provincial arsenal be distributed to the people. Eden had agreed, on the advice of his Lordhip's Council of State, to "commit the care of the arms to the custody of such gentlemen of the militia (regularly appointed by myself) as they most place confidence in." As he wrote his brother, "They expressed great satisfaction with this." He might have added that his decision had kept up the appearance of harmony between constituted authority and the new extralegal bodies now beginning to taste power.

—13—

William Eddis, minor official and bon vivant of Annapolis, gives a running account of events in the years of 1774 to 1776. Vivid and somewhat at variance with convention and court records, the Eddis commentary provides a valuable insight into the transformation that occurred in these months. During his first five years in Maryland he viewed his surroundings from his vantage point at the capital where he enjoyed the oasis culture of a civilized community set in a vast province of toilers and tillers of the soil, a kind of desert broken only by a gracious country home here and there. Eddis had identified with the elite and his outlook resembled that of the British ruling class, comfortably at home in their London houses or country seats, surrounded by poorer farmers and artisans of the countryside and small towns of England. He wrote of balls, entertainments, and pastimes of the elite, though he thoroughly understood the workings of governmental machinery.*

Then on 28 May 1774 his tone changes abruptly. "All America is in a flame!" he tells his correspondent. "I hear strange language every day. The colonists are ripe for any measures that will tend to the preservation of what they call their natural liberty." Clearly Eddis had not penetrated far beneath the surface characteristics of Maryland society to the tough fibre below. As an Englishman he felt a sense of

*His letter of 17 Febuary 1772 describes the land system with textbook accuracy.

shock at the rhetoric he heard from the very companions—all of the "better sort"—who frequented the fashionable taverns and attended carefree meetings of his favorite Homony Club. Baffled at first, he tried to probe this Maryland breed who spoke his tongue, carefully copied London fashions, and in so many ways resembled Englishmen at home save in this odd aberration about "natural liberty."

By November 1774 his letters had become apprehensive. The Continental Congress had addressed the king and Parliament, he heard, in a "masterly performance, firm, explicit, and respectful." But after reading both addresses "with impartial attention" Eddis decided that he was not "competent to determine their respective merits." He could easily perceive that cessation of trade had reduced his income from fees, as business slowed. In April of 1775 the shooting "at a place called Lexington" disquieted him: "With the most dreadful anxiety we are now waiting for further and more circumstantial intelligence." Nor could he describe the governor's consent to distribution of provincial arms as anything more than a sop to the aroused populace: "In these turbulent times something must be yielded to the clamor of an infatuated multitude."

Gradually Eddis came to comprehend that the enchanted ball which he, like Cinderella, had relished was drawing near the hour of harsh realities when the magic spell would end. In July of 1775 he wrote a British friend, "Speech is become dangerous . . . the sword is drawn . . . . Before this letter is received, you will have heard of the action at *Bunker Hill* . . . the inhabitants of this province are incorporated under military regulations . . . in Annapolis there are two complete companies."

His reference was to the decisions of the fourth convention that met at Annapolis in July of 1775 to take the most drastic steps yet. The convention took its cue from the Second Continental Congress, which had assembled in Philadelphia on 10 May and appointed George Washington to command the troops at Boston. Thomas Johnson, a Maryland delegate, nominated Washington, and Congress unanimously settled on him as commander-in-chief of continental troops. The Maryland convention at once drew up an "Association of the Freemen of Maryland," pledging all signers "to repel force by force." Copies went to all the counties for signatures with further directions for compiling lists of non-associators. By explicit words, the Association undertook the "maintenance of good order and the public peace, to support the civil power in the due execution of the laws . . . and to defend, with our utmost power, all persons from every species of outrage to themselves or their property." With the formation of the Association, supreme power passed to the convention, when in session, and for interim periods between meetings of the whole body to a Council of Safety of sixteen members, eight from each shore. The acts of the convention before adjournment were themselves expressions of supreme power: a regular organization for provincial militia and an issue of paper money in the amount of $264,666 in such denominations as sixteen, eight, and four dollar bills and fractional currency of two-thirds of a dollar.

With the fourth convention the world of William Eddis collapsed. "It seems but yesterday that I considered my situation permanent. Every flattering prospect appeared before me. . . . Alas! my brother, how cruelly the scene is reversed." He sent his family back to England and accepted with some embarrassment Governor Eden's offer of shelter. The governor remained at his post. "Considering the wild, unsettled times, he is uncommonly popular," wrote Eddis.

After the departure of his family Eddis, in residence at the governor's mansion, watched Eden at close range. He surely could not have failed to note the governor's nerve, though little of it rubbed off on him. Eden's composure appeared unruffled by the fifth convention which met in Annapolis on 7 December 1775 for a sitting that lasted through mid-January 1776. He still had friendly relations with several leaders of the "incindiaries," as Eddis dubbed them, including among others Charles Carroll of Carrollton and Daniel of St. Thomas Jenifer. Carroll's star had been in the ascendant since he had vanquished Daniel Dulany in the First Citizen-Antilon newspaper war. Jenifer, a member of his Lordship's Council of State, had already accepted election as delegate to the convention with the announcement, "Things are gone so far people ought to risque everything." But privately he told Eden that he was accepting "only for the sake of being instrumental in preventing Disorder, and Violence." Secretive, sensitive, and devious beyond compare, Jenifer had actually spoken the truth in both statements.

In fact Governor Eden, behind his boisterous bonhomie, watched his colleagues, the friendly and the ill disposed alike, with a shrewd eye. His confidential letters indicate an understanding of political maneuver denied his house guest. An excellent observer, Eddis reported what he saw: he had sight without insight. Eden had both. He correctly surmised that the fourth convention in the previous July had set proprietary power aside. He had yielded "to the storm when I could not resist it, to preserve some hold of the helm of government, that I might steer . . . clear of those shoals which all here must sooner or later, I fear get shipwreck'd upon." Now in midwinter the fifth convention confirmed his reading.

By this time the precedent of government by convention had become the accepted mode. Its resolutions were in fact law, enforced by county committees and at the provincial level by the Committee of Safety. By easy stages the convention had replaced the Assembly. Like its predecessors, the December convention declared loyalty to the crown, expressed hope for reconciliation on a "just constitutional basis," then moved to actual legislation under the transparent guise of resolutions. The resolutions moved the fifth convention a long step further toward what one observer called "an independent state," using the term "state" in the same sense as twentieth century commentators use "status." With a show of unanimity the delegates improved the defense posture of the province by creating five military districts, each commanded by a brigadier, to expedite recruitment and drilling of troops. Then followed two practical moves to support the militia: provision "for raising clothing and victualling the forces to be raised" and the establishment of a gun factory in Frederick. These actions, and the authorization of additional paper money, followed the example of earlier conventions. But January brought a novelty, the "Test" as it soon came to be called. The convention instructed the counties to enroll all non-associators. Those freeman who refused to sign the Association were to be deprived of their arms or be permitted to leave the province, taking their property with them. Thenceforth subscribing to the Association, with its assertions of American rights and its enjoinder to resist British encroachments by arms, was to be the test of loyalty to the colonial cause. But lest anyone misconstrue this drastic move, the convention gave positive instructions to provincial delegates in the second Continental Congress sitting in Philadelphia: "Do not without the previous knowledge and approbation of the Convention of this province assent to any proposition to declare these colonies independent of the crown of Great Britain."

Between June of 1774 and January 1776, when the latest meeting of delegates adjourned, Eddis and Eden witnessed five conventions. For Eddis these extralegal assemblies and the rhetoric that accompanied them were cause for real alarm. For Eden they were, of course, a concern but more practically a problem, a departure from traditional ways of administering the province. His cool head and his continued popularity as a person had enabled him to remain nominally at the helm while functionaries and bodies foreign to duly constituted authority made decisions and took action repugnant to his conceptions of propriety. He survived without being able to prevail. Eden's pattern of conduct differed in kind from the course of his counterpart across the Potomac, Lord Dunmore, who declared war on the Virginia elite, leaders of resistance to parliamentary rule. By contrast Eden remained on civil terms with Maryland leaders who, whether he sensed it or not, were going through a crisis of their own.

—14—

Behind the facade of unanimity the Maryland elite experienced the anguish of an embattled minority in the years 1774–1776. For the first time the resistance movement, with its apparatus of conventions, committees, and out-of-door political gatherings, challenged the dominion of the ruling families long accustomed to ordering the course of provincial affairs as officeholders and as elected representatives of their local precincts in the Assembly. For decades the leading families had indulged in a certain amount of competition for place; in-fighting was hardly a novelty. Yet, the wealthy families that made up the elite had much in common, far more than their personal feuds indicate: a whig political philosophy, similar conceptions of property rights, and a clear conviction that the well-being of society demanded their continued control. Even the division between court and country parties was bridged by this outlook.

In the years after 1770, as proprietary control slackened, a coalition gradually formed around a handful of leaders, mostly old country party hands with a sprinkling of aspiring upstarts: Matthew Tilghman, Samuel Chase, Charles Carroll, Barrister, Thomas Johnson, and, tardily, William Paca. During the fee controversy they had pulled together and, when Charles Carroll of Carrollton spoke up as "First Citizen," they welcomed him as a kindred spirit, a spokesman who as yet had no political power. Even before the first convention, observers of the provincial scene spoke of them as the "Patriots." This nucleus and their well-wishers carried the elections to the first convention of June 1774 and dominated its proceedings much to the chagrin of other former luminaries of the country party, John Hall and Matthias Hammond.

In succeeding months Hall and Hammond attempted to improve their political fortunes by a course that thoroughly frightened the Patriots. They led the violent element in the meeting that compelled Anthony Stewart to burn the *Peggy Stewart*. Soon they were cooperating with advocates of radical measures in Baltimore Town, Charles Ridgely and Samuel Purviance, both of them merchants who had assumed leadership roles in that rapidly growing but politically unstable community. Once the Hall-Hammond faction found they could rouse artisans, small tradesmen and poorer planters with slogans and radical proposals, they had a powerful weapon against their wealthy and conservative opponents, who viewed with growing alarm any combination that threatened the kind of social change likely to deprive the elite of leadership. The result would be an "ungovernable and revengeful Democracy."

In actual fact the Patriot coalition managed to dominate each of the conventions. Their uneasiness grew out of something more general than mistrust of an opposing faction that had shown itself ready to associate with poorer freemen and their radical yearnings. Each convention had assumed more authority, had taken more decisive steps toward actual control of provincial affairs. Yet the conventions proper met for periods of no more than three or four weeks, and during long intervals between sessions the execution of its mandates fell to county committees supervised only by the provincial Council of Safety at Annapolis. Not even the convention, much less local committees, had a constitutional basis. As long as authority continued in this uncertain state, any determined knot of men might assert their own wishes and defy the mandates and precepts so carefully worked out by the right-minded Patriots. Adventurers like Hall and Hammond had ample opportunities to scheme and perhaps turn the resistance movement into some kind of revolution, with the bottom rail on top.

The militia, a creation of the convention, gave unsettling evidence of the dangers inherent in extralegal, self-appointed government resting on the popular will. At first the militia units elected their junior officers, the lieutenants and captains of company units. The rank and file, many of them men with next to no property, had a kind of franchise for the first time. Shortly they were demanding a voice in selecting field grade officers, battalion commanders with the rank of major and colonel, whose appointment the convention had specifically reserved for itself. In Queen Anne's County, the 20th Battalion refused to acknowledge field officers appointed by the convention and elected its own colonel and lieutenant colonel, neither of them from the elite of the county. This kind of conduct, if permitted to continue, threatened the control of the province by the better sort. The next step might easily be a democracy, abandonment of deference in politics, and an opening of the floodgates of social revolution.

—15—

The course ahead for the Patriots in the early months of 1776 was far from clear. News of the burning of Norfolk, Virginia, by order of Lord Dunmore indicated royal determination to suppress American resistance. Tom Paine's powerful pamphlet, *Common Sense*, advocated independence from Britain: "The blood of the slain, the weeping voice of Nature cries, 'Tis time to part." The New Hampshire and South Carolina provincial congresses had framed temporary governments for regulating internal policy until the unnatural differences between colonies and mother country could be accommodated. At least one Maryland voice had come out for independence. Charles Carroll of Carrollton, now identified as one in the Patriot coalition, put the case in black and white about mid-March: "I am satisfied peace with Great Britain is at a great distance . . . we must either be totally independent or totally dependent." Six months later he regretted his brashness.

But others among the Patriot leaders saw problems. Undisciplined militia was merely one. Poorer whites spoke more boldly in criticism of the privileged element and the Council of Safety heard these messages clearly. One Robert Gassaway, small farmer from Frederick County, told his fellows in the militia: "It was better for the poor people to lay down their arms and pay the duties and taxes laid on them by the king and Parliament than to be brought into slavery and to be commanded and ordered about as they were [by convention appointees]." The bitterness of the deprived, heretofore below the surface, emerged in speech and overt action. American liberties were taking on new meanings in times of dearth brought on by non-exportation and by confusion of authority.

In early spring a bizarre kidnapping attempt tested the provisional government of Maryland. General Charles Lee, who had just assumed command of the Continental army in the southern department, came into possession of dispatches from British Colonial Secretary, Lord George Germain, to Governor Eden. The dispatches, captured on the person of a merchant coming from Lord Dunmore's fleet, indicated that Eden had been sending Germain secret intelligence, including information on the feasibility of military landings in Maryland and Virginia. Lee immediately wrote his friend, Samuel Purviance, chairman of the Baltimore Committee of Observation, urging the arrest of Governor Eden. Lee bypassed the Maryland Council of Safety, the executive authority for the entire province, in favor of Purviance, whom he knew to be aggressive and quite as impatient with foot dragging of both Virginia and Maryland leaders as he was himself. Already Lee had labelled provincial leaders in both colonies as "namby pambys." Purviance, he knew, was quite able to do the job.

Purviance acted in accordance with Lee's recommendation. He immediately sent Lee's letter together with the captured documents on to John Hancock, president of Continental Congress, and made plans to seize the "person and papers of Governor Eden." Within two days Purviance had Hancock's order authorizing the seizure, and on 18 April he dispatched an armed detail of Baltimore militia under Captain Samuel Smith to Annapolis to take the governor. Captain Smith did not succeed in his mission; the Council of Safety sent him packing. After extracting a promise from Eden that he would not leave the province, the Council then dealt with Purviance and Hancock. Purviance, an internal threat to its authority, received a tongue lashing for going beyond his province and authority; "the assumption of power intrusted to another body was a high-handed and dangerous offence." To Hancock, the external threat, the Council wrote, "To dissolve the government and subvert the constitution by the seizure and imprisonment of the governor, we conceive to be a measure of too much delicacy and magnitude to be adopted without calling and consulting the convention of this province." In short the Council of Safety served

notice on local committees and on Continental Congress to stay within
proper bounds.

—16—

After mid-April the Patriot coalition sailed between Scylla and Cha-
rybdis. Determined to prevent radicals from steering the province toward "an ungovernable and revengful democracy," the Patriots resisted
increasing calls for declaring independence from Great Britain. The
future looked too uncertain to cut loose. The sixth convention, which
met at Annapolis on 8 May, completely vindicated the action of the
Council of Safety in condemning Purviance. Under the presidency of
Charles Carroll, Barrister, a leading Patriot, the delegates resolved that
Eden had been guilty of no "unfriendly intent" in discharging his
duties. Nevertheless, they continued, "the public quiet and
safety . . . require that he leave this province." Accordingly, "he is at
full liberty to depart peaceably with his effects." But on the subject
of independence the convention was adamant: by unanimous voice
Maryland's delegates to Continental Congress were instructed to oppose
separation from Great Britain.

After adjournment of the sixth convention on 25 May the Patriots
had four weeks of intense anxiety. Four colonies took decisive stands
for independence: North Carolina, Rhode Island, Massachusetts, and
Virginia. On 7 June Richard Henry Lee of the Virginia delegation
introduced a resolution in the Continental Congress declaring that all
political connection between the United Colonies and Great Britain
"is, and ought to be, totally dissolved." Maryland's own delegates
wrote asking for instructions, one of them, Thomas Stone, the most
conservative of the Patriots, with genuine misgivings. The time had
come for final decisions.

—17—

On 21 June the seventh and last convention assembled to declare the
sense of the people. Three days after Matthew Tilghman took the chair
as president of the convention Governor Robert Eden bade farewell to
Maryland. A group of gentlemen accompanied him to the Severn River

where H.M.S. *Fowey* rode at anchor. His popularity had lasted until the skiff pushed off the shore to take him aboard. Only his personal baggage remained heaped up for transportation by the ship's tender. Unfortunately the friendliest of farewells ended in rancor. During the preceding night seven white servants and a deserter from the militia had taken asylum on board the *Fowey*. The Council of Safety sent a demand for their return to the captain, who peremptorily refused on the ground that he had orders "to receive all persons well affected and give them every protection." Asked by the Council to intervene, Eden explained that his "interposition . . . must prove ineffectual against the King's orders." In reprisal the Council refused to put the baggage on board, forcing the *Fowey* to sail on 26 June without it.

Eden's departure symbolically ended proprietary government in Maryland. In fact his real authority had ended two years previously when the first convention met in June of 1774. Eden held the last meeting of his Council of State on 12 June, a purely ceremonial affair. And yet the courts and offices continued to do some business under proprietary appointees long after his departure. Ben Dulany, son and deputy of Daniel the Younger, remained county clerk in Frederick County until May of 1777. A younger brother of Daniel, Dennis Dulany, who was clerk in Kent County, continued a month longer. In Queen Anne's County the court held sessions in the name of the Lord Proprietor until 1777.

—18—

In the seven days after Eden's departure the convention moved Maryland from a proprietary province to a free state. On 28 June the assembled delegates released their representatives to Continental Congress from former restrictions and instructed them to "concur with the other United Colonies, or a majority of them, in declaring the United Colonies free and independent States." Thus far the convention merely expressed a consensus of county meetings held earlier to select delegates to the Annapolis meeting. Then, after a flurry of committee meetings and reports, the convention adopted on 3 July 1776 a Maryland declaration of independence and set the date for election of delegates to a constitutional convention to frame a new form of government for what was shortly to be called the Free State of Maryland.

12

THE FREE STATE

The formal break with England had come without serious jolts. Six days elapsed between the decision to instruct the Maryland delegates in the Continental Congress to vote for independence and the adoption on 3 July of a unilateral declaration of Maryland independence by the last provincial convention. During those six days the delegates heard snatches of flaming oratory, a few unsettling rumors of insubordination in the military, some disturbing reports of opposition to the patriot cause from the Eastern Shore, and a great deal of commonplace chatter about appropriate steps that the convention should take next. Doubts and uncertainties yielded to the determination of the Patriots, who pushed through the formal declaration of independence and, as a next and logical step, issued a call for a constitutional convention.

—1—

By comparison with Thomas Jefferson's magic prose, "A Declaration of the Delegates of Maryland" sounds flat. Neither in felicity of expression nor in elegance of logic does the Maryland document approach the draft that Jefferson produced for the United States in Congress assembled. Yet some arresting similarities catch the eye. The Maryland declaration catalogued British abuses and ennunciated a philosophy so similar to the more famous draft that Jefferson's claim to have stated the common sense of the matter is amply demonstrated. The operative sentence in the Maryland declaration reads "We, the Delegates of Maryland, in convention assembled, do declare, that the king of Great Britain has violated his compact with his people, and they owe no allegiance to him." This one statement presupposes radical principles: the right of revolution, government by the consent of the governed. Such was the document adopted on 3 July.

The next order of business, the call for a constitutional convention, carefully qualified the glowing expression, "his people" as used in the Declaration. Not everyone was to have a hand in fashioning the new order. Election rules provided for exactly the same property qualifications that restricted the suffrage under the old proprietary government. All males above twenty-one years of age with freeholds of not less than fifty acres or with visible estates of £40 sterling were qualified to elect four deputies from the county of their residence or two deputies if they lived in the cities of Annapolis or Baltimore. Natural rights with its radical implications was the philosophy elaborated in the Maryland declaration of independence, but clearly the practice was to be a continuation of elite control of government. The election order did, however, redress former inequities by giving Baltimore Town two deputies and by dividing the huge western area, once Frederick County, into three election districts, each with the right to elect four representatives to the constitutional convention.* With these minor alterations of time-honored procedure the convention set 1 August as election day for delegates to the constituent Assembly and on 6 July adjourned *sine die*.

—2—

The next few months were anxious times for the Patriot coalition. They had pressed for cutting all formal ties with both the Lord Proprietor and Great Britain. In Whig theory the province had reverted to a "state of nature" with the breaking of these contracts. In practice, government continued as it had during the two years of convention rule: a curious combination of traditional proprietary offices and courts acting in concert with extemporized councils and committees that had, with convention approval, grasped legislative and executive functions in 1774. Over these two years of policy making and administration the central

---

*Later in 1776 these three districts became counties: Montgomery, Washington and Frederick.

Council of Safety and the county Committees of Observation had acquired considerable self-confidence and generally enjoyed the respect
of provincials. Certainly the supreme authority, the convention, had
sufficient confidence in the Council of Safety to leave general oversight
to it until a government under the expected constitution could take
office. Nevertheless, uncertainties perplexed leaders and followers alike
as they looked to the future.

One doubt grew out of the unclear political complexion of the
constituent convention to be elected on 1 August. A small but energetic
faction led by William Fitzhugh, John Hall, and the two Hammonds,
Matthias and Rezin, had unaccountably taken a radical position on
voting for delegates. Wealthy and prominent in provincial society and
politics, all four had fallen into disagreements with the Patriot leadership that had steered the course over the preceding two years. Facing
a crucial election that would determine the form of government for
years to come, the Hall-Hammond faction began preaching the doctrine
of broader suffrage, of giving the ballot to all persons bearing arms
without regard to their property holdings. Rezin Hammond went so
far as to advise "the people to lay down their arms if they were denied
the privilege of voting, for it was their right." Such democratic precepts
threatened to undermine the political base of Western Shore Patriot
leaders: the two Carrolls, Thomas Johnson, Samuel Chase, and William
Paca. Matthew Tilghman and Robert Goldsborough, both from the
Eastern Shore, appeared to be in no danger of defeat, though their area
had shown an alarming number of families loyal to the king and not
only mistrustful of the new authority in Maryland but actually defiant.
Some even threatened cooperation with Lord Dunmore, the ousted
royal governor of Virginia, just then carrying on military operations
against Virginians from his shipboard refuge. His highly objectionable
tactics included freeing all slaves who would desert their masters to
join his forces. But loyalism and a radicalized militia, while undoubted
threats, took second place to insuring a sound body of delegates to the
constitutional convention. Beyond question many freemen, disfran-
chised by the high property qualifications, listened with interest to
the radical doctrine that all men bearing arms deserved the ballot.
Most militiamen fell in this category, not to mention scores of activists
who had supported the county committees by demonstrations and as
informants. In this reservoir of discontented persons the Hammonds

saw their support and to them made their appeal. Viewing the prospects of radical maneuvering a week before balloting, Charles Carroll of Carrollton warned, "should their schemes take place, and it is probable they will unless vigorously counteracted by all honest men, anarchy will follow as a certain consequence . . . and this province in a short time will be involved in all the horrors of an ungovernable and revengeful Democracy and will be dyed with the blood of its best citizens."

—3—

When the constitution makers assembled at Annapolis on Wednesday, 14 August, Carroll might easily have concluded that his fears were soon to be realized. Among the seventy-six delegates only thirty-three had attended a previous convention; forty-three were untried in politics. All four leading radicals had managed to get themselves elected: Fitzhugh, the Hammonds, and John Hall. Several of their known sympathizers were also delegates. But leaders of the Patriot coalition were also in attendance in full numbers: Matthew Tilghman, Samuel Chase, William Paca, Thomas Johnson, Robert Goldsborough, George Plater, and the two Charles Carrolls.

From the outset, however, these conservative members dominated proceedings. Matthew Tilghman took the chair almost by prescriptive right. They succeeded first in dismissing delegates from five counties where voting irregularities had occurred and ordering new elections with strict attention to property qualifications violated in the initial balloting. Although the new elections did not result in substantial changes in delegations returned, the Patriot leadership had served notice that laws and regulations were not to be flouted. More indicative of the direction the convention was to take, every place on the "Committee to propose a Declaration and Charter of Rights and a Form of Government" went to a member of the Patriot coalition: Tilghman, Paca, Chase, Plater, Goldsborough, and the two Carrolls. Conceiving their task as the search for a vanishing authority, the committeemen took counsel behind closed doors.

Proceedings of deliberative bodies make notoriously dull reading, and the Maryland constitutional convention of September 1776 does not violate the rule. Only in retrospect does the monotonous recital of sittings and risings, of committee reports and formal votes take on the character of a play, skillfully produced by adroit management and by the deceptions that make good drama. In effect the seven-man committee wrote the script and directed the action, profoundly aware that the realization of their vision of the future state depended on their handiwork. Their drafting task was twofold: to produce a declaration of rights that amply stated their Whig philosophy and at the same time to structure a government that would continue the elite domination of the years before independence. They succeeded brilliantly. After ten days behind closed doors the committee brought in a forty-two article Declaration of Rights. Exactly two weeks later, on 10 September, a Constitution and Form of Government followed. In just over three weeks the committee had completed its assigned task. Thereafter its members, individually and collectively, were cast in the role of managers or directors.

The Form of Government was a remarkable performance. Even the committee members feared that delegates would not approve of it, although they prepared to push hard for adoption. To avoid the dangers of a "revengeful democracy" they had imposed property restrictions on both voting and officeholding. Only those persons with fifty-acre freeholds or personal property worth £30 current money (approximately £20 sterling) qualified as voters. But the qualifications for holding public office were so much higher that only persons with extensive material wealth were eligible: for membership in the lower house of the legislature £500 current money real or personal property, for the upper house, £1000, for governor £5000. Other offices—Executive Council member, delegate to Continental Congress, sheriff—required estates of £1000. These restrictions in practice deprived over one third of the free adult males of the suffrage. The drastically high property qualifications confined eligibility for the most important offices to about 11 percent of the adult male population.

Structurally the Form of Government retained familiar features of proprietary days, with a few variations required by the disappearance of a Lord Proprietor who had held major appointive authority. The lower house remained essentially the same; four delegates from each county elected on a restricted franchise. For an upper house the constitution provided a novel election procedure to replace the former proprietary appointments. Voters in each county chose electors who in turn selected the senators—nine from the Western Shore and six from the Eastern Shore—each to serve a five-year term. Finally the two houses jointly elected the governor for a term of one year.

By contrast with the conservative constitution, the Declaration of Rights contained in its forty-two articles the fullest statement of Whig philosophy. Article one set the tone: "All Government of right originates from the people, is founded in compact only, and instituted solely for the good of the whole." Succeeding articles recited the positive precepts: freedom of speech, right of petition, trial by jury, subordination of the military to civil control, frequent elections, separation of powers, freedom from unwarranted searches and seizures, and freedom of the press. Other articles contained the prohibitions enshrined in the Whig pantheon: against "cruel and unusual pains and penalties," ex post facto laws, attainders, self-incrimination, quartering soldiers on civilians in times of peace, excessive bail, standing armies, and the ancient grievance of plural officeholding.

With these documents before it the convention spent the month of October debating the provisions in a committee of the whole. Day after day the knot of radical spokesmen attempted without major success to change specific provisions, particularly to lower property qualifications for voting. The few alterations in the text were mainly details. The basic structure emerged without modification, even the clumsy electoral college for the senate, which was a device for removing senators from direct dependence on the popular vote and consequently from the danger of being put under binding instructions by their constituencies. On 3 November the convention adopted the final text of the Declaration of Rights. Five days later the same body agreed to The Constitution and Form of Government. The victory of the Patriots was complete. The constitution called for no referendum to voters of the state. By provision of Article 61, elections were scheduled for 25 November and the first meeting of the two houses for 10 February 1777.

—4—

The fathers of Maryland independence and founders of the new government carried into the new day traditions that ran back beyond memory of living men. True heirs of the provincial country party, they added revolutionary rhetoric to the Whig principles they had always professed. But these principles did not include such democratic vagaries as universal suffrage, or even suffrage for all taxpayers. Joseph Dashiell, member of a prominent Worcester County family, expressed the elite attitude toward the propertyless and poverty-stricken, who lived in "wretched hut[s] crowded with children, naked, hungry and miserable without bread or a penny of money to buy any." Continuing, he remarked, "They appear as objects almost too contemptible to excite the public resentment: yet these are the wretches who set up to be the arbiters of government." Obviously he felt such people ought to be governed, rather than governors. The authors of the new Form of Government had insured that this view would prevail.

Yet the masses had lived with the litany of freedom and had understood it in their own way. Rank and file in the militia, most of them poor and some illiterate, had become restive. Some ordinary citizens had resisted the authority of interim revolutionary committees, most not quite as coarsely as one Baltimorean who called them "a parcel of roguish, damned, sons-of-bitches," adding that they "might kiss his arse and be damned" as he graphically pulled his coat apart behind. Few responsible Patriot leaders would have agreed to the corrective for this manifest defiance suggested by a hothead of the wealthy Chew family who declared that "no poor man was entitled to a vote, and those that would insist on voting, if he had his way, should be put to death." Nor would they have subscribed to the dictum of Chew's brother: "A poor man was not born to freedom but to be a drudge on earth." The proper antidote prescribed by the Patriot leadership, more nearly resembled the pronouncement of Governor Benedict Leonard Calvert uttered half a century previously: the "end for which government was instituted [is] an authoritative influence for the good order of society." In that mood they had written and pushed through the convention the Form of Government, without a bow toward any such democratic gesture as a referendum.

—5—

If the authors of the Maryland constitution had played the role of hard-nosed elitists, they had not lost their feeling for the realities. For decades their kind had conducted campaigns against proprietors and more recently against the entire British establishment with cool-headed pragmatism. None of them imagined that the mere writing of a constitution either ended their labors or earned them their just reward. Some even doubted whether their handiwork would endure. The implementation of a constitution on paper remained ahead. And looking toward this future one of the most active and sensitive of the participants, Daniel of St. Thomas Jenifer, wrote several of his colleagues a letter of caution:

> I find objections that appear to me insuperable as to the new form of government. . . . In attempting to excell, there have been so many gradations and Exclusions that there will not be men enough found of sufficient abilities to turn the machine with that velocity which the present exigencys of our affairs require. Besides the Senate does not appear to me to be a Child of the people at Large, and therefore will not be Supported by them longer than there Subsists the most perfect Union between the different Legislative branches. How long that may be, you, who know mankind full as well as I do, may easily determine. . . . The two houses are composed of 89 members, 8 of whom have it in their power to counteract 81. Will they submit?

The test came as soon as the general Assembly convened in February of 1777 and completed the organization of the new government by electing as first governor of the state Thomas Stone, a leader in the Patriot coalition. Within two months the legislators, all of them upper class, had put on the books an astounding law, more radical and broader in social implications than the like in any other state. Quite simply the act made paper money legal tender for all debts, including those contracted in sterling before the separation from England.

When first proposed, the tender act met violent opposition from several important citizens including the elder Charles Carroll, who declared "it will surpass in iniquity all the acts of the British Parliament against America." Paper currency had depreciated in value and might in time be entirely worthless, Carroll said. He added that he was perfectly prepared to give poor debtors reasonable relief, but certainly not so much as the proposed act, which permitted debtors to pay off their creditors in currency worth only a fraction of sterling value. He advised his famous son, Charles Carroll of Carrollton, the richest man in Maryland and recently elected to the senate, "to draw up a strong and nervous protest against the law."

Wiser counsel prevailed. The younger Carroll, more astute than his father, had different priorities. "I have long considered our personal estate, I mean the money part of it, to be in jeopardy," he told his father. "If we can save a third of that and all our land and negroes, I shall think ourselves well off." Daniel of St. Thomas Jenifer also tried to pacify the rich old patriarch. Agreeing that the law was evil and corrupt, Jenifer wrote "I think you had better bend to the times." Jenifer and young Carroll spoke in behalf of the bargain that the elite leadership was striking with the people to make a conservative constitution acceptable. Theirs was the wisdom of sacrifice, or as Charles Carroll of Carrollton put it, "the price of Revolution."

EPILOGUE

If official pronouncements mark beginnings and terminal points, the history of colonial Maryland ends on 3 July 1776 with the state declaration of independence. But the events of that day seem in perspective neither more important nor memorable than those of several other dates between 1774 and 1777. Months before the formal declaration, Marylanders had in fact conducted their affairs in accordance with provincial sentiment, without regard to proprietary wishes or commands. Months after 3 July 1776 some proprietary officials were still carrying on the business of their offices, in one instance in the Lord Proprietor's name.

Such is the unity and coherence of Maryland colonial history that something more significant than a date seems called for as the final cadence. I see this endpoint in the constitution of 1776, a document that completes a pattern running through a century and a half of Maryland history. In the constitution of 1776 provincial leaders reduced to written form the propositions that represented their deepest political and social convictions. The document that they produced in convention, an elected convention to be sure but elected on a limited franchise, has little that can be properly called democratic. Moreover, it was never submitted to a referendum of any kind.

It may seem strange to readers two hundred years later that out of the rhetoric of natural rights could come such results. To the fathers of the Maryland constitution any other result would have seemed strange, perhaps unreasonable, and even dangerous. They had set down exactly what they and their forbears had fought for for over half a century. They turned deaf ears to advocates of untried political ideas—

such as manhood suffrage—that almost surely would have upset the entire social order.

At the same time they perceived that the unprivileged, who took the rhetoric of freedom in a different sense, might prove a dangerous element, a potential threat to the stability of the new government. Accordingly, conservative legislators under a conservative constitution made the necessary sacrifice—passing radical tender law—to preserve a political and social order that grew out of their history.

APPENDIX A

LORD PROPRIETORS
OF MARYLAND

George Calvert, First Baron of Baltimore	(c. 1580–1632)*
Cecilius Calvert, Second Baron	(1605–1675)
Charles Calvert, Third Baron	(1637–1715)
Benedict Leonard Calvert, Fourth Baron	(1679–1715)
Charles Calvert, Fifth Baron	(1699–1751)
Frederick Calvert, Sixth Baron	(1732–1771)
Henry Harford	(1760–1834)

---

*Never de jure Lord Proprietor, he died while his charter was going through the seals.

APPENDIX B

GOVERNORS OF MARYLAND

First Proprietary Period

The formal title of the chief magistrate (governor) in the first proprietary period was "Lieutenant General, Admiral, Chief Captain and Commander."

Leonard Calvert	1634–1643
Giles Brent (vice Leonard Calvert, absent from the province)	1643–1644
Leonard Calvert	1644–1647
Thomas Greene	1647–1649
William Stone	1649–1652
Commissioners of Parliament	1652 (29 March–28 June)
William Stone	1652–1654
Deputies of the Commissioners of Parliament	1654–1658
Josias Fendall	1658–1660
Philip Calvert	1660–1661
Charles Calvert	1661–1676
Jesse Wharton, for Cecilius Calvert, infant	1676
Thomas Notley, for Cecilius Calvert, infant	1676–1679
Charles Calvert, Lord Baltimore	1679–1684
Board of Deputy Governors, for Benedict Leonard Calvert, infant	1684–1689

Royal Period

During the royal period governors bore the style, "Captain General and Governor in Chief, Chancellor, and Vice Admiral."

Convention of the Freemen of Maryland	1689–1692
Lionel Copley	1692–1693
Sir Thomas Lawrence	1693
Sir Edmund Andros	1693–1694
Nicholas Greenberry	1694
Sir Thomas Lawrence	1694
Frances Nicholson	1694–1698
Nathaniel Blakiston	1698–1702
Thomas Tench	1702–1704
John Seymour	1704–1709
Edward Lloyd	1709–1714
John Hart	1714–1715

Second Proprietary Period

Governors had the official title during this period, "Lieutenant and Chief Governor, Chancellor, Admiral, Captain General and Commander." In most correspondence, even official, the form used was "Lieutenant Governor."

John Hart	1715–1720
Thomas Brooke II	1720
Charles Calvert	1720–1727
Benedict Leonard Calvert	1727–1731
Samuel Ogle	1731–1732
Charles Calvert, Lord Baltimore	1732–1733
Samuel Ogle	1733–1742
Thomas Bladen	1742–1747
Samuel Ogle	1747–1752
Benjamin Tasker	1752–1753
Horatio Sharpe	1753–1769
Robert Eden	1769–1774
Richard Lee (vice Eden, absent from the province)	1774
Robert Eden	1774–1776
Richard Lee (vice Eden, departed from the province)	1776

APPENDIX C

COUNTIES ESTABLISHED DURING THE
PROPRIETARY PERIOD

St. Mary's	1637
Kent	1642
Anne Arundel	1650
Calvert	1650
Charles	1658
Baltimore	1659
Talbot	1662
Somerset	1666
Dorchester	1668
Cecil	1674
Prince George's	1695
Queen Anne's	1706
Worcester	1742
Frederick	1748
Caroline	1773
Harford	1773

BIBLIOGRAPHY

BIBLIOGRAPHICAL REFERENCES AND GUIDES

No systematic bibliography for Maryland comparable to Nelson Burr's for New Jersey has yet been compiled. But several special works, each excellent in its own way, can be helpful to serious students. On imprints, mostly European, concerning Maryland to 1700, Elizabeth Baer, comp., *Seventeenth Century Maryland, A Bibliography* (Baltimore, 1949) is complete and has splendid reproductions of title pages. Less complete, John W. Garrett, "Seventeenth Century Books Relating to Maryland," in *Maryland Historical Magazine* XXXIV (March 1939), pp. 1–39, lists a selection of books in all languages with brief sketches of their contents. Lawrence C. Wroth, *A History of Printing in Colonial Maryland, 1686–1776* (Baltimore, 1922) not only lists all known Maryland imprints from William Nuthead's first broadside to the Declaration of Independence but contains so much background matter that it qualifies as an excellent cultural history as well. Useful for the late colonial period, Paul H. Giddens, "Bibliography on Maryland during the Time of Governor Horatio Sharpe, 1753–1769," in *Maryland Historical Magazine* XXXI (March 1936), pp. 6–16, lists both primary and secondary materials. The first two volumes of Thomas D. Clark, *Travels in the Old South: A Bibliography*, 3 vols. (Norman, Oklahoma, 1956) contain many references to accounts by visitors in the seventeenth and eighteenth centuries. For the vast storehouse of largely unpublished scholarship see Richard R. Duncan and Dorothy M. Brown, *Master's Theses and Doctoral Dissertations on Maryland History* (Baltimore, 1970). Periodically, listings in the *Maryland Historical Magazine* update this list.

PRIMARY SOURCES

Two great depositories contain the richest veins of early Maryland materials: The Maryland Hall of Records at Annapolis and the Maryland Historical Society in Baltimore. The Hall of Records is unique among American archival institutions in its Assembly of central and local (county, parish, and city) records for the whole colonial period under a single roof. Among the outstanding series are the Proceedings of the General Assembly, Proceedings of the Council, the Patent (land) Records, proceedings of the central courts (chancery, court of appeals, provincial court, and the testamentary or probate court), and all the existing county court proceedings. The Hall of Records Commission has authorized a number of guides and aids to research, including calendars of the State Papers in the "Rainbow Series," named for their colorful leather bindings:

> *Calendar of Maryland State Papers No. 1: The Black Books* (Annapolis, 1943)
> *Calendar of Maryland State Papers No. 2: The Bank Stock Papers* (Annapolis, 1947)
> *Calendar of Maryland State Papers No. 3: The Brown Books* (Annapolis, 1948)
> *Calendar of Maryland State Papers No. 4: The Red Books*, Parts 1, 2, and 3 (Annapolis, 1950–55)

Other valuable aids to research include Elizabeth Hartsook and Gust Skordas, comps., *Land Office and Prerogative Court Records of Colonial Maryland* (Annapolis, 1946); Phebe R. Jacobsen, *Quaker Records in Maryland* (Annapolis, 1967); and a pair of unusual volumes: *The County Court Houses and Records of Maryland, Part One, The Courthouses* (Annapolis, 1960) and *The County Courthouses and Records of Maryland, Part Two, The Records* (Annapolis, 1963).

Holdings of the Maryland Historical Society, including the magnificent set of Calvert Papers, are described in Avril J. M. Pedley, comp., *The Manuscript Collections of the Maryland Historical Society* (Baltimore, 1968).

Important series of official records have been printed by the Maryland Historical Society in the stately set, *The Archives of Maryland* (Baltimore, 1883–   ), 72 volumes. The *Archives* include the proceedings of the general Assembly, the council proceedings, letterbooks of Governor Horatio Sharpe, and several volumes of provincial and county court proceedings. The Society has also published a one volume guide to the Calvert Papers and two volumes of selected documents under the title *The Calvert Papers*, I (Fund Publication No. 28, Baltimore, 1889) and II (Fund Publication No. 35, Baltimore, 1899).

Among other collections of manuscripts most valuable are those in the Library of Congress (particularly the transcripts from the Public Record Office of Great Britain), the Pennsylvania Historical Society, and the University of Virginia Library.

Beside the massive printed sources in the *Archives of Maryland* several single volumes contain important primary materials for the social, intellectual, and religious history of the colony. William S. Perry, ed., *Historical Collections of the American Colonial Church, IV, Maryland* (Hartford, 1878) prints rare letters and memorials. Thomas Bacon (c. 1700–1768) left a mass of writings collected years later as *The Writings of the Rev. Thomas Bacon* (Philadelphia, 1843) and *Four sermons, preached at the parish church of St. Peter in Talbot County, in the province of Maryland. . . .* (London, 1750). These sermons to servants and slaves went through several editions up into the nineteenth century.

The *Maryland Gazette* (William Parks, 1727–1734, and Jonas Green and successors, 1745–1789) came out weekly in the periods covered. Both sets are available on microfilm in most research libraries. Parks also printed the important tract by Daniel Dulany [the Elder], *The Right of the Inhabitants of Maryland to the Benefit of the English Laws* (Annapolis, 1728), conveniently reprinted in St. George L. Sionssat, *The English Statutes in Maryland and the Public Services of Daniel Dulany, the Elder (Johns Hopkins University Studies in Historical and Political Science* XXXI, Baltimore, 1903). Two other pamphlets, Daniel Dulany [the Younger], *Considerations on the Propriety of Imposing Taxes on the British Colonies. . . .* (Annapolis, 1765) and *The Right to the Tonnage* (Annapolis, 1765) came from the press of Jonas Green. Dulany's *Considerations* is reprinted in *Maryland Historical Magazine* VI (December 1911), pp. 374–406, and VII (March 1912), pp. 26–59. Dr. Alexander Hamilton's delightful *Itinerarium* appears in two editions, by Albert B. Hart (St. Louis, 1907) and by Carl Bridenbaugh under the title *Gentleman's Progress: The Itinerarium of Dr. Alexander Hamilton* (Chapel Hill, 1948). Two commentaries on the late colonial scene contain valuable insights: Jonathan Bouchier, ed., *Reminiscences of an American Loyalist, 1738–1789, being the Autobiography of the Rev'd Jonathan Boucher* (Boston, 1925) and William Eddis, *Letters from America* (London, 1792), more accessible in the John Harvard Library, ed. by Aubrey C. Land (Cambridge, 1969). Bernard C. Steiner, *Early Maryland Poetry* (Maryland Historical Society, Fund Publication No. 36, Baltimore, 1900) contains *The Sotweed Factor* and other verse. Clayton C. Hall, *Narratives of Early Maryland, 1633–1684* (New York, 1910) reprints all the best known eyewitness accounts and a few not so well known. Two other volumes print sources of first importance for the legal history of colonial Maryland: Carroll T. Bond, ed., *Proceedings of the Maryland Court of Appeals* (Washington, 1933) and Thomas Bacon, *Laws of Maryland at Large. . . .* (Annapolis, 1765), a masterpiece of early American bookmaking.

SECONDARY SOURCES: General Studies

There is no contemporary history of provincial Maryland. The oldest histories of Maryland came from the pens of talented amateurs who wrote well after the Revolution. Noteworthy for their times, these works are today almost curiosities. John V. L. MacMahon, *An Historical View of the Government of Maryland from its Colonization to the Present Day* (Baltimore, 1849) covers the period decade by decade in summary form. William Hand Brown, *Maryland: The History of a Palatinate* (Boston, 1884), one of the American Commonwealths series, presents a sketch of colonial Maryland rather more modern in feeling than previous single volume accounts, but extremely brief. The massive work in three volumes of John Thomas Scharf, *History of Maryland from Earliest Times to the Present Day* (Baltimore, 1879) is an old-fashioned, leisurely history filled with antiquarian digressions, but useful for the many letters and documents printed in full. Amazingly industrious, Scharf also produced a two volume *History of Western Maryland* (Philadelphia, 1882) and a seven hundred page *History of Baltimore City and County* (Philadelphia, 1881), both with the same lack of form and system, though useful as compendiums. Charles B. Clark, ed., *The Eastern Shore of Maryland and Virginia*, 3 vols. (New York, 1950) has chapters by specialists on local history, industries, and prominent personalities.

Modern scholarship on Maryland begins with Newton D. Mereness, *Maryland as a Proprietary Province* (New York, 1901), the standard institutional study. A more popularly written narrative account, Matthew Page Andrews, *The Founding of Maryland* (New York, 1933) covers in detail and less critically the years up to 1689. An earlier work of Andrews, *History of Maryland: Province and State* (Garden City, 1929) deals extensively with both the seventeenth and eighteenth centuries, but suffers from a lack of design and a tendency to ramble. Clayton C. Hall, *The Lords Baltimore and their Maryland Palatinate* (Baltimore, 1904), although thin in subject matter, does sketch the relationships between proprietor and province. Another early twentieth century volume, William T. Russell, *Maryland: the Land of Sanctuary* (Baltimore, 1907) covers the colonial period chronologically, but haphazardly and at times un-critically.

For the seventeenth century the hundred pages in Charles M. Andrews, *The Colonial Period of American History*, II (New Haven, 1936), chapters VIII and IX, pp. 274–379, are the surest guide through the five and a half decades preceding the fall of the proprietary. Wesley F. Craven, *The Southern Colonies in the Seventeenth Century, 1607–1689* (Baton Rouge, 1949) has three thoughtful chapters (7, 8, and 9) that present critical accounts of major turning points in early Maryland history.

Two superlative books cover the eighteenth century: Wroth, *History of Printing*, mentioned above, and Charles A. Barker, *The Background of the Revolution in Maryland* (New Haven, 1940). For the years 1720 to 1774 Barker's work is a model of research and analysis written in a vigorous style.

Covering both centuries, Richard B. Davis, *Intellectual Life in the Colonial South, 1585–1763*, 3 vols. (Knoxville, 1978) has brought into a majestic set a lifetime of perceptive investigation into life and letters in the early South. Every chapter has informed and accurate comment on Maryland, and some chapters are indispensable: Vol I, chapter 3, on "Formal Education"; Vol II, chapter 4 on "Books, Libraries, Reading, and Printing"; and chapter 6 on "The Sermon and the Religious Tract."

SECONDARY SOURCES: Special Studies

The paucity of general studies is offset by the wealth of monographs and articles that supplied much of the matter for the present volume. Some dry and pedestrian, others engaging and stimulating, collectively they are the storehouse that students draw on for special periods or topics of interest. The largest number of monographs appear in the *Johns Hopkins Studies in Historical and Political Science* (hereafter abbreviated *JHUS*), the *Maryland Historical Magazine* (hereafter abbreviated *MHM*) containing by far the largest number of articles, and the *William and Mary Quarterly* (hereafter abbreviated *W&MQ*) which has published several seminal studies.

Several economic studies with an institutional cast cover the entire colonial period, even though their titles seem to limit them to briefer time spans. On the basic factor of land Clarence P. Gould, *The Land System of Maryland, 1720–1765, JHUS* XXXI (Baltimore, 1913) is sound and far more readable than the title suggests. Beverly W. Bond, *The Quit-Rent System in the American Colonies* (New Haven, 1919) deals clearly with this complex part of the land system. Two excellent financial studies help the reader through the long battles over money problems: Clarence P. Gould, *Money and Transportation in Maryland, 1720–1765, JHUS* XXXIII (Baltimore, 1915) and Kathryn Behrens, *Paper Money in Maryland, 1727–1789, JHUS* XLI (Baltimore, 1923). On the staple crop the standard authority is Vertrees J. Wyckoff, *Tobacco Regulation in Colonial Maryland, JHUS*, Extra Volume, New Series, No. 22 (Baltimore, 1936).

For a subject of such importance, major books on religion are few: Henry S. Spalding, *Catholic Colonial Maryland* (Milwaukee, 1931) and Nelson W. Rightmyer, *Maryland's Established Church* (Baltimore, 1950). Though excellent factually, both are written from a sectarian point of view. Briefer studies are listed at appropriate places in the suggested readings for individual chapters.

On unfree labor two older works cover the entire colonial period: Eugene I. McCormac, *White Servitude in Maryland, 1634–1820, JHUS* XXII (Baltimore, 1904) and Jeffrey R. Brackett, *The Negro in Maryland: A Study of the Institution of Slavery, JHUS*, Extra Volume, No. 10 (Baltimore, 1889). Abbot E. Smith, *Colonists in Bondage: White Servitude and Convict Labor in America, 1607–1776* (Chapel Hill, 1947), written in a more modern manner, contains new material to supplement the history of the unfree.

On justice in early Maryland the fare is meagre: Conway W. Sams and Elihu S. Riley, *The Bench and Bar of Maryland*, 2 Vols. (Chicago, 1901), is essentially a reference work and weak on the colonial period; Raphael Semmes, *Crime and Punishment in Early Maryland* (Baltimore, 1938), is entertainingly written but restricted to the seventeenth century. One special tribunal has found an ideal historian, Carroll Taney Bond, *The Court of Appeals of Maryland, a History* (Baltimore, 1928).

Architectural and urban history are treated accurately and attractively in several outstanding volumes: John W. Reps, *Tidewater Towns: City Planning in Colonial Virginia and Maryland* (Williamsburg, 1972), is a lavish production; Morris L. Radoff, *Buildings of the State of Maryland at Annapolis* (Annapolis, 1954) and *The County Court Houses and Records of Maryland, Part One: The Courthouses* (Annapolis, 1960), are accurate and well illustrated; and Walter B. Norris, *Annapolis, Its Colonial and Naval Story* (New York, 1925), is charmingly written.

For a province rich in personalities, biographers have treated only two persons adequately. Kate Mason Rowland, *The Life of Charles Carroll of Carrollton, 1737–1832, with his Correspondence and Public Papers*, 2 Vols. (New York, 1898), an old-fashioned life and times, still remains the most satisfactory. More recent biographies, though shorter, miss the mark: Ellen H. Smith, *Charles Carroll of Carrollton* (Cambridge, Massachusetts, 1942) and Thomas O. Hanley, *Charles Carroll of Carrollton: The Making of a Revolutionary Gentleman* (Washington, 1970). Aubrey C. Land, *The Dulanys of Maryland* (Baltimore, 1955; new edition, 1968) puts this important family in perspective.

A special kind of biographical work now in progress will add a new dimension to knowledge about Maryland political leadership: Edward C. Papenfuse, Alan F. Day, David W. Jordan, and Gregory A. Stiverson, comps., *A Biographical Dictionary of the Maryland Legislature, 1635–1689*, Volume One; A-H (Baltimore, 1978). A second volume shortly to be produced will complete the series.

Beginnings of a Province

Readers may follow the unfolding age of exploration and discovery in Samuel E. Morison's epic, *The European Discovery of America: The Northern Voyages, A.D. 500–1600* (New York, 1971) and David B. Quinn's *North America from Earliest Discovery to First Settlements* (New York, 1977). The three folio volumes of Richard Hakluyt, *The Principal Navigations, Voyages, Traffiques & Discoveries of the English Nation* are magnificently reprinted in twelve volumes by James MacLehose (Glasgow, 1903–1905). The English background of early settlers has fascinated scholars from Edward P. Cheney, *European Background of American History, 1300–1600* (New York, 1904) to Carl Bridenbaugh, *Vexed and Troubled Englishmen, 1590–1642* (New York, 1968). Wallace Notestein, *The English People on the Eve of Colonization, 1603–1630* (New York, 1954) and J. E. Christopher Hill, *The World Turned Upside Down* (London, 1972) have specially appealing insights.

The Maryland physical setting has tempted several descriptive and anecdotal pens: Frederick Gutheim, *The Potomac* (New York, 1949) and Hulbert Footner, *Rivers of the Eastern Shore* (New York, 1944), both in the Rivers of America series edited by

Hervey Allen and Carl Carmer. Paul Wilstach, *Tidewater Maryland* (New York, 1931) ranges the upper Bay for scenery and the whole colonial period for yarns.

Recent study of the American Indian has changed perceptions of the classifications and culture of native Americans. For cultural analysis Harold E. Driver, *Indians of North America* (2d. ed., Chicago, 1969) is up-to-date. Alfred L. Kroeber, *Cultural and Natural Areas of Native North America* (University of California Publications in American Archeology and Ethnology, XXXVIII, Berkeley, 1939) is a safe guide to distribution. Francis Jennings, *The Invasion of America* (Chapel Hill, 1975), typical of new writing on the Indian, is critical of European behavior toward the natives. Henry F. Dobyns, "Estimating Aboriginal American Population: An Appraisal of Techniques with a New Hemispheric Estimate," *Current Anthropology* VII (October 1966), pp. 395–449 faults previous estimates for being too low. Mechanisms of population reduction are treated by Alfred W. Crosby, "Virgin Soil Epidemics as a Factor in Aboriginal Depopulation of America, *W&MQ* XXXIII (April 1976), pp. 289–299. The primer on Maryland Indians is Raphael Semmes, "Aboriginal Maryland, 1608–1689," *MHM* XXIV (June and September 1929), pp. 157–172 (Eastern Shore) and pp. 195–209 (Western Shore).

Older lives of George Calvert that run to filiopietism are William H. Browne, *George Calvert and Cecilius Calvert* (New York, 1890) and Lewis W. Wilhelm, *Sir George Calvert: Baron of Baltimore* (Baltimore, 1874). Modern revisionists that have given more objective if piecemeal accounts are John D. Krugler, "Sir George Calvert's Resignation as Secretary of State and the Founding of Maryland," *MHM* LXVIII (Fall 1973), pp. 239–254; Thomas D. Coakley, "George Calvert and Newfoundland: The Sad Face of Winter," *MHM* LXXI (Spring 1976), pp. 1–19; and James W. Foster, "George Calvert: His Yorkshire Boyhood," *MHM* LV (December 1960), pp. 261–274. The monograph of Bernard C. Steiner, *Beginnings of Maryland, JHUS* XXI (Baltimore, 1903), is factually correct and leans heavily on the Claiborne episodes. Lawrence C. Wroth, "The Maryland Colonization Tracts" in *Essays Offered to Herbert Putnam*, ed. by William W. Bishop and Andrew Keogh (New Haven, 1929) gives an ample account of Calvert promotional literature. John H. Latané, *The Early Relations between Maryland and Virginia, JHUS* XII (Baltimore, 1895) covers the years to 1657. The great troublemaker has his own biography: Nathiel C. Hale, *Virginia Venturer: A Historical Biography of William Claiborne, 1600–1677* (Richmond, 1951).

For comparative reading Theodore K. Rabb, *Enterprise and Empire: Merchant and Gentry Investment in the Expansion of England, 1575–1630* (Cambridge, Massachusetts, 1967) has instructive material on the financial hazards of colonization. Ruth A. McIntyre, "William Sanderson: Elizabethan Financier of Discovery," *W&MQ* XIII (April 1956), pp. 184–201 organizes similar enterprises around a single person.

The Rim of Christendom

The opening section of Arthur P. Middleton, *Tobacco Coast: A Maritime History of the Chesapeake* (Newport News, Virginia, 1953) describes land and water of the Bay area with charm and insight. For flavor of the times nothing quite replaces contemporary narratives such as "A Relation of Maryland, 1635" in Hall, *Narratives of Early Maryland* (New York, 1910), pp. 70–112. In a more modern and scientifically accurate manner, the physical features, fauna, flora, and climate are described by William B. Clark, "Outline of the Present Knowledge of the Physical Features of Maryland," *Maryland Geological Survey* I (1897), pp. 139–228, and "The Geography of Maryland," *ibid.* X (1918), pp. 39–167. On cartography Henry Gannett and Edward B. Mathews, "The Maps and Map-Makers of Maryland," *Maryland Geological Survey* II (1898), pp. 337–488, is complete and well illustrated; Louis D. Scisco, "Notes on Augustine Herman's Map," *MHM* XXX (September 1935), pp. 343–351, comments on the most notable map of early Maryland. Earl L. W. Heck, *Augustine Herrman* (Richmond, 1941) is the fullest biography.

A guide through the pitfalls of population estimates, Arthur E. Karinen, "Maryland Population, 1631–1730: Numerical and Distributional Aspects," *MHM* LIV (December 1959), pp. 365–407, is based on the author's unpublished Ph.D. dissertation, "Numerical and Distributional Aspects of Maryland Population, 1631–1840" (University of Maryland, 1958). An important population determinant is discussed in Darrett B. Rutman and Anita H. Rutman, "Of Agues and Fevers: Malaria in the Early Chesapeake," *W&MQ* XXXIII (January 1976), pp. 31–60. Lois Green Carr, " 'The Metropolis of Maryland': A Comment on Town Development along the Tobacco Coast," *MHM* LXIX (Summer 1974), pp. 124–145, describes the population center. Russell R. Menard et al., "Opportunity and Inequality: The Distribution of Wealth on the Lower Western Shore of Maryland, 1638–1705," *MHM* LXIX (Summer 1974), pp. 169–184, and Russell R. Menard, "From Servant to Freeholder: Status Mobility and Property Accumulation in Seventeenth Century Maryland," *W&MQ* XXX (January 1937), pp. 37–64, analyze the fragile society of the early decades.

Raphael Semmes, *Captains and Mariners of Early Maryland* (Baltimore, 1937) contains lore on Indians, trade, and warfare drawn in detail from seventeenth century records. Biographical data on two men of consequence appear in Edwin W. Beitzell, "Thomas Copley, Gentleman," *MHM* XLVII (September 1952), pp. 209–223, and, by the same author, "Thomas Gerard and His Sons-in-Law," *ibid.* XLVI (September 1951), pp. 189–206.

A Time of Troubles

Factual and political, Bernard C. Steiner, *Maryland During the English Civil Wars*, Part I, *JHUS* XXIV (Baltimore, 1906) and Part II, *JHUS* XXV (Baltimore, 1907) chronicles major and minor episodes. Steiner's *Maryland Under the Commonwealth*, *JHUS* XXIX (Baltimore, 1911) carries the chronicle to 1660. On the same period George Petrie, *Church and State in Early Maryland*, *JHUS* X (Baltimore, 1892) and Daniel R. Randall, *A Puritan Colony in Maryland*, *JHUS* IV (Baltimore, 1886) are helpful. Carl N. Everstine, "The Establishment of Legislative Power in Maryland," *Maryland Law Review* XII (Spring 1951), pp. 99–121, analyzes the initial legislative deadlock. The hundred, county, and town are fully treated in Lewis W. Wilhelm, *Local Institutions of Maryland*, *JHUS* III (Baltimore, 1885).

Biographical data on early settlers are difficult to find. McHenry Howard, "Some Early Colonial Marylanders," *MHM* XIV (December 1919), pp. 284–399; *ibid.* XV (March, June, September, December 1920), pp. 65–71, 168–180, 292–304, 312–324; *ibid.* XVI (March, June 1921), pp. 19–28, 179–189, provides short lives of nine important men. A sketch of the most famous woman in early Maryland is found under "Margaret Brent" in Edwin L. James, ed., *Notable American Women, 1607–1950*, Vol. I (Cambridge, Massachusetts, 1971).

Hall, *Narratives of Early Maryland* reprints the five most important tracts of the 1650s on pp. 167–308. Donnell M. Owings, "Private Manors: An Edited List," *MHM* XXXIII (December 1938), pp. 307–334, lists all sixty-two private manors patented between 1634 and 1684 with details of ownership and ultimate fates of these anamolous institutions.

The little-known tension between proprietor and an important Catholic power in early Maryland is covered in Alfred P. Dennis, "Lord Baltimore's Struggle with the Jesuits, 1634–1649," *Annual Report of the American Historical Association for the year 1900*, Vol. I (Washington, 1901), pp. 107–125.

The Formative Years

For religious history of the formative years readers must shop about among studies of the sects: J. William McIlvain, *Early Presbyterianism in Maryland*, *JHUS* VIII (Baltimore, 1980) and a supplementary article, Bernard C. Steiner, "Presbyterian Beginnings," *MHM* XV (December 1920), pp. 305–311; Kenneth L. Carroll, "Maryland Quakers in the Seventeenth Century," *MHM* XLII (December 1952), pp. 297–313, and "Talbot County Quakerism in the Colonial Period," *MHM* LIII (December 1958), pp. 326–370, and "Persecution of Quakers in Early Maryland,

1658–1661," *Quaker History* (1954), pp. 67–80. Phebe R. Jacobsen, *Quaker Records in Maryland* (Annapolis, 1966), has detailed sketches of each meeting preceding the bibliographical data. Lawrence C. Wroth, "The First Sixty Years of the Church of England in Maryland, 1632–1692," *MHM* XI (March 1916), pp. 1–41, describes the low estate of the established church.

Much of the new research in economic history of the period is yet unpublished. Russell R. Menard, "Farm Prices of Tobacco, 1659–1710," *MHM* LXVIII (Spring 1973), pp. 80–85, is a small sample of "Economy and Society in Early Colonial Maryland" (unpublished Ph.D. dissertation, Iowa, 1975). Paul G. E. Clemens, "From Tobacco to Grain: Economic Developments on Maryland's Eastern Shore" (unpublished Ph.D. dissertation, University of Wisconsin, 1974) and Gloria L. Main, "Personal Wealth in Colonial America: Explorations in the Use of Probate Records from Maryland and Massachusetts, 1650–1720" (unpublished Ph.D. dissertation, Columbia University, 1972) both touch significant themes. Henry J. Berkeley, "Extinct River Towns of the Chesapeake Region," *MHM* XIX (June 1924), pp. 125–134, accounts for the failure of town legislation. Vertrees J. Wyckoff, "The Sizes of Plantations in Seventeenth Century Maryland," *MHM* XXXII (December 1937), pp. 331–339, and "Ships and Shipping of Seventeenth Century Maryland," *MHM* XXXIII (December, 1938), pp. 334–342; XXXIV (March, September, December 1939), pp. 46–63, 270–283, 349–361, are enlightening statistical studies. On the difficult subject of payments to labor see Manfred Jonas, "Wages in Early Colonial Maryland," *MHM* LI (March 1956), pp. 27–38.

First fruits of new explorations of Maryland social history include Lois Green Carr and Lorena S. Walsh, "The Planter's Wife: The Experience of White Women in Seventeenth Century Maryland," *W&MQ,* XXXIV (October 1977), pp. 542–571; William A. Reavis, "The Maryland Gentry and Social Mobility, 1637–1676," *W&MQ* XIV (July 1957), pp. 418–428; and Lorena Walsh and Russell R. Menard, "Death in the Chesapeake: Life Tables for Men in Early Colonial Maryland," *MHM* LXIX (Summer 1974), pp. 211–227. Raphael Semmes, *Crime and Punishment in Early Maryland* (Baltimore 1938), a colorful account, treats this side of colonial life with careful reference to court records.

Susan R. Falb, *Advice and Ascent: The Development of the Maryland Assembly, 1635–1689* (unpublished Ph.D. dissertation, Georgetown, 1976) has a wealth of data on political leaders. Susan R. Falb, "Proxy Voting in Early Maryland Assemblies," *MHM* LXXIII (September 1978), pp. 217–225 clearly describes the representative character of these first meetings of the provincial legislature.

The master study of British mercantilism, Charles M. Andrews, *The Colonial Period of American History*, Vol. IV (New Haven, 1938), subtitled "England's Commercial and Colonial Policy," presents the broad sketch with many details on Maryland.

The Royal Administration

On the Revolution of 1688–89 in Maryland, Bernard C. Steiner, "The Protestant Revolution in Maryland," *Annual Report of the American Historical Association for the Year 1897,* Vol. I (Washington, 1898), pp. 281–353, has important factual matter. Analysis of tensions and leadership begins with Michael Kammen, "The Causes of the Maryland Revolution of 1689," *MHM* LV (December 1960), pp. 293–333; and Lois Green Carr and David W. Jordan, *Maryland's Revolution of Government, 1689–1692* (Ithaca, 1974), carry Kammen's analysis through 1692. Michael G. Hall, Lawrence H. Leder, and Michael Kammen, eds., *The Glorious Revolution in America* (Chapel Hill, 1964) contains relevant documents; David S. Lovejoy, *The Glorious Revolution in America* (New York, 1972) is a connected narrative of the period with two chapters on Maryland. David W. Jordan, "John Coode, Perennial Rebel," *MHM* LXX (Spring 1975), pp. 1–28, gives a thoughtful sketch of a leader in the rebellion; and Anne L. Sioussat, "Lionel Copley, First Royal Governor of Maryland," *MHM* XVII (June 1922), pp. 163–177, presents a vignette on a duly appointed authority.

Margaret S. Morriss, *Colonial Trade of Maryland, 1689–1715, JHUS* XXXII (Baltimore, 1914) covers the economy of the entire royal period. Gary B. Nash, "Maryland's Economic War with Pennsylvania," *MHM* LX (September 1965), pp. 231–244, recounts the ups and downs during this period of disorganization, 1690–1715. For special aspects there are Jonathan W. Alpert, "The Origin of Slavery in the United States: The Maryland Precedent," *American Journal of Legal History* XIV (1970), pp. 189–221; and Winthrop D. Jordan, "American Chiaroscuro: The Status and Definition of Mulattoes in the British Colonies," *W&MQ* XIX (April 1962), pp. 183–200. The monumental work of Richard B. Morris, *Government and Labor in Early America* (New York, 1946) distinguishes between slavery and servitude. Donald D. Wax, "Black Immigrants: The Slave Trade in Colonial Maryland," *MHM* LXXIII (Spring 1978), pp. 30–45, has the most up-to-date figures on this commerce. For comparative reading consult Richard S. Dunn, *Sugar and Slaves: The Rise of the Planter Class in the West Indies, 1624–1713* (Chapel Hill, 1972).

Thomas Bray's labors are detailed and interpreted by several scholars. Samuel C. McCullough, "Dr. Thomas Bray's Commissary Work in London, 1696–1699," *W&MQ* II (October 1945), pp. 333–348, comments on his organization of the Society of the Promotion of Christian Knowledge. A companion piece by the same author, "Dr. Thomas Bray's Trip to Maryland: A Study in Militant Anglican Humanitarianism," *W&MQ* II (January 1945), pp. 15–32, assigns the origin of the even more important Society for the Propagation of the Gospel to Bray's Maryland experiences. For a sketch of Bray's life see John W. Lydekker, "Thomas Bray (1658–1730): Founder of Missionary Enterprise, *Historical Magazine of the Protestant Episcopal Church* XII

(September 1932), pp. 187–214. On Bray libraries there are two quite different studies, Bernard C. Steiner, "Rev. Thomas Bray and the American Libraries," *American Historical Review* II (October 1896), pp. 59–75; and Joseph T. Wheeler, "Thomas Bray and the Maryland Parochial Libraries," *MHM* XXXIV (September 1939), pp. 246–265. Bernard C. Steiner, *Rev. Thomas Bray* (Maryland Historical Society Fund Publication, No. 37: Baltimore, 1901) reprints selected works relating to Maryland.

Two vivid administrations of the royal period, those of Nicholson and Seymour, still await proper treatment. Chellis N. Evanson, "Sir Francis Nicholson: A Royal Governor in the Chesapeake Colonies During the Period 1690–1705" (unpublished Ph.D. dissertation, University of Iowa, 1930) focusses narrowly on politics. The picturesque move of the capital is briefly described by Eugenia C. Holland, "Anne Arundel Takes Over from St. Mary's," *MHM* XLIV (March 1949), pp. 42–51. Charles B. Clark, "The Career of John Seymour, Governor of Maryland, 1704–1709," *MHM* XLVIII (June 1953), pp. 134–159, is brief. Sidelights of Seymour's reformation of the bar appear in Alan F. Day, "Lawyers in Colonial Maryland, 1660–1715," *American Journal of Legal History* XVII (April 1973), pp. 145–165; and E. Alfred Jones, *American Members of the Inns of Court* (London, 1924). For facts on Annapolis annalistically arranged without evaluation of the little or great, there is David Ridgely, *Annals of Annapolis* (Baltimore, 1841).

The Second Restoration (1714–1734)

The title accurately describes the contents of Bernard C. Steiner, "The Restoration of the Proprietary of Maryland and the Legislation Against the Roman Catholics during the Administration of Capt. John Hart (1714–1720)," *Annual Report of the American Historical Association for the Year 1899*, Vol. I (Washington, 1900), pp. 229–307, a factual, detailed monograph. On the beginnings of the constitutional battle, St. George L. Sioussat, *The English Statutes in Maryland*, *JHUS* XXI (Baltimore, 1903), puts the discussion in legalistic terms, leaving economic implications to a companion study. This monograph conveniently reprints Dulany's pamphlet and the Bradford edition of the Resolutions of 1722. In *Economics and Politics in Maryland, 1720–1750*, *JHUS* XXI (Baltimore, 1903), Sioussat builds his treatment around Daniel Dulany, the Elder.

Classic studies of population, Evarts B. Greene and Virginia D. Harrington, *American Population Before the Federal Census of 1790* (New York, 1932), and Stella H. Sutherland, *Population Distribution in Colonial America* (New York, 1936) are now supplemented by a work with the refinements of quantification, Robert V. Wells, *The Population of the British Colonies in North America Before 1776: A Survey of Census Data* (Princeton, 1975), which breaks down gross figures to show racial and sexual components. A vignette, Aubrey C. Land, "Governor Blakiston Numbers the People, or Bureaucracy Confounded," *MHM* LXII (December 1967), pp. 419–421, describes the procedure in the unique census of 1700.

The first six chapters of Walter B. Norris, *Annapolis, Its Colonial and Naval History* (New York, 1925) are a cultural account. These may be supplemented by Lawrence C. Wroth, *William Parks* (Richmond, 1926) and by the same pen, "The Maryland Muse by Ebenezer Cooke," *Proceedings of the American Antiquarian Society*, New Series, Vol. 44 (Worcester, Massachusetts, 1935) which reproduces in facsimile *The Sot-Weed Factor*. Edward H. Cohen, *Ebenezer Cooke: The Sot-Weed Canon* (Athens, Georgia, 1975) has the fullest account of Cook's life and references to the original imprints as well as accessible contemporary reproductions. Wroth runs the history of printing back several decades in "The St. Mary's City Press: A New Chronology of American Printing," *MHM* XXXIII (March 1938), pp. 91–112. A. Owen Aldridge, "Benjamin Franklin and the Maryland Gazette," *MHM* XLIV (September 1949), pp. 177–189, recounts Franklin's service in preserving the "Plain Dealer" essays printed in lost issues of the *Gazette*.

The Politics of Tension

Fullest general accounts of Baltimore's visit and its consequences are found in Barker, *Background of the Revolution in Maryland*, and Land, *Dulanys of Maryland*. Paper money, fully discussed by Behrens, *Paper Money in Maryland*, brought a problem pointed out by Kenneth Scott, "Counterfeiting in Colonial Maryland," *MHM* LI (June 1956), pp. 81–100. A curious consequence of Baltimore's visit appears in Aubrey C. Land, "Lord Baltimore and the Maryland County Courts," *Maryland Law Review* XX (Spring 1960), pp. 133–140.

Jacob M. Price, "The Rise of Glasgow in the Chesapeake Tobacco Trade, 1707–1775," *W&MQ* XI (April 1954), pp. 179–199, broke new ground when published. His masterly study, *France and the Chesapeake: A History of the French Tobacco Monopoly, 1674–1791, and of its Relationship to the British and American Tobacco Trades*, 2 vols. (Ann Arbor, 1973), puts the tobacco trade in an international setting. Tommy R. Thompson, "Debtors, Creditors, and the General Assembly in Colonial Maryland," *MHM* LXXII (Spring 1977), pp. 59–77, reveals the role of legislators in developing a code that demanded responsibility from debtors and creditors alike while affording both equal protection in the years from 1720 to 1770.

Husbandry of the first producers may be more fully explored in a great classic, Lewis C. Gray, *History of Agriculture in the Southern United States to 1860*, 2 vols. (Washington, 1933), particularly Vol. I, chapters 2, 10, 11, and 12. An anonymous contemporary account, *American Husbandry* (London, 1775) more readily available in an edition edited by Harry J. Carman (New York, 1939) has four ample chapters on the Chesapeake tobacco colonies. Aubrey C. Land, "The Planters of Colonial Maryland," *MHM* LXVII (Spring 1972), pp. 109–128, attempts to put the small producer in his historic role. Aspects of bond labor in the planting society appear in Russell R. Menard, "The Maryland Slave Population, 1658 to 1730: A Demographic Profile of Blacks in Four Counties," *W&MQ* XXXII (January 1975), pp. 29–54, and Basil Sollers, "Transported Convict Laborers in Maryland during the Colonial Period," *MHM* II (March 1907), pp. 17–47.

Like many other eminent Marylanders, Dr. Charles Carroll has not found a biographer. Materials for his life are printed as "Extracts from the Letter and Account Books of Dr. Charles Carroll," *MHM* XVIII to XXVII (September 1923–December 1932). R. Bruce Harley, "Dr. Charles Carroll—Land Speculator, 1730–1755," *MHM* XLVI (June 1951), pp. 93–107, follows one thread of his career. Carroll, with others, also interested himself in iron manufacturing, for which see Keach Johnson's two articles, "The Baltimore Company Seeks English Subsidies for the Colonial Iron Industry," *MHM* XLVI (March 1951), pp. 27–43, and "The Baltimore Company Seeks English Markets: A Study of the Anglo-American Iron Trade, 1731–1755," *W&MQ* XVI (January 1959), pp. 37–60. Aubrey C. Land, "Genesis of a Colonial Fortune," *W&MQ* VII (April 1950), pp. 255–269, associates iron with fortune building.

In a large literature on the Maryland-Pennsylvania boundary dispute the most accessible pieces are Edward B. Mathews, "History of the Boundary Dispute Between the Baltimores and the Penns Resulting in the Original Mason and Dixon Line," *Maryland Geological Survey* VII (1908), pp. 105–205, illustrated with early maps. Somewhat lighter is Walter A. Powell, "Fight of a Century Between the Penns and Calverts," *MHM* XXIX (June 1934), pp. 83–101. Lawrence C. Wroth, "The Story of Thomas Cresap, A Maryland Pioneer," *MHM* IX (March 1914), pp. 1–37, has the characteristic touch of this master. Kenneth P. Bailey, *Thomas Cresap, Maryland Frontiersman* (Boston, 1944) is fuller and contains many contemporary documents.

Beginnings of the Golden Age

On tobacco legislation the authority is Vertrees J. Wyckoff, *Tobacco Regulation in Colonial Maryland*, *JHUS*, Extra Volumes, New Series, No. 22 (Baltimore, 1936). Barker, *Background of the Revolution*, puts the Act of 1747 in its historical setting.

Historians of architecture have served Maryland well. For broad coverage see Hugh Morrison, *Early American Architecture from the First Colonial Settlements to the National Period* (New York, 1952). The recognized specialist on Maryland houses and gardens is Henry C. Forman, *Maryland Architecture: A Short History from 1634 through the Civil War* (Cambridge, Maryland, 1968) and *Tidewater Maryland Architecture and Gardens* (New York, 1956). A shorter study, Henry C. Forman, "The Transition in Maryland Architecture," *MHM* XLIV (December 1949), pp. 275–281, traces the steps from medieval types first built in the colony to the splendors of Georgian. Gary Carson,

"The 'Virginia House' in Maryland," *MHM* LXIX (Summer 1974), pp. 185–196, discusses the beginnings of vernacular architecture in Maryland. Deering Davis, *Annapolis Houses, 1700–1775* (n.p.,1947) contains a full pictorial record. Particular houses received fuller treatment in Charles Scarlett, Jr., "Governor Horatio Sharpe's Whitehall," *NHM* XLVI (March 1951), pp. 8–26; Rosamond R. Beirne, "The Chase House in Annapolis," *MHM* XLIX (September 1954), pp. 177–195; L. Morris Leisenring, "Tulip Hill, Anne Arundel County," *MHM* XLVII (September 1952), pp. 188–208; and Raymond B. Clark, Jr., "The Abby, or Ringgold House, at Chestertown, Maryland," *MHM* XLVI (June 1951), pp. 81–92. Costs of construction, rarely found, are computed for one mansion in J. Donnell Tilghman, "Bill for the Construction of the Chase House," *MHM* XXXIII, (March 1938), pp. 23–26. Rosamond R. Beirne and John H. Scarff, *William Buckland, 1734–1774, Architect of Virginia and Maryland* (Baltimore, 1958; reprinted 1970) is a full study of a famous architect. Ms. Beirne has a shorter account, "William Buckland, Architect of Virginia and Maryland," *MHM* XLI (September 1946), pp. 199–218. Reliable information about furniture is difficult to obtain. Henry C. Forman's *Old Buildings, Gardens, and Furniture in Tidewater Maryland* (Cambridge, Maryland, 1967) is a work that shows the seamy side as well as the glamorous. Henry J. Berkeley, Jr., "A Register of Cabinet Makers and Allied Trades in Maryland as shown by the Newspapers and Directories, 1746 to 1820," *MHM* XXV (March 1930), pp. 1–27, enumerates these artisans by types of work. On artisans the standard volume is Carl Bridenbaugh, *The Colonial Craftsman* (Chicago, 1961). John. B. Boles, *Maryland Heritage: Five Baltimore Institutions Celebrate the American Bicentennial* (Baltimore, 1976) reproduces in color the iconography, furniture, and objets d'art of eighteenth century Maryland. J. Hall Pleasants and Howard Sill, *Maryland Silversmiths, 1715–1830* (Harrison, New York, 1972) is definitive. For a prominent limner see George C. Croce, "John Wollaston (fl. 1736–67): A Cosmopolitan Painter in the British Colonies," *The Art Quarterly* XV (Summer, 1952), pp. 133–148.

On libraries and reading interests Joseph T. Wheeler did basic research embodied in "Literary Culture in Eighteenth Century Maryland, 1700–1776" (unpublished Ph.D. dissertation, Brown University, 1930). Fortunately, important parts came into the public domain as a series of articles: "Reading and Other Recreations of Marylanders, 1700–1776," *MHM* XXXVIII (June 1943), pp. 37–55, 167–180; "Literary Culture in Eighteenth Century Maryland, 1700–1776," *ibid.* XXXVIII (September 1943), pp. 273–276; "Reading Interests of Maryland Planters and Merchants, 1700–1776," *ibid.* XXXVII (March, September 1942), pp. 26–41, 291–310; "Reading Interests of the Professional Classes in Colonial Maryland, 1700–1776," *ibid.* XXXVI (June 1941), pp. 184–201, 281–301; "Books Owned by Marylanders, 1700–1776," *ibid.* XXXV (December 1940), pp. 337–353; and "Booksellers and Circulating Libraries in Colonial Maryland," *ibid.* XXXIV (June 1939), pp. 111–137.

J. A. Leo Lemay, *Men of Letters in Colonial Maryland* (Knoxville, Tennessee, 1972) had a section on letters and clubs at mid-century. Club life, for all its color, has not had adequate treatment. Elaine G. Breslaw, "Wit, Whimsey, and Politics: The uses of Satire by the Tuesday Club of Annapolis, 1744 to 1756," *W&MQ* XXXII (April 1975), pp. 295–306, presents a new view of the club antics. See also her essay, "The Chronicle as Satire: Dr. Hamilton's History of the Tuesday Club," *MHM* LXX (Summer 1975), pp. 129–148, as well as Lemay's chapter, "Dr. Alexander Hamilton— Wit." Lawrence C. Wroth, "A Maryland Merchant and his Friends in 1750," *MHM* VI (September 1911), pp. 213–224, gives the rural counterpart of urban club life. Kathryn A. Jacob, "The Woman's Lot in Baltimore Town: 1729–97," *MHM* (Fall 1976), pp. 283–295, makes a beginning on the analysis of the legal, social, and cultural role of women in colonial Maryland.

Prized by Annapolis society, the theatre has had only slight notice by historians of Maryland. Some material, not always accurate, appears in George O. Seilhamer, *History of the American Theatre* (Philadelphia, 1888) and a more recent work, Arthur Hornblow, *A History of the Theatre in America from its Beginning to the Present Time*, Vol. I (Philadelphia, 1919). Background of the colonial theatre—plays, dramatists, and actors—can be pieced together from the monumental work, William Van Lennep, ed., Vol. I, *The London Stage, Part 4: 1747–1776* (Carbondale, Illinois, 1965). Katheryn P. Ward, "The First Professional Theatre in Maryland in its Colonial Setting," *MHM* LXX (Spring 1975), pp. 29–44, has full details on the season of 1752.

Sports, too, have been generally neglected. William Woodward, "The Thoroughbred Horse and Maryland," *MHM* XVII (June 1922), pp. 139–162, is a brief sketch. Francis B. Culver, *Blooded Horses of Colonial Days* (Baltimore, 1922) includes Maryland stables.

The Germans have their historian in Dieter Cunz, *The Maryland Germans* (Princeton, 1948). Suggestive on everyday life of this ethnic element is James O. Knauss, *Social Conditions Among the Pennsylvania-Germans in the Eighteenth Century as Revealed in the German Newspapers in America* (Lancaster, Pennsylvania, 1922). A classic statement on German husbandry is made by Richard Shryock, "British Versus German Traditions in Colonial Agriculture," *Mississippi Valley Historical Review*, XXVI (June 1939), pp. 39–54. Aubrey C. Land, "A Land Speculator in the Opening of Western Maryland," *MHM* XLVIII (September 1953), pp. 191–203 has supplementary data on the German element.

Conflicting Imperatives

Maryland historians have paid little attention to the proprietary court in London despite its considerable importance to the colony. Hall, *The Lords Baltimore* concentrates on the Proprietor himself and scarcely mentions his "privy councillors."

Governor Sharpe still awaits a biographer. The older volume, Lady Matilda Edgar,

A Colonial Governor in Maryland, Horatio Sharpe and his Times, 1753–1773 (London, 1912) has errors of fact and interpretation. A scholarly study, Paul H. Giddens, "The Public Career of Horatio Sharpe, Governor of Maryland, 1753–1769," is an unpublished Ph.D. dissertation (University of Iowa, 1930). Giddens has, however, published several important parts: "Land Policies and Administration in Colonial Maryland, 1753–1769," *MHM* XXVIII (June 1933), pp. 142–171; "Trade and Industry in Colonial Maryland, 1753–1769," *Journal of Economic and Business History* IV (1931–1932), pp. 512–538; "Governor Sharpe and his Maryland Government," *MHM* XXXII (June 1937), pp. 156–174. A very human side of this talented administrator appears in Aubrey C. Land, ed., "The Familiar Letters of Governor Horatio Sharpe," *MHM* LXI (September 1966), pp. 189–209.

For the background of the last intercolonial war the modern authority is Lawrence H. Gipson, *The British Empire Before the American Revolution* (Caldwell, Idaho and New York, 1936–70), Vols. V, VI, VII, and VIII. Francis Parkman's classic, *Montcalm and Wolfe*, 2 Vols. (Boston, 1884) is briefer. Two somewhat different points of view on Maryland participation in the French War are presented in Arthur M. Schlesinger, "Maryland's Share in the Last Intercolonial War, *MHM* VII (June, September 1912), pp. 119–149, 243–268, and Paul H. Giddens, "The French and Indian War in Maryland, 1753–1756," *MHM* XXX (December 1935), pp. 281–310. Charles A. Barker, "Property Rights in the Provincial System of Maryland: Proprietary Revenues," *Journal of Southern History* II (May 1936), pp. 211–232, gets to the root of the tension that prevented more ample financial support of the war. Henry I. Stegmaier, Jr., et al., *Allegany County: A History* (Parsons, W. Virginia, 1976) has a full account of this critical area. The governor's shrewd reading of the state of affairs just after the war is candidly stated in Aubrey C. Land, ed., "Sharpe's Confidential Report on Maryland, 1765," *MHM* XLIV (June 1949), pp. 123–129. One older study, J. William Black, *Maryland's Attitude in the Struggle for Canada*, *JHUS* X (Baltimore, 1892) puts the onus for inaction on the Assembly.

Basil Sollers, "The Acadians (French Neutrals) Transported to Maryland," *MHM* III (March 1908), pp. 1–21, has a reasonably full account of this sad episode. The background is urbanely sketched by John B. Brebner, *New England's Outpost: Acadia Before the Conquest of Canada* (New York, 1927), a volume that should be better known.

No one has surpassed Barker, *Background of the Revolution* (especially chapter IV) in analyzing the material as well as the psychic costs of the proprietary establishment. Without doubt the proprietor defaulted in managing his Maryland government, as shown by James Haw, "The Patronage Follies: Bennet Allen, John Morton Jordan, and the Fall of Horatio Sharpe," *MHM* LXXI (Summer 1976), pp. 134–150. David C. Skaggs, "Thomas Cradock's Sermon on the Governance of Maryland's Established Church," *W&MQ* XXVII (October, 1970), pp. 630–653, puts this famous sermon in its setting. The role of the vestry in church affairs is in Gerald E. Hartdegen, "Vestry and Clergy in the Anglican Church of Colonial Maryland," *Historical Magazine of the Protestant Episcopal Church* XXXVII (December 1968), pp. 371–396; his article, "The Vestry as a Unit of Local Government in Colonial Maryland," *MHM* LXVII (Winter 1972), pp. 363–368, clears up uncertain points; and several specific problems are dealt with in his "The Anglican Vestry in Colonial Maryland: Organizational Structure and Problems," *Historical Magazine of the Protestant Episcopal Church* XXXVIII (December 1969), pp. 349–360.

An intelligent supporter of the Proprietor has an unpublished biography: Joseph C. Morton, "Stephen Bordley of Colonial Annapolis" (Ph.D. dissertation, University of Maryland, 1964).

A Search for Direction

For the beginnings of the imperial troubles, Edmund S. and Helen Morgan, *The Stamp Act Crisis* (rev. ed., 1963) paints a broad canvas with an especially incisive chapter on Maryland. Land, *Dulanys of Maryland* has a section on an outstanding figure. A sidelight on a minor figure is in Aubrey C. Land, "The Subsequent Career of Zachariah Hood," *MHM* LI (September 1956), pp. 237–242. Paul H. Giddens, "Maryland and the Stamp Act Controversy," *MHM* XXVII (June 1932), pp. 79–98, has a straightforward account of the troubles.

The Bennet Allen episode is robustly reported by Josephine Fisher, "Bennet Allen, Fighting Parson," Part 1, *MHM* XXXVIII (December 1943), 299–322, and Part II, *ibid.* XXXIX (March 1944), pp. 49–72. For a contrast to the Bennet Allen type, see David C. Skaggs, "Thomas Cradock and the Chesapeake Golden Age," *W&MQ* XXX (January 1973), pp. 93–116. Nelson W. Rightmyer, "The Character of the Anglican Clergy of Colonial Maryland," *MHM* XLIV (December 1949), pp. 229–250, argues that the Bennet Allen type was the exception.

The question of discipline in the established church and the fears created in America by rumors that a bishop might be appointed are the subject of two impressive studies: Arthur L. Cross, *The Anglican Episcopate and the American Colonies* (Harvard Historical Studies IX, London, 1902) and Carl Bridenbaugh, *Mitre and Scepter: Transatlantic Faiths, Ideas, Personalities, and Politics, 1689–1775* (New York, 1962). Bridenbaugh gives American fears of ecclesiastical establishment a prominent place in conditioning American minds for revolution.

The importance of the voluntary associations and out-of-doors politics has been stressed by Barker in his *Background of the Revolution*. Otherwise these years have had less analysis than they deserve. One primary source puts contemporary feeling and practice in a bright light, Richard D. Fisher, ed., "The Case of Good Intent," *MHM* III (June, September, December 1908), pp. 141–157, 240–256, 342–363, which reprints committee proceedings as they were issued by Anne Catherine Green.

The Contours of Freedom

The perennial interest in our revolutionary impulse has resulted in several careful monographs of recent years. Ronald Hoffman, *A Spirit of Dissention: Economics, Politics, and the Revolution in Maryland* (Baltimore, 1973) explains the curious blend of conservatism and radicalism exhibited by Maryland leaders. David C. Skaggs, *Roots of Maryland Democracy, 1753–1776* (Westport, Connecticut, 1973) untangles the skeins of radicalism prior to the final break.

The conflicts accompanying the Fee Proclamation have attracted much attention. Barker, *Battleground of the Revolution*, and Land, *Dulanys of Maryland* devote space to the details. Three quarters of a century ago Elihu S. Riley edited *The Correspondence of "First Citizen"—Charles Carroll of Carrollton—and "Antilon"—Daniel Dulany, Jr., 1773* (Baltimore, 1902), but a more available edition, Peter S. Onuf, *Maryland and the Empire, 1773: The Antilon First Citizen Letters* (Baltimore, 1976) has an extensive introduction and incisive explanatory notes in addition to the full text. Shorter studies of concurrent disputes include Anne Y. Zimmer, "The 'Paper War' in Maryland, 1772–73: The Paca-Chase Political Philosophy Tested," *MHM* LXXI (Summer 1976), pp. 177–193 recounts the exchanges between Jonathan Boucher and two country party stars; and Neil Strawser, "Samuel Chase and the Annapolis Paper War," *MHM* LVII (September 1962), pp. 177–194, has a different perspective.

The literature on business enterprise on the eve includes Jacob N. Price, "Joshua Johnson in London, 1771–1775: Credit and Commercial Organization in the British Chesapeake Trade" in Anne Whitman et al, eds., *Statesmen, Scholars and Merchants, Essays . . . Presented to Dame Lucy Sutherland* (Oxford, 1973). Edward C. Papenfuse, *"In Pursuit of Profits: The Annapolis Merchants on the American Revolution, 1763–1805* (Baltimore, 1975) surveys the provincial economic scene; his "Planter Behavior and Economic Opportunities in a Staple Economy," *Agricultural History* XLVI (April 1972), pp. 297–311, tests the Craven thesis against data from Prince George's county. Clarence P. Gould, "The Economic Causes of the Rise of Baltimore," in *Essays in Colonial History Presented to Charles McLean Andrews* (New Haven, 1931) accounts for the new economic center. As yet no one has systematically studied the third focal point, Fredericktown. Paul K. Waller, "Business and Commerce in Baltimore on the Eve of Independence," *MHM* LXXI (Fall 1976), pp. 296–309, treats several merchant houses. More general, Aubrey C. Land, "Economic Behavior in a Planting Society: The Eighteenth-Century Chesapeake," *Journal of Southern History* XXXIII (November 1967), pp. 469–485, reaches back several decades to explain stratification and mobility. A case study, Paul G. E. Clemens, "The Operation of an Eighteenth-Century Chesapeake Tobacco Plantation" *Agricultural History* XLIX (July 1975), pp. 517–531, details cost and diversification. Allan Kulikoff, "The Social and Economic History of the Chesapeake: Toward a Synthesis," a paper delivered at the Southern Historical Association Annual Meeting in New Orleans, 1977, is an ambitious attempt to bring to coherent statement many strands of recent research. (This paper is scheduled for future publication in the *Journal of Southern History*.) A micro-study by Kulikoff, "The Beginnings of the Afro-American Family in Maryland" in Aubrey C. Land et al., eds., *Law, Society and Politics in Early Maryland* (Baltimore, 1977), pp. 171–196, offers keen new insights into a hitherto dark area. Gregory Stiverson, *Poverty in a Land of Plenty: Tenancy in Eighteenth Century Maryland* (Baltimore, 1977) has written a new chapter, long overdue, in Chesapeake social and economic history. An important mechanism of social control is treated in detail by C. Ashley Ellefson, "The County Courts and the Provincial Court in Maryland, 1733–1763" (unpublished Ph.D. dissertation, University of Maryland, 1963).

Few of the revolutionary fathers have biographies at all. W. Stull Holt, "Charles Carroll, Barrister: The Man," *MHM* XXXI (June 1936), pp. 112–126, may be read with "Extracts from the Letter and Account Books of Charles Carroll, Barrister," *MHM* XXI–XXXVIII (March 1926 to December 1943) for an understanding of a leading figure. Edward S. Delaplaine, *The Life of Thomas Johnson* (New York, 1924) brings the insights of a learned judge to the biographer's chore. For other leaders the reader must discover their roles in the essays and monographs on the Revolution. Three thoughtful pieces deserve reading: Charles A. Barker, "The Revolutionary Impulse in Maryland," *MHM* XXXVI (June 1941), pp. 125–138; James Haw, "Maryland Politics on the Eve of the Revolution: the Provincial Controversy, 1770–1773," *ibid.* LXV (Summer 1970), pp. 103–129; and Herbert E. Klingelhofer, "The Cautious Revolution: Maryland the Movement Toward Independence, 1774–1776," *ibid.* LX (September 1965), pp. 261–313. Tommy R. Thompson, "Personal Indebtedness and the American Revolution in Maryland," *MHM* LXXIII (Spring 1978), pp. 13–29, urges indebtedness as a grievance strongly conditioning the revolutionary impulse in Maryland. All these are more adventuresome than the older standard authorities who give straight factual accounts: John A. Silver, *The Provisional Government of Maryland (1774–1777)*, *JHUS* XIII (Baltimore, 1895), and Bernard C. Steiner, *Life and Administration of Sir Robert Eden*, *JHUS* XVI (Baltimore, 1898).

The Free State

The introductory chapter of Philip A. Crowl, *Maryland During and After the Revolution: A Political and Economic Study* (Baltimore, 1943) has a fine sketch of the country party and its makeup in the last years of colonial dependency. Ronald Hoffman, *A Spirit of Dissension* is full on the compromise that insured elite dominance in the final crisis. Hoffman's article, "Popularizing the Revolution: Internal Conflict and Economic Sacrifice in Maryland, 1774–1780," *MHM* LXVIII (Summer 1973), pp. 125–139, carries this theme well into the war years. A short study, Gordon Wood, "Rhetoric and

Reality in the American Revolution," *W&MQ* XXIII (January 1966), pp. 3–32, explains some matters that William Eddis misunderstood. John C. Rainbolt, "A Note on the Maryland Declaration of Rights and the Constitution of 1776," *MHM* LXVI (Winter, 1971), pp. 420–435, follows the changes that whittled away some of the elitist provisions.

INDEX